# BRADMAN
# THE GREAT

# BRADMAN
# THE
# GREAT

## B.J. Wakley

MAINSTREAM
PUBLISHING
EDINBURGH AND LONDON

Copyright © B.J. Wakley, 1959
All rights reserved
The moral right of the author has been asserted

This edition published in Great Britain in 1999 by
MAINSTREAM PUBLISHING COMPANY (EDINBURGH) LTD
7 Albany Street
Edinburgh EH1 3UG

ISBN 1 84018 236 9

First published in Great Britain in 1959 by
Nicholas Kaye Ltd, London

A catalogue record for this book is available from the British Library

Typeset in Garamond
Printed and bound in Great Britain by Butler & Tanner Ltd

# CONTENTS

## PART II: SUMMARY AND STATISTICS OF BRADMAN'S CAREER IN FIRST-CLASS CRICKET, 1927–49

### Section 1. Batting Averages

### Section 2. Centuries and Double Centuries

## Section 3. *Percentage of Side's Total Runs (Excluding Extras)*

## Section 4. *Analysis of Bradman's Scores*

## Section 5. *Bradman in Partnership*

## Section 6. *Speed of Scoring*

### Section 7. Boundaries

### Section 8. Dismissals and Chances

### Section 9. Bradman on Rain-affected Wickets

### Section 10. Miscellaneous

# PREFACE

W ho was the greatest batsman in the history of cricket is a question which will, I hope, be discussed and argued by cricketers for as long as the game is played; and it is one to which – fortunately – no final answer can ever be given, for the conditions under which great batsmen of different generations and different countries have played, and the quality of the bowling opposed to them, have been so different and variable that it is impossible to find any common standard for comparison.

This chronicle of Sir Donald Bradman's career is not, therefore, in any sense intended to prove a point, one way or the other, for facts and figures by themselves cannot do so; though if they are as remarkable as Bradman's, they may be, to say the least, suggestive.

I did not have the good fortune to watch W.G. Grace, K.S. Ranjitsinhji or V.T. Trumper bat, and I saw Sir John Hobbs only towards the end of his great career; all I can say, therefore, is that in my opinion Bradman is, by a very big margin, the finest batsman that I have ever seen.

This book was originally compiled for my own spare-time amusement, and it has given me almost as much enjoyment as I used to get from watching his glorious batting; I hope that those who read it will also find that it revives some of the pleasure which he used to give to so many lovers of cricket in England and Australia.

Sir Donald himself is not, of course, in any way responsible, either for the idea of the book or for any of its contents; but he has been kind enough to spare the time to read through the manuscript, for which I am most grateful to him.

I have obtained the detailed information from a number of sources. First and foremost, by the kindness of Mrs Ferguson, I have had the opportunity of studying some of the original score-books of the late Mr W.H. Ferguson, BEM. Mr Ferguson had the formidable, if pleasant, task of recording 201 of Sir Donald's 338 innings and 16,020 of the 28,067 runs he made, and it was a privilege to be allowed to peruse his beautifully kept score-books.

Miss Diana Rait-Kerr, the curator of the MCC Library, was, as always, most kind and helpful in very many ways, and especially in allowing me access to score-books and other books in the MCC's collection. I am also most grateful to the secretaries of many of the County Clubs for providing me with information from their records.

I have consulted the files of a large number of contemporary English and Australian newspapers in the search for information, and I must acknowledge my indebtedness to all of them, as well as to the staff of the British Museum

Newspaper Library, Colindale, for their patience and efficiency in supplying my needs.

Among the many books on cricket to which I have referred, to the authors of all of which I am indeed grateful, *Wisden's Cricketers' Almanack* is, of course, pre-eminent, and like so many other writers, I have found it indispensable.

Several members of the Cricket Society have been most helpful in answering my queries and in other ways; I tender my thanks to them, and to all others who have assisted me – and most especially to my wife for her continual help and encouragement.

B.J. WAKLEY

NOTE: All facts, figure and records are stated as at 1 October 1958.

# INTRODUCTION

DONALD GEORGE BRADMAN was born on 27 August 1908, at Cootamundra, in New South Wales, and spent most of his early life at Bowral, some 80 miles from Sydney.

His introduction into first-class cricket, at the age of 19, occurred at a time when there was a great opportunity for young batsmen of ability, both in New South Wales and Australian XIs. Australia, under the captaincy first of W.W. Armstrong and then of H.L. Collins, had easily won the first three Test match series against England after the 1914–8 war, but England had become steadily stronger, and in 1926 at last recovered the Ashes; and of the leading batsmen in the 1926 Australian team, most had reached or were approaching the end of their cricket careers.

Of these, C.G. Macartney, W. Bardsley, J.M. Taylor, H.L. Collins and T.J.E. Andrews were all from New South Wales, as also was C.E. Kelleway, another veteran who had failed to gain inclusion in the 1926 team; and this left A.F. Kippax, who certainly deserved to have been but also was not selected for the 1926 side, as the only experienced batsman in the New South Wales XI with any promise for the future. The New South Wales selectors took energetic steps to fill these vacancies at the top of the state's batting order, and the first of their discoveries was A.A. Jackson, who in his first season for New South Wales in 1926–7, at the age of 17, made 500 runs, average 50.00, and who died in 1933 at the age of 23, after a short and brilliant career; another was S.J. McCabe, who first appeared for New South Wales in 1928–9, at the age of 18. Between these two came Bradman, who, after missing selection for New South Wales' first two matches of the 1927–8 season (*v* the New Zealanders and Queensland), was chosen for the next, *v* South Australia at Adelaide, in the absence of Jackson owing to illness.

Nor were the future prospects of Australia much brighter than those of New South Wales, for the Australian selectors too had to find virtually a new batting order; indeed, there were then in Australia only two batsmen of proved Test match quality who held any promise for the future, the Victorian opening pair of W.M. Woodfull and W.H. Ponsford.

At the time that Bradman was coming to the fore, Ponsford was the leading batsman in Australia; he was a great player, with a vast appetite for runs. High scoring had prevailed, especially on Australian wickets, for many years before the appearance of Ponsford or Bradman (up to the beginning of the 1927–8 season, when Bradman made his début, 81 double centuries had been scored in Australia, against 388 in England, despite the limited amount of first-class cricket played in an Australian season), but it was Ponsford who, in the consistency of his huge scoring, set the example to Bradman.

Ponsford had made 429 for Victoria *v* Tasmania in 1922–3, at the age of 22, in his fourth innings in first-class cricket, thereby passing A.C. MacLaren's record score of 424, set up in 1895, and had played in all five Test matches *v* England in 1924–5, making centuries in his first two Tests; he had then had a rather less successful time in England in 1926 where, handicapped by illness, he made only 901 runs at an average of 40.95, and found a place in the Australian team in only two of the Test matches. On his return to Australia, however, he opened a vein of high scoring which even Bradman never surpassed; counting his 102 for the Australians *v* Western Australia at the end of the 1925–6 season, he made centuries in 11 consecutive matches in Australia, and many of his scores were colossal. In 1926–7, in six matches, he made 214 and 54, 151, 352, 108 and 84, 12 and 116, 131 and 7 – 1,229 runs, average 122.90; and in 1927–8, he started with 133, 437, 202 and 38, and 336, before finishing with 6 and 2, and 63. That season in Australia he made 1,217 runs, average 152.12, and by the end of it his record on Australian wickets was: 63 innings, twice not out, 5,653 runs, average 92.67.

He made his 437 for Victoria *v* Queensland at Melbourne, in ten hours 21 minutes, at the same time as Bradman was making his first appearance for New South Wales at Adelaide; this 437 broke Ponsford's own record score in a first-class match of 429, and stood as a record for just over two years, until Bradman himself broke it with a score 452 not out; but even Bradman only made one score of over 400, and never made 1,000 runs in a month in Australia, as Ponsford did that December (1,146 runs in five innings), nor did he ever make as many as 1,013 runs in four consecutive innings. Ponsford never reached the same form again, though he often batted finely for Victoria and for Australia, and it was not long before Bradman himself eclipsed him, both in consistency and in size of scores.

Whereas Australia, therefore, had almost completely to rebuild her Test match XI, especially in regard to the batsmen, England's position was much happier. In addition to possessing a powerful opening attack in H. Larwood and M.W. Tate, England's batting had seldom been stronger; commencing with such great batsmen as J.B. Hobbs, H. Sutcliffe, F.E. Woolley and E. Hendren, there were other experienced players of an ability only slightly inferior to theirs, and at least three young men of the richest promise in W.R. Hammond, K.S. Duleepsinhji and M. Leyland. It looked, therefore, as if, in the normal course of events, England should retain the Ashes from Australia for some time to come.

That was the aspect of the world of cricket when Bradman made his first appearance; he was soon to alter it dramatically.

# PART I

# Bradman in First-Class Cricket

# 1927–49

# 1927–8

## AGED NINETEEN

———◆◆✕◆◆———

1. **NEW SOUTH WALES** *v* **SOUTH AUSTRALIA**, at Adelaide, 16, 17, 19 and
   20 December 1927

SCORES: New South Wales 519 (A.F. Kippax 143, D.G. Bradman 118, N.E.
Phillips 112, T.J.E. Andrews 58) and 150 (C.V. Grimmett 8 for 57);
South Australia 481 (K.J. Schneider 108, V.Y. Richardson 80, G.W.
Harris 77) and 189 for 9 wickets (R.L.A. McNamee 5 for 53). New South
Wales lost by 1 wicket.

| | |
|---|---|
| D.G. BRADMAN c. N.L. Williams b J.D. Scott | 118 |
| b. C.V. Grimmett | 33 |

Bradman faced a stern test in his first first-class match, for the opposing bowlers
included Grimmett, then perhaps the best bowler in Australia, as well as other
useful performers such as Scott and P.K. Lee; moreover, he was suffering from an
injured hand. He went in just before tea on the first day at number seven, with the
score 250 for 4 (Kippax had previously retired ill), and promptly hit two fours off
Grimmett in his first over. He reached 50 in 67 minutes, but thereafter went more
slowly, being 65 not out at the close of play after one and three-quarter hours'
batting.

He soon settled down again next morning, and reached his century after two
hours 41 minutes at the wicket, by pulling Lee to the fine-leg boundary. He had a
stand of 111 for the eighth wicket with Kippax, when the latter resumed his
innings, and was last out, just before lunch, caught in the gully after a stay of three
hours eight minutes; he hit eight fours, gave no chance, and saw 269 runs added
while he was in. The best feature of his innings was the confident way in which he
used his feet to play the bowling of Grimmett. He was the 20th Australian
batsman to make a century on his début in first-class cricket.

In the second innings, the wicket gave Grimmett some help, and he dominated
all the batsmen. Bradman, going in before lunch on the last day with the score 61
for 4, took part in the only stand of the innings, adding 65 for the fifth wicket with
G. Morgan, whose 34 was top score; he batted for 64 minutes before being bowled

off his pads soon after lunch. After his dismissal at 126 for 5, Grimmett quickly finished off the innings, and gave South Australia the opportunity to seize a thrilling victory; the winning runs were four byes from a ball which just missed the off-stump.

## 2. NEW SOUTH WALES *v* VICTORIA, at Melbourne, 23, 24, 26 and 27 December 1927

SCORES: Victoria 355 (W.H. Ponsford 202, W.M. Woodfull 99, R.L.A. McNamee 7 for 77) and 386 for 7 wickets dec. (W.M. Woodfull 191*, H.L. Hendry 59, J.A. Scaife 54); New South Wales 367 (T.J.E. Andrews 110, G. Morgan 93, H. Ironmonger 5 for 108) and 152 (T.J.E. Andrews 53, D.D.J. Blackie 6 for 32). New South Wales lost by 222 runs.

| | | |
|---|---|---|
| D.G. BRADMAN | lbw. b. A.E.V. Hartkopf | 31 |
| | b. D.D.J. Blackie | 5 |

Bradman went in after tea on the second day, with the score 257 for 4, and when he was out the total had been raised to 318 for 7. He used his feet confidently to the slow bowlers, but he should have been stumped off Blackie when about 20, and he should also have been easily run out just before his dismissal. His innings lasted 46 minutes.

His second innings began at 106 for 4, on the last afternoon, and at 113 for 5, after ten minutes, Blackie yorked him, the performance of the New South Wales batsmen being very disappointing. On the other hand, Bradman had a close and prolonged view of Woodfull and Ponsford.

## 3. NEW SOUTH WALES *v* QUEENSLAND, at Sydney, 31 December 1927, 2, 3, 4 and 5 January 1928

SCORES: New South Wales 639 (A.F. Kippax 315*, G. Morgan 121, J.M. Gregory 63) and 100 for 8 wickets (O.E. Nothling 5 for 39); Queensland 276 (L. Litster 82, O.E. Nothling 74) and 590 (R.L. Higgins 179, W. Rowe 147, F.C. Thompson 68, L.E. Oxenham 50). Drawn.

| | | |
|---|---|---|
| D.G. BRADMAN | b. F.J. Gough | 0 |
| | c. L.P. O'Connor b. O.E. Nothling | 13 |

Going in on the second morning at 467 for 6, after a stand of 253 between Kippax and Morgan, Bradman watched Kippax score a single to mid-on, and was bowled first ball in trying to emulate the stroke, playing across a rather faster

---

* not out

one. Kippax played a magnificent innings.

Forced to follow on, 363 behind, Queensland made a great recovery, and set New South Wales 228 to win; and then, on the last morning, Nothling made such good use of a rain-affected wicket that, when Bradman went in, with 74 minutes left to play, his side was 60 for 6 and struggling to avoid defeat. He batted cautiously for 66 minutes, showing excellent defence and judgement on an unpleasant pitch, before being caught at the wicket at 99 for 8, eight minutes from the close, after having done much to save New South Wales from defeat.

## 4. NEW SOUTH WALES *v* SOUTH AUSTRALIA, at Sydney, 6, 7, 9 and 10 January 1928

SCORES: New South Wales 291 (A.A. Jackson 131) and 368 (A.A. Jackson 122, D.G. Bradman 73, A.F. Kippax 58, J.D. Scott 5 for 108); South Australia 248 (W.C. Alexander 58, C.V. Grimmett 54, A. Hack 50, C.O. Nicholls 5 for 115) and 293 (V.Y. Richardson 86, K.J. Schneider 54). New South Wales won by 118 runs.

| | |
|---|---|
| D.G. BRADMAN c. and b. D.G. McKay | 2 |
| st. A. Hack b. C.V. Grimmett | 73 |

This match was a triumph for Jackson who, a year younger than Bradman, hit a century in each innings. Bradman's first innings was very poor; he went in at 190 for 4, on the first afternoon, gave a stumping chance off Grimmett from his first ball, snicked his second for 2, and was out off his third, at 193 for 5; he tried to turn a full-pitch to leg and hit it with the edge of his bat. His second innings, however, was much better; going in early on the third morning, at 224 for 4, he started rather scratchily against Grimmett, but thereafter was very brilliant, using his feet to that bowler, and on one occasion hitting him for 18 in an over. He reached 50 in 48 minutes, and was batting altogether for only 79 minutes, hitting ten fours. He should have been stumped, yards down the pitch, off Grimmett when 51 and he was out in this way in the end, again after stepping out to drive; the score had then been raised to 351 for 7.

## 5. NEW SOUTH WALES *v* VICTORIA, at Sydney, 26, 27, 28, 30 and 31 January 1928

SCORES: New South Wales 533 (A.F. Kippax 134, G. Morgan 110, C.O. Nicholls 110, W.A. Oldfield 101, E.L. a'Beckett 6 for 119) and 353 for 8 wickets dec. (D.G. Bradman 134*, D.D.J. Blackie 6 for 101); Victoria 422 (H.L. Hendry 138, J.S. Ryder 106, W.M. Woodfull 94) and 205 for 1 wicket (K.E. Rigg 110*, W.M. Woodfull 81*). Drawn.

D.G. BRADMAN st. J.L. Ellis b. D.D.J. Blackie     7
          not out                       134

Bradman's contribution to the big first-innings score, when he went in at 276 for 4 on the first evening, was again a modest one, and he was out at 290 for 5, after struggling for half an hour; but again he redeemed himself in the second innings. Going in at 86 for 4, at a time of some danger to New South Wales, just before lunch on he fourth day, he should have been easily run out when 8; his partner refused his call and he was stranded in mid-wicket, only a poor return enabling him to scramble back. Apart from this, he proceeded to play another chanceless innings; he reached 50 in 98 minutes and 100 in three hours 17 minutes. His stand with Oldfield realised 118 for the seventh wicket, and by the close of play he had made 134, including 13 fours, in three and three-quarter hours, off bowlers who included E.L. a'Beckett, D.D.J. Blackie and H. Ironmonger. New South Wales declared overnight, but there was no prospect of a result in the two and a half hours remaining.

This was the first-class match in which eight centuries were scored, a record which stood until nine were recorded in the match between Maharashtra and Bombay, at Poona, in 1948–9; but W.H. Ponsford's contribution to the huge number of runs scored were 6 and 2.

## SUMMARY, 1927–8

| | Matches | Innings | NO | HS | Runs | Average | Centuries |
|---|---|---|---|---|---|---|---|
| All First-class Matches | | | | | | | |
| Sheffield Shield Matches | 5 | 10 | 1 | 134* | 416 | 46.22 | 2 |
| All Matches for NSW | | | | | | | |

Thirteen Australians had higher first-class batting averages than Bradman's, and 11 had more runs, W.H. Ponsford being easily first with 1,217 runs, average 152.12, including four centuries. A.F. Kippax was the leading New South Wales batsman, with 926 runs, average 84.18, and also four centuries, but, after him, A.A. Jackson's and T.J.E. Andrews' batting averages of 46.40 (for 464 runs) and 42.67 (for 509 runs) were only fractionally higher than Bradman's. Kippax (119 and 0*), Jackson (104) and Andrews (134) all improved their figures at the expense of the New Zealanders, so that in Sheffield Shield matches only, Bradman's aggregate and average were second best to Kippax's for New South Wales.

He just missed selection for the Australian team which, under the captaincy of V.Y. Richardson, toured New Zealand in February and March 1928; the team included Ponsford, Woodfull, Kippax and Jackson.

# 1928–9

## AGED TWENTY

———◆➤✕◆◆———

The MCC team, under the captaincy of A.P.F. Chapman, which toured Australia this season, was one of the strongest ever to visit Australia.

### 6. REST OF AUSTRALIA *v* AUSTRALIA (Test match trial), at Melbourne, 19, 20 and 22 October 1928

SCORES: Rest of Australia 111 and 244 (O.E. Nothling 62*, G.W. Harris 51, R.K. Oxenham 6 for 62); Australia 398 (W.H. Ponsford 79, W.A. Oldfield 58). Rest of Australia lost by an innings and 43 runs.

| | | |
|---|---|---|
| D.G. BRADMAN | c. W.A. Oldfield b. C.V. Grimmett | 14 |
| | b. R.K. Oxenham | 5 |

This was a disappointing match, not least for Bradman. In the first innings he batted for 34 minutes on the first afternoon, and helped to raise the score from 79 for 4 to 100 for 6, before being caught at the wicket; while on the third afternoon, he went in at 124 for 4, was 5 not out when rain stopped play at tea-time ten minutes later, and was yorked by the first ball after the resumption, to make the score 133 for 7. He made his 5 in one stroke, a pull off Grimmett, without assistance from any overthrow.

### 7. NEW SOUTH WALES *v* QUEENSLAND, at Brisbane (Exhibition Ground), 27, 29, 30, 31 October and 1 November 1928

SCORES: Queensland 324 (L.P. O'Connor 72, F.J. Gough 67, R. Higgins 58, J.E.H. Hooker 6 for 46) and 322 (F.C. Thompson 158*); New South Wales 248 (D.G. Bradman 131, A.A. Jackson 50, H.M. Thurlow 6 for 59) and 401 for 4 wickets (D.G. Bradman 133*, A.F. Kippax 96, A.A. Jackson 71). New South Wales won by 6 wickets.

| | | |
|---|---|---|
| D.G. BRADMAN | c. L.P. O'Connor b. H.M. Thurlow | 131 |
| | not out | 133 |

New South Wales' victory was a triumph for Bradman, who made a century in each innings, the first of the four occasions on which he did so. Going in on the second morning with the score 7 for 1, he added 113 with Jackson for the second wicket; reaching 50 in 77 minutes, he was 95 not out at tea-time, and completed his century in two hours 44 minutes. He batted altogether for three hours 32 minutes, and hit 14 fours; his only vestige of a mistake was a very hard c. and b. chance to R.K. Oxenham at 32. He was caught at the wicket with the score 246 for 5, and the last five wickets thereafter fell for the addition of only two more runs; he thus scored 54 per cent of his side's total (apart from extras). Bradman, Jackson and Kippax (47) scored all but 12 of their side's runs from the bat, the next highest innings being 5.

Being 76 behind on the first innings, New South Wales were set to make 399 to win. Bradman went in soon after lunch on the fourth day at 121 for 1, and had reached 88 not out by the close of play, after two hours 57 minutes' batting; he was missed in the slips off Thurlow when he was 38, but otherwise gave no chance; his 50 came in one hour 54 minutes, and his third-wicket stand with Kippax put on 185 in two hours 31 minutes.

Next morning he took 34 minutes to complete his second century of the match, after batting for three hours 31 minutes, and went on to give New South Wales victory, with 65 minutes to spare, having batted altogether for four hours 22 minutes; his eleventh four, an on-drive, was the winning hit. The Queensland bowlers included P.M. Hornibrook, H.M. Thurlow, R.K. Oxenham and O.E. Nothling, all of whom played for Australia at one time or another.

A hundred in each innings had been scored on only ten previous occasions in Sheffield Shield matches, four of these being by New South Wales batsmen; Bradman did this again in 1937–8, for South Australia.

## 8. NEW SOUTH WALES *v* MCC TEAM, at Sydney, 9, 10, 12 and 13 November 1928

SCORES: MCC Team 734 for 7 wickets dec. (W.R. Hammond 225, E. Hendren 167, D.R. Jardine 140, H. Sutcliffe 67); New South Wales 349 (C.E. Kelleway 93*, D.G. Bradman 87, A.F. Kippax 64, A.P. Freeman 5 for 136) and 364 for 3 wickets (A.F. Kippax 136*, D.G. Bradman 132*). Drawn.

D.G. BRADMAN  b. A.P. Freeman     87
               not out          132

After fielding out to MCC's huge score for almost two days, New South Wales had lost 3 wickets for 38 when Bradman went in to bat, in indifferent light, ten minutes before the close of play. Getting 6 not out overnight, he reached 50 next morning in 85 minutes; after lunch, however, he was by no means comfortable against Freeman, who appealed several times for lbw. against him before causing him to play on, the ball coming off his bat, on to his foot, and thence on to his wicket. He batted for two hours 11 minutes, and hit eight fours, being fifth out at 196.

An even better display was his second innings; going in soon after lunch on the last day, at 115 for 3, he reached 50 in 65 minutes and 100 in two hours eight minutes; and when bad light stopped play 20 minutes early, he and Kippax had put on 249 undefeated for the fourth wicket, in two hours 36 minutes. Bradman hit 14 fours, mostly hard drives, in a brilliant and chanceless innings; the bowlers whom he mastered included H. Larwood, M.W. Tate, A.P. Freeman and W.R. Hammond.

This 249 is still the record for the fourth wicket for New South Wales *v* MCC, the previous best being 138 by C.G. Macartney and T.J.E. Andrews in 1920–1; at the time it was also a record for the fourth wicket against any touring team in Australia and against an English touring team anywhere, the previous highest being 198 by Macartney and J.M. Gregory, for Australia, 1920–1, and 198 by H.S. Love and R.L. Park, for Victoria, 1922–3. In 1937–8, I.S. Lee and R.G. Gregory passed this with a stand of 262 for Victoria *v* MCC.


9. **AN AUSTRALIAN XI *v* MCC TEAM**, at Sydney, 16, 17, 19 and 20 November 1928

SCORES: An Australian XI 231 (D.G. Bradman 58\*) and 243 (A.A. Jackson 61, G.W. Harris 56); MCC Team 357 (E. Tyldesley 69, M.W. Tate 59, J.B. Hobbs 58, C.P. Mead 58) and 118 for 2 wickets (J.B. Hobbs 67\*). An Australian XI lost by 8 wickets.

| | | |
|---|---|---|
| D.G. BRADMAN | not out | 58 |
| | lbw. b. M.W. Tate | 18 |

Bradman's first innings was one of his slowest, averaging only 18 runs an hour. Going in at 81 for 3 just before lunch on the first day, he took two hours 45 minutes (the slowest of his career) to reach 50, and he was undefeated when the Australian XI was all out 20 minutes from time, after batting soundly for three hours 13 minutes. The MCC bowlers, and in particular J.C. White, flighting the ball into a strong wind, bowled with great accuracy and pinned Bradman down for long periods; he hit a five and four fours.

In the second innings, he had to go in at 128 for 3 after tea on the third day, and had not scored when bad light stopped play two minutes later. He stayed next morning until the score was 171 for 4, before Tate had him lbw.; he batted for 39 minutes.


10. **AUSTRALIA *v* ENGLAND**, First Test match, at Brisbane (Exhibition Ground), 30 November, 1, 3, 4 and 5 December 1928

SCORES: England 521 (E. Hendren 169, H. Larwood 70, A.P.F. Chapman 50) and 342 for 8 wickets dec. (C.P. Mead 73, D.R. Jardine 65*, C.V. Grimmett 6 for 131); Australia 122 (H. Larwood 6 for 32) and 66. Australia lost by 675 runs.

| | | |
|---|---|---|
| D.G. BRADMAN | lbw. b. M.W. Tate | 18 |
| | c. A.P.F. Chapman, b. J.C. White | 1 |

Bradman's introduction to Test match cricket was an unhappy experience; Australia suffered the heaviest defeat in her history, and he himself failed in each innings. In the first, he went in on the third morning at 71 for 5, and batted quite well for 33 minutes and 40 balls, hitting four fours, before falling, at 101 for 6, to Tate's slower ball; his 18 was, in fact, the third highest score, and he shaped as well as anyone. In the second innings, the wicket was difficult, after overnight rain, followed by hot sunshine, when he went in at 47 for 4 on the fifth morning, and he had been in for only four minutes when, off his fifth ball, he cocked up a defensive stroke to give a gentle catch to Chapman at silly point, to be fifth out at 49.

In playing in a Test match after only nine previous first-class matches, Bradman did not create a record, even for Australia, but until then no Australian batsman had made such a swift rise to Test match status since the very early days; those who played Test cricket even earlier in their careers were all either bowlers or all-rounders. E.H. Bromley's first Test in 1932–3 was his eighth appearance in first-class cricket, and A.R. Morris's in 1946–7 was also his eighth, though owing to the war he was then aged 24, having played his first-class match six years previously.

\*\*\*

Bradman was one of the 12 chosen for the Australian team for the second Test match at Sydney on 14–20 December 1928, but he was, on the morning of the match, excluded from the XI and made twelfth man – a decision on the part of the Australian selectors which was by no means as absurd as, in retrospect, it now appears to be. However, he had a lot of work to do; W.H. Ponsford broke a bone in his finger when batting in Australia's first innings, and Bradman therefore had to field all through the England innings of 636, including 251 from W.R. Hammond. Australia lost in the end by 8 wickets.

11. **NEW SOUTH WALES** *v* **VICTORIA**, at Melbourne, 22, 24, 25, 26 and 27 December 1928

SCORES: Victoria 376 (J.S. Ryder 175, E.L. a'Beckett 113) and 251 for 6 wickets dec. (E.L. a'Beckett 95, H.L. Hendry 69*); New South Wales 420 (A.F. Kippax 260*, J.E.H. Hooker 62) and 156 for 2 wickets (D.G. Bradman 71*). Drawn.

D.G. BRADMAN   b. H.L. Hendry     1
           not out           71

Going in on the second evening at 54 for 3, and being out one run and three minutes later, Bradman failed in the first innings, in common with many others; New South Wales were later, in fact, 113 for 9, before Kippax and Hooker added 307 for the last wicket – a world record.

On the last morning, New South Wales were set to make 208 to win in two and a half hours, but they were already well behind the clock when Bradman went in, with the score 17 for 1 after 47 minutes' batting; there was therefore little chance of a definite result, and Bradman enjoyed some batting practice; he reached 50 in 74 minutes, and altogether was at the wicket for one hour and 43 minutes. He hit four boundaries.

12. **AUSTRALIA** *v* **ENGLAND**, Third Test match, at Melbourne, 29 and 31 December 1928, 1, 2, 3, 4 and 5 January 1929

SCORES: Australia 397 (J.S. Ryder 112, A.F. Kippax 100, D.G. Bradman 79) and 351 (D.G. Bradman 112, W.M. Woodfull 107, J.C. White 5 for 107); England 417 (W.R. Hammond 200, D.R. Jardine 62, H. Sutcliffe 58, D.D.J. Blackie 6 for 94) and 332 for 7 wickets (H. Sutcliffe 135). Australia lost by 3 wickets, and England won the rubber and retained the Ashes.

D.G. BRADMAN   b. W.R. Hammond        79
           c. G. Duckworth b. G. Geary    112

Bradman fully justified his return to the Australian XI. In the first innings, he had to wait while Ryder and Kippax added 161 for the fourth wicket, going in 46 minutes from the end of the first day with the score 218 for 4; he was 26 not out overnight, and reached his 50 on the second morning after a further hour. Being 60 not out at lunch, he batted altogether for three hours 14 minutes for his 79 before being bowled by a yorker. He and a'Beckett added 86 for the seventh wicket, and the score had been raised to the respectability of 373 for 7 when Bradman was out; he hit nine fours and scored his runs, at the rate of 24 an hour, off 233 balls.

His second innings, also chanceless, was even better, and he reached his first century in Test match cricket. Going in at 12.36 p.m. on the fifth day, when Australia were only 143 for 4, he was all but bowled by White when 7; very cautious to start with, he was 9 not out at lunch, took two hours 23 minutes to reach 50, and was 60 at tea. Thereafter, as the bowlers tired, he brightened up considerably; whereas before he had played back to J.C. White, and been in some difficulty, he now began to use his feet to jump out to drive, with the result that his second 50 took only 83 minutes, the century taking three hours 46 minutes altogether; he reached it at 5.30 p.m., after an anxious wait at 96, by forcing White, off his back foot, past mid-on for 4 all run. He was finally caught at the wicket at 345 for 8, nine minutes from time, after batting for four hours seven minutes, and hitting seven fours; he received 282 balls, and carried the latter part of the innings on his shoulders against such bowlers at Larwood, Tate, Geary, White and Hammond. He and R.K. Oxenham added 93 for the eighth wicket.

Up till that time, he was the youngest player ever to make a century in a Test match; he was then 20 years 129 days, the previous youngest being 20 years 317 days – C. Hill in 1897–8. In the next Test match, A.A. Jackson performed this feat at the age of 19 years 152 days, while the present record is 19 years 121 days – H.G. Vivian and R.N. Harvey. Since the very early days of Test matches, when C. Bannerman scored 165* in the first Test match of all in 1876–7, in his seventh first-class match, but at the age of 25, after being for several years the best Australian batsman of the day, no Australian batsman had up till then scored a Test match century with so little first-class experience behind him as only 11 matches, R.A. Duff (12 previous matches) being the previous best; A.R. Morris (aged 24) and R.N. Harvey have since hit Test centuries in their eleventh first-class games, while G.A. Headley did so for the West Indies in his seventh.

That England won in the end was due to superb batting on a sticky wicket by Hobbs, Sutcliffe and Jardine; but no side should have been permitted to get 332 runs in such conditions.

## 13. NEW SOUTH WALES *v* SOUTH AUSTRALIA, at Adelaide 11, 12, 14, 15 and 16 January 1929

SCORES: New South Wales 402 (A.A. Jackson 162, A.F. Kippax 107) and 313 (A.A. Jackson 90, C. Andrews 87); South Australia 304 (C.V. Grimmett 71*) and 351 (W.C. Alexander 79, D.G. McKay 74). New South Wales won by 60 runs.

| D.G. BRADMAN | c. C.V. Grimmett b. T.W. Wall | 5 |
| | b. T.W. Wall | 2 |

This match had a curiously far-reaching effect on Bradman's career, for he was tried as an opening batsman and, failing in each innings, was never thereafter seriously considered for that position, though he occasionally opened the innings in later matches. On the first morning he failed to get over a rising ball and was caught at square-leg with only 7 on the board, after batting for ten minutes; while, when New South Wales' second innings began after lunch on the third day, he was bowled in the first over with the score 2.

This was one of the only two matches in his career in which he was dismissed twice for single figures.

## 14. NEW SOUTH WALES *v* VICTORIA, at Sydney, 24, 25, 26, 28 and 29 January 1929

SCORES: New South Wales 713 for 6 wickets dec. (D.G. Bradman 340*, A.G. Fairfax 104, S.J. McCabe 60, A. Marks 56); Victoria 265 (B.A. Onyons 61, J.E.H. Hooker 6 for 42) and 510 for 7 wickets (B.A. Onyons 131, L.S. Darling 96, J.A. Scaife 91, T. Bird 63). Drawn.

D.G. BRADMAN not out    340

This was the match in which Bradman first displayed his potentialities as a record-breaker and his ruthless dominance in building up a colossal score. Going in shortly before lunch on the first day at 76 for 1, he reached 50 in 85 minutes, and 100 in three hours nine minutes, being 129 not out at the close of play after three hours 51 minutes.

Soon after the start next morning, when he was 133, he completed 1,000 runs for the season for the first time in his career. He had reached 196 by lunch-time, having slowed up as he approached 200; this score took him five hours 57 minutes. The 300, which he reached just before tea, took seven hours 33 minutes, and when New South Wales declared, he had been at the wicket for eight hours eight minutes and had hit 38 fours.

He helped to add 161 with Fairfax for the second wicket, 118 with McCabe for the fourth wicket, 120 with R.H. Bettington (40) for the sixth wicket, and 111 unfinished for the seventh wicket with J.H. Fingleton (25*); and he was in while 637 was added to the score. He gave no chance, and the only criticism of his innings was in regard to his running between the wickets; he should, in fact, have been easily run out when 69, 76 and 310, poor returns enabling him to scramble home after bad calling had put his wicket into jeopardy. Among the bowlers who suffered at his hands were H.I. Ebeling and H. Ironmonger.

The highest score then in any Sheffield Shield match by a New South Wales player was 340* (previous best, 315* by A.F. Kippax *v* Queensland, 1927–8, which was the only previous treble century); it was the highest score *v* Victoria in any match, the highest score by a New South Wales batsman *v* Victoria in a Sheffield Shield match (previous best, 281 by M.A. Noble for New South Wales, 1905–6). Bradman himself later broke most of these records again, either with his 452* for New South Wales *v* Queensland in 1929–30, or his 357 for South Australia *v* Victoria in 1935–6; but this 340* still remains the highest score for New South Wales *v* Victoria.

At eight hours eight minutes, this was in point of time the longest innings he ever played, and it is the longest ever played for New South Wales in a Sheffield Shield match; the previous longest in a Shield match for New South Wales was seven hours 12 minutes by Kippax, 271* *v* Victoria, 1925–6, though H. Moses, in 1887–8, batted ten and a half hours for 297* *v* Victoria, before the start of the Shield competition.

Bradman was the first batsman to reach 1,000 runs this season; he reached it on

25 January, the earliest until then by a New South Wales batsman, W. Bardsley, on 17 February, being the previous best, in 1910-1, though Bradman several times improved upon this date in later seasons. At 20 years 151 days, he was the youngest batsman ever to reach 1,000 runs in an Australian season, the previous best being C. Hill, 20 years 340 days; N.C. O'Neill was also 20 years 340 days when he completed 1,000 runs for the 1957–8 season.

At 20 years 151 days, he was also then the youngest batsman to play an innings of 300 and over, V.T. Trumper, at 21 years 269 days, being the previous youngest (300* for Australians *v* Sussex, 1899), and W.H. Ponsford, at 22 years 109 days, being the previous youngest to do so in Australia (429 for Victoria *v* Tasmania, 1922–3); Bradman remains the youngest Australian to perform this feat, and the youngest to do so in Australia, but F.M. Worrell was only 19 years 199 days when he made 308* in the West Indies in 1943–4. His 340* is still the highest score ever made by a batsman under 21 (previous best, 224 by W.G. Grace, 1866; by an Australian and in Australia, 206* by C. Hill, 1895–6; next best, 314* by C.L. Walcott, in the West Indies, 1945–6; next best by an Australian and in Australia, 274 by C.L. Badcock, 1933-4). This was then, in fact, only the fifth time that a batsman under the age of 21 had made a score of 200 and over, Hill having done so twice. It has now been done 22 times, including thrice by R.S. Modi in India; but only Bradman, Worrell and Walcott have gone on to reach 300.

Bradman is the only batsman to make a treble century as well as a hundred in each innings, both before reaching the age of 21; W.G. Grace, G.A. Headley and Hanif Mohamed are the only other batsmen to make a double century as well as a hundred in each innings while still under 21.

Bradman was also then the youngest batsman to make a score of 200 or over for New South Wales; Trumper was 21 years 38 days old when he made 292* *v* Tasmania in 1898–9, and I.D. Craig only 17 years 205 days when he made 213* *v* the South Africans, 1952–3; Bradman is still the youngest to make a double century for New South Wales in a Sheffield Shield match (previous best, Trumper, 23 years 94 days when he made 230 *v* Victoria, 1900–1; next best, N.C. O'Neill, 20 years 340 days when he made 233 *v* Victoria, 1957–8).

H.L. Collins (1912-3) and Hanif Mohamed (1957–8) are the only other batsmen to have had a share in four century partnerships in the same innings. Bradman in his innings was in while 637 runs were added to the score, the most until then for New South Wales in a Sheffield Shield match; M.A. Noble, with 281 out of 565 in 1905–6, was the previous best, but Bradman next season broke his own record by helping to add as many as 739. He was the tenth batsman and the fifth Australian to make his first double century into a treble century; nine more batsmen, but no Australians, have done so since. Bradman's previous highest score was 134*, which he now improved upon by 206.


15. **AUSTRALIA** *v* **ENGLAND**, Fourth Test match, at Adelaide, 1, 2, 4, 5, 6, 7 and 8 February 1929

SCORES: England 334 (W.R. Hammond 119*, J.B. Hobbs 74, H. Sutcliffe 64, C.V. Grimmett 5 for 102) and 383 (W.R. Hammond 177, D.R. Jardine 98); Australia 369 (A.A. Jackson 164, J.S. Ryder 63, J.C. White 5 for 130) and 336 (J.S. Ryder 87, D.G. Bradman 58, A.F. Kippax 51, J.C. White 8 for 126). Australia lost by 12 runs.

| | |
|---|---|
| D.G. BRADMAN  c. H. Larwood b. M.W. Tate | 40 |
| run out | 58 |

Bradman's first innings began early on the third day, with the score 145 for 4; 34 not out at lunch, he was dismissed soon afterwards, being caught in the slips, the ball being deflected off the wicket-keeper's gloves. He batted rather streakily for 80 minutes and 97 balls, but helped Jackson, who played a magnificent innings, to add 82 valuable runs. In making 40, he carried his season's aggregate to 1,247, thus passing the previous record by an Australian for a season's aggregate in Australia, 1,246 by V.T. Trumper in 1910–11.

His second innings was much sounder, and all but won the match for Australia. Wanting 349 to win, Australia had lost 4 wickets for 211 when he went in on the sixth evening; he batted for 68 minutes for 16 not out overnight, but completed his 50 next morning after another 43 minutes. With three wickets to fall and the score 320, he was batting with such skill and assurance that, despite White's magnificent bowling, Australia seemed to have the game in their grasp; but then Oldfield threw Bradman's wicket away with a most ill-judged call. Off the last ball of an over, Oldfield, instead of leaving the bowling to Bradman, played the ball straight to Hobbs at cover, and called; Bradman responded, but Hobbs' return was too good and Bradman was run out. His 58 was made in two hours 18 minutes (25 runs an hour) off 119 balls, and included four fours. Thereafter England just managed to win in a desperately close finish.

## 16. NEW SOUTH WALES *v* MCC TEAM, at Sydney, 16, 18 and 19 February 1929

SCORES: New South Wales 128 (J.C. White 5 for 48); MCC Team 144 for 4 wickets (E. Tyldesley 68*). Drawn.

D.G. BRADMAN  c. E. Tyldesley b. J.C. White        15

This game was ruined by rain. When it was possible to start, at 3 p.m. on Saturday, New South Wales were put in to bat; and on a none-too-easy wicket Bradman, going in at 45 for 3, was not at all comfortable before giving an easy catch to square-leg, being fourth out at 66, after staying for 20 minutes.

17. **NEW SOUTH WALES** *v* **SOUTH AUSTRALIA**, at Sydney, 1, 2, 4, 5 and 6 March 1929

SCORES: New South Wales 326 (A. Marks 92, F. Jordan 65, J.E.H. Hooker 62) and 399 for 9 wickets dec. (D.G. Bradman 175, C.V. Grimmett 5 for 116); South Australia 280 (G.W. Harris 107) and 385 (G.W. Harris 94, H.E.P. Whitfield 91, A. Hack 79, V.Y. Richardson 56). New South Wales won by 60 runs.

| | |
|---|---|
| D.G. BRADMAN  c. C.W. Walker b. C.V. Grimmett | 35 |
| c. C.W. Walker b. T.A. Carlton | 175 |

In the first innings, Bradman went in early on the first morning at 12 for 1 and batted soundly for 73 minutes before being well caught at the wicket on the leg side at 69 for 4.

His second innings was very brilliant; going in at 65 for 1, on the third afternoon, he soon got on top of the bowling, his first 50 taking one and a half hours and his second only 37 minutes. Being 125 not out at the close of the third day, after two hours 31 minutes, he added another 50 in 59 minutes next morning and was then caught at the wicket. He altogether batted three and a half hours, hit 14 fours, and had seen the score raised to 340 for 5; his fourth-wicket stand with S.J. McCabe (27) was worth 109. He gave no chance, and among the bowlers he mastered were T.W. Wall, J.D. Scott and C.V. Grimmett. A.G. Fairfax (41) was the next highest scorer.

18. **AUSTRALIA** *v* **ENGLAND**, Fifth Test match, at Melbourne, 8, 9, 11, 12, 13, 14, 15 and 16 March 1929

SCORES: England 519 (J.B. Hobbs 142, M. Leyland 137, E. Hendren 95) and 257 (J.B. Hobbs 65, M.W. Tate 54, M. Leyland 53*, T.W. Wall 5 for 66); Australia 491 (D.G. Bradman 123, W.M. Woodfull 102, A.G. Fairfax 65, G. Geary 5 for 105) and 287 for 5 wickets (J.S. Ryder 57*). Australia won by 5 wickets.

| | |
|---|---|
| D.G. BRADMAN  c. M.W. Tate b. G. Geary | 123 |
| not out | 37 |

Against England's big first-innings score, Australia were again in a critical situation when Bradman went in to bat directly after lunch on the fourth day, at 203 for 3, and again he played a splendid innings. Driving and cutting beautifully, he reached 50 in 71 minutes, was 62 not out at the tea interval, and at 5.38 p.m. completed his century in two hours 52 minutes, being 109 not out, after three hours one minutes, when bad light stopped play 13 minutes early. He gave one very sharp chance; when he had made 46, a hard on-drive off White went through the hands of deep mid-on.

Next morning he continued his fifth-wicket partnership with Fairfax until they had added 183, in three hours 33 minutes; Bradman was then caught at short-leg, after batting for three hours 37 minutes, by which time Australia, at 386 for 5, had been taken much of the way towards safety. He hit eight fours off 247 balls, and when he had made 5 he passed the aggregate record for an Australian season – 1,534 by G.A. Faulkner (South Africa) in 1910–1.

This stand of 183 was then a record for Australia's fifth wicket in any Test match; the previous highest was 143 by W.W. Armstrong and V.T. Trumper *v* South Africa, in Australia, 1910–1, and (*v* England) 142 by S.E. Gregory and J. Darling in Australia in 1894–5. This 183 was equalled in 1930–31 by W.H. Ponsford and W.M. Woodfull *v* the West Indies, and easily passed by Bradman and S.G. Barnes in Australia in 1946–7, when they added 405 for the fifth wicket *v* England. In scoring 123 out of 183 added while he was in (67 per cent), Bradman achieved the highest proportion of his career for Test match centuries.

Set 286 to win, Australia had reached 204 for 5 when Bradman went in on the eighth morning. He should have been stumped off J.C. White when he was 5, but thereafter he made no mistake and, 22 at lunch, he stayed with Ryder until the latter made the winning hit 20 minutes after the interval. Bradman's 37 took an hour and 12 minutes and was made off 89 deliveries. England's bowlers were again Larwood, Tate, Geary, White and Hammond.

## SUMMARY, 1928–9

| | Matches | Innings | NO | HS | Runs | Average | Centuries |
|---|---|---|---|---|---|---|---|
| All First-class Matches | 13 | 24 | 6 | 340* | 1690 | 93.88 | 7 |
| Test Matches | 4 | 8 | 1 | 123 | 468 | 66.85 | 2 |
| All Matches *v* MCC Team | 7 | 13 | 3 | 132* | 778 | 77.80 | 3 |
| Sheffield Shield Matches | 5 | 9 | 3 | 340* | 893 | 148.83 | 4 |
| All Matches for NSW | 7 | 12 | 4 | 340* | 1127 | 140.87 | 5 |

England won the Test match series by four matches to one and retained the Ashes.

New South Wales won the Sheffield Shield.

Bradman's aggregate of 1,690 remains a record for an Australian season, the previous best being 1,534 by G.A. Faulkner in 1910–1, and (by an Australian and a New South Wales batsman) 1,246 by V.T. Trumper, also in 1910–1; R.N. Harvey came close to it in 1952–3 with 1,659 runs.

In all first-class matches, W.M. Woodfull averaged 85.40, and A.F. Kippax scored 1,079 runs, each with four centuries, these being the next Australians to

Bradman in average, aggregate and centuries respectively; J.S. Ryder was the only other Australian to score 1,000 runs, but three members of the MCC team, W.R. Hammond, D.R. Jardine and E. Hendren, reached this total. Hammond's figures were 1,553 runs, average 91.35, he too passing Faulkner's record aggregate.

Hammond, like Bradman, scored seven centuries during the season; until then, six centuries (by W.H. Ponsford in 1926–7) had been the most ever scored in an Australian season, though Bradman himself twice later scored seven, and in 1947–48 made eight hundreds.

Bradman was second for Australia in the Test match batting averages, A.A. Jackson, in four innings, being top with an average of 69.00; Ryder, 492 runs, average 54.66, and Woodfull, 491 runs, average 54.55, including three centuries, both scored more runs than Bradman, no one else exceeding 400 for Australia. For England, however, Hammond scored 905 runs, average 113.12, both aggregate and average being records which Bradman beat in 1930; and Hendren scored 472 runs, average 52.44.

Bradman's aggregate of 468 was the highest on record for any Test series by a batsman under the age of 24 (previous best, 452 by C. Hill, 1897–8); in 1929–30, G.A. Headley made 703 runs, average 87.87, for the West Indies *v* England, but Bradman's performance is still the best for Australia, in Australia, and in an England *v* Australia series, for a batsman so young.

His aggregate of 893 runs in Sheffield Shield matches was then a record for New South Wales, the previous best being 888 by Kippax in 1926–7; Bradman twice later broke this record, with 894 in 1929–30 and 922 in 1933-4, and in 1957–58 N.C. O'Neill made 1,005. Only Kippax (in 1926–7) had previously scored four centuries in a season for New South Wales in Sheffield Shield matches only; Bradman did this again in 1933–4, and in 1948–9 A.R. Morris made five. Bradman's average 148.83 for Shield matches was also a record for New South Wales (previous best, 134.00 by Kippax, 1924–5), in 1932–3 and 1933–4, Bradman's Shield average was 150.00 and 184.40, the latter still being the record. His average of 140.87 in all matches for New South Wales was the highest on record, the previous best being 112.75 by J.R.M. Mackay in 1905–6; in 1933–4 Bradman increased this to 148.00, which is still the highest for New South Wales.

Bradman's 1,127 runs are still the record for all matches in a season for New South Wales, Mackay's 902 in 1905–6 being the previous best; Bradman shares with Mackay and Morris the record for the number of centuries (five) in a season in all matches for New South Wales, and with Mackay and Kippax the distinction of scoring centuries in the same season *v* Victoria, South Australia and Queensland; Kippax (1927–8) and Bradman did so in Sheffield Shield matches. W.H. Ponsford (1926–7 and 1927–8), G.W. Harris (1928–9) and A.L. Hassett (1946–7) are the only other batsmen to make Shield centuries *v* all three other States in the same season 1926–7 (when Queensland first took part) and 1947–8 (when Western Australia first came into the competition); Bradman did this in three later seasons for South Australia.

***

Bradman celebrated his twenty-first birthday on 27 August 1929, and by that time his record in first-class cricket (all in Australia) was: matches 18, innings 34, not out 7, highest score 340*, total runs 2,106, average 78.00, with nine centuries.

Of those who have played over 20 innings, his average of 78.00 was then a record for batsmen under the age of 21; the previous best was as far back as W.G. Grace, whose average up to 18 July 1869 was 49.23 for 2,511 runs – a magnificent record, considering the wickets he had to play on. The previous best Australian was C. Hill, 3,280 runs, average 40.00; later, N.C. O'Neill averaged 61.72 while under 21, his average in Australia being 60.46. In India, up to his twenty-first birthday in 1945, R.S. Modi actually averaged 101.27 (2,228 runs in 26 innings, with four not-outs), thus easily beating Bradman's 78.00 which, however, remains the record for Australian batsmen.

Bradman's aggregate of 2,106 was then a record for a batsman of under 21 for runs scored in Australia (previous best, 2,084 by C. Hill, who, however, also scored 1,196 runs in England in 1896 while still under 21). A.A. Jackson, a year younger than Bradman, had commenced his first-class career a year earlier, and by the end of 1928–29 had scored 1,956 runs in Australia; in 1929–30, his fourth season, at the age of 20, he took this aggregate to 2,586 runs in Australia (in 54 innings), thus passing Bradman's record.

Bradman made nine centuries in first-class cricket before he was 21; W.G. Grace had also made nine hundreds before reaching 21, the most on record, and C. Hill, with eight (including two in England) was the previous best among Australians. To the end of 1928–9, Jackson had made seven first-class centuries (his first at the age of 17 years three months, then the youngest in history), all in Australia; he made two more in 1929–30, thus equalling Bradman's record for Australian wickets, and he made another in England in 1930, his tenth in all first-class cricket before his twenty-first birthday. D.C.S. Compton later made 11 centuries before his coming-of-age, which is still the record.

Two of Bradman's centuries were made in Test matches between England and Australia, and this remains a record; before 1928–9, only Hill and J.W. Hearne had made even one Test century before their twenty-first birthdays. G.A. Headley made four hundreds for the West Indies v England in 1929–30, when only 20, and R.N. Harvey, for Australia, made one v India and one v England when only 19.

# 1929–30

## AGED TWENTY-ONE

———●▸◖◂●———

The MCC team, under A.H.H. Gilligan, played matches in Australia against the five leading States early this season before going on to New Zealand.

19. **NEW SOUTH WALES** *v* **QUEENSLAND**, at Brisbane (Exhibition Ground), 8, 9, 11 and 12 November 1929

SCORES: New South Wales 373 (A.A. Jackson 80, S.J. McCabe 77, R.K. Oxenham 5 for 72) and 198 (D.G. Bradman 66, A. Marks 51); Queensland 273 (F.J. Gough 69) and 275 (R.K. Oxenham 117). New South Wales won by 23 runs.

| | |
|---|---|
| D.G. BRADMAN run out | 48 |
| c. L.P. O'Connor b. F.M. Brew | 66 |

In the first innings, Bradman went in at 72 for 1 just before lunch on the first day and hit up 48 in 66 minutes, before being run out, his partner failing to respond to his call; he was second out at 148.

His second innings was one of his most dour; going in on the third morning at 37 for 3, he took two hours 35 minutes to reach 50, and batted for three hours 29 minutes altogether before being caught at the wicket. When he was out, the score had been raised to 185 for 7; he hit only one boundary, and his average rate of scoring was only 18 runs an hour, but the value of his innings was proved by the narrow margin of his side's victory.

20. **NEW SOUTH WALES** *v* **MCC TEAM**, at Sydney, 22, 23, 25 and 26 November 1929

SCORES: New South Wales 629 for 8 wickets dec. (D.G. Bradman 157, A. Allsopp 117, A.F. Kippax 108, S.J. McCabe 90) and 305 for 3 wickets dec. (A.A. Jackson 168*, A. Allsopp 63*); MCC Team 469 (F.E. Woolley 219, M.J. Turnbull 100) and 204 for 2 wickets (E.W. Dawson 83*). Drawn.

D.G. BRADMAN  b. T.S. Worthington          157
             (did not bat)                 –

Bradman started this feast of run-getting on a perfect wicket with a brilliant innings, punishing the bowling of F. Barratt, M.J.C. Allom, T.S. Worthington, E.H. Bowley and F.E. Woolley with devastating power. Going in at 26 for 1 on the first morning, he ran to 50 in three-quarters of an hour, and was 71 not out at lunch; his century was achieved in one hour 43 minutes, and when he was bowled by the last ball before tea, he had batted only two hours 55 minutes, without giving the slightest chance; he had slowed down just before being out, which may have been a factor in his dismissal. He hit 16 fours, and features of his innings were his masterly placing and his power off the back foot; he helped to add 117 in 76 minutes with Jackson (49) for the second wicket, and 149 in 97 minutes with Kippax for the third; the score was 292 for 3 when he was out.

### 21. W.M. WOODFULL'S XI *v* J.S. RYDER'S XI (Test trial match), at Sydney, 6, 7, 9, 10 and 11 December 1929

SCORES:  J.S. Ryder's XI 663 (A.A. Jackson 182, W.H. Ponsford 131, R.K. Oxenham 84*, A. Marks 83, H.E.P. Whitfield 68) and 191 for 9 wickets; W.M. Woodfull's XI 309 (D.G. Bradman 124, K.E. Rigg 73, R.K. Oxenham 5 for 42) and 541 (D.G. Bradman 225, A.F. Kippax 170, C.V. Grimmett 7 for 173). Woodfull's XI lost by 1 wicket.

D.G. BRADMAN  c. A.A. Jackson b. R.K. Oxenham     124
              lbw. b. C.V. Grimmett               225

In another high-scoring match, Bradman's contributions were again outstanding. Starting his first innings late on the second day, at 85 for 2, he made a rather hesitant start but reached 50 in 58 minutes just before the close, and was 54 not out overnight. Next morning his century came up in two minutes over two hours altogether, and he was last out, just before lunch, for a chanceless 124, caught in the slips after batting two hours 46 minutes; he hit 16 fours and helped Rigg to put on 171 for the fifth wicket, the only stand of the innings.

After lunch, when his side was forced to follow on 354 runs behind, Woodfull took Bradman in first with him, and he carried on from where he had left off, to be 205 not out at the close of the third day's play. He reached 50 in 80 minutes, 100 in two hours 18 minutes, and 200 in three hours 34 minutes, five minutes before the close; after passing 150 he indulged in some rather fortunate slogging, going from 150 to 200 in only 26 minutes. He gave two chances, a very hard c. and b. to Grimmett when 36, and a skier to the deep field off Grimmett when 203. He made 275 runs altogether during the day in five hours 25 minutes – the most he ever scored in one day in Australia.

33

Rather stiff the next morning, he never settled down, being very uncomfortable against Grimmett, who, after 33 minutes' play, had him lbw. for 225; his whole innings took only four hours 12 minutes, and he hit a five and 28 fours. He and Kippax added 218 for the third wicket in two hours 14 minutes, and when he was out at 378 for 3, the innings defeat had just been avoided.

Ryder's bowlers included H.H. Alexander, as well as Oxenham and Grimmett, and Bradman became the first Australian to perform this feat more than once, in Australia in 1910–1 and in England in 1912. Since then, R.A. Hamence, W.R. Hammond, A.R. Morris and C. Pinch have also scored two hundreds in a match in Australia twice, while Bradman has performed the feat on four occasions altogether (he did it again in 1937–8 and 1947–8). W.W. Armstrong (157* and 245 in 1920–1) is the only other Australian to make a century and a double century in the same match, and the only other batsman to perform this feat in Australia. Bradman is the only Australian to complete two centuries in the same match on the same day, and he thus almost rivalled the feat of K.S. Ranjitsinhji who, in 1896 in England, made 100 and 125*, all the runs being made on the same day.

This was also his third century in successive innings, the sixteenth time that his had been done by an Australian in Australia, no one ever having (till then) made more than three; Bradman altogether made three hundreds (or more) in succession ten times.

## 22. NEW SOUTH WALES v SOUTH AUSTRALIA, at Adelaide, 19, 20, 21, 23 and 24 December 1929

SCORES: New South Wales 314 (A. Allsopp 77, S.J. McCabe 69, H.L. Davidson 52) and 434 (D.G. Bradman 84, A.A. Jackson 82, A. Allsopp 73, S.J. McCabe 70, C.V. Grimmsett 7 for 136); South Australia 508 (D.E. Pritchard 148, B.W. Hone 126, V.Y. Richardson 64) and 244 for 5 wickets (D.E. Pritchard 75, B.W. Hone 61). New South Wales lost by 5 wickets.

| D.G. BRADMAN | run out | 2 |
|---|---|---|
| | lbw. b. C.V. Grimmett | 84 |

Bradman, in at 34 for 1 on the first morning, was easily run out in the first innings, his partner failing to answer his call; Bradman, slipping, was unable to get back. He was second out at 40 after a stay of five minutes.

In the second innings, he went in first with Jackson and they put on 172 for the first wicket before Bradman was out just before the end of the third day. He made 50 in an hour and 42 minutes, and batted for two hours 22 minutes in all; Grimmett, bowling well, caused him the most difficulty. He hit only five fours.

## 23. NEW SOUTH WALES *v* VICTORIA, at Melbourne, 26, 27, 28, 30 and 31 December 1929

SCORES: Victoria 229 (W.H. Ponsford 65, S.C. Everett 5 for 57) and 343 (H.L. Hendry 103, J.A. Scaife 60*, E.L. a'Beckett 50, A.G. Fairfax 5 for 104); New South Wales 402 (D.G. Bradman 89, A.F. Kippax 80, S.J. McCabe 70, A. Marks 69) and 145 for 2 wickets (S.J. McCabe 50*). Drawn.

| D.G. BRADMAN | b. H.H. Alexander | 89 |
| | not out | 26 |

Going in soon after the start of the second day at 8 for 1, Bradman soon settled down to another good innings, his 50 coming up in 68 minutes. He gave a very hard c. and b. chance to Blackie at 72, and at lunch was 85 not out. After the interval, however, he glanced Alexander for 4, and in trying to repeat the shot, had his leg stump hit. His 89 took a hundred minutes and included 12 fours; he was out at 151 for 3, having added 127 with Kippax for the third wicket.

The 85 not out he made before lunch in this innings was the nearest he ever got in Australia to a century before lunch after starting his innings the same morning; though he four times added over 100 runs before lunch to an overnight not-out century, the first of these being in his very next match, and he also four times made a hundred before lunch in England, twice on the first morning of a match. In Australia, of course, there is normally one and three-quarter hours' play, at most, before lunch.

Set 171 to win in two hours on the fifth morning, New South Wales made no effort to go for the runs. Bradman had only 22 minutes' batting, hitting up 26 and increasing the score with McCabe from 103 for 2 to 145 for 2; but it was too late by then.

## 24. NEW SOUTH WALES *v* QUEENSLAND, at Sydney, 3, 4, 6 and 7 January 1930

SCORES: New South Wales 235 (C. Andrews 56) and 761 for 8 wickets dec. (D.G. Bradman 452*, A.F. Kippax 115, A. Allsopp 66, S.J. McCabe 60, A. Hurwood 6 for 179); Queensland 227 (V. Goodwin 67, E.C. Benstead 51, S.J. McCabe 5 for 36) and 84 (S.C. Everett 6 for 23). New South Wales won by 685 runs.

| D.G. BRADMAN | c. H. Lerson b. A. Hurwood | 3 |
| | not out | 452 |

Bradman opened the first innings, but was caught at the wicket after seven minutes, with only 3 runs scored, a failure he redeemed in the most convincing manner in the second innings.

Going in at 22 for 1 soon after lunch on the second day, he completed 50 in 51 minutes, 100 in an hour and 44 minutes, and 200 in three hours five minutes, to be 205 not out at the close of play ten minutes later. He completed 1,000 runs for the season when 176; 4 January was the earliest date that, until then, a New South Wales batsman had ever reached this aggregate, 21 days earlier than his own record of 1928–9; and he took only 11 innings, Kippax's 13 in 1926–7 being the previous best, though W.H. Ponsford in 1927–8 took only five innings to reach 1,000 on 30 December.

Refreshed by Sunday's rest, he carried on without any trouble on the third day to pass Ponsford's two-year-old record score of 437, till then the highest score ever made in first-class cricket. He reached 300 in four hours 48 minutes, was 310 not out at lunch (having added 105 before the interval), achieved 400 in six hours 17 minutes, and 29 minutes later broke the record. An off-drive off H.M. Thurlow took him from 430 to 434; two scoreless balls followed, and then, with a savage hook to the square-leg boundary off Thurlow, he carried his score to 438. When New South Wales declared at the tea interval (leaving over one and a half days to dismiss Queensland again), he appeared to be still perfectly fresh, after batting for six hours 55 minutes (415 minutes, Ponsford having taken 621 minutes). He hit 49 fours and made only two mistakes, neither of which was quite a chance; at 264 mid-on failed to move in quickly enough when he put up a ball from W. Rowe's bowling, and at 345 the wicket-keeper obstructed first slip in trying for a snick off Thurlow. He had stands of 272 (in two hours 25 minutes) with Kippax for the third wicket, 156 (in 81 minutes) with McCabe for the fourth wicket, and 180 (in 90 minutes) with Allsopp for the sixth wicket; and he was in while 739 was added to the score. Only Hurwood, who bowled well, gave him any trouble; the remainder he dealt with as he liked, with strokes of tremendous power all round the wicket. He was, however, fortunate in that his partners survived long enough to give him his opportunity of breaking the record.

His 452* still remains the highest score ever made in a first-class match, though B.B. Nimbalkar, in India in 1948–9, came very close indeed to it, making 443* before the other side conceded the match.[1] It is also the highest score ever made in a first-class match in Australia, the highest score in a first-class match by an Australian batsman, the highest in a Sheffield Shield match, and the highest ever made against Queensland (previous best, Ponsford's 437); it is the highest for New South Wales in any Sheffield Shield match, and the highest in any first-class match on the Sydney ground (previous best, Bradman's 340* in 1928–9); it is the highest for New South Wales *v* Queensland in a Sheffield Shield match (previous best, 315* by Kippax in 1927–8), and the highest in a second innings of any first-class match (previous best, 344 by W.G. Grace in 1876; by an Australian, and in Australia, 275* by W.H. Ponsford, 1928–9; for New South Wales in a Sheffield

---

[1] In 1958–9, Hanif Mohamed broke Bradman's record by making a score of 499 in Pakistan.

Shield match, 235 by W. Bardsley, 1920–1); and he became the only New South Wales batsman twice to make a score of over 300. His match aggregate of 455 is also the highest on record, Ponsford's 437 being the previous best; A.E. Fagg made 446 in 1938, with two innings of 244 and 202*. At 21 years 132 days, he was the youngest player ever to make 400 (previous best, Ponsford at 22 years 109 days when making his 429).

His partnership of 272 with Kippax for the third wicket was a record for matches between New South Wales and Queensland, and in any match against Queensland (previous best, 232 by Kippax and H.C. Steele, 1926–7); Kippax and O.W. Bill added 280 for the third wicket *v* Queensland in 1930–1, but in 1933–4 Bradman and Kippax regained the record with a partnership of 363. Until Kippax and Bill added their 280 in 1930–1, it was also the highest for many wicket for matches between New South Wales and Queensland (previous best, 256 by N. Callaway and C.G. Macartney, 1914–5, for the fifth wicket; in a Sheffield Shield match, 253 for the sixth wicket, by Kippax and G. Morgan, 1927–8).

His time for reaching 400 (six hours 17 minutes) is the fastest ever achieved, Ponsford, 400 in seven hours 17 minutes *v* Tasmania, 1922–3, being the previous quickest. His time for reaching 300 (four hours 48 minutes) is the fastest for New South Wales (previous best, five and a half hours by C.W. Gregory *v* Queensland, 1906–7; in a Sheffield Shield match, six hours 20 minutes in 1927–8 by Kippax, the only other batsman to make 300 for New South Wales in a Shield match).

His 49 fours are the highest number of boundaries in an innings ever hit in a Sheffield Shield match, and his 196 are the most runs scored in boundaries; Ponsford's 42 fours (168 runs) in his 437 were the previous best, while J.S. Ryder, in his innings of 295 in 1926–7, also scored 168 runs in boundaries, with six sixes and 33 fours; for New South Wales, the previous best was 41 fours (164 runs) by Kippax in his 315* in 1927–8, though in a non-Shield match, C.W. Gregory hit 55 fours in his 383.

Bradman out-scored the next highest scorer, Kippax with 115, by 337 runs, then the biggest margin on record in any first-class match, and still the biggest by an Australian and in Australia; Ponsford, with 308 (437 to 129) was the previous best, and in 1952–3, in New Zealand, B. Sutcliffe (385) scored 356 more than the next highest scorer.

He was in while 739 runs were added to the score, a record for New South Wales; Gregory, 383 out of 691, was the previous best, and in a Sheffield Shield match, Bradman's 340* out of 637 in 1928–9 was until then the record for New South Wales.

## 25. NEW SOUTH WALES *v* SOUTH AUSTRALIA, at Sydney, 9, 10, 11 and 13 January 1930

SCORES: New South Wales 535 (A. Allsopp 136, S.J. McCabe 81, S.C. Everett 62,

H.C. Chilvers 52, H.E.P. Whitfield 5 for 106); South Australia 215 and 100. New South Wales won by an innings and 220 runs.

D.G. BRADMAN  c. V.Y. Richardson b. H.E.P. Whitfield     47

Going in at 27 for 1 on the first morning, Bradman tried to open his score with a short single, was sent back by his partner, and cover-point's return hit him on his head, as a result of which he had to retire hurt. Resuming during the afternoon, when New South Wales were in trouble at only 163 for 5, he was obviously still far from well. T.A. Carlton missed a c. and b. chance when he was 3, and soon afterwards, when he was about 10, short-leg failed to hold a hard catch off Grimmett's bowling. However, he struggled on for 89 minutes before being caught at slip, having helped to raise the score to 285 for 7; he did not field when South Australia batted.

Bradman had thus scored 499 runs in his last two innings before he was dismissed, up till then the highest on record for a series of not-out innings; in 1901, K.S. Ranjitsinhji made 489 (with successive scores of 285* and 205), while W.H. Ponsford's single innings of 437 was the most in Australia, and by an Australian, and A.F. Kippax with 398 (271*, 127) in 1925–6–7 made the most for New South Wales. Five days after this, in the West Indies, E. Hendren completed 514 runs in succession before being dismissed (233*, 211* and 80), and a month later, Hendren made 630 in three innings (205*, 254*, 171) before being dismissed; in 1933–4 Bradman raised the Australian and New South Wales records to 517. The present record was made in 1947–8, in India, when K.C. Ibrahim scored 709 runs in succession before being out.

The most ever scored in two consecutive innings for New South Wales is 499, the previous best being 406 by H. Moses in 1887–8.

## 26. NEW SOUTH WALES *v* VICTORIA, at Sydney, 28 and 29 January 1930

SCORES: New South Wales 330 (D.G. Bradman 77, A. Allsopp 65, A.G. Fairfax 64); Victoria 222 for 3 wickets (J.S. Ryder 100*, H.L. Hendry 95). Drawn.

D.G. BRADMAN  c. R.N. Ellis b. H. Ironmonger     77

Rain prevented play on the first three days, and next morning New South Wales were sent in to bat on a difficult drying wicket. However, despite some early disasters to his side, Bradman was at his best; going in at 14 for 1, he reached 50 in one and a quarter hours, and hit up 77 in one hour forty-three minutes, with eight fours, before being caught at forward short-leg; the score was then 149 for 5 and the wicket had eased considerably.

Bradman thus scored 579 runs in January 1930, more than any New South

Wales batsman had ever scored in a month in Australia, the previous best being 563 by M.A. Noble in December 1903; Bradman's 579 remained a record for New South Wales until December 1948, when A.R. Morris made 585. Bradman himself twice made 593 in a month for South Australia (in December 1937 and December 1938), but all these totals look puny beside the 1,146 runs scored by W.H. Ponsford in December 1927.

His 576 runs (452*, 47, 77) are the most ever made in three consecutive innings for New South Wales, A.F. Kippax's 529 in 1925-6–7 being the previous best.

## 27. AUSTRALIANS v TASMANIA, at Launceston, 8, 10 and 11 March 1930

SCORES: Tasmania 157 (J. Atkinson 50) and 158; Australians 311 (S.J. McCabe 103, W.M. Woodfull 50*, T. James 5 for 97) and 6 for no wicket. Australians won by 10 wickets.

D.G. BRADMAN lbw. b. L.J. Nash    20
        (did not bat)         –

Going in at 163 for 3 on the second morning, with his side already in the lead on the first innings, Bradman played a comparatively modest part, batting for only 24 minutes before being out at 199 for 4.

## 28. AUSTRALIANS v TASMANIA, at Hobart, 14 and 15 March 1930

SCORES: Tasmania 131 (C.V. Grimmett 5 for 30) and 174 for 5 wickets (L.J. Nash 93); Australia 419 for 4 wickets dec. (W.H. Ponsford 166, D.G. Bradman 139, A.F. Kippax 53*). Drawn.

D.G. BRADMAN c. A.W. Rushforth b. J. Atkinson    139

Bradman enjoyed a big stand with Ponsford, whom he joined at 36 for 1; this was the first time that Ponsford and he had batted together. He reached 50 in 67 minutes and was 70 not out at the close of the first day after 80 minutes' batting; he was, however, missed in the slips – a very hot chance – when 16, off the bowling of L.J. Nash, a fast bowler who later played for Australia. Next morning, Ponsford reached his century first, and when Bradman had followed him, after two hours seven minutes at the wicket, the pair launched a tremendous attack on the bowling; at one stage, off five overs and in 15 minutes, they added 62. Both fell at 332, Ponsford being first, after they had added 296 for the second wicket; Bradman batted for two hours 32 minutes and hit 15 fours before being caught in the deep.

## 29. AUSTRALIANS *v* WESTERN AUSTRALIA, at Perth, 21, 22 and 24 March 1930

SCORES: Western Australia 167 (C.V. Grimmett 6 for 75) and 132; Australians 324 (A.F. Kippax 114). Australians won by an innings and 25 runs.

D.G. BRADMAN   c. R. Bryant b. A. Evans      27

Bradman had five minutes' batting before bad light stopped the first day's play, after he had gone in at 52 for 1; 4 not out overnight, he batted brightly next morning for another 23 minutes before being caught at cover, with the score 83 for 3, having made 27 out of 31 added while he was in (87 per cent – the highest proportion he ever achieved).

### SUMMARY, 1929–30

| | Matches | Innings | NO | HS | Runs | Average | Centuries |
|---|---|---|---|---|---|---|---|
| All First-class Matches | 11 | 16 | 2 | 452* | 1586 | 113.28 | 5 |
| Match *v* MCC Team | 1 | 1 | 0 | 157 | 157 | – | 1 |
| Sheffield Shield Matches | 6 | 10 | 2 | 452* | 894 | 111.75 | 1 |
| All Matches for NSW | 7 | 11 | 2 | 452* | 1051 | 116.77 | 2 |

In all first-class matches, S.J. McCabe's total of 844 runs was next highest to Bradman's, while A.A. Jackson's 70.00 was the next best average. A.F. Kippax and W.H. Ponsford each hit three centuries, the next best to Bradman's five.

His aggregate of 894 in Sheffield Shield matches passed by one run the record for New South Wales which he had established the previous season; in 1933–4 he increased this to 922, and in 1957–8, N.C. O'Neill made 1,005. His average in all first-class matches of 113.28 was also the highest, up till then, by any New South Wales batsman in a season, the previous best being 112.75 by J.R.M. Mackay in 1905–6. Bradman twice later improved on these figures.

# 1930

## AGED TWENTY-ONE

———◆━◆✕◆━◆———

Bradman was a member of the seventeenth Australian team to tour England, under the captaincy of W.M. Woodfull.

### 30. AUSTRALIANS *v* WORCESTERSHIRE, at Worcester, 30 April, 1 and 2 May 1930

SCORES: Worcestershire 131 and 196 (C.V. Grimmett 5 for 46); Australians 492 for 8 wickets dec. (D.G. Bradman 236, W.M. Woodfull 133). Australians won by an innings and 165 runs.

D.G. BRADMAN  c. C.F. Walters b. G.W. Brook    236

Making the most successful début on English wickets of any batsman in history, Bradman soon showed form as convincing as anything he had done in Australia. He went in after tea on the first day at 67 for 1, and though at first playing himself in with some care, he scored fast enough to reach 50 in an hour, and at the close of play, after one and a half hours' batting, was 75 not out.

Equally confident next morning, he reached his century in a further half hour and brought his score to 173 by lunch-time, having added 98 in the two hours before lunch; his stand with Woodfull had by then been broken, after they had added 208 for the second wicket in two and a quarter hours. He completed 200 in four hours ten minutes, and then indulged in some big hitting to give his wicket away. He gave Brook a very hard chance off his own bowling when 215, and at 236 was well caught at short-leg off a skier. He was in for four hours 36 minutes, gave only the one chance, hit 28 fours and helped to raise the score to 480 for 8; despite the strangeness of the wicket, he displayed his whole range of strokes, his off-driving and cutting being particularly attractive. The Worcestershire bowlers included C.F. Root, who had played against Australia in 1926.

The previous highest score made by any batsman on his first appearance on English wickets was 206 by H.H. Massie for the Australians *v* Oxford in 1882, while A.C. MacLaren's 228 in Australia in 1894–5 was the previous best by any batsman touring any other country; Bradman's 236 still remains the record in both respects, though in 1948 G.H.G. Doggart made 215* on his début. Bradman's

236 was also the highest score *v* Worcestershire, and on the Worcester ground, made on behalf of an Australian or any other touring side (previous best, 195* by C.E. Pellew for the AIF in 1919, 176* by W. Bardsley in 1912); Bradman himself made 258 in 1938.

It was also the highest score made by a visiting batsman in his first innings of a tour of England (previous best, Massie's 206 in 1882), until Bradman made 258 in his first innings of the 1938 tour, and then K.R. Miller made 281* *v* Leicestershire in 1956.

Bradman was until then the only Australian to make a century in his first matches both in Australia and in England; A.C. MacLaren also achieved this feat, and K.R. Miller and A.R. Morris have since done so; Morris also scored centuries in his first matches in South Africa and the West Indies, and Miller also did so in his first matches in Ceylon and New Zealand.

At 21 years 247 days old, Bradman was then the youngest player from overseas to score a double century in England; V.T. Trumper, the previous youngest, was 21 years 269 days old when he made 300* in 1899. Bradman is still the youngest Australian to do so, but for the East Indians, G. Sobers was only 20 years 301 days old when he made 219* in 1957.

## 31. AUSTRALIANS *v* LEICESTERSHIRE, at Leicester, 3 and 5 May 1930

SCORES: Leicestershire 148 (A. Shipman 63, L.G. Berry 50, C.V. Grimmett 7 for 46); Australians 365 for 5 wickets (D.G. Bradman 185*, V.Y. Richardson 100). Drawn.

D.G. BRADMAN  not out  185

Bradman had 40 minutes' batting at the end of the first day, after going in at 18 for 1, and was only 9 not out at the close. Next morning, accurate bowling again put him for a long time on the defensive; when 44, he gave Shipman a very hard return chance and, spending a long time in the forties, he was two and a quarter hours at the wicket before he reached 50. After lunch, however, he cast off this restraint and gradually mastered the bowlers, who included G. Geary and W.E. Astill. His century was attained after three and three-quarter hours, and when rain stopped play at 5.30 p.m. he had batted for five hours 17 minutes for 185 not out, including 16 fours; his stand with Richardson for the fifth wicket added 179 in two and a half hours after the Australians had lost 4 wickets for 80, and after that partnership was broken, A.G. Fairfax (21*) helped him to add 106 unfinished for the sixth wicket.

Bradman thus equalled the performance of Woodfull in 1926, who made a double century and a century in his first two innings in England.

Rain prevented any play on the third day.

## 32. AUSTRALIANS *v* YORKSHIRE, at Sheffield, 10 and 12 May 1930

SCORES: Yorkshire 155 (H. Sutcliffe 69, C.V. Grimmett 10 for 37); Australians 320 (W.M. Woodfull 121, D.G. Bradman 78). Drawn.

D.G. BRADMAN  c. and b. G.G. Macaulay      78

After a superb piece of bowling by Grimmett had routed Yorkshire, the Australians had scored 35 for 1 when Bradman went in on the first evening, and rain and bad light interfered to such an extent that he had only 38 minutes' batting, during which he made 24 not out.

Play did not start until 2.15 p.m. next day, and he carried on with delightful ease and certainty. The wicket was extremely wet and slow, though dead and easy – probably the slowest on which, so far, he had ever batted; and the Yorkshire bowlers were E. Robinson, W.E. Bowes, G.G. Macaulay and W. Rhodes, one of the strongest combinations in the country. Despite this, he scarcely bothered to play himself in, and by his beautiful timing made batting on a slow wicket look perfectly simple; he made 50 in 70 minutes, and when he was caught and bowled, that was his first false stroke and the first occasion on which had lifted a ball off the ground. He made 78 out of 107 for the second wicket with Woodfull in an hour and 40 minutes, and hit eight fours; he had so far scored 499 runs on the tour and been out twice.

Rain prevented any play on the third day.

## 33. AUSTRALIANS *v* LANCASHIRE, at Liverpool, 14, 15 and 16 May 1930

SCORES: Lancashire 176 (P.T. Eckersley 54, C.V. Grimmett 6 for 57) and 165 (P.M. Hornibrook 5 for 38); Australians 115 and 137 for 2 wickets. Drawn.

D.G. BRADMAN  b. E.A. McDonald        9
             not out                48

The Australians were 29 for 1 when Bradman went in on the first evening and he found McDonald, the ex-Australian fast bowler, at his best; bowling at great pace, he knocked Bradman's leg stump out of the ground after he had been in for 19 minutes, with the score 49 for 2. By the close of play, the Australians were 63 for 5, and McDonald had dismissed three of them.

Despite these setbacks, the Australians on the third day had two hours 40 minutes to make 227 to win, but although the wicket was now easy, they made no attempt to achieve victory. Going in after lunch at 67 for 1, Bradman helped himself to an hour and 29 minutes' batting practice and, at the end, to some rather easy runs.

## 34. AUSTRALIANS *v* MCC, at Lord's, 17, 19 and 20 May 1930

SCORES: Australians 285 (W.H. Ponsford 82*, D.G. Bradman 66, W.M. Woodfull 52, M.J.C. Allom 5 for 67) and 213 (A.A. Jackson 64); MCC 258 (K.S. Duleepsinhji 92, A.G. Fairfax 6 for 54). Drawn.

| | | |
|---|---|---|
| D.G. BRADMAN | b. M.J.C. Allom | 66 |
| | lbw. b. G.T.S. Stevens | 4 |

A strong MCC side included five bowlers, G.O. Allen, M.J.C. Allom, I.A.R. Peebles, A.S. Kennedy and G.T.S. Stevens, and against them, Bradman had to exercise considerable caution. Going in at 0 for 1 soon after the start, he was 47 at lunch, reached 50 in an hour and 25 minutes – after a long time in the forties – and made 66 altogether in an hour and 50 minutes, hitting six fours; he and Woodfull added 119 for the second wicket. Bradman, second out, played on to an in-swinger which he was attempting to force on the off side.

His second innings began at 14 for 1, late on the second day, and he spent a very unhappy 20 minutes; when 1, he was missed off Allen by Stevens in the slips, and that fielder shortly afterwards atoned by getting him lbw. with a googly, at 23 for 2.

## 35. AUSTRALIANS *v* DERBYSHIRE, at Chesterfield, 21, 22 and 23 May 1930

SCORES: Derbyshire 215 (T.S. Worthington 79, H. Storer 65, P.M. Hornibrook 6 for 61) and 181 (P.M. Hornibrook 6 for 82); Australians 348 (W.H. Ponsford 131, A.A. Jackson 63) and 52 for no wicket. Australians won by 10 wickets.

| | | |
|---|---|---|
| D.G. BRADMAN | c. H. Elliott b. T.S. Worthington | 44 |
| | (did not bat) | – |

Bradman went in at 127 for 1 on the second morning (which was bitterly cold and rather wet) and helped Ponsford add 106 for the second wicket in 65 minutes. He himself was hardly at his best, being 85 minutes at the wicket for 44, before being caught by the wicket-keeper, standing back, on the leg side, at 253 for 3; his timing was by no means as certain as usual.

## 36. AUSTRALIANS *v* SURREY, at the Oval, 24 May 1930

SCORES: Australians 379 for 5 wickets (D.G. Bradman 252*, W.M. Woodfull 50); Surrey did not bat. Drawn.

D.G. BRADMAN not out    252

Rain restricted play to the first day, and Bradman was on view for almost the whole of it, playing a superb innings on a soft but easy wicket against a Surrey attack which, apart from M.J.C. Allom and P.G.H. Fender, was rather weak; the light was bad and the weather gloomy, all day, but after a rather anxious start, when he had some difficulty in playing Allom, he was in no trouble. Going in at 11 for 1, he played himself in with great care, having made 28 in an hour by lunch; after the interval, he completed 50 in one and a half hours, and 100 in two hours 25 minutes, thereafter scoring at such a pace that his second century took only another 80 minutes. When rain stopped play at 6.25 p.m., he had scored 252 in four hours 50 minutes, including 29 fours; he had stands of 116 for the second wicket with Woodfull, 113 in 65 minutes for the third wicket with V.Y. Richardson (32), and 129 unfinished for the sixth wicket with A.G. Fairfax (28*); during the latter, Bradman at one time scored 51 out of 52. He gave no chance until he reached 207, when a hard hook off Allom might have been caught low down at short-leg. His best stroke was the cut, but once he had settled down he also scored many runs with forcing strokes on the leg side.

This is still the highest score for an Australian or any other touring team *v* Surrey (previous best, 162 by H.L. Collins, 1921; next best, 240 by S.J. McCabe, 1934); it was also the highest score for an Australian or any other touring team at the Oval (previous best, 211 by W.L. Murdoch, *v* England, 1884), until in 1934 W.H. Ponsford made 266 in the Test match there. J. Darling (1896), M.A. Noble (1899), V.T. Trumper (1899) and A.R. Morris (1948) are the only others to have taken part in three-century partnerships in one innings on behalf of an Australian or other touring team in England.

## 37. AUSTRALIANS *v* OXFORD UNIVERSITY, at Oxford (Christ Church ground), 28 and 29 May 1930

SCORES: Australians 406 for 2 wickets dec. (W.H. Ponsford 220*, S.J. McCabe 91, A.F. Kippax 56*); Oxford University 124 (C.V. Grimmett 5 for 48) and 124. Australians won by an innings and 158 runs.

D.G. BRADMAN  b. H.M. Garland-Wells     32

Having so far scored 922 runs this season, Bradman had an admirable opportunity to complete 1,000 runs before the end of May; however, although McCabe and Ponsford, in an opening stand of 172, had extracted such sting as there was from the bowling, he took an hour to score 32 out of 89 before being bowled just before tea on the first day, by a well-pitched off-break to which he played back. The only feature of his innings worthy of mention was that when I.A.R. Peebles bowled him a no-ball, he hit for the first six of his career.

## 38. AUSTRALIANS *v* HAMPSHIRE, at Southampton, 31 May and 2 June 1930

SCORES: Hampshire 151 (G Brown 56, C.V. Grimmett 7 for 39) and 175 (C.V. Grimmett 7 for 56); Australians 334 (D.G. Bradman 191, S.J. McCabe 65, G.S. Boyes 6 for 90). Australians won by an innings and 8 runs.

D.G. BRADMAN  c. C.P. Mead b. G.S. Boyes               191

Requiring 46 runs to complete his 1,000 runs on the last day of May, Bradman owed his opportunity to do so, after the Australians had lost the toss, partly to Grimmett for so speedily dismissing Hampshire, and partly to his own brilliant fielding when he threw out Brown. Woodfull sent him in first at 3.30 p.m., and he proceeded cautiously to 28 by tea-time, when rain held up the game; when play was at last resumed, he took his score to 39 before more rain began to fall. However, two generous deliveries on the leg side from J. Newman were each hit for four, to make his score 47 and his aggregate 1,001, before the players dashed for the pavilion in torrential rain.

He is the only touring batsman ever to complete his 1,000 runs before the end of May, a feat he repeated in 1938; this was his eleventh innings of the season, against the ten required by W.G. Grace in 1895. In 1938 he reached 1,000 in his seventh innings on 27 May, and in 1948 he did so in his tenth innings on 12 June; while in 1912 C.G. Macartney made 776 runs by the end of May, reaching 1,000 in his nineteenth innings on 19 June; this was the previous best by an Australian batsman, though in 1934 S.J. McCabe reached 1,000 in his thirteenth innings on 11 June, and for the New Zealanders in 1949, W.M. Wallace made 910 runs before June. W.L. Murdoch, in 1882, and Macartney, in 1912, are the only other overseas batsmen to reach 1,000 runs for the season ahead of any English player; Bradman did this again in 1938 and 1948. The total of 926 runs which Bradman made actually in May this year is the most in any month by any Australian or other touring batsman in England; Macartney in 1921 made 871 in June, this being the previous best, and all his 776 in 1912 were scored actually in May, while in 1938 W.A. Brown got 888 runs in June and, for the 1949 New Zealanders, B. Sutcliffe made 911 runs in August, and 828 of Wallace's runs were made in May. Bradman is the youngest batsman ot make 1,000 runs before the beginning of June, at 21 years 277 days; W.R. Hammond was nearly 24 when he achieved the feat in 1927, and W.J. Edrich was just over 22 when he did so in 1938.

Next morning, Bradman completed his 50 (in one and a quarter hours) off Newman's uncompleted over, and thereafter continued in his most brilliant form. He reached 100 in a further hour, and was 156 at lunch, having added 109 in two hours; and when he was last out, caught at slip (only just failing to carry his bat through the innings), he had scored 191 out of 325 from the bat (58 per cent) in four hours, including a six off Boyes and 26 fours; he and McCabe added 141 in 70 minutes for the fifth wicket, the only stand of the innings. Bradman gave no chance, though at 157 a snick off Boyes only just failed to carry to slip; for much of the second day, the wicket was decidedly helpful to the bowlers, and Boyes, the slow left-hander, was very difficult to play; but this made little difference to Bradman's mastery, his quick footwork being much in evidence, and he was just as severe on A.S. Kennedy.

For the only time in his career he was on the field for the whole of the match.

## 39. AUSTRALIANS *v* MIDDLESEX, at Lord's, 4, 5 and 6 June 1930

SCORES: Middlesex 103 (P.M. Hornibrook 7 for 42) and 287 (E. Hendren 138); Australians 270 (A.F. Kippax 102, G.O. Allen 6 for 77) and 121 for 5 wickets. Australians won by 5 wickets.

| | | |
|---|---|---|
| D.G. BRADMAN | b. J.W. Hearne | 35 |
| | b. G.T.S. Stevens | 18 |

On a wicket which assisted the bowlers and took a good deal of spin, Bradman on the first afternoon batted well for three-quarters of an hour, making a confident 35 before Hearne bowled him with a vicious googly. He helped to raise the score from 13 for 1 to 58 for 2, thus scoring 77 per cent of the runs added while he was in.

On the third afternoon, he went in at 16 for 1, and, after batting for 40 minutes, on an easier wicket, appeared to have settled down when he was bowled, hitting over a slow yorker, at 45 for 2.

## 40. AUSTRALIANS *v* CAMBRIDGE UNIVERSITY, at Cambridge, 7, 9 and 10 June 1930

SCORES: Cambridge University 145 and 225 (F.R. Brown 52); Australians 504 for 8 wickets dec. (W.M. Woodfull 216, S.J. McCabe 96). Australians won by an innings and 134 runs.

| | | |
|---|---|---|
| D.G. BRADMAN | c. T.W.T. Baines b. R.H.C. Human | 32 |

Going in after tea on the first day at 13 for 1, Bradman scored mainly on the leg side until he was caught in the slips when trying to cut a very wide ball; he was second out at 79, having batted for 50 minutes. In this match he had unusual success as a bowler, with analyses of 11–1–35–3 and 17–3–68–3, the best of his career.

## 41. AUSTRALIA *v* ENGLAND, First Test match, at Nottingham, 13, 14, 16 and 17 June 1930

SCORES: England 270 (J.B. Hobbs 78, A.P.F. Chapman 52, R.W.V. Robins 50*,

C.V. Grimmett 5 for 107) and 302 (J.B. Hobbs 74, E. Hendren 72, H. Sutcliffe 58*, C.V. Grimmett 5 for 94); Australia 144 (A.F. Kippax 64*) and 335 (D.G. Bradman 131). Australia lost by 93 runs.

| | | |
|---|---|---|
| D.G. BRADMAN | b. M.W. Tate | 8 |
| | b. R.W.V. Robins | 131 |

Overnight rain prevented play on the second day until after lunch, and when the Australian first innings began shortly after 3 p.m., hot sun made the wicket decidedly helpful to Tate, who soon took the first three wickets. Bradman went in at 6 for 2, after Woodfull and Ponsford had both been dismissed, and the score was raised to only 16 when he too was out, bowled by an in-swinger which kept rather low; he was in for a quarter of an hour and had 22 balls.

His second innings was a much better display. At the end of the third day, Australia were set to make 429 to win, and Bradman, going in at 12 for 1, had 35 minutes' batting and made 31 not out, his only mistake being a lucky snick over the slips' heads off Larwood from his first ball.

Playing with great care on the last day, he almost succeeded in winning the match for Australia; he took 65 minutes to make 19 runs to complete his 50 (in one hundred minutes altogether), and was 88 not out at lunch; when he was 60, he missed at the wicket off R. Tyldesley. He spent half an hour in the nineties and reached his century at 2.45 p.m., after batting for three hours 35 minutes. Shortly afterwards, Australia were in the favourable position of wanting exactly 200 to win in three and a quarter hours, with 7 wickets in hand and Bradman and S.J. McCabe well set; but McCabe was out to a fantastic catch by an unknown substitute fielder, and then Bradman too was dismissed. At 3.30 p.m., when he had made 131, he played no stroke while watching a sharply turning googly from Robins hit his off-stump; he had batted for four hours 20 minutes, hit ten fours, and gave only the one chance. When he was out to his 287th ball, the score was 267 for 5, and England thereafter always had the match in hand.

He was the first Australian to score a century in a Test match at Nottingham, the previous best being 80 by C. Hill in 1899; in 1938, McCabe made 232 there. Bradman was also only the fourth Australian to make a century in his first Test match against England in England; since 1930, the only other Australian to join this list has been R.N. Harvey.

## 42. AUSTRALIANS *v* SURREY, at the Oval, 18, 19 and 20 June 1930

SCORES: Surrey 162 (T. Shepherd 56, C.V. Grimmett 6 for 24) and 249 for 2 wickets (J.B. Hobbs 146*, T. Shepherd 65*); Australians 388 for 5 wickets dec. (W.M. Woodfull 141, E.L. a'Beckett 67*). Drawn.

| | |
|---|---|
| D.G. BRADMAN c. M.J.C. Allom b. T. Shepherd | 5 |

When Bradman went in after lunch on the second day, the Australians were already in a strong position at 115 for 1. He was, however, caught at short-leg, high up and left-handed, in trying to hook; he was dismissed at 127 for 2 after batting for ten minutes.

## 43. AUSTRALIANS v LANCASHIRE, at Manchester, 21, 23 and 24 June 1930

SCORES: Australians 427 (A.F. Kippax 120, A.G. Fairfax 63, A.A. Jackson 52) and
79 for 1 wicket; Lancashire 259 (F. Watson 74). Drawn.

| | | |
|---|---|---|
| D.G. BRADMAN | c. G. Duckworth b. F.M. Sibbles | 38 |
| | not out | 23 |

Going in after lunch on the first day at 59 for 1, Bradman was very much out of touch on a wicket affected by rain, taking an hour and 56 minutes to make 38. Just before tea, when 33, he might have been caught at the wicket, and just before he was out, after tea, he was missed when 35 in the slips off J. Iddon; he was then well caught at the wicket on the leg side, with the score 144 for 3. His rate of scoring was only 19 runs an hour.

With only three-quarters of an hour left for play when the Australian second innings began, on the third afternoon, the cricket was not taken seriously. The Australians lost a wicket at 17, and Bradman thereafter enjoyed 25 minutes' batting practice.

## 44. AUSTRALIA v ENGLAND, Second Test match, at Lord's, 27, 38, 30 June, 1 July 1930

SCORES: England 425 (K.S. Duleepsinhji 173, M.W. Tate 54) and 375 (A.P.F. Chapman 121, G.O. Allen 57, C.V. Grimmett 6 for 167); Australia 729 for 6 wickets dec. (D.G. Bradman 254, W.M. Woodfull 155, A.F. Kippax 83, W.H. Ponsford 81) and 72 for 3 wickets. Australia won by 7 wickets.

| | | |
|---|---|---|
| D.G. BRADMAN | c. A.P.F. Chapman b. J.C. White | 54 |
| | c. A.P.F. Chapman b. M.W. Tate | 1 |

Bradman's first innings was one of the most perfect that he ever played. After Woodfull and Ponsford had worn down the English bowling in an opening stand of 162, he went in at 3.30 p.m. on the second day, and at once attacked and mastered the bowling. Scarcely bothering to play himself in, he went yards down the wicket to his first ball, from J.C. White, to off-drive it powerfully for a single; he took only 45 minutes to reach 50 (out of 66 while he was in), his fastest in a Test match, was 54 at tea adjournment, and went on to complete his century at

5.30 p.m. (out of 152 while he was in) in one and three-quarter hours. Against an attack consisting of G.O. Allen, M.W. Tate, White, R.W.V. Robins and W.R. Hammond, his brilliant footwork enabled him to score more or less as he pleased, and he not only gave no chance, but never even made a false stroke or lifted the ball off the ground. When Woodfull was dismissed, just before the close of play, for 155, the pair had added 231 for the second wicket in two hours 40 minutes, and at the close, Bradman was 155 not out, after batting for only two and three-quarter hours; he had added 101 in one and three-quarter hours since tea. He had just caught up with Woodfull, who had had 78 runs and two hours 50 minutes' start.

Playing himself in again with more care on Monday morning, he took another 80 minutes to reach 200 (at 12.50 p.m., after four hours five minutes altogether); the one false stroke of his innings was made just before then, when he was 191, and that too was safely along the ground. At lunch, he was 231; afterwards, just when he seemed certain to break R.E. Foster's 27-year-old record score of 287, the highest ever made in a Test match between England and Australia, a wonderful right-handed catch by Chapman at extra-cover sent him back. This was the first ball he had hit in the air, in a superb and chanceless innings which lasted five hours 20 minutes; he hit 25 fours and helped Kippax to add 192 for the third wicket in two hours 38 minutes. When he was out at 2.50 p.m., the score was 585 for 3, and Australia were well on the way to their highest score in a Test match; his 254 was thus made out of 423 added while he was in, off 376 deliveries.

Up till that time, only 14 double centuries had been made in all Test cricket, only six in Tests between England and Australia, and only five by Australians in all test matches, three of these being made against England. This score of 254 was therefore the highest score ever made in a test match in England (previous best, 211 by J.B. Hobbs *v* South Africa, 1924, and 211 by W.L. Murdoch for Australia *v* England, 1884, these being the only two Test match double centuries scored in England prior to 1930), the highest score by an Australian in any Test match anywhere (previous best, 214* by V.T. Trumper *v* South Africa, 1910–1), the highest score against England in a Test match (previous best, 223 by G.A. Headley, for West Indies, 1929–30), and the highest by an Australian in a Test match in England, and in any Test against England (previous best, 211 by Murdoch, 1884); all these records lasted less than a fortnight, Bradman himself breaking them in the next Test match. However, it remains the ground record for a Test Match at Lord's (previous best, 211 by Hobbs; by an Australian, and in an England *v* Australia Test match, 193* by W. Bardsley, 1926; next best, 240 by W.R. Hammond, 1938); and until Ponsford made 281* *v* MCC there in 1934, it was the highest score made at Lord's by an Australian or other touring batsman (previous best, 248* by W.W. Armstrong, 1905). He also remains the youngest batsman (as he later also became the oldest) to score a double century in a Test match for Australia, and in an England *v* Australia Test, the previous youngest having been S.E. Gregory, who was over 24 when he made 201 in 1894–5; Bradman was now 21 years 307 days old.

His time for reaching 200 (four hours five minutes) was quicker than that for either of the other two Test match double centuries scored in England, Hobbs with four and a half hours being the previous best, though Bradman improved considerably on this time in the next Test match.

He thus made 385 in two consecutive Test innings (131, 254), a record for Australia (previous best, 373 by Trumper, 1910–1; *v* England, 289 by J.S. Ryder, 1924–5); Bradman later made 466 (1931–2) and 548 (1934) in two successive innings. His 393 in three consecutive Test innings (8, 131, 254) equalled the record for Australia *v* England, by C.G. Macartney, 1926, Bradman easily passing this record in the next Test match. His last five Test innings (123, 37*, 8, 131, 254) totalled 553, which was an Australian Test record for a few weeks, until he himself thrice beat it; the previous best was 495 by Trumper, 1910–1, and *v* England, 493 by Macartney, 1921–6.

Late on the fourth day, Australia had one and a half hours to make 72 to win, but lost 3 wickets for 22 before Woodfull and S.J. McCabe steered them to victory. Bradman, in at 16 for 1, survived only two balls before he was again out to a brilliant catch by Chapman, this time in the gully, low down, off a hard cut, with the score 17 for 2.


## 45. AUSTRALIANS *v* YORKSHIRE, at Bradford, 2, 3 and 4 July 1930

SCORES: Australians 302 (W.H. Ponsford 143) and 7 for no wicket; Yorkshire 146 (C.V. Grimmett 6 for 75) and 161 (C.V. Grimmett 5 for 58). Australians won by ten wickets.

D.G. BRADMAN lbw. b. E. Robinson   1
               (did not bat)       –

On a rather damp wicket, Bradman went in at 4 for 1 and was soon lbw., he and Woodfull both being out in the first 20 minutes of the game with only 11 runs scored. Bradman's innings lasted eight minutes.


## 46. AUSTRALIA *v* ENGLAND, Third Test match, at Leeds, 11, 12, 14 and 15 July 1930

SCORES: Australia 566 (D.G. Bradman 334, A.F. Kippax 77, W.M. Woodfull 50, M.W. Tate 5 for 124); England 391 (W.R. Hammond 113, C.V. Grimmett 5 for 135) and 95 for 3 wickets. Drawn.

D.G. BRADMAN c. G. Duckworth b. M.W. Tate    334

Another magnificent innings by Bradman was the main feature of this match, and on this occasion he passed the record to which he had come so close at Lord's, R.E. Foster's 287. He went in at 11.38 on the first morning, when A.A. Jackson was out in the second over with the score at 2, was all but bowled by his first ball from Tate, and thereafter batted as brilliantly as at Lord's. He completed 50 in 49 minutes, out of 61 while he was in, and after 99 minutes, he hit Larwood to leg for 4 to reach his century; he thus joined V.T. Trumper (1902) and C.G. Macartney (1926) in scoring a century before lunch on the first day of a Test match, being 105 at lunch out of a total of 136 for 1, in an hour and 52 minutes.

Woodfull, after a cautious innings, was out after helping Bradman to add 192 for the second wicket in two hours 39 minutes, Bradman's score being 142; and Kippax then shared in another long partnership. Bradman went from 150 to 200 in 40 minutes and reached 200 at 4 p.m., out of a total of 268 for 2, after batting for only three hours 34 minutes; at 202, however, he made a weak stroke off R. Tyldesley, which skied the ball over mid-on's head, though this was not quite a chance. By the tea interval his score was 220.

He carried on afterwards in the same wonderful form, though at 273 he gave a hard chance at the wicket off Geary. He made his score 287 by on-driving Tate for 4, and next ball scored a single to leg; so that at 6 p.m., after batting five hours 14 minutes, he broke Foster's record (Foster had batted for six hours 59 minutes). Shortly afterwards he lost Kippax, who had helped to add 229 for the third wicket in two hours 43 minutes, Bradman's share being 151. Reaching 300 after five hours 36 minutes, he ended the day eight minutes later with 309 not out, out of a total of 458 for 3; off the last ball of the day, he reached his 2,000 runs for the season with a superb off-drive for 4.

Only two batsmen, both English (T. Hayward and W.R. Hammond), have reached an aggregate of 2,000 runs for a season before 11 July, and the earliest until then by any touring batsman was 10 August, by C.G. Macartney in 1921; though in 1938 Bradman reached 2,000 on 19 July, Macartney took 33 innings to reach 2,000 in 1921, the previous fewest by a touring batsman, whereas this was Bradman's 23rd innings of the season, which equalled the previous best by any player, Hayward in 1906; Bradman himself improved upon this in 1938 by reaching 2,000 for the season in his 21st innings, and in 1934 and 1948 he took 27 and 29 innings respectively. Only Trumper (1902) and W. Bardsley (1912), among overseas batsmen, had beaten al Englishmen to the 2,000 for the season, until Bradman this year and again in 1938.

Bradman, at 21 years 318 days, was the youngest batsman in history to reach an aggregate of 2,000 runs in an English season, C.L. Townsend at the age of 22, in 1899, being the previous youngest; Trumper, 24 in 1902, was the previous youngest among Australians or other visiting batsmen. W.J. Edrich and L. Hutton in 1937, and D.C.S. Compton in 1939, were all only just over 21 when they reached this aggregate for the first time, but Bradman remains the youngest among touring batsmen to do so, as he later also became the oldest.

His total of 309 runs in a single day's play broke several Test match records; it is still the most made in one day in any Test match anywhere (previous best, 214 by Foster, for England v Australia, in Australia, 1903–4; next best, 295 by Hammond, in New Zealand, 1932–3), the most made in a day in any Test match by an Australian (previous best, 206 by Trumper, v South Africa, 1910–1), the most made in a day in any Test match in England (previous best, 199 by J.B. Hobbs, v South Africa, 1924), the most made in a day in any England v Australia Test match by an Australian (previous best, 182 by C. Hill, 1897–8; in England, 173 by Bardsley, 1926, this being the previous best for either country in England).

This was only the seventh time in all first-class cricket that a batsman had made over 300 in a day's play; it has now been done 12 times, including twice in Australia and nine times in England.

His time for reaching 100 (99 minutes) is still the fastest on record by an Australian in a Test match in England, the previous best being an hour and 43 minutes by C.G. Macartney (1926). His time for reaching 200 (three hours 34 minutes) is the fastest in any Test match (previous best, three hours 46 minutes by Trumper v South Africa, 1910–1; v England, and in an England v Australia Test match, four hours two minutes by S.E. Gregory, 1894–5; in any Test match in England, four hours five minutes, by Bradman, 11 days earlier; S.J. McCabe, v England in 1938, reached 200 in three hours 43 minutes, this being the next fastest time to Bradman's). His time for reaching 300 (five hours 36 minutes) was much faster than that taken by A. Sandham (nine and a half hours), the only other player till then to reach 300 in a Test match; but in 1932–3, Hammond reached 300 for England v New Zealand in four hours 48 minutes, Bradman's time being still the best by an Australian, the best in an England v Australia Test match, and the best in a Test in England.

His partnership of 229 for the third wicket with Kippax broke the record for that wicket against England, passing the 207 added in 1884 by W.L. Murdoch and H.J.H. Scott; this record has since been beaten twice by Bradman, in company first with McCabe in 1936–7 (249) and then with A.L. Hassett in 1946–7 (276), both in Australia. It remains the highest third-wicket stand in Tests between England and Australia in England, and until 1947, when A. Melville and A.D. Nourse put on 319 for South Africa, it was the highest for that wicket by any country against England in England.

When he was 138, he completed 1,000 runs in Test matches, all against England, in his seventh Test and his 13th innings; H. Sutcliffe reached 1,000 runs in all Test matches in his ninth Test, though it took him only 12 innings to do so, and v Australia he reached this total in his tenth Test match and his 15th innings; Hammond, later in this Test match, reached 1,000 runs in his eighth Test and his 14th innings against Australia. The previous best for Australia was (v England) Woodfull, with his 16th run in the present match, in his 13th Test and his 21st innings, and (in all Tests), H.L. Collins, in his twelfth Test and his 18th innings, and W. Bardsley, in his eleventh Test and 21st innings. A.R. Morris later made his 1,000th run v England in his ninth Test and his 16th innings, while in all Tests S.G. Barnes did so in his eleventh match and 17th innings, and for the West Indies, E.D. Weekes, like Sutcliffe, took nine Tests and 12 innings.

At 21 years 318 days, Bradman was then the youngest ever to reach 1,000 runs in Test cricket, C. Hill, at 24, being the previous youngest; G.A. Headley, in 1931, reached 1,000 when 38 days younger than Bradman, who remains, however, the youngest to do so in England *v* Australia Tests, and the youngest Australian.

Next morning, Bradman continued until 11.39 a.m., and added another 25 runs before being caught at the wicket, to make the score 508 for 6. He was in for six hours 23 minutes (an average of 52 runs an hour) and hit 46 fours, scoring with equal facility all round the wicket off bowlers who included Larwood, Tate, Geary and R. Tyldesley; he gave only the one chance, at 273, and though he put the ball into the air rather more often than at Lord's, and made a few more false strokes than in his 254 there, it was nevertheless a wonderful display. He scored his runs off 436 balls.

His 334, which was 60 per cent of Australia's total (apart from extras) and 66 per cent of the runs added while he was at the wicket, broke numerous records; in addition to passing R.E. Foster's score of 287 as the highest score for either side in an England–Australia Test match, it was the highest score in any Test match anywhere (previous best, 325 by A. Sandham, *v* West Indies, 1929–30), and the highest score in any Test match in England (previous best, 254 by Bradman, 12 days before), though these records were later again broken, first by W.R. Hammond's 336* *v* New Zealand, in New Zealand, 1932–3, then by L. Hutton's 364 for England *v* Australia, in England, 1938, and now by G. Sobers' 365* for the West Indies *v* Pakistan, 1957–8. It remains the highest score ever made by an Australian in any Test match, in any Test match on behalf of any country against England, and by an Australian in any Test match in England (previous best, 254 by Bradman; next best, 304 by Bradman, 1934). It is also the highest score ever made in a first-class match on the Leeds ground, beating W. Rhodes' 267* in 1921, and, in a Test match, C.G. Macartney's 151 in 1926, which was also the previous ground record for an overseas batsman in any first-class match.

Bradman's match aggregate (also 334) was then the highest for any Test match between England and Australia (previous best, Foster with 287 and 19 = 306; by an Australian, J.S. Ryder, 201* and 88 = 289); Hutton of course broke this record too with his 364, though Bradman's 334 is still the best by an Australian in any Test match.

His single innings of 334 was also then the most runs scored in succession in Test matches by any batsman before being dismissed (previous best, J.B. Hobbs' 126* and 187 = 313 in 1911–2; by an Australian, Ryder's 201* and 88 = 289). In 1932–3 and 1933, Hammond (336* and 29) passed this with 365, and the present record is 490, by Sobers in 1957–58 (365* and 125); while for Australia, in 1947–8 and 1948, A.L. Hassett (198* and 137) made 335 runs in succession before being dismissed. Hutton, with his 364, also passed this record of Bradman's for England *v* Australia Tests, but Bradman's 334 still remains the most runs in succession for Australia in Test *v* England.

Bradman also made 720 in four successive Test innings (131, 254, 1, 334), then a record for all Tests (previous best, Hammond, with 602; by an Australian, 435 by Trumper, 1910–1; *v* England, 432 by Macartney, 1926); Bradman's 720 is still a record for Australia and for tests between England and Australia, but Hammond later made 739 in four succesive innings in all Tests.

Bradman became the first player to make two double centuries in tests in England and against England, and the first Australian to make more than one Test-match double century; previously, Hammond was the only player of any country to make more than one such score in Test matches, and Bradman finished with 12 against Hammond's seven. This was his fourth double century in first-class matches in England, more than any other Australian batsman had achieved before; the previous best was three by W. Bardsley, in four tours, and though since then W.H. Ponsford and K.R. Miller have both made four such scores, and E.D. Weekes, for the West Indians, has made five, Bradman later took his total to 12.

In making over 200 in two successive Tests, he did something which only Hammond had done before, in 1928–9 (his being in consecutive innings); Bradman did this three times altogether, all against England, and Hammond did so on one other occasion, v New Zealand.

Bradman had now made 589 runs in three successive Test innings (254, 1, 334), then a Test match record (previous best, 483 by Hammond, 1928–9; by an Australian, 407 by V.T. Trumper, 1910–1; v England, 393 by Macartney, 1926, which Bradman had equalled in the previous match). Hammond later made 638 in three successive innings in all Tests, and Bradman made 625 v England in 1934.

Bradman also made 720 in four successive Test innings (131, 254, 1, 334), then a record for all Tests (previous best, Hammond, with 602; by an Australian, 435 by Trumper, 1910–1; v England, 432 by Macartney, 1926); Bradman's 720 is still a record for Australia and for Tests between England and Australia, but Hammond later made 739 in four successive innings in all Tests.

Bradman's 728 in five successive Test innings (8, 131, 254, 1, 334) was an Australian record (previous best, his own 553 completed in the previous Test match) for a few weeks, until he himself raised the figure to 734 and then to 835.

He is still the only batsman to score a treble century in a first-class match both in England and Australia; Hammond, who did so in England and New Zealand, is the only other player to make 300 or over in more than one country; while W.L. Murdoch, V.T. Trumper and W.H. Ponsford all got close to Bradman's feat, Murdoch making 321 in Australia and 286* in England, Trumper making 292* in Australia and 300* in England (as well as 293 in New Zealand), and Ponsford making four treble centuries in Australia with a highest score of 281* in England. Bradman also made four such scores in Australia as well as two in England.

Bradman is still the youngest, at 21 years 318 days, to make a score of 300 in an England v Australia Test match, and until Sobers made his 365* in 1957–8, at the age of 21 years 216 days, he was the youngest to make a score of 300 in any Test match; the only previous such score was made by Sandham when he was 39, and Hutton was over 22 when he made his 364.

Bradman's 46 fours remain a record number of boundaries for all Test matches; Foster, in his 287, hit 37 fours, this being the previous record, while Bradman hit two sixes and 43 fours in his 304 v England, 1934; Hammond, in his 336* v New

Zealand in 1932–3, hit ten sixes and 34 fours, this 196 being the most runs scored in boundaries in a Test match innings, though Bradman's 184 in this innings and in his 304 remains the most by an Australian and the most in an England *v* Australia Test match.

In helping to increase the total by 506 while he was in, he broke the record for Test matches between England and Australia; Foster made his 287 out of 504, and, in England for Australia, W.L. Murdoch made 211 out of 479. In 1934, Bradman made 304 out of 511 and, also in 1934, W.H. Ponsford made 266 out of 574 while he was at the wicket; then, in 1938, L. Hutton was batting until the score reached 770.

Bradman out-scored the next highest scorer, Kippax with 77, by 257 runs, which was a Test match record (previous best in any Test match, Foster with 185; by an Australian, 160 by V.T. Trumper (214*), *v* South Africa, 1910–1; by an Australian *v* England, 193 - 39 = 154, by W. Bardsley, 1926). Hammond (336*) scored 276 more than his nearest rival *v* New Zealand in 1932–3, but Bradman's margin of 257 remains a record for Australia and for matches between England and Australia. It is also a record for first-class matches by a touring batsman in England, Macartney's 245 (345 - 100) in 1921 being the previous best.

This was the sixth successive Test match, all *v* England, in which he exceeded 50 in one innings or the other; in England *v* Australia Test matches, only four Englishmen and four Australians (C. Hill, H.L. Collins, J.M. Gregory and J.S. Ryder) had ever done this in as many as four successive Tests. S.J. McCabe later increased the record to seven, and Bradman, in 1936–48, actually made at least 50 in 14 successive Tests *v* England in which he batted. In all Tests, G.A. Faulkner made at least 50 in seven successive Tests, and Bardsley did so in six successive Tests; Bradman, in 1931–3, made at least 50 in eight successive Tests in which he batted, and in 1936–47 did so in 13 successive Tests in which he batted.

It was also the fourth successive Test in which he had made a century, all *v* England; J.B. Hobbs (twice), C.G. Macartney and W.R. Hammond were the previous best, with centuries in three consecutive Tests; Bradman later did so in five, and then in eight successive Tests.

Rain prevented the chance of an Australian victory, but England had to follow on and in the second innings Hobbs was run out by a magnificent piece of fielding by Bradman.

## 47. AUSTRALIANS *v* SCOTLAND, at Edinburgh, 16 July 1930

SCORES: Scotland 129 for 3 wickets (G.W.A. Alexander 51); Australians did not bat. Drawn.

Rain restricted this match to less than three hours' play on the first day and washed out play entirely on 17 and 18 July.

## 48. AUSTRALIA *v* ENGLAND, Fourth Test match, at Manchester, 25, 26 and 28 July 1930

SCORES: Australia 345 (W.H. Ponsford 83, W.M. Woodfull 54, A.F. Kippax 51, C.V. Grimmett 50); England 251 for 8 wickets (H. Sutcliffe 74, K.S. Duleepsinhji 54). Drawn.

D.G. BRADMAN  c. K.S. Duleepsinhji b. I.A.R. Peebles    14

Bradman's experience in this match was far less successful than in the previous Test matches; going in on the first afternoon at 106 for 1, he scored a single off Tate and was then completely beaten by his first ball from Peebles. When 10, he gave a hard chance at slip off that bowler, who beat him again next ball; soon afterwards, in trying to cut, he was caught at second slip, off his 26th ball. He was out with the score 138 for 2, having survived uneasily for half an hour; the wicket was slow but dead and it was fine bowling on Peebles' part to give Bradman so much difficulty and finally to dismiss him.

He thus scored 734 in his last five Test innings (131, 254, 1, 334, 14), just beating his own Australian record of 728 set up in the third Test match; at the Oval he easily passed this with 835.

## 49. AUSTRALIANS *v* SOMERSET, at Taunton, 30 and 31 July 1930

SCORES: Somerset 121 and 81 (C.V. Grimmett 7 for 33); Australians 360 (A.A. Jackson 118, D.G. Bradman 117, A. Young 5 for 70). Australians won by an innings and 158 runs.

D.G. BRADMAN  c. and b. A. Young    117

Going in before tea on the first day at 13 for 1, Bradman took 18 minutes (the second-longest time of his career) to open his score, and 95 minutes to reach 50. At 71 not out overnight, after two hours 13 minutes' batting, he completed his century next morning after three hours five minutes at the wicket, and when he was second out at 244, he and Jackson had added 231 in three hours 35 minutes for the second wicket. Bradman gave no chance and hit 13 fours, off bowlers who included A.W. Wellard and J.C. White.

## 50. AUSTRALIANS *v* GLAMORGAN, at Swansea, 2, 4 and 5 August 1930

SCORES: Australians 245 (D.G. Bradman 58, W. H. Ponsford 53, S.J. McCabe 53, F. Ryan 6 for 76)and 71 for 1 wicket dec.; Glamorgan 99 and 197 for 7 wickets (W.E. Bates 73, M.J. Turnbill 52). Drawn.

| D.G. BRADMAN | b. F. Ryan | 58 |
| | not out | 19 |

Play not starting until 4.20 p.m. on the first day owing to rain, Bradman, going in at 93 for 1, had 47 minutes' batting overnight and made 27 not out on a dead wicket. Next morning, on a wicket which soon began to give Ryan, the slow left-hander, assistance, he and McCabe took their stand for the third wicket to 101 in 86 minutes, but once they were separated the last seven wickets added only 49, Ryan making full use of the difficult wicket. Bradman's 50 took an hour and 44 minutes, and he batted altogether for exactly two hours before being bowled, playing back, at 215 for 5. He hit five fours.

In the second innings the pitch again helped the bowlers, and Bradman, going in at 27 for 1, hit out brightly for 31 minutes before the Australians' declaration at lunch on the third day.

### 51. AUSTRALIANS *v* NORTHAMPTONSHIRE, at Northampton, 9, 11 and 12 August 1930

SCORES: Northamptonshire 249 (A.H. Baskwell 84, J.E. Timms 78); Australians 93 (V.W.C. Jupp 6 for 32) and 405 for 8 wickets (W.M. Woodfull 116, V.Y. Richardson 116, A.A. Jackson 52). Drawn.

| D.G. BRADMAN | b. V.W.C. Jupp | 22 |
| | c. A.P.R. Hawtin b. A.L. Cox | 35 |

Caught on a sticky wicket on the second day, the Australians failed badly against fine off-spin bowling by Jupp. Bradman, although uncomfortable, made the top score and helped Woodfull to take the score from 15 for 1 to 51 for 2 before dragging a ball on to his wicket in trying to cut, just after lunch; his innings lasted 55 minutes.

Forced to follow on, the Australians, on an improved wicket, had little difficulty in saving the game, and Bradman, on the third morning, batted soundly for 78 minutes before mis-timing a pull and being caught at forward short-leg. He took the score from 106 for 2, past the 156 needed to avoid an innings defeat, to 173 for 3.

### 52. AUSTRALIA *v* ENGLAND, Fifth Test match, at the Oval, 16, 18, 19, 20 and 22 August 1930

SCORES: England 405 (H. Sutcliffe 161, R.E.S. Wyatt 64, K.S. Duleepsinhji 50) and 251 (W.R. Hammond 60, H. Sutcliffe 54, P.M. Hornibrook 7 for 92); Australia 695 (D.G. Bradman 232, W.H. Ponsford 110, A.A. Jackson 73, W.M. Woodfull 54, S.J. McCabe 54, A.G. Fairfax 53*, I.A.R.

Peebles 6 for 204). Australia won by an innings and 39 runs, and won the rubber and the Ashes.

D.G. BRADMAN  c. G. Duckworth b. H. Larwood                    232

Rain and bad light held up play on the second day, and Bradman's innings began at 5.12 p.m., after Woodfull and Ponsford had taken the score to 159 for 1. At 27 not out overnight, after 60 minutes at the wicket, Bradman batted the whole of the third day, which was again interfered with by rain; he completed 50 in an hour and 39 minutes, and his fourth century of the series at 1.05 p.m. (with a lovely late cut for 4 off Larwood) in three hours and five minutes. He gave a hard chance at the wicket off Hammond when 82, but otherwise batted very soundly. After lunch, when he was 112, rain and bad light stopped play until 3 p.m., and again at 3.50, when he was 129; but the odd decision was taken to resume play at 6.22. Bradman added one more run off the 14 balls delivered in the remaining eight minutes, and at the close was 130 not out, after four hours 28 minutes' batting.

The rain had made the wicket difficult on the fourth morning and Larwood and Hammond were for a time able to make the ball fly in a most unpleasant manner. Bradman, when 175, received a hard blow in the chest from Larwood, and although just after that he showed for a short time some inclination to draw away and spar at rising balls, he and Jackson mastered the conditions in courageous fashion. At 12.55 p.m. Bradman reached 200 – his third double century of the series – in six hours 23 minutes, and he and Jackson put on 243 for the fourth wicket in four and three-quarter hours before Jackson was out.

With a score of 228 at lunch, having added 98 in two and a half hours, Bradman was 20 minutes afterwards caught at the wicket, in trying to square-cut Larwood; he made his runs off 408 balls, in seven hours 18 minutes (his longest innings in England) and he hit 16 fours. He gave only the hard chance at 82, scarcely ever lifted a ball, and if he did not show the same brilliance as at Lord's and Leeds – he scored mainly by cutting and placing the ball to leg – he had played an innings of immense value to Australia, who were 570 for 5, or 165 ahead, when he was out. His defence, even during the period when the wicket was all in favour of the faster bowlers, was perfect, and his relentless determination to make a big score in the interests of his side was never more apparent. Peebles, who had caused him such trouble in the previous Test match, was the best of the England bowlers, who also included Larwood, Tate and Hammond; and this was the first time that Larwood ever took his wicket.

When he was 164, he took his aggregate for the series to 906, past the 905 made by Hammond in 1928–9, the previous record for any Test match series. He finished with an aggregate of 974 in seven innings and, including his 37* in the second innings of the fifth Test match, 1928–9, he made 1,000 runs in six matches and eight innings in succession, all against England; Hammond, in 1928–9 and 1929, also made 1,000 runs in six matches *v* Australia and South Africa, but took

11 innings to do so, while the best Australian achievement of this nature was by Woodfull, who made 1,000 runs in 11 matches and 17 innings between 1926 and 1930, all *v* England. Bradman again made 1,000 runs in Test cricket in six matches and eight innings in 1930–1–2, and in 1936–7–8 he did so in five matches and nine innings.

His 232 was at that time the highest in any Test match at the Oval (previous best, 211 by W.L. Murdoch for Australia *v* England, 1884); in 1934, Bradman made 244 and then Ponsford scored 266, while in 1938 L. Hutton made 364.

Bradman's and Jackson's partnership of 243 for the fourth wicket broke the records for Test matches between England and Australia, and for all Test matches against England, for Australia, and in England, previously held by S.E. Gregory and G.H.S. Trott, who added 221 for that wicket in England in 1896; it also equalled the highest for any wicket by Australia in any Test match (243 for the eighth, by C. Hill and R.J. Hartigan, *v* England in Australia, 1907–8), and passed the highest for any wicket by Australia in any Test match in England (242 for the third wicket by W. Bardsley and C.E. Kelleway, for Australia *v* South Africa in England, 1912), and for either side in a Test between England and Australia in England (235 by Woodfull and C.G. Macartney, for the second Australian wicket, 1926). All these records lasted for only four years at most, until Bradman helped Woodfull put on 274 for the second wicket *v* South Africa in Australia in 1931–2, and then assisted Ponsford to put on 388 for the fourth wicket and 451 for the second wicket in England in 1934.

His last five Test innings this season thus totalled 835 (254, 1, 334, 14, 232), which still remains a Test match record, the previous best being 779 by W.R. Hammond in 1928–9, and for Australia, his own figure of 734 set up in the fourth Test a few weeks before.


## 53. AUSTRALIANS *v* GLOUCESTERSHIRE, at Bristol, 23, 25 and 26 August 1930

SCORES: Gloucestershire 72 and 202 (W.R. Hammond 89, P.M. Hornibrook 5 for 49); Australians 157 (W.H. Ponsford 51, T.W. Goddard 5 for 52) and 117 (C.W.L. Parker 7 for 54). A Tie.

| | | |
|---|---|---|
| D.G. BRADMAN | c. R.S. Sinfield b. C.W.L. Parker | 42 |
| | b. C.W.L. Parker | 14 |

The wicket was difficult all through this match and Gloucester's spin bowlers, Parker and Goddard, made the fullest use of it. Bradman went in before lunch on the second day, at 42 for 1, and apart from Ponsford was the only Australian to make any effective resistance on a wicket all against the batsman. He batted for an hour and 42 minutes and was eighth out at 131, having hit only one boundary; he fell to a good catch at silly mid-off.

Requiring 118 to win on the last day, the Australians seemed to have the situation well under control when Bradman went in just before lunch at 63 for 2, but after the interval, Parker and Goddard bowled superbly on a wicket which was now at its worst, and the score had slumped to 81 for 6 when Bradman was bowled, after batting for 32 minutes; amid tremendous excitement, the last wicket fell with the scores level.

When Bradman had made 7, he carried his aggregate for the tour to 2,571, past the record for an Australian on tour in England, 2,570 by V.T. Trumper in 1902.

## 54. AUSTRALIANS v KENT, at Canterbury, 27, 28 and 29 August 1930

SCORES: Australians 181 (A.P. Freeman 5 for 78) and 320 for 3 wickets dec. (D.G. Bradman 205*, A.A. Jackson 50*); Kent 227 (T.W. Wall 5 for 60) and 83 for 2 wickets (F.E. Woolley 60*). Drawn.

| | | |
|---|---|---|
| D.G. BRADMAN | lbw. b. A.P. Freeman | 18 |
| | not out | 205 |

Bradman's twenty-second birthday on the first day was not marked by any great personal success for, after going in at 39 for 1, he was lbw., to a leg-break from Freeman just before lunch, after that bowler had caused him some perplexity during his 32-minute stay. The score was then 78 for 3.

Bradman played Freeman to much better effect in the second innings; going in before tea on the second day at 18 for 1, he drove and pulled him so hard that he completed 50 in 59 minutes. He and Woodfull (45) put on 105 for the second wicket, and at the close Bradman was 68 not out, having slowed down in the last half-hour and thus having batted for 103 minutes altogether.

In hot weather next morning, with the Australians still in some danger of defeat, he continued to score unusually slowly, against some very good bowling by Freeman, and took one and a half hours to make the 32 needed to reach his century; he took 25 minutes to go through the nineties, and his 100 took him three hours 13 minutes. Thereafter he brightened up, and his second century took only one and a half hours (four hours 43 minutes altogether), as, with the game well saved, he used his brilliant strokes and quick footwork to entertain himself and the crowd. When Woodfull declared at the end of the over, Bradman had been in four and three-quarter hours for 205, made without a chance and including 28 fours; he and Jackson had an unfinished partnership of 195 for the fourth wicket. This was his sixth double century of the season, one more than the previous best, by K.S. Ranjitsinhji in 1900.

His 205* is still the highest score v Kent on behalf of an Australian or any other touring team, and the highest on the Canterbury ground, the previous best being 189 by V.S. Ransford, 1909.

## 55. AUSTRALIANS *v* AN ENGLAND XI, at Folkestone, 3, 4 and 5 September 1930

SCORES: An England XI 403 for 8 wickets dec. (L.E.G. Ames 121, W.R. Hammond 54, R.E.S. Wyatt 51, M.W. Tate 50) and 46 for 1 wicket; Australians 432 (A.A. Jackson 78, W.H. Ponsford 76, D.G. Bradman 63, E.L. a'Beckett 53). Drawn.

D.G. BRADMAN  lbw. b. M.J.C. Allom               63

Bradman went in 50 minutes from the end of the second day at 117 for 1, and was 30 not out at the close; next morning, he completed 50 in 71 minutes, but soon afterwards, at 222 for 4, was lbw. in trying to drive the new ball. He made 63 in 80 minutes, including six fours, and he and Jackson put on 103 for the fourth wicket in 74 minutes.

## 56. AUSTRALIANS *v* MR H.D.G. LEVESON-GOWER'S XI, at Scarborough, 10, 11 and 12 September 1930

SCORES: Mr Leveson-Gower's XI 218 for 9 wickets dec. (A. Sandham 59, P.M. Hornibrook 5 for 69) and 247 (J.B. Hobbs 59, M. Leyland 50); Australians 238 (D.G. Bradman 96, A.F. Kippax 59, W. Rhodes 5 for 95). Drawn.

D.G. BRADMAN  b. C.W.L. Parker               96

Mr Leveson-Gower's XI was a strong one, including Larwood, Tate, Parker and Rhodes, who was playing in his last first-class match at the age of 52; rain, however, interfered with the cricket, as well as giving Parker and Rhodes considerable assistance. Bradman started his innings on the second day at 30 for 1 and had reached 73 in an hour and 48 minutes before bad light stopped play; his 50 came up after only 51 minutes. He enjoyed some luck, however, for he might have been caught at mid-off first ball, and at 60 he gave a chance of stumping and was dropped off a skier at mid-on, Rhodes being the sufferer on all three occasions.

Next morning, he ought to have been run out at 74, but carried his score to 96 before being bowled off his pads in trying to hook a ball which kept very low. Fourth out at 214, he batted for exactly two and a half hours, hit seven fours and with Kippax added 113 for the third wicket in 91 minutes. The wicket was again rather difficult, helping Rhodes and Parker with spin and lift, and the last six Australian wickets collapsed for 24 runs.

| | Matches | Innings | NO | HS | Runs | Average | Centuries |
|---|---|---|---|---|---|---|---|
| All First-class Matches | 27 | 36 | 6 | 334 | 2960 | 98.66 | 10 |
| Test Matches | 5 | 7 | 0 | 334 | 974 | 139.14 | 4 |

Australia won the Test match series by two matches to one with two drawn and regained the Ashes. Bradman's aggregate of 2,960 in all first-class matches remains the record for any overseas batsman touring England (previous best, 2,570 by V.T. Trumper in 1902; next best, 2,627 by B. Sutcliffe, for the New Zealanders, 1949). It is also, of course, a record for an overseas batsman on his first tour of England (previous best, 2,072 by W. Bardsley in 1909; next best, Sutcliffe's 2,627); Bardsley is the only other Australian to make more than 2,000 runs on his first tour of England, though Sutcliffe (New Zealand), G.A. Headley (West Indies) and E.D. Weekes (West Indies) have also done so.

This season, the next highest aggregate by an Australian was 1,451 by A.F. Kippax, while among Englishmen K.S. Duleepsinhji made most runs, 2,562. Eleven Englishmen scored over 2,000 runs.

Bradman's average of 98.66 was the highest ever achieved in an English season up till then; the previous best was 91.23 by R.M. Poore in 1899. H. Sutcliffe had an average of 96.96 in 1931, while Bradman himself did even better than this in 1938, when he averaged 115.66. Up to 1930, the best average by a touring batsman was C.G. Macartney's 59.41 in 1921, and the previous best average by one making a first visit to England, 57.65 by W.M. Woodfull in 1926; while this season, the next best by an Australian was 58.06 by A.F. Kippax, also on his first visit, and the next best by an Englishman was Sutcliffe's 64.22.

Of Australian or other touring batsmen, only Bardsley (1909) had previously had an average higher than any Englishman's; Bradman later also headed the English batting averages on his other three visits. Only Trumper (1902) and Bardsley (1912) had previously finished an English season with the highest aggregate of any batsman, English or Australian.

Bradman's ten centuries were the most by a touring batsman on his first visit to England (previous best, eight by Woodfull in 1926), though he just failed to equal Trumper's 11 centuries (in 53 innings) on his second visit in 1902, a record which Bradman broke in 1938. Woodfull, with six centuries, was the next Australian to Bradman this summer, while Duleepsinhji, with nine, scored more hundreds than any other English batsman.

Woodfull, in 1926, had scored his eight centuries in 34 innings, or 23 per cent, the highest proportion by any visiting batsman; Bradman's ten in 36, or 27 per cent, was better than this, though not so good as the 50 per cent (13 centuries in 26 innings) he achieved in 1938, or his 35 per cent in 1948.

Bradman's six double centuries remain a record for an English season (previous best, five by K.S. Ranjitsinhji in 1900; previous best by an Australian, two each by

W.W. Armstrong in 1905 and Bardsley in 1909; next best, five by Weekes for the West Indians in 1950; next best by an Australian, three each by W.H. Ponsford in 1934, and by Bradman in 1934 and 1938).

Bradman's aggregate of 974 for the Test match series remains a record; the previous highest was W.R. Hammond's 905 in 1928–9, and the previous best *v* England was 703 by Headley for the West Indies in 1929–30; while the previous highest by an Australian was 661 by Trumper *v* South Africa in Australia, 1910–1, and (*v* England) 574 by Trumper in 1903–4; in England, the previous best were, (in any series) 513 by H. Sutcliffe *v* South Africa in 1929, (in an England *v* Australia series) the Hon. F.S. Jackson's 492 in 1905, and (by an Australian, and in any series against England in England) 473 by Macartney in 1926. In 1934, Bradman made 758 runs in a series, this being the next highest to his 974, for a Test series in England; while his aggregate of 810 in Australia in 1936–7 is the next highest in one rubber against England anywhere.

His average of 139.14 was also a record for a Test match rubber; the previous highest in any Test match series was 132.66 by E. Hendren *v* South Africa, in England, 1924, and by an Australian, 113.66 by Bardsley *v* South Africa, 1912 – though Bradman himself, by averaging 201.50 *v* South Africa in 1931–2, raised the figure even higher, and his 139.14 now is a record only for any Test series in England and against England. It also remains the record for an England *v* Australia Test match series (previous best, 113.12 by Hammond in 1928–9; in England, and by an Australian batsman, 94.60 by Macartney, 1926, this being the previous highest average in any Test series against England).

His feat of scoring three double centuries in one series also remains a record; only Hammond had previously made as many as two such scores, both *v* Australia in 1928–9.

He also became the first Australian to score four centuries in one series, and is still the only Australian to do so against England, and the only batsman to do so in an England *v* Australia series in England; Sutcliffe, in 1924–5, and Hammond, in 1928–9, both made four centuries in a series for England *v* Australia in Australia, G.A. Headley (West Indies) did so *v* England in 1929–30, and Sutcliffe also performed this feat *v* South Africa in England, 1929; for Australia in England, only Macartney, in 1926, had previously scored as many as three centuries in one series, though Bradman in 1938 and A.R. Morris in 1948 also scored three. In 1955, for West Indies *v* Australia, C.L. Walcott broke all previous records by making five centuries in a series, while Bradman made four in a series on two later occasions in Australia, *v* South Africa (1931–2) and India (1947–8). D.C.S. Compton (*v* South Africa, 1947) is the only batsman apart from Sutcliffe and Bradman to make four in a series in England.

This season, Woodfull, 345 runs, average 57.50, was second to Bradman in the Australian Test match batting averages; for England, Sutcliffe was first, with 436 runs, average 87.20. No one else on either side scored more than one century.

In the year from 1 November 1929 to 31 October 1930, Bradman made a total of 4,546 runs, the most on record by a batsman in the space of one year; he took

52 innings to do this. The previous best was 4,378, by Hammond (1928 and 1928–9), in 66 innings, and, by an Australian, 3,480 by Macartney (59 innings), from 19 November 1920 to 18 November 1921. In 1932 and 1932–3, Sutcliffe broke Bradman's record with 4,681 runs (74 innings), and in 1946–7 and 1947, D.C.S. Compton, in 81 innings, amassed 5,476 runs; Bradman's is still the record for an Australian, R.N. Harvey having come closest to it with 3,699 runs in 1952–3 and 1953, in 62 innings.

# 1930–1

## AGED TWENTY-TWO

——————◆◆◆◆◆◆——————

The first West Indian team, under G.C. Grant, toured Australia this season.

### 57. NEW SOUTH WALES v SOUTH AUSTRALIA, at Sydney, 7, 8, 10 and 11 November 1930

SCORES: New South Wales 228 (A.G. Fairfax 62, D.G. Bradman 61, J.E.H. Hooker 54) and 396 (D.G. Bradman 121, A.F. Kippax 104, A. Allsopp 93); South Australia 124 (J.E.H. Hooker 5 for 28) and 287 (H.C. Nitschke 141). New South Wales won by 213 runs.

D.G. BRADMAN  c. D.E. Pritchard b. C.S. Deverson      61
              c. M.G. Waite b. C.S. Deverson         121

Bradman was some way below his best form in his first innings, being troubled by some accurate medium-paced bowling, especially from Waite. Going in at 8 for 1 on the first morning, he took 96 minutes to reach 50, just before lunch; he had been missed at the wicket off B.J. Tobin when 35. Soon after the interval, he was brilliantly caught at first slip, having batted for an hour and 48 minutes and hit seven fours; the score was 126 for 5 when he was out, and he had carried his aggregate in four consecutive innings for New South Wales to 637 (452*, 47, 77, 61), the most on record (previous best, 600 by Kippax, 1925–6–7); in 1933–4, Bradman made 645 in four successive innings for that State.

His second innings was much better; he went in at 7 for 1, just after lunch on the second day, reached 50 in 72 minutes, and was 87 at tea-time. His century came soon afterwards, in two hours five minutes, and after that he lashed out and threw his wicket away, being caught at cover off a hard drive. He was out at 228 for 3, after he and Kippax had added 219 in two and a quarter hours for the third wicket; he batted for only two hours 22 minutes, gave no chance, and hit 13 fours, his cover-driving being particularly powerful.

In five consecutive innings for New South Wales, he had thus made 758 runs a record for that State (452*, 47, 77, 61, 121); the previous best was 694 by J.R.M. Mackay in 1905–6.

## 58. AUSTRALIA *v* REST OF AUSTRALIA (J.S. Ryder Testimonial), at Melbourne, 14, 15 and 18 November 1930

SCORES: Rest of Australia 293 (G.W. Harris 108, C.V. Grimmett 5 for 89) and 191 for 3 wickets dec. (K.E. Rigg, 74, J.S. Ryder 65*); Australia 367 (D. Bradman 73, A.F. Kippax 70, W.M. Woodfull 53) and 96 for 5 wickets. Drawn.

| | | |
|---|---|---|
| D.G. BRADMAN | b. A.A. Mailey | 73 |
| | c. and b. A.A. Mailey | 29 |

The Rest of Australia's bowlers included H.H. Alexander, D.D. J. Blackie, H. Ironmonger and A.A. Mailey, the last three of whom, though veterans, showed that they still possessed much skill; and Mailey in particular bowled well enough to trouble Bradman and to dismiss him twice.

In the first innings, he went in on the second morning, at 9 for 1, got his 50 in 95 minutes, and was then completely beaten by one ball from Mailey and bowled by the next – a leg-break to which he played back. He was in for two hours eight minutes, hit four fours, and added 105 for the third wicket with Kippax; he was dismissed at 129 for 3.

Rain having washed out the third day's play, Ryder's declaration on the last day left Australia 85 minutes to score 118 runs to win. Bradman opened, in an endeavour to force the pace, but so well did the Rest's bowlers bowl, that he took an hour to score 29, and failed to reach the boundary; at 61 for 3, he hit a ball very hard back to Mailey, who took a good catch.

## 59. NEW SOUTH WALES *v* WEST INDIANS, at Sydney, 21, 22, 24 and 25 November 1930

SCORES: West Indians 188 and 241 (G.A. Headley 82, L.N. Constantine 59, H.C. Chilvers 5 for 73); New South Wales 206 (D.G. Bradman 73) and 224 for 6 wickets (A.A. Jackson 62). New South Wales won by 4 wickets.

| | | |
|---|---|---|
| D.G. BRADMAN | c. I. Barrow b. G.N. Francis | 73 |
| | c. G.A Headley b. F.R. Martin | 22 |

Bradman began his first innings 35 minutes from the close of the first day's play and had reached 39 not out when stumps were drawn. Next morning, he completed his 50 in 49 minutes, but thereafter went more slowly, until he was deceived by a slower ball from Francis and was caught at the wicket, off the inside edge, when apparently not attempting a stroke. He made 73 in an hour and 28 minutes, hit ten fours, and saw the total raised from 20 for 1 to 135 for 5.

In the second innings, he went in at 97 for 1 on the third evening, and was well caught in the deep after batting for 25 minutes; he was fourth out, just before the end of the day, at 131, and after his departure New South Wales had to struggle hard to win.

## 60. AUSTRALIA *v* WEST INDIES, First Test match, at Adelaide, 12, 13, 15 and 16 December 1930

SCORES: West Indies 296 (E.L. Bartlett 84, C.A. Roach 56, G.C. Grant 53\*, C.V. Grimmett 7 for 87) and 249 (G.C. Grant 71\*, L.S. Birkett 64); Australia 376 (A.F. Kippax 146, S.J. McCabe 90) and 172 for no wicket (W.H. Ponsford 92\*, A.A. Jackson 70\*). Australia won by 10 wickets.

D.G. BRADMAN   c. C.G. Grant b. H.C. Griffith        4
               (did not bat)                         –

Bradman went in at 55 for 1 after lunch on the second day, and failed badly, being caught at third slip, cutting at a wide ball, with the score 64 for 3; he was in for quarter of an hour without ever looking secure. In the West Indies' second innings, Bradman obtained his first wicket in a Test match, dismissing I. Barrow lbw. in the last over of the third day.

## 61. NEW SOUTH WALES *v* SOUTH AUSTRALIA, at Adelaide, 18, 19, 20 and 22 December 1930

SCORES: New South Wales 610 (D.G. Bradman 258, A.A. Jackson 166, C.V. Grimmett 5 for 180); South Australia 166 (H.C. Nitschke 69, W.A. Hunt 5 for 36, H.C. Chilvers 5 for 68) and 310 (H.C. Nitschke 102). New South Wales won by an innings and 134 runs.

D.G. BRADMAN  b. V.Y. Richardson              258

Going in on the first morning at 24 for 1, Bradman assisted Jackson in a brilliant partnership which added 334 for the second wicket in three hours 43 minutes. Bradman, after lunch, reached 50 in 79 minutes, and 100 in two hours eight minutes; he later hit so hard that he went from 150 to 200 in 38 minutes, completing 200 in three hours 54 minutes soon after Jackson was out. When he was bowled, at 448 for 3, just before the close of play, he had been at the wicket for four hours 49 minutes without giving a chance, and had hit 37 fours; the bowlers who suffered from his and Jackson's treatment included T.W. Wall, T.A. Carlton, P.K. Lee, C.V. Grimmett and M.G. Waite.

This partnership of 334 remains a record for the second wicket in a Sheffield Shield match, *v* South Australia in a Shield match, and for New South Wales in any match, the previous best being 314 by W.H. Ponsford and H.L. Hendry for Victoria *v* Queensland in 1927–8, 283 by M.A. Noble and A.J. Hopkins for New South Wales *v* South Australia in 1908–9, and 304 by W. Bardsley and M.A. Noble for New South Wales *v* Victoria in 1908–9. Bradman's 258 came within 13 of the highest score for New South Wales *v* South Australia in a Sheffield Shield match.

This was the tenth double century of Bradman's career, more than any other Australian had ever made; Ponsford, the previous best, had until then made nine such scores, and although he added four more before he retired in 1934, Bradman had by then established a clear lead over all Australians with 21 double centuries and had almost caught up with W.R. Hammond, who then held the world record for the number of double centuries.

Bradman took 3 wickets for 54 in South Australia's second innings.

## 62. NEW SOUTH WALES *v* VICTORIA, at Melbourne, 24 and 29 December 1930

SCORES: Victoria 185 (W.H. Ponsford 109*); New South Wales 97 for 6 wickets (A.A. Jackson 52*). Drawn.

D.G. BRADMAN  c. H.L. Hendry b. E.L. a'Beckett          2

Rain prevented play for most of the first day and all of the second and third, but on the fourth day the wicket was slow and by no means difficult. Bradman went in during the afternoon at 29 for 1, and was caught in the slips at 33 for 2, after a stay of nine minutes.

During the year 1930, Bradman amassed a total of 4,368 runs (52 innings) in all first-class matches in England and Australia, more than anyone had ever made in one calendar year before; W.R. Hammond, in 1928, made 3,971 runs (66 innings), while the previous best by an Australian was 3,152 (74 innings) by V.T. Trumper in 1902. In 1933, Hammond broke this record of Bradman's with 4,445 runs (69 innings), while in 1947 D.C.S. Compton put together as many as 4,962 runs (69 innings); Bradman's 4,368 is still the most in a calendar year by an Australian, his own 3,838 (in 40 innings) in 1938 being the next best.

## 63. AUSTRALIA *v* WEST INDIES, Second Test match, at Sydney, 1, 3 and 5 January 1931

SCORES: Australia 369 (W.H. Ponsford 183, W.M. Woodfull 58); West Indies 107 and 90. Australia won by an innings and 172 runs.

D.G. BRADMAN  c. I. Barrow b. G.N. Francis          25

69

Bradman went in at 12 for 1, early on the first day, and was settling down confidently, having been in for 40 minutes, when he was caught at the wicket off a rising ball, at 52 for 2.

He thus brought his Test match aggregate since 14 June 1930 to 1,003 in 201 days – until then the quickest 1,000 runs ever scored in Test matches; the previous best was 248 days, by J.B. Hobbs, in 1911 and 1912, and by an Australian, 312 days by C. Hill in 1902. Bradman's remains the best performance of this nature by an Australian, but for England, W.R. Hammond made 1,003 runs in only 122 days in 1932 and 1933. In 1954 and 1955, R.N. Harvey made 1,000 runs for Australia in 205 days, the next best time to Bradman's.

## 64. AUSTRALIA *v* WEST INDIES, Third Test match, at Brisbane (Exhibition Ground), 16, 17, 19 and 20 January 1931

SCORES: Australia 558 (D.G. Bradman 223, W.H. Ponsford 109, A.F. Kippax 84); West Indies 193 (G.A. Headley 102*) and 148 (C.V. Grimmett 5 for 49). Australia won by an innings and 217 runs, and won the rubber.

D.G. BRADMAN  c. C.G. Grant b. L.N. Constantine                      223

Going in at 1 for 1, early on the first day, Bradman all but achieved a third consecutive failure in the Test matches, for he gave a sharp chance in the slips, trying to cut Constantine, when only 4. After that, he batted brilliantly and faultlessly; he completed 50 in 80 minutes, being 51 at lunch; his century took him two hours 22 minutes, and his second-wicket stand with Ponsford added 229 in two hours 42 minutes. At tea, he was 129; afterwards, he reached 200 in four hours 11 minutes, and at the close of play, after batting for four hours 50 minutes, he was 223 not out, having passed V.T. Trumper's 214* *v* South Africa, 1910–1, previously the highest score by an Australian batsman in a home Test match. He and Kippax added 193 for the third wicket in two minutes less than two hours.

By scoring 223 runs in a day, he made the most runs ever scored in one day's play in a Test match in Australia (previous best, 214 by R.E. Foster, 1903–4; by an Australian, 206 by Trumper, *v* South Africa, 1910–1); this remains a record. This was the second time that he had scored more than 200 in a day's play in a Test match; up till then, no one else had done so more than once, Trumper and H.L. Collins being the only other Australians in a list of five batsmen, including Bradman. Bradman did this six times altogether, and W.R. Hammond four times.

On a drying wicket next morning, Bradman stayed for only seven minutes and did not add to his score, being caught off a skier at square-leg in trying to hook a bumper, at 434 for 4. Batting for four hours 57 minutes, he hit 24 fours, off bowlers who included G.N. Francis, H.C. Griffith, O.C. Scott, L.N. Constantine and F.R. Martin.

His 223 remained a record for an Australian in a Test match in Australia for less than a year, Bradman himself, with scores of 226 and 299*, twice passing it *v*

South Africa in 1931–2. It remains the record for either side in Tests between Australia and the West Indies, passing W.H. Ponsford's 183 in the previous Test match; the next best are 219 by D. Atkinson and 204 by R.N. Harvey, both in the West Indies in 1955. It is also still the highest score against a West Indian team on tour in Australia (previous best, 187 by Ponsford, for Victoria, 1930–1); and the highest in a Test Match on the Exhibition Ground, Brisbane, the previous best being 169 by E. Hendren, for England in 1928–9; this was the second and last Test match played on this ground, the Brisbane Cricket Ground being used from 1931–2 onwards.

His partnership of 229 with Ponsford was up till then the highest for the second wicket in any Test match in Australia (previous best, 224 by W. Bardsley and C. Hill, for Australia *v* South Africa, 1910–1); Woodfull and Bradman passed this with 274 *v* South Africa in 1931–2, and C.C. McDonald and A.L. Hassett added 275 *v* South Africa in 1952–3. It was also the record for a second-wicket partnership in any Test match *v* West Indies (previous best, 148 by A. Sandham and R.E.S. Wyatt, for England. 1929–30), and remained so until P. Roy and V.L. Manjrekar put on 237 for India in 1952–3, and then in 1957 P.E. Richardson and T.W. Graveney added 266 for England. It remains the highest second-wicket stand for either side in any Australia *v* West Indies Test match.

His partnership of 193 with Kippax equalled the highest for the third wicket for Australia in a Test match in Australia (J. Darling and J. Worrall also added 193 for the third wicket *v* England in 1897–8); Bradman and S.J. McCabe passed this with 249 *v* England in 1936–7, and Bradman and A.L. Hassett added 276 *v* England in 1946–7. It was also the record for a third-wicket partnership in any Test match *v* West Indies (previous best, 168 by A. Sandham and E. Hendren, 1929–30) until, in England in 1939, L. Hutton and W.R. Hammond added 264. It remains the highest third-wicket stand for either side in an Australia *v* West Indies Test match in Australia, though in the West Indies in 1955, R.N. Harvey and K.R. Miller put on 224 for Australia, and then C.L. Walcott and E.D. Weekes added 242 for the West Indies, both for the third wicket.

In helping to add 433 runs to the total, he broke the record for an Australian in any Test match in Australia, 420 by C.E. Kelleway, *v* England, 1920–1; next season, Bradman raised this record to 504, and in 1946–7, S.G. Barnes increased it to 564.

## 65. NEW SOUTH WALES *v* VICTORIA, at Sydney, 24, 26, 27 and 28 January 1931

SCORES: New South Wales 196 and 417 for 9 wickets dec. (D.G. Bradman 220, O.W. Bill 100, D.D.J. Blackie 5 for 101); Victoria 318 (L.P. O'Brien 119) and 202 for 6 wickets (K.E. Rigg 98). Drawn.

| | | |
|---|---|---|
| D.G. BRADMAN | c. B.A. Barnett b. H.H. Alexander | 33 |
| | c. K.E. Rigg b. H. Ironmonger | 220 |

Bradman went in at 14 for 1 early on the first morning and made a confident start to his first innings, hitting 33 in 47 minutes, before being brilliantly caught at the wicket on the leg side by Barnett, who, standing back, had to make a great deal of ground; he was second out at 68.

Led by 122 on the first innings, New South Wales opened their second with Bradman and McCabe early on the third day. Bradman reached 50 in 87 minutes and 100 in two hours 54 minutes shortly before tea; at 76 he completed his 1,000 runs for the season, being again the first batsman to do so. Afterwards he continued to bat soundly, and completed 200 in four hours 42 minutes, six minutes before the close of play, being 208 not out overnight. He gave no chance, but had several narrow escapes when assaulting the bowling after passing 150. Next morning, he stayed for another 20 minutes until, at 415 for 7, he tried to score off a very wide ball, and gave a catch to cover, after batting for five hours eight minutes; he hit 13 fours and he and Bill added 234 for the fifth wicket in two hours ten minutes. H.H. Alexander, E.L. a'Beckett, H. Ironmonger and D.D.J. Blackie were among the bowlers to suffer. This was his third double century of the season.

The partnership of 234 with Bill is still the highest for the fifth wicket against Victoria, the previous best being 190 for South Australia in 1920–1, by P.D. Rundell and D.M. Steele; for New South Wales *v* Victoria, 159 by A.C.K. McKenzie and L.W. Pye in 1897–8. It is also still the highest on either side in a match between New South Wales and Victoria, the previous best for the fifth wicket being 187 by R.L. Park and J.S. Ryder for Victoria in 1920–1.

In being for the third time the first (or only) batsman to reach 1,000 in an Australian season, he surpassed the performances of C. Hill and W.H. Ponsford (and later, H. Sutcliffe and A.R. Morris), each of whom twice was the first batsman of the season to complete 1,000 runs. Bradman did so eight times altogether in Australia.

## 66. AUSTRALIA *v* WEST INDIES, Fourth Test match, at Melbourne, 13 and 14 February 1931

SCORES: West Indies 99 (H. Ironmonger 7 for 23) and 107; Australia 328 for 8 wickets dec. (D.G. Bradman 152, W.M. Woodfull 83). Australia won by an innings and 122 runs.

D.G. BRADMAN c. C.A. Roach b. F.R. Martin                    152

The wicket on the first day was perfect, and after the West Indies had failed, Australia took full advantage of it. Going in after tea at 50 for 1, Bradman at once attacked the bowling, reaching 50 in 45 minutes, his fastest in a Test match, and when stumps were drawn he had batted only 78 minutes to be 92 not out. After overnight rain, the wicket was sticky next morning, and before he had added to his score Bradman was missed at silly point off Martin. After that he mastered the conditions and continued to bat brilliantly, reaching 100 in 102 minutes; and when he was caught in the deep at 286 for 5, he had made 152 in two hours 34 minutes, including two fives and 13 fours, with only the one chance; the last 60 of them came in 76 minutes on the second morning on a wicket all against good batsmanship. His stand with Woodfull realised 156 for the second wicket, in 91 minutes. The West Indian bowlers again included G.N. Francis, H.C. Griffith, O.C. Scott, L.N. Constantine and F.R. Martin. At 59 runs an hour, this was his fastest Test match century.

## 67. NEW SOUTH WALES *v* WEST INDIANS, at Sydney, 21, 23, 24 and 25 February 1931

SCORES: West Indians 339 (G.A. Headley 70, J.E.D. Sealey 58, C.A. Roach 55) and 403 for 9 wickets dec. (L.N. Constantine 93, J.E.D. Sealey 92, O.C. Scott 67*, F.R. Martin 56); New South Wales 190 (L.N. Constantine 6 for 45) and 466 (A.F. Kippax 141, S.J. McCabe 100, D.G. Bradman 73). New South Wales lost by 86 runs.

| D.G. BRADMAN | b. L.N. Constantine | 10 |
| | lbw. b. H.C. Griffith | 73 |

Bradman went in at 36 for 1 on the second morning, but with the score 48 for 2, after eight minutes, a fine off-break hit his off-stump; while in the second innings he scored 73 for the third time this season. New South Wales were set 553 to win, and made a great effort; Bradman, going in an hour before the close of the third day, at 33 for 1, reached 50 in 50 minutes and was 63 not out (in 62 minutes) overnight, though there was a confident lbw. appeal against him when he was 55. Next morning he stayed for 16 more minutes before being lbw., at 140 for 3, to a ball which kept low. He batted for only 78 minutes and hit nine fours.

## 68. AUSTRALIA *v* WEST INDIES, Fifth Test match, at Sydney, 27, 28 February, 2 and 4 March 1931

SCORES: West Indies 350 for 6 wickets dec. (F.R. Martin 123*, G.A. Headley 105, G.C. Grant 62) and 124 for 5 wickets dec.; Australia 224 (A.G. Fairfax 54) and 220 (A.G. Fairfax 60*). Australia lost by 30 runs.

| D.G. BRADMAN | c. G.N. Francis b. F.R. Martin | 43 |
| | b. H.C. Griffith | 0 |

The West Indies declared twice and twice caught Australia on a sticky wicket. Bradman went in soon after tea on the second day, at 7 for 1, when the pitch was at its most spiteful, and played a brilliant innings, displaying sure judgement of which ball to hit and which to leave alone. He made 43 in 51 minutes (50 runs an hour) before being well caught in the slips, off a ball which kicked viciously, the score then being 66 for 2. Apart from an escape from being run out at 21, he gave no chance, and he scored his runs out of 59 added while he was in (72 per cent).

On the fourth morning, he went in at 49 for 1, when the wicket was rather easier than in the first innings, but still unpleasant after more rain and sun; and, pinned down by Griffith, he swung wildly across a straight good-length ball and was bowled for his first 'duck' in a Test match; he was third out at 53, after staying for ten minutes.

## SUMMARY, 1930–1

| | Matches | Innings | NO | HS | Runs | Average | Centuries |
|---|---|---|---|---|---|---|---|
| All First-class Matches | 12 | 18 | 0 | 258 | 1422 | 79.00 | 5 |
| Test Matches | 5 | 6 | 0 | 223 | 447 | 74.50 | 2 |
| All Matches *v* West Indians | 7 | 10 | 0 | 223 | 625 | 62.50 | 2 |
| Sheffield Shield Matches | 4 | 6 | 0 | 258 | 695 | 115.83 | 3 |
| All Matches for NSW | 6 | 10 | 0 | 258 | 873 | 87.30 | 3 |

Australia won the Test match series by four matches to one.

This was the third consecutive Australian season in which Bradman made more than 1,000 runs, a feat he performed 12 times altogether. E. Hendren completed 1,000 runs on three consecutive MCC tours, but no one else, English or Australian, had up to that time reached this aggregate more than twice; A.R. Morris has since done so three times, not in consecutive seasons, but no one except Bradman has yet done so more often than thrice. A.F. Kippax was until then the only New South Wales batsman to reach this aggregate twice, and W.H. Ponsford and Morris are still the only other Australian batsmen to make 1,000 runs in as many as two consecutive seasons.

In making three double centuries this season, Bradman equalled the performance of Ponsford (1927–8) and W.R. Hammond (1928–9); no one else, and no New South Wales batsman, has made more than two double centuries in one Australian season, but Bradman made three on five occasions altogether. Only M.A. Noble (1908–9) and W. Bardsley (1920–1) had previously made two double centuries in the same season for New South Wales; Bradman did this again in 1933-4, and Morris did so in 1951–2.

This season, G.A. Headley, of the West Indies, was the only other batsman to make 1000 runs; his total was 1,066, and the next highest by an Australian was 902 by Kippax. F.C. Thompson's average of 79.16 (for 475 runs in nine innings, with three not-outs to help him) slightly exceeded Bradman's; Ponsford also averaged 70, he, Kippax and Headley all hitting four centuries.

Ponsford just headed Bradman for first place in the Test match aggregates and averages, with 467 runs, average 77.83; these two were a long way ahead of any other batsman on either side. He, Bradman and Headley each scored two Test match centuries; Ponsford's and Bradman's two centuries remained a record for Australia *v* West Indies until 1955, when R.N. Harvey and K.R. Miller each scored three in one series, the latter having previously made one century *v* West Indies in 1951–2. Only Bradman and Harvey have made a double century for Australia *v* West Indies, and on Bradman, Ponsford and A.L. Hassett have made two centuries for Australia *v* West Indies in Australia.

In the year between 1 April 1930 and 31 March 1931, Bradman scored 1,421 runs in Test matches, the most on record for any period of one year; the previous best was 1,257, by Hammond, between 1 November 1928 and 31 October 1929, and, by an Australian 1,106 runs by C. Hill, between 1 December 1901 and 30 November 1902; while Bradman himself, in 1947–8 and 1948, made 1,223 runs in Test cricket in less than one year.

# 1931–2

## AGED TWENTY-THREE

———◆·▸◀·◆———

The South African team which toured Australia this season, under H.B. Cameron, was the second to do so, the first visit having been as long ago as 1910–1.

69. **NEW SOUTH WALES** *v* **QUEENSLAND**, at Brisbane, 6, 7, 9, and 10 November 1931

SCORES: Queensland 109 (G.S. Amos 5 for 22) and 85; New South Wales 432 (S.J. McCabe 229*, J.H. Fingleton 93). New South Wales won by an innings and 238 runs.

D.G. BRADMAN  c. L. Waterman b. E. Gilbert          0

On the first afternoon, after Queensland's batting failure, Gilbert, the aboriginal fast bowler, bowled at a tremendous pace on a fast wicket, and took two wickets in his first over before a run had been scored. O.W. Bill was caught at the wicket off his first ball, and Bradman, after being in the gravest difficulty for four balls, was caught at the wicket off the sixth.

70. **NEW SOUTH WALES** *v* **SOUTH AFRICANS**, at Sydney, 13, 14, 16 and 17 November 1931

SCORES: South Africans 425 (H.W. Taylor 124, E.L. Dalton 87, H.B. Cameron 74) and 190 for 3 wickets dec. (S.H. Curnow 79*); New South Wales 168 and 430 for 3 wickets (D.G. Bradman 135, J.H. Fingleton 117, S.J. McCabe 79*). Drawn.

D.G. BRADMAN  c. and b. Q. McMillan          30
　　　　　　　c. A.J. Bell b. D.P.B. Morkel          135

Bradman's first innings was not one of his best; he went in just before lunch on the second day and batted for 87 minutes, before giving an easy return catch. He helped to raise the score from 1 for 1 to 98 for 3, and his 30 was the second highest score to McCabe's 37.

Declaring at the end of the third day, the South Africans gave New South Wales a day (five hours) to make 448 to win – an average of 90 an hour – and thanks largely to Bradman, they came within 18 runs of victory with 7 wickets in hand. Going in just after lunch, at 81 for 1, he batted in his most brilliant form; he reached 50 in only 37 minutes and 100 in 100 minutes, just before tea, and when he was well caught at backward point, he had batted for only two hours eight minutes. He was out at 297 for 2, having put on 216 for the second wicket with Fingleton; he hit 15 fours and gave only one chance, in the slips off Morkel when he was 120. In addition to Morkel and McMillan, the South African bowlers included A.J. Bell, C.L. Vincent and X. Balaskas.

Bradman is the only Australian to score a century in his first match against both English (1928–9) and South African touring teams in Australia; he also scored a century in his first match *v* the Indians in 1947–8, though the West Indians got him out for 73 and 22 in his first match against them in 1930–1.

His 135 was then the highest for New South Wales against a South African team (previous best, 126 by C.G. Macartney, 1910–11); later this season, Bradman passed this with an innings of 219.


71. **AUSTRALIA** *v* **SOUTH AFRICA**, First Test match, at Brisbane, 27, 28 November, 2 and 3 December 1931

SCORES: Australia 450 (D.G. Bradman 226, W.M. Woodfull 76, W.A. Oldfield 56*); South Africa 170 (B. Mitchell 58, H. Ironmonger 5 for 42) and 117 (T.W. Wall 5 for 14). Australia won by an innings and 163 runs.

D.G. BRADMAN lbw. b.C.L. Vincent                226

Going in at 32 for 1 on the first morning, on a very fast wicket, Bradman made a dreadful start to his big innings; at 3 he might have been caught at square-leg in hooking N.A. Quinn, though this was not a chance, and at 11 and 15 he was missed in the slips, both times again off Quinn's bowling. After that, he found the pace of the pitch, and completely mastered the South African attack, showing no further signs of fallibility until just before he was out. Being 30 not out at lunch, he reached 50 in 62 minutes, then, slowing up, took a further hour and 22 minutes to reach three figures. He was 108 at tea, and reached 200, just before the close of play, in four hours 13 minutes, being 200 not out overnight; he took some time to pass through the 190s, good fielding keeping the value of his strokes down to singles. His stand of 163 with Woodfull for the second wicket took two hours 17 minutes, and that of 81 with McCabe (27) for the fourth wicket only three-quarters of an hour; his hooking and his forcing shots to the on were particularly devastating. This was the third time, out of six altogether, that he made 200 or more in a day's play in a Test match; and when he was 111, he reached an aggregate of 2,000 runs in all Test matches.

Hitting out next morning, he soon passed V.T. Trumper's 214*, made in 1910–1, which had been the highest score in Tests between Australia and South Africa, against South Africa in any Test match, and against any South African side in Australia; and he then overtook his own 223 *v* the West Indies the previous season, which had been the highest score by an Australian batsman in a home Test match. However, at 224 he might have been stumped off Vincent, and two balls later he was lbw. to that bowler in trying to force him to the on. His innings (51 per cent of Australia's total from the bat) lasted four hours 37 minutes and included 22 fours; he was out at 380 for 7. In addition to C.L. Vincent and N.A. Quinn, the South African bowlers were A.J. Bell, D.P.B. Morkel and Q. McMillan.

This was his ninth century in all Test matches; Trumper made eight, previously the most Test centuries made by any Australian batsman, though Bradman altogether made 29. He is the only batsman to make a double century in his first Test match *v* South Africa, the previous best being 142 by C. Hill, for Australia, 1902–3; Hill and W. Bardsley were till then the only Australians to make a century in their first Test matches *v* South Africa, though four others have since done so, in addition to Bradman.

This was the first Test match to be played on the Brisbane Cricket Ground (the two previous Brisbane Tests having been played on the Exhibition Ground), and his 226 remains a ground record for Test matches there; the best in a Test match on the Exhibition Ground was his own 223 *v* West Indies in 1930–1.

## 72. NEW SOUTH WALES *v* SOUTH AFRICANS, at Sydney, 7 and 8 December 1931

SCORES: New South Wales 500 (D.G. Bradman 219, S.F. Hird 101, Q. McMillan 6 for 189); South Africans 185 for 1 wicket (S.H. Curnow 81*, D.P.B. Morkel 70*). Drawn.

D.G. BRADMAN c. S.H. Curnow b. Q. McMillan       219

Bradman was again in brilliant form and gave no chance in making his second successive double century against the tourists. He made 50 in 66 minutes, 100 in two hours seven minutes, 200 in three hours 34 minutes, and altogether batted for six minutes under four hours for his 219, the highest score for New South Wales *v* the South Africans (previous best, his own 135 earlier in the season; next best, 213* by I.D. Craig, 1952–3).

His innings saved his side; 8 for 1 when he went in early on the first day, the score was at one time 159 for 5, but it had been raised to 348 for 7 when he was out, caught in the deep when hitting out recklessly. He hit 15 fours, being especially severe on the slow bowler, McMillan, whom he scarcely allowed to bowl a length; the other bowlers were A.J. Bell, D.P.B. Morkel, C.L. Vincent and N.A. Quinn. His stand with Oldfield for the sixth wicket lasted 70 minutes and put on 99, Oldfield's share being 29.

Rain prevented any play on what should have been the first and fourth days and made the outfield very slow.

Up till then, the only batsmen to score two double centuries in successive innings in Australia were W.H. Ponsford and W.R. Hammond; in fact, it had been done only nine times in the whole of cricket history up to then. Bradman altogether performed this feat on three other occasions, twice in Australia and once in England. This was also his third century in succession, the second of the ten occasions he accomplished this performance.

### 73. AUSTRALIA v SOUTH AFRICA, Second Test match, at Sydney, 18, 19 and 21 December 1931

SCORES: South Africa 153 and 161; Australia 469 (K.E. Rigg 127, D.G. Bradman 112, S.J. McCabe 79, W.M. Woodfull 58, A.J. Bell 5 for 140). Australia won by an innings and 155 runs.

D.G. BRADMAN  c. K.J. Viljoen b. D.P.B. Morkel                112

In hitting his fourth successive century, all off the South Africans, Bradman continued in magnificent form. When he went in just before lunch on the second day, the score was already 143 for 2, only ten runs behind the South African first-innings total; 11 not out at lunch, he reached 50 in 85 minutes and was 90 not out at the tea interval. Afterwards, he reached 100 in two hours 27 minutes, being finally out caught in the deep (he again virtually threw his wicket away), after being in for only two hours 35 minutes; he hit ten fours, and gave no chance. He put on 111 in 93 minutes for the third wicket with Rigg, and when the latter was out McCabe helped him put on 93 in an hour for the fourth wicket, Bradman being out at 347 for 4. A strained leg, causing him to limp considerably, affected his mobility to some extent, but did not restrict his brilliant stroke-play; the bowlers included A.J. Bell, N.A. Quinn, L.S. Brown and C.L. Vincent, in addition to Morkel. This was his first Test match century at Sydney; he did not make another there until 1946–7.

To score four or more centuries in successive innings is an uncommon feat (this was the 14th time it had been done in first-class cricket), and Bradman is the only batsman to perform it off a touring team's bowling; the previous best was three in succession by C.G. Macartney in 1910–1, also v the South Africans in Australia. Moreover, he is the only Australian batsman to perform this feat in Australia; Macartney did it in England in 1921, and W.R. Hammond (1936–7) and D.C.S. Compton (1946–7) later did it in Australia for the MCC. In 1938–9, Bradman scored six centuries in successive innings, and in 1948 and 1948–9, in England and Australia, he again made four in succession.

## 74. AUSTRALIA v SOUTH AFRICA, Third Test match, at Melbourne, 31 December 1931, 1, 2, 4, 5 and 6 January 1932

SCORES: Australia 198 (K.E. Rigg 68, A.F. Kippax 52, A.J. Bell 5 for 69) and 554 (D.G. Bradman 167, W.M. Woodfull 161, S.J. McCabe 71, A.F. Kippax 67); South Africa 358 (K.J. Viljoen 111) and 225 (J.A.J. Christy 63, C.V. Grimmett 6 for 92). Australia won by 169 runs and won the rubber.

| | | |
|---|---|---|
| D.G. BRADMAN | c. H.B. Cameron b. N.A. Quinn | 2 |
| | lbw. b. C.L. Vincent | 167 |

Going in at 11 for 1 on the first morning, on a perfect wicket, Bradman took ten minutes to open his score, and after another four minutes was caught at the wicket at 16 for 2.

He redeemed this failure convincingly in the second innings, which Australia started on the third day 160 behind. Bradman went in just after tea, at 54 for 1, and promptly attacked and mastered the bowling, driving and pulling in his most brilliant form. He reached 50 in 64 minutes and when stumps were drawn 34 minutes later, he was 97 not out; and Australia were 206 for 1, having easily cleared off the arrears.

He drove the first ball of the next day for 3, to complete his third century of the series, 98 minutes being the fastest time in which he ever reached his hundred in a Test match. Thereafter he was rather less brilliant, but when he was out at 328 for 2, just before lunch, he and Woodfull had put on 274 for the second wicket in three hours three minutes, and he had scored his runs at a rate of 54 an hour. He hit 18 fours, and gave no chance, off bowlers who included A.J. Bell and Q. McMillan in addition to Quinn and Vincent.

His partnership of 274 with Woodfull for the second wicket was at that time the highest second-wicket stand in all Test cricket, the previous best being 235 by Woodfull and C.G. Macartney v England in 1926; the previous best in Australia was 229 by W.H. Ponsford and Bradman v the West Indies in 1930–1, and the previous best v South Africa was 230 by H. Sutcliffe and E. Tyldesley for England in 1927–8, and (for Australia v South Africa) 224 by W. Bardsley and C. Hill in Australia in 1910–1. It was also the highest for any wicket for Australia in any Test match (previous best, 243 for the eighth wicket by Hill and R.J. Hartigan v England in Australia, 1907–8, and 243 for the fourth wicket by Bradman and A.A. Jackson v England in England, 1930), the highest for any wicket for either side in a Test match between Australia and South Africa (previous best, 242 for the third wicket by Bardsley and C.E. Kelleway, for Australia, in England, 1912; in Australia, 224 for the second wicket by Bardsley and Hill, 1910–1), and the highest for any wicket against South Africa in a Test match (previous best, 268 by J.B. Hobbs and H. Sutcliffe, for the first wicket for England, 1924).

All these records have since been broken; in 1934, in England, Ponsford and Bradman added 388 for the fourth wicket and then 451 for the second wicket *v* England; in 1936–7, Bradman and J.H. Fingleton added 346 for the sixth wicket *v* England; in 1938–9, P.A. Gibb and W.J. Edrich added 280 for the second wicket for England *v* South Africa; and in 1952–3, C.C. McDonald and A.L. Hassett put on 275 for the second wicket for Australia *v* South Africa, in Australia.

The total of 274 was then also the highest for any wicket against any touring team in Australia (previous best, 270 for the second wicket by H.L. Collins and T.J.E. Andrews *v* MCC, 1924–5; *v* a South African team in Australia, 224 for the second wicket by Bardsley and Hill, 1910–1), and the highest for the second wicket against any South African touring team anywhere (previous best, 225 by T. Hayward and J.T. Tyldesley, in England, 1907). All these records have since been broken, either by C.L. Badcock and W. Horrocks, who added 306 for the second wicket *v* MCC, 1936–7, or by McDonald's and Hassett's partnership of 275 for the second wicket *v* South Africa, 1952–3. The present record for any wicket against any touring team in Australia is 405 for the fifth wicket, by Bradman and S.G. Barnes, *v* England, 1946–7.

## 75. NEW SOUTH WALES *v* VICTORIA, at Sydney, 22, 23, 25 and 26 January 1932

SCORES: New South Wales 348 (S.J. McCabe 106) and 389 for 4 dec. (D.G. Bradman 167, S.J. McCabe 103*); Victoria 204 and 294 (H.H. Oakley 93*, J. Thomas 70). New South Wales won by 239 runs.

| | | |
|---|---|---|
| D.G. BRADMAN | c. S.A. Smith b. H. Ironmonger | 23 |
| | b. L.E. Nagel | 167 |

In his first innings, Bradman went in at 72 for 1, just before lunch on the first day, and was all but run out before scoring; he batted for 49 minutes before being caught at short-leg, when failing to get hold of a long hop, at 119 for 3.

He made a cautious start to his second innings; going in at 28 for 1, early on the third morning, he took 37 minutes to reach double figures and one and a half hours to get to 50; he was missed, when 44, at slip off Ironmonger, who bowled well and caused him considerable trouble. However, after lunch, he gradually mastered him and ran to his century in two hours 46 minutes; hitting out after that, he used the last over before tea to score 20 runs off L.S. Darling. Soon after tea, his leg stump was hit when he was going for another big hit, the ball keeping low; he batted for three hours 44 minutes, hit 22 fours, and gave only one chance. He added 110 with Kippax (44) for the third wicket, and when he was out New South Wales, at 303 for 4, were in a strong position; he completed 1,000 runs for the season when 86, in his tenth innings, one fewer than his own previous record for New South Wales set up in 1929–30. The Victorian bowlers, in addition to Ironmonger and Nagel, included E.L. McCormick and E.L. a'Beckett.

76. **AUSTRALIA** *v* **SOUTH AFRICA**, Fourth Test match, at Adelaide, 29, 30 January, 1 and 2 February 1932

SCORES: South Africa 308 (H.W. Taylor 78, B. Mitchell 75, H.B. Cameron 52, C.V. Grimmett 7 for 116) and 274 (B. Mitchell 95, H.W. Taylor 84, J.A.J. Christy 51, C.V. Grimmett 7 for 83); Australia 513 (D.G. Bradman 299*, W.M. Woodfull 82, A.J. Bell 5 for 142) and 72 for no wicket. Australia won by 10 wickets.

D.G. BRADMAN  not out                      299
         (did not bat)                      –

Bradman continued his overpowering mastery over the South African bowlers with another magnificent innings, his seventh century in seven successive matches, and his sixth *v* the South Africans. Going in at 9 for 1, ten minutes before lunch on the second day, he scored 2 before the interval. Afterwards, he attacked the bowling and reached 50 in 62 minutes; 84 not out at tea, he completed his fourth century of the series in two hours 13 minutes, having just previously run Kippax out in an endeavour to get his 100th run, before that unfortunate batsman had received a ball. Thereafter, he hit the bowling even more fiercely and had made a chanceless 170 not out at the close of play after being in for only three hours 24 minutes. His stand with Woodfull for the second wicket added 176 in two hours six minutes; and when he had made 109, he completed 1,000 runs for the season (including six centuries) off the South African bowling alone. He had now scored a Test match century at Sydney, Melbourne and Adelaide, as well as on both Brisbane grounds; no one else has done this, though A.L. Hassett and R.N. Harvey have since hit hundreds on four different Australian grounds.

Next morning he played himself in again with the utmost caution, taking 80 minutes to make the 30 he needed for his third double century off the tourists' bowling. When 185, he was missed in the slips off Bell, and for a long time was most uncomfortable, surviving several appeals; he eventually reached 200 with a late-cut for an all-run 4, after being in for four hours 44 minutes. He put on 114 with K.E. Rigg (35) for the fifth wicket in 88 minutes.

After lunch, when he was 219 not out, he recovered his best form, but began to run out of partners; however, when 226, he passed G.A. Faulkner's record aggregate of 732 for an Australia–South Africa Test series, set up in 1910–1, and then, cleverly shielding his partners, of whom W.J. O'Reilly (23) helped him with 78 for the ninth wicket, went after the record for the highest score in a Test match in Australia, 287 by R.E. Foster in 1903–4. This record he also broke, with the last man, H.M. Thurlow, as his partner; but when he was 298, they ran 1 for a hit to leg, Bradman called for an impossible second, sent Thurlow back, and the latter was easily run out. That left Bradman with 299 not out (61 per cent of Australia's total from the bat – the highest he ever achieved in a Test match), made in six hours 36 minutes, and including 23 fours; he saw 504 added to the score, and apart from the troubled period during the third morning, he was at his best throughout. On the third day he added 129 in three hours 12 minutes and gave only one sharp chance. A.J. Bell, N.A. Quinn, C.L. Vincent, Q. McMillan and D.P.B. Morkel were the South African bowlers.

His 299* remains the highest score ever made in any Test match in Australia; it also passed his own 226, made two months earlier, and is still the highest score ever made by an Australian in a Test match in Australia, the highest for either side in Tests between Australia and South Africa, and the highest ever made in any Test match v South Africa; and it is the highest against any South African touring team anywhere (previous best, 229 by G.J. Bryan in England, 1924), as well as the highest against any touring team in Australia (previous best, 280 by A.J. Richardson v MCC, 1922–3; v the South Africans, his own 226).

The previous highest score in a Test match at Adelaide was V.T. Trumper's 214* v South Africa in 1910–1.

This was the ninth double century he had scored in Australia; W.H. Ponsford, with eight at that time, had previously scored most double centuries in Australia, and though he caught Bradman up next season, the latter went ahead again the next day; Ponsford finished with nine double centuries in Australia, Bradman with 25.

His stand of 78 with O'Reilly remains the highest ninth-wicket partnership in any Test match v South Africa (previous best, 71 by H. Wood and J.T. Hearne, for England, 1891–2; for Australia, 54 by R.A. Duff and J.J. Kelly, in South Africa, 1902–3; for Australia in Australia, 39 by W.A. Oldfield and T.W. Wall, first Test match, 1931–2). It is also the highest ninth-wicket stand for either side in Tests between Australia and South Africa, the previous best being the 54 by Duff and Kelly in 1902–3, and also 54 by J.M. Blackenberg and E.P. Nupen, for South Africa, 1921–2. In 1957–8, K. Mackay and I. Meckiff in South Africa, also added 78 for the ninth Australian wicket.

Bradman out-scored the next highest scorer by 217 runs, the highest in any Test in Australia (previous best, 185 by R.E. Foster; by an Australian, 160 by Trumper, v South Africa, 1910–1). His match aggregate (299) is the highest by an Australian in a Test match in Australia (previous best, 201 and 88 = 289 by J.S. Ryder, 1924–5).

In remaining at the wicket while 504 runs were added to his side's total, he equalled the record set up by R.E. Foster, and broke that for an Australian in any home Test match, the 433 which he helped to add in 1930–1; in 1946–7 S.G. Barnes helped to take the Australian score to 564 before being out.

Bradman finished this match with a Test aggregate for the series of 806, and including his 152, 43 and 0 in the last two Tests v West Indies in 1930–1, he had made over 1,000 Test runs in six matches and eight innings – the second time he had achieved this feat. The first time he scored all his runs against England; this time he scored all his runs in Australia. In 1936–7 and 1938, he took only five Tests to make 1,000 runs, though then he took nine innings.

His last two Test innings thus totalled 466, then a record (previous best, 451 by W.R. Hammond in 1928–9, and, for Australia, his own 385 in 1930); in 1934, Bradman made 548 in two successive Test innings, while in 1932–3, Hammond made 563 *v* New Zealand.

### 77. AUSTRALIA *v* SOUTH AFRICA, Fifth Test match, at Melbourne, 12 and 15 February 1932

SCORES: South Africa 36 (H. Ironmonger 5 for 6) and 45 (H. Ironmonger 6 for 18); Australia 153. Australia won by an innings and 72 runs.

D.G. BRADMAN  absent hurt                                –

Bradman strained a ligament in his ankle as a result of a fall in the dressing-room just before going out to field and took virtually no part in the match, apart from fielding on the second day during the South Africans' second innings. However, Australia were able to win by an innings without his assistance, on a 'glue-pot' wicket on which the South Africans were hopelessly outclassed.

### 78. NEW SOUTH WALES *v* SOUTH AUSTRALIA, at Sydney, 19, 21 and 22 March 1932

SCORES: South Australia 272 (A.R. Lonergan 68, H.E.P. Whitfield 51, W.J. O'Reilly 5 for 68) and 225 (H.C. Nitschke 119, W.J. O'Reilly 5 for 59); New South Wales 247 (O.W. Bill 76*, J. Donnelly 57) and 118. New South Wales lost by 132 runs.

D.G. BRADMAN  b. T.A. Carlton              23
              b. T.W. Wall                  0

Bradman began and ended this season with a 'duck', this being the second year in succession that his final innings was 0. In the first innings, going in at 11 for 3, early on the second morning, he might have been caught at the wicket off Grimmett when 12, and was bowled off his pads by a break-back after 42 minutes at the wicket; he was out at 55 for 4. In the second innings he went in on the third afternoon at 15 for 1, and to his fifth ball, and his first from Wall, played over an in-swinging yorker, one run later.

| | Matches | Innings | NO | HS | Runs | Average | Centuries |
|---|---|---|---|---|---|---|---|
| All First-class Matches | 10 | 13 | 1 | 299* | 1403 | 116.91 | 7 |
| Test Matches | 5 | 5 | 1 | 299* | 806 | 201.50 | 4 |
| All Matches v South Africans | 7 | 8 | 1 | 299* | 1190 | 170.00 | 6 |
| Sheffield Shield Matches | 3 | 5 | 0 | 167 | 213 | 42.60 | 1 |
| All Matches for NSW | 5 | 8 | 0 | 219 | 597 | 74.62 | 3 |

Australia won the Test match series by five matches to nil.

Bradman's aggregate of 806 for the Test match series was the highest by an Australian in any series in Australia, and by any batsman in a series v South Africa (previous best, 661 by V.T. Trumper in 1910–1); it was also the highest in any rubber between Australia and South Africa (previous best, 732 by G.A. Faulkner for South Africa, 1910–1). These records have, however, since gone, Bradman making 810 v England in 1936–7, and R.N. Harvey making 834 (in nine innings) v South Africa in Australia in 1952–3. Bradman's 974 in England in 1930 remains, of course, the record for any batsman in any Test match series, and W.R. Hammond's 905 in 1928–9 remains the highest by any batsman in a series in Australia.

As the only Test matches between Australia and South Africa in Australia have been in 1910–1, 1931–2 and 1952–3, and none of the players on either side took part in more than one of these series, Bradman's aggregate of 806 was, of course, also the highest total of runs scored in Australia in all Test matches between the two countries by a batsman on either side, until Harvey made his 834 in 1952–3.

His average of 201.50 is still the highest on record for any Test match rubber (previous best, Bradman's 139.14 v England in 1930; v South Africa, 132.66 by E. Hendren, 1924; by an Australian v South Africa, 113.66 by W. Bardsley, in England, 1912; in a series in Australia, 113.12 by W.R. Hammond in 1928–9, and by an Australian in Australia, 94.42 by Trumper v South Africa, 1910–1). In 1947–8, Bradman had an average of 178.75 v India, and in 1949–50, Harvey averaged 132.00 v South Africa in South Africa.

He had a century average this season both for the Test series and for all first-class matches which had never been done in any country before; he did so twice more, in England in 1938 and in Australia in 1947–8.

For the second time in his career, he scored four centuries in a series of Test matches, the first Australian to do so; H. Sutcliffe performed this feat for England v Australia (1924–5) and v South Africa (1929). Bradman also scored four centuries v England in 1930, and four centuries v India in 1947–8, and Harvey, the only other Australian to do so, made four centuries v South Africa twice, in 1949–0 and 1952–3. Until Harvey's performances, Bradman's four centuries were the most by any Australian batsman in all Tests v South Africa, C. Hill and W. Bardsley being next best with three each.

He remains the only batsman of any country to score more than one double century in all Tests *v* South Africa; in scoring two double centuries in a rubber in Australia, he equalled Hammond's performance in 1928–9, Bradman also doing this *v* England in 1936–7. Bradman, of course, made three double centuries in a series in England in 1930 and two in 1934, while Hammond also made two in a series *v* New Zealand in 1932–3, but no one else had ever made more than one score of 200 and over in any Test match series until, for India *v* New Zealand, V. Mankad made two double centuries in 1955-6.

His total of 1,190 runs is still the most ever made in one season anywhere off any touring team's bowling; even D.C.S. Compton, in his great season of 1947, took only 1,187 runs off the South Africans in England, in 14 innings, average 84.78, and the previous best were 891, average 81.00, by G.A. Headley, *v* MCC in the West Indies, 1929–30, and in Australia, 833, average 92.55, by W.M. Woodfull, off MCC in 1928–9; against the South Africans, the best was 830, average 74.75, by Trumper in 1910–1; Bradman's average of 170.00 is much higher than any of these. The only other seasons in which over 1,000 runs have been scored off a touring team are 1947–8, when Bradman made 1,081 *v* the Indians, and 1957–8, when G. Sobers made 1,007 runs in the West Indies *v* the Pakistanis; the next best in Australia is 942 by Harvey *v* the South Africans in 1952–3.

His total of six centuries against the South Africans is also a record against any touring team; in 1929, Sutcliffe scored five centuries off the South Africans in England, and in 1928–9, Woodfull scored four off the MCC in Australia, as did A.R. Morris *v* MCC in 1946–7 and 1950–1; while Compton in 1947 and Bradman in 1947–8 also scored six. This season *v* South Africa, Bradman's six centuries were in consecutive matches *v* the tourists.

He also made three double centuries *v* the South Africans, two of them in successive innings; Weekes made two (also in succession) *v* the Indians in the West Indies in 1952–3, and Mankad made two *v* the New Zealanders in India in 1955–6, but otherwise no one except Bradman has ever made more than one double century in a season off a touring team's bowling. Bradman also made two *v* MCC in 1936–7.

This was the second Australian season in which he made seven centuries and three double centuries, feats which no one else had achieved more than once; his seven centuries were made in seven successive matches. It was also the fourth consecutive Australian season in which he exceeded 1,000 runs, thereby breaking Hendren's record which he had equalled in 1930–1. W.W. Armstrong had previously been the only player twice to make five or more centuries in a season in Australia; this was the fourth time (out of ten altogether) that Bradman had done so.

Bradman was easily first in the Australian first-class averages and aggregates this season; S.J. McCabe had the next best average, 87.80, and J.A.J. Christy, the South African, with 909, and V.Y. Richardson, with 873, had the next highest aggregate. No one else scored more than three centuries during the season. Bradman's average of 116.91 in all first-class matches was the highest on record by a New South Wales player, the previous best being his 113.28 in 1929–30; in 1933–4, he had an average of 132.44.

W.M. Woodfull, 421 runs, average 70.16, was second to Bradman in aggregate and average in the Test matches, in which no one else hit more than one century. Woodfull made 0 in the fifth Test match, and it is fair to say that if Bradman had been able to take his innings on that difficult wicket his average for the series would probably not have remained as high as 201.50.

There was a marked difference this season between his extraordinary success against the South Africans and his relative failure in Sheffield Shield matches – despite which New South Wales won the Shield.

Bradman was married on 30 April 1932, and soon afterwards, accompanied by his wife, took part in the tour of A.A. Mailey's Australian team in Canada and America. None of the matches was first-class, but Bradman was in great form, his figures being: 51 innings, 14 times not out, highest score 260, total runs 3,782, average 102.21, with 18 centuries. His score of 260 was the highest ever made in Canada.

# 1932–3

## AGED TWENTY-FOUR

The MCC team which toured Australia this season, under D.R. Jardine, brought with it four fast bowlers, H. Larwood, W. Voce, G.O. Allen and W.E. Bowes. Larwood was a greatly improved bowler, both in pace and accuracy, compared with 1928–9 and 1930, when Bradman had scored readily off him; in fact, in 1932–3, he was probably both the fastest bowler and the best fast bowler of this century. It was soon apparent that Jardine's plan to regain the Ashes was to use Larwood and Voce to bowl what became known as 'body-line', or fast leg-theory, in order to restrict the run-getting of Bradman and other leading Australian batsmen; this consisted of fast bowling directed at or outside the leg stump, a great proportion of the balls being short of a length and rising chest or head high, to a field set mainly on the leg side. Bradman himself was the chief, though not the only, target for this extremely dangerous form of attack.

79. **COMBINED AUSTRALIAN XI** *v* **MCC TEAM**, at Perth, 27, 28 and 29 October 1932

SCORES: MCC Team 538 for 7 wickets dec. (H. Sutcliffe 169, Nawab of Pataudi 129, D.R. Jardine 98, W.R. Hammond 77); Combined Australian XI 159 (H. Verity 7 for 37) and 139 for 4 wickets (J.H. Fingleton 53*). Drawn.

| | | |
|---|---|---|
| D.G. BRADMAN | c. W.R. Hammond b. H. Verity | 3 |
| | c. Nawab of Pataudi b. G.O. Allen | 10 |

Bradman, for the only time in his career, had the melancholy experience of being dismissed twice in a day; after the MCC had used a good wicket for nearly two days, overnight rain made the conditions ideal for Verity on the third day. In the first innings, Bradman went in soon after the start at 61 for 1, and at 67 for 2 was out to a brilliant right-handed catch at second slip off a ball which jumped viciously and which he could not quite avoid, after batting for seven minutes. In the follow-on, on a slightly easier wicket, he went in during the afternoon at 0 for 1, and was in for 22 minutes before being caught at short-leg at 19 for 2.

The weakness of the Combined XI's bowling is indicated by the fact that Bradman bowled 19 eight-ball overs – the longest spell of his career. He took two wickets (Jardine and G.O. Allen) for 106.

## 80. NEW SOUTH WALES *v* VICTORIA, at Sydney, 4, 5, 7 and 8 November 1932

SCORES: Victoria 404 (W.H. Ponsford 200, W.M. Woodfull 74, W.J. O'Reilly 5 for 81) and 150 (W.M. Woodfull 83, S.F. Hird 6 for 56); New South Wales 475 (D.G. Bradman 238, S.J. McCabe 56, A.F. Kippax 52, H.H. Alexander 7 for 95) and 82 for 1 wicket (D.G. Bradman 52*). New South Wales won by 9 wickets.

| D.G. BRADMAN c. L.P. O'Brien b. L.O'B. Fleetwood-Smith | 238 |
|---|---|
| not out | 52 |

Bradman played two superb innings, and soon showed that there was little the matter with his form. Going in at 16 for 1 just after lunch on the second day, he took only half an hour (the fastest of his career) to complete 50, and only 73 minutes to reach his century; continuing to score at a great pace, his 200 took two hours 52 minutes, and when, just before the close of play, he was fourth out with the score at 355, caught at long-off, he had batted for only three hours 20 minutes and scored 70 per cent of the total added while he was in, as well as 51 per cent of New South Wales' eventual total (excluding extras). He hit 32 fours and gave no chance, though a weak stroke off Fleetwood-Smith, when he was in the forties, went over the bowler's head and might have been caught at mid-on by a more athletic fieldsman. He added 128 with Kippax for the third wicket, and 134 with McCabe for the fourth wicket; he hit all the bowlers impartially, but his great speed of foot enabled him to be particularly severe upon Fleetwood-Smith, whom he scarcely ever permitted to bowl a length. Alexander, H. Ironmonger and D.D.J. Blackie, too, all came in for heavy punishment.

Ponsford, on the first day, with his ninth (and last) double century in Australia, had again caught up with Bradman's total, but Bradman wasted no time in hitting his tenth such score in Australia, and thereafter left Ponsford's double centuries in Australia far behind.

His time for reaching 200 in this match, two hours 52 minutes, was up to then the fastest ever achieved in a Sheffield Shield match (previous best, 200 in two hours 58 minutes by R.B. Minnett, for New South Wales *v* Victoria, 1911-2); this is still the fastest in a Sheffield Shield match for New South Wales, though in 1935–6, Bradman, playing for South Australia, improved upon this time by four minutes.

His second innings started at 19 for 1, soon after the start of the fourth day's play, and lasted only 41 minutes; his eighth boundary was the winning hit. He scored his 52 out of 63 added while he was at the wicket (82 per cent).

## 81. AN AUSTRALIAN XI *v* MCC TEAM, at Melbourne, 18, 19, 21 and 22 November 1932

SCORES: MCC Team 282 (H. Sutcliffe 87, R.K. Oxenham 5 for 53) and 60 (L.E. Nagel 8 for 32); Australian XI 218 and 19 for 2 wickets. Drawn.

| | | |
|---|---|---|
| D.G. BRADMAN | lbw. b. H. Larwood | 36 |
| | b. H. Larwood | 13 |

The MCC bowlers included Larwood, Voce and Bowes, and Bradman found himself faced with their 'body-line' attack for the first time, a very big proportion of the balls bowled to him being short bumpers; Larwood in particular used these tactics and bowled at a great pace. Bradman's first innings, starting at 51 for 1 on the second afternoon, lasted 46 minutes before he was lbw. in trying to turn a straight ball to leg, and though he played some brilliant strokes, he was clearly disconcerted by the fast leg-theory. He helped to take the score to 105 for 2, his 36 being the second highest score to L.P. O'Brien's 46.

After some splendid bowling by Nagel, the Australian XI had all the last day to try to make 125 to win, but rain had made the wicket vicious and Larwood and Allen, bowling at a tremendous pace, and in poor light, were able to make the ball fly dangerously from a length. Woodfull was out at 0, and Bradman had a most unhappy 17 minutes' batting, making some very streaky shots before being bowled, attempting to draw away and cut a straight ball. Soon after he was out at 18 for 2 rain put an end to further play.

## 82. NEW SOUTH WALES *v* MCC TEAM, at Sydney, 25, 26, 28 and 29 November 1932

SCORES: New South Wales 273 (J.H. Fingleton 119*, S.J. McCabe 67, G.O. Allen 5 for 69) and 213 (F.S. Cummins 71, W. Voce 5 for 85); MCC Team 530 (H. Sutcliffe 182, L.E.G. Ames 90, R.E.S. Wyatt 72, Nawab of Pataudi 61, S.F. Hird 6 for 135). New South Wales lost by an innings and 44 runs.

| | | |
|---|---|---|
| D.G. BRADMAN | lbw. b. M.W. Tate | 18 |
| | b. W. Voce | 23 |

Although Larwood was not playing, Bradman again failed twice, and it was obvious that his confidence was shaken by the fast bowling. In the first innings, going in at 43 for 1 on the first morning, he had 41 minutes of mainly defensive batting, without showing much sign of being likely to build up a big score; he was out at 75 for 2.

Suffering from a chill, he spent the third day in bed and batted early on the fourth day when still far from well. On this occasion he lasted for 53 minutes and appeared to have settled down before Voce bowled him a very short ball; expecting it to bump, Bradman went over to the off to left it fly past, but instead it kept low and bowled him. He then returned home to bed after helping to raise the score from 90 for 4 to 161 for 6.

***

Bradman was unable to play in the first Test match early in December, owing to ill health, and in his absence Australia lost by ten wickets, despite a superb innings of 187* by S.J. McCabe. Bradman had signed a contract with a newspaper to report the Test matches, which had brought him into dispute with the Australian Board of Control, and he had for some weeks been the centre of a heated controversy on the subject. This, coupled with his failures against the MCC – he had so far scored 103 runs in six innings against them – affected his health to such an extent that he became thoroughly run down and in need of rest. The 'player-writer' controversy was eventually solved by the newspaper in question releasing Bradman from his contract, and he played no cricket for nearly a month while he attempted to recover his health.

### 83. NEW SOUTH WALES v VICTORIA, at Melbourne, 26 and 27 December 1932

SCORES: New South Wales 388 (D.G. Bradman 157, J.H. Fingleton 85, H. Ironmonger 5 for 87) and 8 for no wicket; Victoria 258 (E.H. Bromley 84, L.P. O'Brien 53). Drawn.

| D.G. BRADMAN c. E.H. Bromley b. H. Ironmonger | 157 |
|---|---|
| (did not bat) | – |

In rather better health after his rest, Bradman took the opportunity of regaining his form. Rain having washed out the first two days' play, New South Wales were sent in to bat, and the score was 67 for no wicket at the lunch interval, during which W.A. Brown retired hurt; Bradman took his place and soon settled down. His first 50 was carefully compiled in one and a half hours, and after tea he reached his century in two hours 37 minutes. He then lashed out in an endeavour to throw his wicket away, making his last 50 in half an hour before being well caught at long-on, at 338 for 4. He batted altogether for three hours 19 minutes, gave no chance, and hit 16 fours; his stand with McCabe (48) realised 103 for the second wicket. The Victorian bowlers included H.H. Alexander, L.E. Nagel, H. Ironmonger and L.O'B. Fleetwood-Smith.

When he was 130, he completed 10,000 runs in all first-class cricket in his

126th innings; W.H. Ponsford, the previous best, took 161 innings to reach this landmark. Despite the very limited amount of first-class cricket Bradman had played, he was then, at 24 years 121 days, the youngest batsman ever to reach 10,000 runs; W.R. Hammond was the previous youngest, at 24 years 355 days, and W.G. Grace had been six days older than that – a tremendous performance on the wicket of those days. Among Australians, the best were C. Hill and V.T. Trumper, both over 27; Hill had had three English tours and Trumper two in that time, while Bradman had had only one season in England. He remains the youngest Australian (next best, R.N. Harvey, 25 years 106 days), but L. Hutton was only 23 years 11 days old when he reached his 10,000 in 1939. Bradman completed this aggregate in five years ten days from his début in first-class cricket, much the fastest of any Australian batsman; Woodfull and Ponsford, the previous best, both took just under ten years to do so, and Harvey, the next fastest, took just under seven years.

## 84. AUSTRALIA v ENGLAND, Second Test match, at Melbourne, 30, 31 December 1932, 2 and 3 January 1933

SCORES: Australia 228 (J.H. Fingleton 83) and 191 (D.G. Bradman 103*); England 169 (H. Sutcliffe 52, W.J. O'Reilly 5 for 63) and 139 (W.J. O'Reilly 5 for 66). Australia won by 111 runs.

| | | |
|---|---|---|
| D.G. BRADMAN | b. W.E. Bowes | 0 |
| | not out | 103 |

Bradman's first innings was perhaps the most spectacular failure of his career. With his previous failures against the MCC, and the other unhappy events of the season, weighing heavily upon him, he went in to bat at 2.57 p.m. on the first day, with the score at 67 for 2, and was bowled first ball; he attempted to hook a ball outside the off-stump which was not nearly short enough to hook, and a wild swing dragged the ball down on to his leg stump.

If that display was one of the worst of his career, his second innings was unquestionably one of his greatest. He went in at 12.54 p.m. on the third morning with the score 27 for 2, with the result of the match depending almost entirely upon him, and he succeeded to such an extent that he virtually won the match off his own bat. He bravely opened his score with a hook for 4 off Bowes, and then played with great care on a wicket which always helped the bowlers, against an all-fast attack consisting of H. Larwood, W. Voce, G.O. Allen, W.R. Hammond and W.E. Bowes; he was 25 at lunch, reached 50 in 93 minutes, and had raised his score to 77 by tea-time. Meanwhile, wickets were falling at the other end, and the last man, H. Ironmonger, came in when his score was 98; Ironmonger survived two balls before Bradman got the bowling again, and then Voce bowled so well that Bradman was unable to score off his first five balls. Off the last ball of the over, however, Bradman scored 3 to leg, completing his century in two minutes over three hours; and three minutes afterwards, at 5 p.m., Ironmonger was run out in trying to give his partner the bowling. Bradman's 103 not out, in a total of 182 from the bat (56 per cent), lasted three hours five minutes, and he hit seven fours off 146 balls, while giving no chance; his defence was magnificent, and his courage in standing up to the 'body-line' bowling was equally admirable.

This was his seventh century *v* England in Tests, one more than the six made by V.T. Trumper and W.M. Woodfull; H.W. Taylor also made seven centuries *v* England for South Africa. This was the fifth successive Test match in which he batted (four *v* South Africa and one *v* England) in which he made a century; his own achievement of four centuries in four consecutive Tests (1928–30) was the previous best, but in 1936–47 he made a century in eight consecutive Tests in which he batted.

## 85. AUSTRALIA *v* ENGLAND, Third Test match, at Adelaide, 13, 14, 16, 17, 18 and 19 January 1933

SCORES: England 341 (M. Leyland 83, R.E.S. Wyatt 78, E. Paynter 77, T.W. Wall 5 for 72) and 412 (W.R. Hammond 85, L.E.G. Ames 69, D.R. Jardine 56); Australia 222 (W.H. Ponsford 85) and 193 (W.M. Woodfull 73*, D.G. Bradman 66). Australia lost by 338 runs.

| D.G. BRADMAN | c. G.O. Allen b. H. Larwood | 8 |
| | c. and b. H. Verity | 66 |

This was certainly the most unpleasant Test match ever played, the 'body-line' attack rousing the crowd to furious barracking, and moving the Australian Board of Control to protest to the MCC. In at 1 for 1, on the second afternoon, Bradman failed again in his first innings, staying for 18 minutes and 17 balls before giving a simple catch to short square-leg in defending his head from a fast rising ball, at 18 for 2.

In the end, Australia were set to make 532 to win on a worn wicket, a hopeless proposition; Bradman came in at 12 for 2, on the fifth evening, and played a brilliant if rather hectic innings. Some of his strokes were amazing, as he sometimes retreated to square-leg to try to hit Larwood's and Voce's leg-theory to the unprotected off side, and also tried to take quick runs off the other bowlers while he could. He hit up 50 in 64 minutes and then, having hit ten fours, drove Verity over the on boundary for 6 (the first he ever hit in Australia, and his first in a Test match) before being caught and bowled next ball. He made 66 in 73 minutes (54 runs an hour), off 71 balls, out of 88 while he was in (75 per cent), the patient Woodfull, who carried his bat through the innings, being his partner.

Bradman also had the distinction of bowling Hammond for 85 with a full pitch just before the close of the fourth day; this was his only wicket in Test matches against England.

### 86. NEW SOUTH WALES *v* MCC TEAM, at Sydney, 26, 27 and 28 January 1933

SCORES: New South Wales 180 (R. Rowe 70, W.A. Brown 69) and 128 (D.G. Bradman 71, W.R. Hammond 6 for 43); MCC Team 199 (R.E.S. Wyatt 63, H.C. Chilvers 5 for 73) and 110 for 6 wickets. New South Wales lost by 4 wickets.

| | | |
|---|---|---|
| D.G. BRADMAN | b. T.B. Mitchell | 1 |
| | c. L.E.G. Ames b. W.R. Hammond | 71 |

On the first morning, Bradman went in at 58 for 1, and, two runs and three minutes later, was bowled by a top-spinner, playing a rather casual stroke.

In the second innings, going in at 11 for 1, he made 10 not out in 23 minutes by the end of the second day, and on the third, after overnight rain, played a very fine innings on a sticky wicket. Hammond, bowling off-breaks to a leg-trap, was able to make the ball spin and lift sharply, but Bradman was never in trouble against him or Verity; he completed 50 in 88 minutes, was 68 not out at lunch, and ten minutes afterwards failed for the first time to get over a lifting ball and gave a catch to short-leg. Eighth out at 122, he batted for two hours three minutes and hit six fours, showing firm defence and complete mastery of the difficult conditions; his 71 was 56 per cent of the runs scored from the bat.

### 87. NEW SOUTH WALES *v* SOUTH AUSTRALIA, at Sydney, 3, 4 and 6 February 1933

SCORES: New South Wales 113 (D.G. Bradman 56, T.W. Wall 10 for 36) and 356 (D.G. Bradman 97, W.A. Brown 79, S.J. McCabe 67); South Australia 114 (W. Howell 5 for 31) and 257 (H.C. Nitschke 105, W.J. O'Reilly 5 for 56). New South Wales won by 98 runs.

| | | |
|---|---|---|
| D.G. BRADMAN | c. A.J. Ryan b. T.W. Wall | 56 |
| | b. P.K. Lee | 97 |

The New South Wales first innings was an extraordinary affair, for, after Bradman and J.H. Fingleton (43) had carried the score without much trouble from 12 for 1 to 87, Wall caused a collapse, as soon as Fingleton was out, by taking the last nine wickets at a personal cost of 5 runs; the next highest was 4.

Bradman completed 50 in one and a half hours, but could get no one to stay with him, and in the end was ninth out at 106; he batted for an hour and 49 minutes, and hit five fours, being caught off a skier at square-leg when mis-hitting a hook. He made his 56 out of 106 from the bat (52 per cent) – the fourth time this season that he had contributed more than half his side's total. The wicket was perfect, and the only assistance Wall had was a stiff breeze to aid his swerve.

Bradman's second innings started just after lunch on the second day, in cold and showery weather, with the score at 95 for 1. He was lucky with a snick off Wall when only 5, this being not quite a chance, but thereafter he batted well. He reached 50 in one and a quarter hours, and was in for two hours 52 minutes altogether before being bowled at 268 for 5, when trying to pull-drive a straight ball; he hit eight fours, and his stand with Brown for the second wicket realised 122. The South Australian bowlers included Grimmett, as well as Wall and Lee.

## 88. AUSTRALIA v ENGLAND, Fourth Test match, at Brisbane, 10, 11, 13, 14, 15 and 16 February 1933

SCORES: Australia 340 (V.Y. Richardson 83, D.G. Bradman 76, W.M. Woodfull 67) and 175; England 356 (H. Sutcliffe 86, E. Paynter 83) and 162 for 4 wickets (M. Leyland 86). Australia lost by 6 wickets and England won the rubber and regained the Ashes.

| D.G. BRADMAN | b. H. Larwood | 76 |
| | c. T.B. Mitchell b. H. Larwood | 24 |

On the first day, Australia made their best start of the series and the score was 133 for 1 when Bradman went to the wicket at 3.25 p.m., in great heat which proved very trying for the fast bowlers. He made a subdued and uncertain start, being 14 at tea-time, but gradually settled down, despite some streaky strokes; he again used his unorthodox square-cut, on the retreat, against the 'body-line' bowling. He completed 50 in 88 minutes and was 71 not out overnight after two hours 16 minutes' batting; Larwood had not taken a wicket all day, and the score was 251 for 3. Bradman, when 48, completed his 1,000 runs for the season.

Next day, Bradman batted for only another 20 minutes and failed to drive home the advantage which Australia had won on the first day, being very uncomfortable against Larwood before that bowler hit his leg stump in his third over, as he again drew away and tried to cut. He was out at 264 for 4, and thereafter, despite the fierce heat, Larwood took on a fresh lease of life and swept aside the tail; Bradman was in for two hours 36 minutes and hit 11 fours, receiving 138 balls.

With the match still in the balance on the fourth evening, Bradman, going in at 46 for 1, continued the same daring tactics, and though he cut Larwood for 10 in an over, he had batted for only 32 minutes when, drawing away again, he lobbed an easy catch to square-cover at 79 for 2, off his 31st ball.

### 89. AUSTRALIA *v* ENGLAND, Fifth Test match, at Sydney, 23, 24, 25, 27 and 28 February 1933

SCORES: Australia 435 (L.S. Darling 85, S.J. McCabe 73, L.P. O'Brien 61, W.A. Oldfield 52) and 182 (D.G. Bradman 71, W.M. Woodfull 67, H. Verity 5 for 33); England 454 (W.R. Hammond 101, H. Larwood 98, H. Sutcliffe 56, R.E.S. Wyatt 51) and 168 for 2 wickets (W.R. Hammond 75*, R.E.S. Wyatt 61*). Australia lost by 8 wickets.

| | | |
|---|---|---|
| D.G. BRADMAN | b. H. Larwood | 48 |
| | b. H. Verity | 71 |

Bradman had to go in very early on the first morning, with the score 0 for 1, and again played a brilliant if rather reckless innings against the fast leg-theory; this time he was bowled, just before the lunch interval, in going over to the off to glance a well-pitched straight ball. He batted for 71 minutes and 56 balls, and the score was only 64 for 3 when he left, his share being 75 per cent. When his score was 28 he reached his 3,000 runs in all Test matches.

The score was again 0 for 1 when Bradman batted on the fourth morning, being 22 not out at lunch, and he was again in daring form, some of his cutting of the 'leg-theory' being most spectacular; but though he reached 50 in 76 minutes and appeared almost to have mastered Larwood, he was in the end deceived by Verity, who yorked him with his faster ball as he jumped in to drive. He and Woodfull added 115 for the second wicket in an hour and 37 minutes, and Bradman hit nine fours, scoring his 71 off 69 balls. After he was out, only Woodfull offered much further resistance, and England had the match well in hand. During his innings, Bradman was hit by Larwood, receiving a painful blow on the arm as he drew away to cut a rising ball; fortunately, it did not interfere with his innings, and this was the only occasion on which he was struck by 'body-line' bowling.

This was Bradman's first Test match *v* England at Sydney; and it was the eighth successive Test (in which he batted) in which he exceeded 50 in one innings or other; up till then, the best performance of that nature had been seven successive Tests by G.A. Faulkner, 1910–2, and by Australians, six, by W. Bardsley (1909–11), Bradman (1928–30) and W.H. Ponsford (1930–1); Bradman, between 1936 and 1947, later made at least 50 in 13 consecutive Tests in which he batted.

### SUMMARY, 1932–3

| | Matches | Innings | NO | HS | Runs | Average | Centuries |
|---|---|---|---|---|---|---|---|
| All First-class Matches | 11 | 21 | 2 | 238 | 1171 | 61.63 | 3 |
| Test Matches | 4 | 8 | 1 | 103* | 396 | 56.57 | 1 |

| | Matches | Innings | NO | HS | Runs | Average | Centuries |
|---|---|---|---|---|---|---|---|
| All Matches *v* MCC Team | 8 | 16 | 1 | 103* | 571 | 38.06 | 1 |
| Sheffield Shield Matches | 3 | 5 | 1 | 238 | 600 | 150.00 | 2 |
| All Matches for NSW | 5 | 9 | 1 | 238 | 713 | 89.12 | 2 |

England won the Test match series by four matches to one and regained the Ashes.

Though for the fifth successive Australian season he completed his 1,000 runs, the 'body-line' bowling certainly achieved its object of reducing his batting average nearer to normal proportions. Nevertheless, and despite ill health, he made more runs than any other Australian and headed the Australian first-class batting averages; E.H. Bromley, 52.40, had the next highest average, and V.Y. Richardson, 924 runs, the next highest aggregate, while L.S. Darling hit one more century than Bradman, H. Sutcliffe, for MCC, made 1,318 runs, average 73.22 and hit five centuries.

In the Test matches, Bradman headed the Australian averages and made the most runs for Australia, S.J. McCabe, 385 runs, including one century, average 42.77, being second; for England, against much less hostile bowling, E. Paynter, in three completed innings, averaged 61.33, and W.R. Hammond and Sutcliffe each scored 440 runs, average 55.00, Hammond's scores including two centuries.

In all matches against the tourists, McCabe averaged 43.66 for 524 runs, and J.H. Fingleton averaged 39.50 for 395 runs, Bradman's 38.06 being third to these two, although he scored the most runs in all matches against the MCC bowling. His average of 38.06 in all matches against the MCC represents about the nearest he ever got to being out of form, and was in marked contrast to his success in Sheffield Shield matches. Larwood took his wicket six times altogether this season, four times in Test matches, and while it would be untrue to say that he was Bradman's master, it would equally be untrue to say that Bradman, hard as he tried, and daringly as he counter-attacked, really mastered Larwood this season, as he had in 1928–9 and 1930. The tactics which Larwood used were, of course, such as to arouse widespread condemnation in Australia, as well as by many people in England, and 'body-line' bowling has now been banned by the Laws of Cricket. The object of these tactics, to win the rubber by reducing the scoring ability of Bradman and other leading Australian batsmen, was certainly attained, such fine players as W.M. Woodfull, W.H. Ponsford and A.F. Kippax having much less success against the MCC team than Bradman had; and, in view of the nature of the bowling to which he was opposed, it was not the least of Bradman's achievements to return an average in the Test matches of 56.67, and to make 50 in one innings or the other of all four Tests in which he played.

By contrast, his average in Sheffield Shield matches, 150.00, was the highest ever achieved for New South Wales, his own 148.83 in 1928–9 being the previous best; next season, he averaged 184.40 in Shield matches. New South Wales again won the Shield this season.

# 1933–4

## AGED TWENTY-FIVE

———◆◆×◆◆———

90. **NEW SOUTH WALES** *v* **QUEENSLAND**, at Brisbane, 3, 4, 6 and 7 November 1933

SCORES: Queensland 183 (E.C. Bensted 70, C.W. Andrews 59, W.J. O'Reilly 6 for 58) and 140 (W.J. O'Reilly 7 for 53); New South Wales 494 for 4 wickets dec. (D.G. Bradman 200, W.A. Brown 154, J.H. Fingleton 53). New South Wales won by an innings and 171 runs.

D.G. BRADMAN  c. C.W. Andrews b. R.M. Levy          200

Bradman started the season in dazzling form, doing what he pleased with some rather mediocre Queensland bowling. He went in on the second morning with the score 101 for 1 and took only 34 minutes to reach 50, and an hour and 32 minutes to complete his century. He gave a difficult chance at the wicket when 103, off the bowling of H.S. Gamble, but otherwise made no sort of mistake, and when he was caught on the long-on boundary just after reaching 200, he had batted for only three hours four minutes; indeed, he went from 150 to 200 in only 24 minutes, and on one occasion took 23 runs in an over off Wyeth's bowling – his best in Australia. He hit 26 fours and he and Brown added 294 for the second wicket in two hours 51 minutes, the score being 426 for 3 when Bradman was out. R.K. Oxenham was Queensland's only Test match bowler.

His partnership of 294 with Brown remains a second-wicket record for matches between New South Wales and Queensland (previous best, 243 by H. Donnan and V.T. Trumper, 1899–1900; in a Sheffield Shield match, 138 by N.E. Phillips and A.F. Kippax in 1926–7); it was also a record for any wicket for matches between New South Wales and Queensland (previous best, 280 for the third wicket by O.W. Bill and Kippax, 1930–1), until Bradman and Kippax added 363 for the third wicket later this season.

91. **V.Y. RICHARDSON'S XI** *v* **W.M. WOODFULL'S XI** (Test trial match,

D.D.J. Blackie and H. Ironmonger Testimonial), at Melbourne, 18, 20, 21 and 22 November 1933

SCORES: V.Y. Richardson's XI 491 for 8 wickets dec. (J.H. Fingleton 105, K.E. Rigg 94, L.P. O'Brien 90, B.A. Barnett 60, D.G. Bradman 55) and 169 for 4 wickets (D.G. Bradman 101); W.M. Woodfull's XI 350 (W.M. Woodfull 118, S.J. McCabe 82, H.I. Ebeling 5 for 72). Drawn.

D.G. BRADMAN   c. W.M. Woodfull b. T.W. Wall          55
               c. L.S. Darling b. D.D.J. Blackie     101

Bradman went in before lunch on the first day at 52 for 1; after the interval, he reached 50 in 55 minutes, and looked quite set and ready to make a big score when he mishit a hook and was caught at mid-wicket. Out at 131 for 2, he batted for 61 minutes and hit six fours.

On the last day, with a draw the only possible result, he played for a long time in a curiously restrained and sedate manner. He went in before lunch at 2 for 1, and took an hour and 49 minutes to reach 50; with two overs to go before the close of play (3.30 p.m.), he still required 25 to complete his century, but he at last hit out, and scored 10 off the first, and 16 (four boundaries) off the first five balls of the second, from Blackie, before being caught off the seventh on the long-on boundary in trying to hit a six. He batted for two hours 46 minutes, hit 12 fours, gave no chance, and, in company with O'Brien (42), added 118 for the third wicket. Woodfull's bowlers in this innings included Fleetwood-Smith in addition to Wall and Blackie.

## 92. NEW SOUTH WALES v REST OF AUSTRALIA, Test trial match (H.L. Collins, T.J.E. Andrews and C.E. Kelleway Testimonial), at Sydney, 24, 25, 27 and 28 November 1933

SCORES: New South Wales 273 (S.J. McCabe 110, R. Rowe 66, H.I. Ebeling 5 for 66) and 390 for 4 wickets dec. (A.F. Kippax 111*, D.G. Bradman 92, J.H. Fingleton 78, R. Rowe 66*); Rest of Australia 255 (W.H. Ponsford 70, P.K. Lee 69) and 409 for 8 wickets (W.M. Woodfull 129, L.S. Darling 77, H.C. Nitschke 76). New South Wales lost by 2 wickets.

D.G. BRADMAN   c. C.W. Walker b. H.C. Chilvers   22
               b. H.I. Ebeling                   92

Bradman's first innings was one of his least happy efforts, for he was in for 42 minutes on the first morning, after going in at 16 for 1, and was greatly troubled for much of that time by Chilvers' spin; that bowler richly deserved his wicket when Bradman was caught by the wicket-keeper in trying to cut a leg-break. He was second out at 51.

His second innings was a better display. He went in at 64 for 1 before lunch on the third day, hit up 50 in 80 minutes, and had batted for two hours 37 minutes when – unusually for him – he was dismissed in the nineties; he played on to a fast break-back which he tried to drive off his back foot, and only dragged on to his wicket. He hit 12 fours, mainly with hard drives, and was out at 224 for 3; he and Fingleton put on 102 for the second wicket.

### 93. NEW SOUTH WALES *v* SOUTH AUSTRALIA (E. Jones Testimonial), at Adelaide, 15, 16 and 18 December 1933

SCORES: New South Wales 108 and 271 (A.F. Kippax 90, D.G. Bradman 76, C.V. Grimmett 5 for 103); South Australia 316 (A.J. Ryan 94*, H.C. Nitschke 82, A.R. Lonergan 50) and 65 for no wicket. New South Wales lost by 10 wickets.

| | | |
|---|---|---|
| D.G. BRADMAN | b. F.H. Collins | 1 |
| | c. T.W. Wall b. C.V. Grimmett | 76 |

In his first innings, Bradman went in at 17 for 1 on the first morning and, his forward defensive stroke failing to find the ball, he was bowled, at 18 for 2, after a three-minute stay.

His second innings was also not one of his best, and for much of the time Grimmett, exploiting a worn spot on the leg stump, had him in great difficulties. Going in at 68 for 1, early on the third day, he gave two very hard chances in one over off Grimmett, when he was 31, to silly mid-off and mid-on, and later, when he was 60, Grimmett should have had him stumped. Having completed 50 in an hour and 12 minutes, he was caught at mid-on, trying to force a rather short ball, after batting for an hour and 44 minutes; the score was then 194 for 3, and he and Kippax added 118 for the third wicket. He hit six fours.

### 94. NEW SOUTH WALES *v* VICTORIA, at Melbourne, 22, 23, 26 and 27 December 1933

SCORES: Victoria 382 (L.S. Darling 91, L.P. O'Brien 86, W.M. Woodfull 60, W. Howell 5 for 97) and 200 (L.S. Darling 5, W.J. O'Reilly 9 for 50); New South Wales 355 (D.G. Bradman 187*, J.H. Fingleton 76, L.O'B. Fleetwood-Smith 7 for 138) and 144 for 1 wicket (D.G. Bradman 77*). Drawn.

| | | |
|---|---|---|
| D.G. BRADMAN | not out | 187 |
| | not out | 77 |

Bradman's batting dominated this match to an extraordinary degree. His first innings commenced just after tea on the second day, at 88 for 1, and a strained back at first compelled him to take things easily. However, he reached 50 in 71 minutes and was 68 not out overnight after 93 minutes' batting.

Next morning, he continued to play Victoria almost single-handed, and the extent to which he took control of the game is shown by the fact that, after the third wicket had fallen at 199, to the last ball of the second day's play, when he was 68, he scored 119 out of the last 156 for the last seven wickets, 79 out of the last 96 for the last four wickets, and 37 out of 39 for the last wicket; and altogether he made 187 out of 267, 70 per cent of the runs added while he was in, and 54 per cent of the total runs from the bat. He showed great skill in keeping the bowling; but despite all his efforts, his side was 27 runs behind on the first innings. His century had been completed in two minutes under three hours (the last eight runs took him a quarter of an hour), and altogether he batted for four hours 54 minutes, hitting 13 fours and never looking like getting out. He showed some respect for Fleetwood-Smith, but the other Victorian bowlers, including H.I. Ebeling, L.E. Nagel and H. Ironmonger, did not cause him any anxiety.

Bradman opened the second innings with Kippax on the fourth evening, when New South Wales had an hour and 43 minutes to make 228 to win; this task never looked likely of accomplishment, but Bradman, completing 50 in 70 minutes, again enjoyed some batting practice. His innings included five fours.

## 95. NEW SOUTH WALES *v* QUEENSLAND, at Sydney, 30 December 1933, 1, 2 and 3 January 1934

SCORES: Queensland 372 (F.C. Thompson 92, T. Allen 86, R.K. Oxenham 51) and 158 (H.C. Chilvers 6 for 62); New South Wales 614 for 6 wickets dec. (D.G. Bradman 253, A.F. Kippax 125, A.G. Chipperfield 84, W.A. Brown 50). New South Wales won by an innings and 84 runs.

D.G. BRADMAN  b. F.M. Brew                    253

With R.K. Oxenham the only Test match bowler in the Queensland side, Bradman was again in devastating form against that unfortunate State. He went in at 94 for 1, just before tea on the second day, and at 118 for 2 he was joined by Kippax in a long partnership. Bradman complete 50 in 56 minutes, 100 in 86 minutes, and was 122 not out, after an hour and 46 minutes, at the close of play; in the last 80 minutes, he and Kippax added 173.

Next morning, he added a further 131 runs before lunch in 98 minutes; he completed 200 in three hours five minutes, and then went from 200 to 250 in 16 minutes. Kippax was out at 481 for 3, the pair having added 363 runs for the third wicket in two hours 52 minutes, and Bradman threw away his wicket six runs later, just before lunch, having batted for three hours 24 minutes; he gave a very hard chance off R.M. Levy at cover when he was 214, but otherwise his display was chanceless despite the rate at which he scored. He hit four sixes (late in his innings – the first he had ever hit at Sydney) and 29 fours; when 189, he completed his 1,000 runs for the sixth successive season, this being his tenth innings, the same as he took in 1931–2 to reach this landmark, which remains the best for New South Wales. The date of 2 January is also still the earliest that a New South Wales batsman has reached 1,000 for the season, two days earlier than his own previous best in 1929–30; Bradman never improved upon this date though, later, for South Australia, he twice took only nine innings.

His partnership of 363 with Kippax was within 12 of the then world record for the third wicket. It was then the highest for the third wicket by any Australians anywhere (previous best, 362 by W. Bardsley and C.G. Macartney, in England, in 1912), though in 1934 W.H. Ponsford and S.J. McCabe passed this with 389; but 363 remains the highest third-wicket partnership in Australia, and a Sheffield Shield record for that wicket (previous best, 345 by Bardsley and J.M. Taylor, for New South Wales v South Australia, 1920–1; v Queensland, 280 by O.W. Bill and Kippax, for New South Wales, 1930–1, who had themselves passed Bradman's and Kippax's previous record third-wicket partnership for New South Wales v Queensland of 272 in 1929–30). It is also the highest partnership for any wicket against Queensland in a Sheffield Shield match (previous best, 314 for the second wicket, by Ponsford and H.L. Hendry, for Victoria, 1927–8; by New South Wales batsmen, 294 by Bradman and W.A. Brown for the second wicket, earlier this season; E.R. Mayne and Ponsford added 456 for the Victoria wicket v Queensland in 1923–4, before Queensland were admitted to the Shield competition).

Added to his scores of 187* and 77* in his previous match, this score of 253 raised the number of runs he had made in successive innings, before he was finally dismissed, to 517, the most in Australia, by an Australian, and for New South Wales; the previous best was 499 by Bradman (452* and 47) in 1929–30, while Ponsford, in England in 1934, came close to this record with 510 (229*, 281*, 0).

The total of 131 was the highest that until then anyone had ever scored before lunch in Australia, R.B. Minnet, for New South Wales v Victoria, in 1911–2, being the previous best with 123; Bradman, in 1935–6, scored 135 before lunch for South Australia v Tasmania, though his 131 in this innings remains a record for New South Wales and a record for the Sheffield Shield competition.

## 96. NEW SOUTH WALES v VICTORIA, at Sydney, 26, 27, 29 and 30 January 1934

SCORES: New South Wales 672 for 8 wickets dec. (W.A. Brown 205, J.H. Fingleton 145, D.G. Bradman 128); Victoria 407 (J.A. Scaife 120, E.H. Bromley 92, W.M. Woodfull 83) and 274 for 5 wickets (L.S. Darling 93, J.A. Scaife 80). Drawn.

D.G. BRADMAN c. L.S. Darling b. L.O'B. Fleetwood-Smith          128

New South Wales ran up a huge score against an attack which included E.L. McCormick, H.I. Ebeling, L.O'B. Fleetwood-Smith and H. Ironmonger, and Bradman, though not in the best of health, hit out with great vigour. When he went in just after lunch on the first day at 148 for no wicket (Fingleton having retired hurt), his partner, Brown, needed 34 to reach his century, and Bradman made it his business to let him get it before the new ball could be claimed at 200. Thus, of the first 50 added, Bradman's share was 13; after Brown had completed his century, Bradman's share of the second 50 added was 44. Despite this early self-effacement (his first 10 runs took 38 minutes), Bradman reached 50 in 57 minutes, completed 100 in 87 minutes, and batted altogether for only an hour an 36 minutes; he finished up by hitting Fleetwood-Smith for three sixes in an over before being caught in the deep, as well as being missed in the deep in the same over, when 122 – his only chance. He hit four sixes and 17 fours, and he and Brown added 192 for the first hour, which thus fell at 340; his own rate of scoring averaged 80 an hour, and, after his slow start, his last 118 runs were actually scored in 58 minutes.

In four successive innings for New South Wales, he thus scored 645 runs (187*, 77*, 253, 128), a record for that State, passing his own 637 in four consecutive innings in 1929–30–1.

## SUMMARY, 1933–4

| | Matches | Innings | NO | HS | Runs | Average | Centuries |
|---|---|---|---|---|---|---|---|
| All First-class Matches | 7 | 11 | 2 | 253 | 1192 | 132.44 | 5 |
| Sheffield Shield Matches | 5 | 7 | 2 | 253 | 922 | 184.40 | 4 |
| All Matches for NSW | 6 | 9 | 2 | 253 | 1036 | 148.00 | 4 |

C.L. Badcock, with an average of 89.22, and W.A. Brown, with 878 runs, were second to Bradman in the first-class averages and aggregates respectively; Badcock, A.F. Kippax and W.M. Woodfull each hit four centuries. This was the sixth successive Australian season in which Bradman had exceeded 1,000 runs, but at the end of it he was again showing signs of not being in the best of health, and he did not play for the Australian touring team in its matches v Tasmania and Western Australia.

This was Bradman's last season with New South Wales; at the end of it he went to live in Adelaide and qualified (by three months' residence) to play for South Australia in Sheffield Shield matches by the beginning of the next Australian season.

His career with New South Wales finished on a high note. His average in all matches of 132.44 for the season is still the highest by any New South Wales batsman (previous best, Bradman's 116.91 in 1931–2), his aggregate of 922 was then the largest for New South Wales in a season in Sheffield Shield matches (previous best, Bradman's 894 in 1929–30), for the second time he made four centuries in a season in Shield matches (previously he did this in 1928–9, and for New South Wales only A.F. Kippax had ever done so, once before), and for the second time he made two double centuries for New South Wales.

With the extension of the Sheffield Shield programme in 1947–8, when Western Australia were admitted to the competition, two of these records have since been beaten, N.C. O'Neill making 1,005 runs for New South Wales in Shield matches in 1957–8 (a season when the Australian Test team was touring South Africa), and A.R. Morris making five Shield centuries, including one *v* Western Australia, in 1948–9.

Morris also made two double centuries for New South Wales in 1951–2; Bradman had previously done this in 1930–1, and only M.A. Noble and W. Bardsley had done so, once each, before. Bardsley is the only other batsman to have scored two double centuries in Shield matches against the same State in the same season, for New South Wales *v* South Australia in 1920–1.

Bradman's average of 184.40 in Shield matches this season is the highest ever achieved by any batsman for any State; the previous highest were 152.25 by C. Hill, 1909–10, 152.12 by W.H. Ponsford, 1927–28 and, for New South Wales, 150.00 by Bradman in 1932–3.

His average of 148.00 is the highest on record for all matches for New South Wales, his own 140.87 in 1928–9 being the previous best.

He made at least 50 in one innings or the other of every match in which he played this season.

# 1934

## AGED TWENTY-FIVE

———◆◆❉◆◆———

Bradman was appointed vice-captain of the 18th Australian team to England, and thus had his first experience of captaincy in first-class cricket; W.M. Woodfull was again captain.

### 97. AUSTRALIANS *v* WORCESTERSHIRE, at Worcester, 2 and 3 May 1934

SCORES: Worcestershire 112 (C.V. Grimmett 5 for 53) and 95 (C.V. Grimmett 5 for 27); Australians 504 (D.G. Bradman 206, W.A. Oldfield 67). Australians won by an innings and 297 runs.

D.G. BRADMAN  b. R. Howorth                    206

As in 1930, Bradman started the tour with a double century at Worcester. He went in at 29 for 1, before tea on the first day, and in fact had a very uncomfortable time for 22 minutes before the interval; he was lucky to avoid playing on to P.F. Jackson when 1. After tea, however, he settled down and batted with great confidence, reaching 50 in 62 minutes, and 100 in a minute less than one and three-quarter hours; at 102, however, he might have been stumped off G.W. Brook. On 112 not out at the close, he had been in for 112 minutes, and his stand with Woodfull (48) for the second wicket was worth 114 before the latter was out.

He thus became the third Australian to make a century on the first day of an English first-class season, C.G. Macartney (1921) and Woodfull (1930) having preceded him; Bradman repeated the performance in 1938.

Next day, he carried on in brilliant form, completing 200 in three hours 28 minutes, and two minutes later, with the score 359 for 6, he deliberately gave his wicket away. He and E.H. Bromley (45) added 111 for the fifth wicket in 63 minutes, and he hit 27 fours in an innings which included only the one stumping chance. His cutting and hooking, especially of R.T.D. Perks' fast bowling, were as powerful as ever, and it was noticeable that he was more willing than in 1930 to hit the ball into the air.

Woodfull had started the 1926 tour with an innings of 201 and that of 1933 with 133; Bradman's feat of starting with 236 in 1930 and 206 in 1934 was an improvement on this, which he carried further by starting with 258 in 1938 and 107 in 1948. No one else, English or Australian, has ever made 200 and over in his first innings of two English seasons; Bradman did so again in 1938. This was Bradman's third century in successive innings, the third of the ten occasions he did this.

His last five innings thus realised 851 (187*, 77*, 253, 128, 206), the best such spell of his career.

## 98. AUSTRALIANS *v* LEICESTERSHIRE, at Leicester, 5, 7 and 8 May 1934

SCORES: Leicestershire 152 (W.J. O'Reilly 7 for 39) and 263 for 9 wickets (E.W. Dawson 91, W.E. Astil 50*); Australians 368 for 5 wickets dec. (S.J. McCabe 108*, A.F. Kippax 89, D.G. Bradman 65). Drawn.

D.G. BRADMAN (capt.)  b. G. Geary                     65

Going in at 25 for 1, 34 minutes from the end of the first day, Bradman had made 25 not out overnight; next morning he completed 50 in 63 minutes, and then was bowled by a fine ball from Geary, a fast out-swinger which knocked his off-stump out of the ground. He batted for one and a half hours and hit seven fours, being third out at 118.

This was Bradman's seventh successive innings of over 50, then an Australian record, beating the six consecutive fifties made by W.M. Woodfull in 1927–8; Bradman himself made eight fifties in succession in 1937–8 and 1938, and in 1947–8 and 1948 equalled E. Tyldesley's world record with ten in succession. This was also the 16th successive match in which he scored at least 50 in one innings or the other – the longest such spell on record (previous best, 13 by H. Sutcliffe in 1928; by an Australian, 12 by W. Bardsley in 1909–10–1; next best, 14  by Bradman in 1937–8 and 1938).

## 99. AUSTRALIANS *v* CAMBRIDGE UNIVERSITY, at Cambridge, 9, 10 and 11 May 1934

SCORES: Australians 481 for 5 wickets dec. (W.H. Ponsford 229*, W.A. Brown 105, L.S. Darling 98); Cambridge University 158 (C.V. Grimmett 9 for 74) and 160 (H.R. Cox 51*). Australians won by an innings and 163 runs.

D.G. BRADMAN  b. J.G.W. Davies                     0

Bradman's first 'duck' in England had little effect on the course of the game, unexpected as it was. Davies, a slow off-spinner, bowled a ball which appeared to drift across from the leg, but did not turn back as Bradman expected, and hit his off-stump. He had gone in at 42 for 1 the first morning and was out to the fourth ball he received, at 46 for 2; he was in for four minutes.

## 100. AUSTRALIANS *v* MCC, at Lord's, 12, 14, and 15 May 1934

SCORES: MCC 362 (E. Hendren 135, R.E.S. Wyatt 72, T.W. Wall 6 for 74) and 182 for 8 wickets (R.E.S. Wyatt 102\*); Australians 559 for 6 wickets dec. (W.H. Ponsford 281\*, S.J. McCabe 192). Drawn.

D.G. BRADMAN (capt.)  c. and b. F.R. Brown          5

The dismissal of Bradman, who went in at 55 for 1, to a very weak shot, just before lunch on the second day, after a six-minute stay, gave Ponsford and McCabe the opportunity to break the then world record for a third-wicket partnership with a stand of 389; they carried the score from 61 for 2 to 450, and also passed the Australian record of 363 set up by Bradman and A.F. Kippax in 1933–4.

## 101. AUSTRALIANS *v* OXFORD UNIVERSITY, at Oxford (Christ Church ground), 19 and 21 May 1934.

SCORES: Australians 319 (L.S. Darling 100, W.H. Ponsford 75, R.G. Tindall 5 for 94); Oxford University 70 (L.O'B. Fleetwood-Smith 5 for 30) and 216 (F.C. de Saram 128, C.V. Grimmett 7 for 109). Australians won by an innings and 33 runs.

D.G. BRADMAN (capt.)  lbw. b. J.H. Dyson          37

Bradman went in at 48 for 1, before lunch on the first day, and played a subdued innings in which he never appeared to be comfortable; after 51 minutes he was lbw. in trying to hook a ball which kept rather low, the score then being 114 for 2.

## 102. AUSTRALIANS *v* HAMPSHIRE, at Southampton, 23, 24 and 25 May 1934

SCORES: Hampshire 420 (W.G. Lowndes 140, C.P. Mead 139, Lord Tennyson 56) and 169 for 7 wickets dec. (J. Arnold 109\*); Australians 433 (A.G. Chipperfield 116\*, L.S. Darling 96, S.J. McCabe 79, A.E.G. Baring 5 for 121) and 10 for 1 wicket. Drawn.

D.G. BRADMAN  c. C.P. Mead b. A.E.G. Baring          0
          (did not bat)                              –

Baring, bowling very fast, had the wickets of W.M. Woodfull, W.A. Brown and Bradman with only 10 runs on the board, before McCabe and Darling rallied the Australians; Bradman went in at 1 for 1 on the second morning and was caught off his second ball in the slips, trying to cut an out-swinger, without addition to the total. He was in for three minutes.

## 103. AUSTRALIANS *v* MIDDLESEX, at Lord's, 26 and 28 May 1934

SCORES: Middlesex 258 (E. Hendren 115, R.W.V. Robins 65) and 114 (C.V. Grimmett 5 for 27); Australians 345 (D.G. Bradman 160, A.F. Kippax 56) and 29 for no wicket. Australians won by 10 wickets.

D.G. BRADMAN c. J. Hulme b. I.A.R. Peebles          160
(did not bat)                                         –

Having made only 42 runs in his last four innings, Bradman now hit his way back to his most brilliant form. Going in at 5.13 p.m. on the first day at 0 for 1, he twice sparred dangerously at C.I.J. Smith in his first over, but thereafter made no sort of mistake in a display of superb strokes. He reached 50 in 49 minutes, and at 6.30, off the last ball of the day, he scored a single to make his score 100 not out, including 19 fours, in a total of 135 for 2.

Next day, his third-wicket stand of 132 with L.S. Darling (37) was soon broken, but he himself stayed for another 47 minutes before being brilliantly caught by Hulme on the long-on boundary. In a stay of only two hours four minutes, he hit a six, a five and 27 fours (119 in boundaries, or 74 per cent), and gave no chance; he was out at 225 for 4, having scored 71 per cent of the runs added while he was in, and among the bowlers whom he treated so harshly were C.I.J. Smith, P.F. Judge, H.J. Enthoven, R.W.V. Robinson and I.A.R. Peebles.

## 104. AUSTRALIANS *v* SURREY, at the Oval, 30, 31 May, 1 June 1934

SCORES: Surrey 475 for 7 wickets dec. (A. Sandham 219, R.J. Gregory 116) and 162 for 2 wickets (R.J. Gregory 59*, F.R. Brown 54*); Australians 629 (S.J. McCabe 240, W.H. Ponsford 125, D.G. Bradman 77, E.H. Bromley 56, A.R. Gover 5 for 147). Drawn.

D.G. BRADMAN c. H.S. Squires b. A.R. Gover          77

This was a very high-scoring game, the result of which always appeared likely to be a draw. Bradman went in after tea on the second day, after Ponsford and McCabe had exhausted the bowling in an opening stand of 239, and scored runs much as he pleased; he reached 50 in 50 minutes, and batted altogether for 73 minutes before being caught, just before the end of the day, at square-leg off a mishit when hooking a bumper from Gover. He hit 11 fours and added 130 for the second wicket with McCabe, the score being 369 for 2 when he was out.

## 105. AUSTRALIA v ENGLAND, First Test match, at Nottingham, 8, 9, 11 and 12 June 1934

SCORES: Australia 374 (A.G. Chipperfield 99, S.J. McCabe 65, W.H. Ponsford 53, K. Farnes 5 for 102) and 273 for 8 wickets dec. (S.J. McCabe 88, W.A. Brown 73, K. Farnes 5 for 77); England 268 (E. Hendren 79, H. Sutcliffe 62, G. Geary 53, C.V. Grimmett 5 for 81) and 131 (W.J. O'Reilly 7 for 54). Australia won by 238 runs.

| | | |
|---|---|---|
| D.G. BRADMAN | c. W.R. Hammond b. G. Geary | 29 |
| | c. L.E.G. Ames b. K. Farnes | 25 |

Bradman contributed less than usual to a convincing Australian victory. In the first innings he went in six minutes before lunch on the first day, at 88 for 2, and hit 11 runs by lunch-time; after the interval, he continued to force the pace rather hectically, hitting six fours (off 31 balls) in 29 minutes altogether before being caught at slip, Ames at the wicket deflecting the ball to Hammond. Spectacular as his innings was, it was a surprise on the first day of a Test match. He was out at 125 for 3, having scored 78 per cent of the runs added while he was in – his highest in a Test match; while his rate of scoring (60 runs an hour) was his fastest in a Test match. His second innings was equally spectacular, and included some brilliant strokes as well as some rather eccentric ones; he went in at 32 for 2 on the third afternoon, at a time when Australia, 106 runs ahead on the first innings, needed runs quickly before declaring, and made 21 in 31 minutes before the tea interval. He batted rather more soberly for 16 minutes thereafter, before being caught at the wicket, playing a defensive stroke to a lifting ball on his off-stump, at 69 for 3. He was in for 39 balls.

## 106. AUSTRALIANS v NORTHAMPTONSHIRE, at Northampton, 13, 14 and 15 June 1934

SCORES: Australians 284 (A.G. Chipperfield 71, D.G. Bradman 65, W.H. Ponsford 56) and 234 (W.A. Brown 113, A.D.G. Matthews 5 for 87); Northamptonshire 187 (A.W. Snowden 105, L.O'B. Fleetwood-Smith 5 for 63) and 133 for 9 wickets (A.H. Bakewell 53, J.E. Timms 50, L.O'B. Fleetwood-Smith 5 for 29). Drawn.

| | | |
|---|---|---|
| D.G. BRADMAN (capt.) | c. A.H. Bakewell b. A.D.G. Matthews | 65 |
| | b. A.D.G. Matthews | 25 |

Owing to a strained thigh, Bradman batted sixth and had a runner. He went in after lunch on the first day, when the Australians had lost 4 wickets for 108, and he and Chipperfield pulled the game round with a sixth-wicket stand of 117. Bradman's injury prevented him from being at his best, but he reached 50 in an hour and 49 minutes, and batted altogether for two hours nine minutes before making a feeble stroke and being caught at short-leg. He hit a five and three fours, and had helped raise the score to the comparative safety of 263 for 8.

The Australians were again in trouble late on the second day, when Bradman went in at 91 for 5; he again needed a runner, and after 35 minutes was 16 not out at the close of play. He went out after a further 20 minutes next morning, attempting to drive an in-swinger, but he had helped Brown raise the score to the relative safety of 148 for 6.

## 107. AUSTRALIA v ENGLAND, Second Test match, at Lord's, 22, 23 and 25 June 1934

SCORES: England 440 (L.E.G. Ames 120, M. Leyland 109, C.F. Walters 82); Australia 284 (W.A. Brown 105, H. Verity 7 for 61) and 118 (H. Verity 8 for 43). Australia lost by an innings and 38 runs.

| | | |
|---|---|---|
| D.G. BRADMAN | c. and b. H. Verity | 36 |
| | c. L.E.G. Ames b. H. Verity | 13 |

For two days this match was played on a perfect wicket, but rain over the weekend made the conditions ideal for Verity; and he, bowling superbly, took full advantage of the helpful surface.

Bradman's first innings was played on the second evening and was another brilliant if rather slapdash affair. In at 68 for 1, he hit seven fours with superb strokes in 46 minutes, before giving a soft return catch off a defensive stroke to a ball which kicked slightly; he was out at 141 for 2, to his 37th ball.

After the weekend rain, Australia failed by 7 runs to avert having to follow on, and that failure virtually cost them the match. As it was, Verity was still making the ball spin and lift during the afternoon, when Bradman went in for his second innings at 43 for 2; and though he batted soundly enough for 28 minutes, he became restless at being chained down by Verity (who was bowling without a deep field), tried to drive him and only succeeded in giving a skied catch to the wicket-keeper. It was perhaps a good idea in theory to try to hit Verity off his length, but the execution of this particular stroke was crude in the extreme, and he fell right into the trap which Verity had cleverly laid for him; he was out to his 26th ball, at 4.15 p.m., with the score 57 for 3, and after that only Woodfull (43) offered much resistance.

## 108. AUSTRALIANS v SOMERSET, at Taunton, 27 and 28 June 1934

SCORES: Somerset 116 (F.S. Lee 59*, W.J. O'Reilly 9 for 38) and 116 (L.O'B. Fleetwood-Smith 6 for 56); Australians 309 (W.M. Woodfull 84, L.S. Darling 79, B.A. Barnett 51, A.W. Wellard 6 for 111). Australians won by an innings and 77 runs.

D.G. BRADMAN  c. W.T. Luckes b. J.C. White       17

Bradman went in at 38 for 1 on the first evening and, after starting steadily, was caught at the wicket in attempting to cut, with the score 62 for 2. He was in for 23 minutes.

## 109. AUSTRALIANS *v* SURREY, at the Oval, 30 June, 2 and 3 July 1934

SCORES: Surrey 175 and 184 (C.V. Grimmett 5 for 33); Australians 251 (W.H. Ponsford 85, A.F. Kippax 50) and 111 for 4 wickets (D.G. Bradman 61*). Australians won by 6 wickets.

D.G. BRADMAN (capt.)  c. E.W.J. Brooks b. E.R.T. Holmes    27
                      not out            61

Bradman went in at 95 for 2, and was out in the last over of the first day, at 136 for 3, being caught at the wicket, after batting well for 32 minutes.

On the third morning, when the Australians wanted 109 to win, he went in at 0 for 1, and at one time 3 wickets were down for 30 runs; however, Bradman batted soundly and prevented any chance of a surprise defeat. He made 50 in 69 minutes, and had been in 76 minutes when he made the winning hit; his innings included nine fours.

## 110. AUSTRALIA *v* ENGLAND, Third Test match, at Manchester, 6, 7, 9 and 10 July 1934

SCORES: England 627 for 9 wickets dec. (M. Leyland 153, E. Hendren 132, L.E.G. Ames 72, H. Sutcliffe 63, G.O. Allen 61, H. Verity 60*, C.F. Walters 52, W.J. O'Reilly 7 for 189) and 123 for no wicket dec. (H. Sutcliffe 69*, C.F. Walters 50*); Australia 491 (S.J. McCabe 137, W.M. Woodfull 73, W.A. Brown 72) and 66 for 1 wicket. Drawn.

D.G. BRADMAN  c. L.E.G. Ames b. W.R. Hammond      30
             (did not bat)          –

Played throughout in very hot weather and on a perfect wicket, this match resolved itself, after England's first innings, into a struggle by Australia to save the follow-on. This they accomplished, despite a throat infection which attacked Bradman and several others of the Australian team.

Bradman was really not well enough to bat, but he went in at 320 for 4 on the third afternoon; he survived until after tea, when he was 25, and batted altogether for 66 minutes and 51 balls, helping Woodfull to raise the score to 328 for 5. When 26, he gave Hammond a sharp return chance; he was caught soon afterwards at the wicket in trying to cut a rather wide ball.

## 111. AUSTRALIANS *v* DERBYSHIRE, at Chesterfield, 11, 12 and 13 July 1934

SCORES: Derbyshire 145 (H.I. Ebeling 5 for 28) and 139 (L.O'B. Fleetwood-Smith 5 for 38); Australians 255 (D.G. Bradman 71, T.B. Mitchell 7 for 105) and 32 for 1 wicket. Australians won by 9 wickets.

| | |
|---|---|
| D.G. BRADMAN  c. H. Elliott b. L.F. Townsend | 71 |
| not out | 6 |

Going in at 12 for 1, Bradman had 78 minutes' batting at the end of the first day and took his score to 49 not out. Completing his 50 off the first ball next morning, he stayed for another 22 minutes, and was then caught at the wicket for 71, the highest score of the match. He batted for an hour and 40 minutes, hit ten fours, and was out at 148 for 5; on a wicket which always took spin, however, Mitchell bowled well enough to cause him a good deal of difficulty and he was by no means at his best.

The Australians, wanting 30 to win, lost a wicket at 17 but, despite rain, soon hit these runs off before lunch on the third day; Bradman had only four minutes at the wicket.

## 112. AUSTRALIANS *v* YORKSHIRE, at Sheffield, 14, 16 and 17 July 1934

SCORES: Yorkshire 340 (A.B. Sellers 104) and 157 (A. Wood 59); Australians 348 (D.G. Bradman 140, W.M. Woodfull 54, W.E. Bowes 7 for 100) and 28 for 1 wicket. Drawn.

| | |
|---|---|
| D.G. BRADMAN  b. M. Leyland | 140 |
| (did not bat) | — |

It was now nearly two months since Bradman had scored a century, the spell of 13 innings without reaching three figures being the longest of his career; and he had not yet, after two and a half months and 20 innings, completed his 1,000 runs for the season though, as his season's average was 53.05 for 955 runs, his failure was only in relation to his own standards.

However, he remedied both these matters in a wonderful innings, against a Yorkshire attack consisting of W.E. Bowes, T.F. Smailes, C.G. Macaulay, C. Turner, H. Verity and M. Leyland. He went in at 2.28 p.m. on the second day, at 16 for 1, and started soundly, taking 74 minutes to reach 50; then he hit out in his most brilliant form and completed his century in a further 26 minutes. He added another 40 in 20 minutes, and then virtually threw his wicket away, going for another big hit, just before tea. He made 140, out of 205 for 2, in exactly two hours, his last 90 coming in 46 minutes; he and Woodfull added 189 for the second wicket, Bradman's share being 74 per cent, and his innings included two sixes and 22 fours, or 100 runs in boundaries (71 per cent). Despite the pace at which he scored and the power of his strokes, he gave no chance, and was never in any difficulty. His 140 is the highest score for the Australians on the Sheffield ground, 121 by Woodfull in 1930 being the previous best.

### 113. AUSTRALIA v ENGLAND, Fourth Test match, at Leeds, 20, 21, 23 and 24 July 1934

SCORES: England 200 and 229 for 6 wickets; Australia 584 (D.G. Bradman 304, W.H. Ponsford 181, W.E. Bowes 6 for 142). Drawn.

D.G. BRADMAN  b. W.E. Bowes                    304

At the start of the second day's play the game was, apparently, evenly poised, with Australia 39 for 3 wickets, all to Bowes, in reply to England's modest score of 200; Bowes still had two balls to bowl of his uncompleted over, they were just short of a length, and Bradman hit them both off the back foot, with a straight bat and perfectly safely, very hard past the bowler for 4 each.

That was the beginning of a day's play which saw Bradman return to his dominance of 1930, and in company with Ponsford gain an overwhelming supremacy over the England bowling; Bowes, W.R. Hammond, T.B. Mitchell, H. Verity and J.L. Hopwood could make no impression upon either of them until, at 5.51 p.m., Ponsford accidentally trod on his wicket when hitting a ball from Verity to the boundary.

Bradman, whose previous five innings in this series added up to only 133 runs, and who had played 11 successive innings in Tests v England without a century, continued cautiously after his forceful start and took 91 minutes to reach 50. When he was 29 he completed 2,000 runs in Tests against England. Just before lunch he gave a very hot chance to square-leg off Bowes, when he was 72 – his only mistake during the day; 76 not out at the interval, he completed his century at 2.58 p.m., in three hours eight minutes and then continued, as in 1930, with remorseless concentration to build up an even larger score.

He had reached 169 at teatime, and at 189 he took his aggregate in all Test matches to 3,413, which exceeded the previous best by any Australian, 3,412 by

C. Hill; Hill played 89 innings in Test matches while this was Bradman's 40th Test innings.

His 200, which he completed at 5.15 p.m., took five hours 41 minutes; and only after the stand had lasted five hours 41 minutes and had put on 388 for the fourth wicket was Ponsford dismissed. Bradman's share was 223 and Ponsford's 159; but Ponsford's innings was a very good one and he scarcely suffered by comparison with his partner.

In the last 35 minutes, Bradman and McCabe batted rather lightheartedly, the former hitting two sixes (his first in a Test match in England), and in that time they took the score from 427 to 494, Bradman at the close being 271 not out, made in six hours 20 minutes. This was the fourth time that he had made 200 runs or more in a Test match in a day's play.

He had a further 50 minutes' batting on the third morning and for the second time reached 300 in a Test match at Leeds; he was, however, rather lucky to do so, as he was missed in the gully off Bowes when 280, and in general did not display the power and certainty of Saturday. However, five minutes after completing his 300, a fine break-back from Bowes removed his leg stump; he had hit two sixes and 43 fours in an innings lasting seven hours ten minutes and 466 balls and, sixth out at 550, had seen 511 runs added to the total, and had scored 53 per cent of the final Australian total (apart from extras). He scored with equal skill all round the wicket, the outstanding features of his performance being the power of his forcing shots off the back foot and his re-acquired concentration; there was no sign of the almost reckless attitude which had characterised some of his earlier Test match innings this season.

Bradman is the only batsman to make two treble centuries in Test matches and only five other batsmen have scored even one; of these, only L. Hutton made his score in a Test match between England and Australia. He is also the only overseas batsman to make two treble centuries in England; apart from him, only C.G. Macartney, W.W. Armstrong and V.T. Trumper, for the Australians, and E.D. Weekes for the West Indians, have made such a score in England.

Bradman's partnership with Ponsford was the highest for any wicket in any Test match (previous best, 323 by J.B. Hobbs and W. Rhodes for the first wicket for England v Australia, in Australia, 1911–2; in England, 268 by Hobbs and H. Sutcliffe for the first wicket for England v South Africa, 1924; against England, 276 for the first wicket by C.S. Dempster and J.E. Mills, for New Zealand, in New Zealand, 1929–30; by Australia in any Test match, 274 by W.M. Woodfull and Bradman v South Africa, in Australia, 1931–2; against England in England, by Australia in England, and by Australia v England anywhere, 243 by Bradman and A.A. Jackson for the fourth wicket, 1930, which equalled the 243 for the eighth wicket by C. Hill and R.J. Hartigan in Australia, 1907–8); these records lasted less than a month, until Ponsford and Bradman put on 451 for the second wicket in the fifth Test match.

The total of 388 was then the fourth-wicket partnership record for any Test match anywhere (previous best, 249 by A. Sandham and L.E.G. Ames v the West

Indies, 1929–30; in England, 243 by Bradman and Jackson, 1930); but P.B.H. May and M.C. Cowdrey passed this in 1957 with a fourth-wicket stand of 411 *v* West Indies. Bradman's and Ponsford's 388 is still the highest for the fourth wicket in Australia in any Test match, against England in any Test match, and for either side in an England *v* Australia Test match (previous best, Bradman's and Jackson 243 in 1930). It also remains a record for the fourth wicket for an Australian or any other touring team in England, the previous best being 291 *v* Notts, 1921, by C.G. Macartney and C.E. Pellew; next best, 377 by K.R. Miller and J.H. de Courcy, 1953.

In helping to increase Australia's score by 511, Bradman broke his own record for England *v* Australia Test matches of 506, set up in 1930; in the next Test match, Ponsford was not dismissed till the score was 574, and in 1938, Hutton batted until 770 runs were on the board.

With two sixes and 43 fours, Bradman scored 184 runs in boundaries, equal to the record set up in his 334 in 1930, for an Australian and for an England *v* Australia Test match.

Later that day Bradman injured his leg while fielding and had to retire, being unable to play any more cricket for nearly a month. A thunderstorm on the last morning saved England when the position was all but hopeless.

114. **AUSTRALIA *v* ENGLAND**, Fifth Test match, at the Oval, 18, 20, 21 and 22 August 1934

SCORES: Australia 701 (W.H. Ponsford 266, D.G. Bradman 244) and 327 (D.G. Bradman 77, S.J. McCabe 70, W.E. Bowes 5 for 55, E.W. Clark 5 for 98); England 321 (M. Leyland 110, C.F. Walters 64) and 145 (C.V. Grimmett 5 for 64). Australia won by 562 runs and won the rubber and the Ashes.

| | | |
|---|---|---|
| D.G. BRADMAN c. L.E.G. Ames b. W.E. Bowes | | 244 |
| b. W.E. Bowes | | 77 |

Bradman's first first-class game for nearly a month found him in the same superb form as at Leeds, and he played another great innings, again in partnership with Ponsford; this time the pair added 451 runs for the second wicket.

Bradman came in at 21 for 1 at 12 noon on the first day, and began quietly, being only 43 at lunch. Afterwards, having reached 50 in 96 minutes, he began to score more rapidly, and his century came up in two hours 50 minutes at 3.37 p.m. At tea he was 150 and in the evening, as the bowlers became tired, he increased the pressure; his 200 (at 5.50) took four hours 43 minutes, and thereafter he scored much as he pleased until, finally, he was out at 6.23 p.m., after five hours 16 minutes at the wicket, when, with the score 472, he tried to hook a very high bumper and only snicked it to the wicket-keeper. The England bowlers included W.E. Bowes, G.O. Allen, E.W. Clark, W.R. Hammond and H. Verity, but none of them could induce him to make a false stroke, let alone give a chance – a matter in which his innings was markedly superior to Ponsford's. In two successive Test matches he and Ponsford had added 839 runs in ten hours 57 minutes, and Bradman's innings – one of the finest which he ever played – included a six and 32 fours; he made his runs off 272 balls and blended sound defence and concentration with a brilliant exhibition of stroke-play all round the wicket.

Ponsford also batted well and contributed 194 to the partnership of 451, being 204* when Bradman was out; next day he carried this to 266, the highest Test match score by any Australian other than Bradman, who exceeded it four times.

This partnership of 451 was at that time the world record for the second wicket, the previous best being 398 by W. Gunn and A. Shrewsbury in 1890; the previous best for the second wicket by Australians was 358 by B.J. Kortlang and C. McKenzie in Australia, 1909–10, and by Australia or any other touring team in England, 303 by C.S. Dempster and C.F.W. Allcott, for the New Zealanders *v* Warwickshire, 1927, and 281 by W.M. Woodfull and W.A. Brown, for the Australians *v* Lancashire, 1934. The world record was broken in 1948–9, when B.B. Nimbalkar and K.V.R. Bhandarkar put on 455 for the second wicket in India; but Ponsford and Bradman's 451 remains a second-wicket record in England, by Australians anywhere, and on behalf of any touring team. It also remains a record for any wicket for Australian or other touring teams in England (previous best, 428 for the sixth wicket, by W.W. Armstrong and M.A. Noble, Australians *v* Sussex, 1902), and was within 5 of the record for any wicket by Australians anywhere.

It is still a record for any wicket for any Test match, beating all the records for any wicket which Ponsford and Bradman had broken when adding 388 for the fourth wicket at Leeds a month before. The second-wicket records for Test matches until then were: for all Test matches 274 by Woodfull and Bradman, for Australia *v* South Africa, 1931–2; in England, against England anywhere, and in all Test matches between England and Australia, 235 by Woodfull and C.G. Macartney, 1926. In 1957–8, for the West Indies *v* Pakistan, C. Hunte and G. Sobers came very close to breaking this record, adding 446 for the second wicket.

This was the second time in first-class cricket that Bradman had made two double centuries in successive innings, and the first and only time that he did so in Test matches; Bradman altogether did this on four occasions in all first-class matches, three times in Australia and once in England. Ponsford is the only other Australian ever to do this, and he did so twice, once in Australia and once in England. W.R. Hammond achieved this feat twice in Test matches, once *v* England and once *v* New Zealand; he and Bradman are the only batsmen to do it in Test matches. Bradman, with his innings, also equalled Hammond's feat in twice making 200 or over in consecutive Test matches. His total of 548 (304, 244) in two successive innings is a Test record for Australia, the previous best being his own 466 in 1931–2, and *v* England, his own 385 in 1930; it is also a record for any batsman in all first-class matches in England (previous best, 538 by Macartney in 1921).

This was also Bradman's third century in successive innings, the fourth time he had done this, and the first time in England. His total of 688 in three successive first-class innings (140, 304, 244) is also a record for an overseas batsman in England (previous best, 653 by Macartney, 1921).

For the fifth time he made 200 or over in a day's play in a Test match; until then the only other Australians to achieve this feat once were V.T. Trumper, H.L. Collins and Ponsford (in this Test match); it has now been done nine times in England, three times by Bradman and twice by Hammond; Ponsford and McCabe are the only other Australians to do so. In England *v* Australia Tests, it has been done only by Bradman (three times), Ponsford, McCabe, Hammond and R.E. Foster.

Although 380 ahead on the first innings, Australia did not enforce the follow-on, but batted again after tea on the third day. Bradman went in at 13 for 1, and again scored easily against bowling which had lost most of its earlier vigour; he had been in for only 23 minutes when, with his score 9, he hooked a short ball from Clark for a huge six. Completing 50 in 78 minutes, he was 76 not out at the close of play, after an hour and 52 minutes' batting.

However, no new records fell to him next morning for, after he had added 1 run off Verity, he attempted to hook Bowes' second ball, it did not rise as much as he expected and he was bowled. He made 77, including a six and six fours, off 100 balls, in an hour and 56 minutes, and added 150 for the third wicket with McCabe in an hour and 34 minutes, the score being 192 for 3 when he was out. The one run he scored on the last morning was, as a matter of fact, the last he ever scored in a Test match at the Oval; in 1938 he was absent injured and did not bat in the Oval Test match, and in 1948 he failed to score in his only innings.

After scoring 133 in five innings in the first three Test matches, he had made a wonderful return to form and consistency with a total of 625 in his last three Test innings (304, 244, 77), which is an Australian record, his own 589 in 1930 being the previous best. His 765 in his last four first-class innings (140, 304, 244, 77) is the most he ever made in four innings and is a record for any overseas batsman in England (previous best, 758 by C.G. Macartney, 1921).

## 115. AUSTRALIANS *v* SUSSEX, at Hove, 25, 27 and 28 August 1934

SCORES: Sussex 304 for 8 wickets dec. (J.H. Parks 60, T. Cook 60, James Langridge 57, L.O'B. Fleetwood-Smith 5 for 114) and 221 (E.H. Bowley 63, John Langridge 53, L.O'B. Fleetwood-Smith 5 for 87); Australians 560 (F. Kippax 250, L.S. Darling 117, A.W.A. Brown 66). Australians won by an innings and 35 runs.

D.G. BRADMAN (capt.)  b. G. Pearce  19

Bradman, suffering from an injured thumb, put himself in seventh and by the time he batted after tea on the second day (his 26th birthday) the score was already

436 for 5, Kippax and Darling having just added 215 for the fifth wicket. Kippax continued to be the dominant partner, and when Bradman played on in trying to cut, after an innings of 41 minutes, the score had been taken to 519 for 7. Of the 83 runs added while he was in, Bradman scored only 19, or 22 per cent – the lowest proportion of his career; he started with 15 singles before hitting a four.

116. **AUSTRALIANS** *v* **KENT**, at Canterbury, 29 and 21 August 1934

SCORES: Kent 21 for 2 wickets dec. and 74 for 7 wickets; Australians 197 for 1 wicket dec. (S.J. McCabe 108, W.H. Ponsford 82*). Drawn.

D.G. BRADMAN (capt.)  (did not bat)                    –

This match was ruined by rain after Bradman had won the toss and put Kent in to bat.

117. **AUSTRALIANS** *v* **AN ENGLAND XI**, at Folkestone, 3 and 4 September 1934

SCORES: An England XI 279 (F.E. Woolley 66, W.R. Hammond 54, L.O'B. Fleetwood-Smith 5 for 137); Australians 365 for 4 wickets (D.G. Bradman 149*, W.A. Brown 73, W.M. Woodfull 62*). Drawn.

D.G. BRADMAN  not out                    149

Bradman went in after lunch on the second (and last) day, at 131 for 3 and, after surviving a chance at the wicket off Woolley when 1, batted in his most attractive style. He completed 50 in 48 minutes, 100 in 87 minutes, and then proceeded from 104 to 134 by hitting Freeman for 30 in an over (4, 6, 6, 4, 6, 4). His innings lasted only an hour and 44 minutes (an average of 85 an hour), included four sixes and 17 fours, and was otherwise chanceless, while his unfinished partnership for the fifth wicket with Woodfull realised 180 in 77 minutes, off the bowling of Jehangir Khan, M.J.C. Allom, Hammond, Woolley and Freeman.

Thirty runs is still the most ever scored by an Australian off one over, the previous best being 26 by C. Hill in New Zealand in 1904–5 and by A. Cotter in Australia in 1905–6, and in England, 24 by C.E. Pellew *v* Notts, 1921; J.H. de Courcy scored 28 in an over for the Australians *v* Essex in 1953, and, for the South Africans in England, H.B. Cameron (1935) and P.L. Winslow (1955) both hit 30 off one over. Thirty was also at that time the most ever scored by any batsman off a six-ball over, the previous best being 28 by G.L. Jessop, twice, in 1904 and 1910; though E. Alletson, in 1911, scored 34 off an over which included two no-balls. Bradman's record of 30 off a six-ball over lasted less than a year, with Cameron equalling it and then C. Smart hitting 32 runs, which is the present record.

Bradman's 149* is the highest score by an Australian on the Folkestone ground (previous best, 81 by H.L. Hendry, 1926).

This was the 50th century of his career, in his 175th innings; the previous best, W.G. Grace, took 282 innings to reach this landmark (a wonderful performance on the wickets of those days), while A.L. Hassett, the next best, took 264 innings. Despite the limited amount of first-class cricket he had played, he was (and still is), at 26 years eight days, the youngest batsman in the history of the game to reach his 50th century; W.R. Hammond, the previous youngest, was 26 years 344 days when he reached his 50th in 1930; W.G. Grace had been 27 years 30 days when he did so in 1875; and the next best, P.B.H. May, was 26 years 195 days when he made his 50th century in 1956. W. Bardsley, the only other Australian then to have made so many hundreds, was 42 when he did so, while R.N. Harvey, the next best Australian, was 29 when he scored his 50th century.

Bradman, moreover, completed 50 centuries in the shortest time from the start of a first-class career; he took only six years 262 days from the date of his début; whereas the previous best, H. Sutcliffe, took eight years 214 days, and P.B.H. May, the next best, took eight years 26 days; Harvey, the next best Australian, took over 11 years from his first appearance in first-class cricket.

## 118. AUSTRALIANS *v* Mr H.D.G. LEVESON-GOWER'S XI, at Scarborough, 8, 10 and 11 September 1934

SCORES: Australians 489 (D.G. Bradman 132, S.J. McCabe 124, W.H. Ponsford 92, A.G. Chipperfield 53, K. Farnes 5 for 132); Mr Leveson-Gower's XI 223 (M.S. Nichols 75) and 218 (L.O'B. Fleetwood-Smith 6 for 90). Australians won by an innings and 48 runs.

D.G. BRADMAN s. G. Duckworth b. H. Verity                                    132

Against an attack consisting of M.S. Nichols, K. Farnes, W.E. Bowes, L.F. Townsend and H. Verity, Bradman played another brilliant innings. He went in early on the first day at 14 for 1, made 50 in 40 minutes, and reached 100 before lunch in 82 minutes. He then added 32 in eight minutes, going from 96 to 127 in five minutes and two overs, including 19 in an over off Verity. He altogether batted for only one and a half hours, hitting a six and 24 fours (102 in boundaries, or 77 per cent – the highest proportion he ever achieved); he gave one chance, in the gully off Farnes when 15, and, when 112, he became the first Australian to complete 2,000 runs for the season. He and Ponsford added 182 for the second wicket before Bradman was out at 196 for 2, Bradman's share being 72 per cent; his average rate of scoring was 88 an hour.

No Australian or other touring batsman has ever scored as many as 132 before lunch on the first day of a match in England, C.G. Macartney's 112* *v* England,

1926, being the previous best by an Australian, and C.A. Roach's 122* for the West Indians *v* Surrey, 1933, being the best for any touring team. This was the second time Bradman had scored a century before lunch in England on the first day of a match; a feat performed twice only by V.T. Trumper among other touring players. In the last seven innings of the season (one not out) he scored 1,065 runs.

## SUMMARY, 1934

|  | Matches | Innings | NO | HS | Runs | Average | Centuries |
|---|---|---|---|---|---|---|---|
| All First-class Matches | 22 | 27 | 3 | 304 | 2020 | 84.16 | 7 |
| Test Matches | 5 | 8 | 0 | 304 | 758 | 94.75 | 2 |

Australia won the Test match series by two matches to one, with two drawn, and regained the Ashes.

In all first-class matches for the Australians, S.J. McCabe (in 37 innings) made most centuries (eight) and most runs (2,078), Bradman being second in each case; but Bradman headed the Australian averages, W.H. Ponsford being second with 77.56 (which is the highest on record for a tour of England by any Australian batsman other than Bradman, who surpassed it on all his four tours, his 84.16 this season being his lowest; for the West Indians, E.D. Weekes averaged 76.65 in 1950, the best by any other touring batsman in England). Nineteen English batsmen completed 2,000 runs, the highest aggregate being 2,654 by H.H. Gibbons; the Nawab of Pataudi averaged 78.75 (for 12 completed innings) and W.R. Hammond's average was 76.32. F.E. Woolley (ten) hit the most centuries.

Bradman's Test match aggregate of 758 was much the largest on either side, Ponsford being next with 569; Ponsford (who did not play at Lord's) had an average of 94.83, which was a fraction higher than Bradman's. He also scored two centuries, while M. Leyland made three for England. Bradman's aggregate is the second highest for any Test rubber in England, his own 974 in 1930 being the record.

Bradman's experience of captaincy was confined to six matches, in none of which, incidentally, did he make a hundred; his highest score was 65 (twice) and his average for these six matches was 49.83 for 299 runs.

\*\*\*

Shortly after the end of the tour, Bradman was taken desperately ill, and had to undergo an emergency operation for appendicitis. His recovery was slow and he did not return to Australia until January 1935; and, of course, owing to his illness he played no cricket during the 1934–5 Australian season.

L.S. Darling, with three centuries and an average of 70.44, was the leading batsman of 1934–5, and J.H. Fingleton (656) scored most runs.

# 1935–6

## AGED TWENTY-SEVEN

———◆◆◆◆◆———

Owing to his illness, Bradman was not available for the Australian tour of South Africa this season, the Australian team being captained by V.Y. Richardson. Bradman, now qualified for South Australia, was appointed captain of that State in place of Richardson and, with the other leading Australian cricketers in either South Africa or India, he had a comparatively easy season. An MCC team, under E.R.T. Holmes, played six matches in Australia before going on to tour New Zealand.

119. **SOUTH AUSTRALIA** *v* **MCC TEAM**, at Adelaide, 8, 9, 11 and 12 November 1935

SCORES: MCC Team 371 (J. Hardstaff 90, J.H. Human 87, J.H. Parks 67, D. Smith 52, M.G. Waite 5 for 42) and 174; South Australia 322 (C.M. Walker 65*, M.G. Waite 58) and 187 (D.G. Bradman 50). South Australia lost by 36 runs.

| | | |
|---|---|---|
| D.G. BRADMAN (capt.) | lbw. b. J.M. Sims | 15 |
| | lbw. b. J.H. Parks | 50 |

In his first match for South Australia, Bradman batted like a man who had had no first-class practice for over a year. In the first innings, going in after lunch on the second day at 64 for 1, he was obviously quite out of touch, but was gradually beginning to time the ball properly once more when he was lbw. to a top-spinner at 90 for 2; he batted for 23 minutes.

South Australia were set to make 224 to win on the last day, with three hours 40 minutes for the task. Bradman went in at 29 for 1, after lunch, and, after being completely beaten by his first ball from Sims, made a painstaking effort to get these runs and to recover his form and confidence. At tea-time, South Australia still wanted 120, in one and three-quarter hours, with six wickets in hand, including that of Bradman, 35 not out; he completed his 50 after an hour and 44 minutes, but was lbw. next over. His 50, in one and three-quarter hours, was the top score, but he failed to reach the boundary, and his score included as many as 32 singles; this was the only innings of 50 or more he ever played in which he did not score at least one boundary.

After his dismissal at 136 for 5, South Australia never looked likely to win, and MCC had 20 minutes to spare at the end.

## 120. SOUTH AUSTRALIA *v* NEW SOUTH WALES, at Adelaide, 18, 19, 20 and 21 December 1935

SCORES: South Australia 575 (C.L. Badcock 150, D.G. Bradman 117, E.J.R. Moyle 98, R. Parker 74); New South Wales 351 (R.H. Robinson 102, R. Little 76, L. Fallowfield 54, F.A. Ward 6 for 127) and 219. South Australia won by an innings and 5 runs.

D.G. BRADMAN (capt.)  c. and b. R.H. Robinson      117

On his first appearance in a Sheffield Shield match, Bradman had made a century for New South Wales *v* South Australia, and now, on his first appearance in a Shield match for South Australia he made another – the only player to do so for two States. He went in after lunch on the first day, at 139 for 1, by which time the edge had been taken off the weak New South Wales bowling and, although rather sedate, he showed that he was now much nearer his normal form and fitness. He completed 50 in an hour and seven minutes, and 100 in two hours 11 minutes, soon afterwards losing Badcock, with whom he had added 202 for the second wicket in two and a half hours. He himself did not last much longer, being out at 349 for 3 after a chanceless innings of two hours 38 minutes which included seven fours. His late-cutting was perhaps the best feature of an innings in which he was content to take runs as they came rather than dominate the bowlers. This was his first century for a side of which he was captain.

His partnership of 202 with Badcock for the second wicket is the highest for South Australia *v* New South Wales in a Sheffield Shield match, the previous best being 175 by D.E. Pritchard and B.W. Hone, in 1929–30; though in 1891–2, before the Sheffield Shield was presented, J.J. Lyons and G. Giffen added 234 for the second wicket *v* New South Wales.

## 121. SOUTH AUSTRALIA *v* QUEENSLAND, at Adelaide, 24, 26, 27 and 28 December 1935

SCORES: South Australia 642 for 8 wickets dec. (D.G. Bradman 233, M.G. Waite 99, C.L. Badcock 91, A.J. Ryan 72, C.W. Walker 71); Queensland 127 (T. Allen 54) and 289 (D. Tallon 88, D. Hansen 80). South Australia won by an innings and 226 runs.

D.G. BRADMAN (capt.)  c. D.T. Tallon b. R.M. Levy        233

Bradman returned to his most brilliant form in making his third successive double century against Queensland, off whose weak bowling he scored almost at will with magnificent strokes; only E. Gilbert, the aboriginal fast bowler, was of sufficient class to cause him much concern. He went in at 32 for 1, before lunch on the first day, and reached 50 in 65 minutes; he ran to his century in one and three-quarter hours and, going from 150 to 200 in 14 minutes, completed 200 in two hours 48 minutes. Being 200 at tea-time, he was finally caught at the wicket after batting for three hours 11 minutes; he hit a six and 28 fours, and was out at 374 for 3, after stands of 183 for the second wicket with Badcock, and 159 (Bradman's share being 125) for the third wicket with Walker. He gave two chances, late in his innings; in the deep when 191 and a stumping chance when 219, both off Levy.

This was the highest score ever made in matches between South Australia and Queensland, passing the 232 made by A.J. Richardson in 1926–7; Bradman himself increased the record to 246 in 1937–8.

In making double centuries in three successive innings off the bowling of one State, Bradman achieved something which no one else has ever done; the next best such feat was by W.H. Ponsford who, in 1926–7 and 1927–8, scored 352 and 202 in successive innings *v* New South Wales, while in 1946–7 and 1947–8 A.L. Hassett made 200 and 204 *v* Queensland.

This was Bradman's eighth double century in Sheffield Shield cricket, one more than the previous best, seven by Ponsford; Bradman made 13 such scores altogether in Shield matches.

His time for reaching 200 in this match, two hours 48 minutes, is the fastest on record for any Sheffield Shield match, Bradman's two hours 52 minutes in 1932–3 (for New South Wales *v* Victoria) being the previous fastest; for South Australia, the previous fastest was three hours 20 minutes by C.E. Pellew *v* Victoria in 1919–20. Two hours 48 minutes was also the fastest in any match for South Australia (previous best, two hours 52 minutes by A.J. Richardson *v* MCC, 1922-3), until Bradman (209* *v* Western Australia, 1939–40) reached 200 in two hours 35 minutes.


## 122. SOUTH AUSTRALIA *v* VICTORIA, at Melbourne, 1, 2, 3 and 4 January 1936

SCORES: South Australia 569 (D.G. Bradman 357, R. Parker 63, C. Welch 5 for 155); Victoria 313 (R.G. Gregory 80, S. Quin 52, I.S. Lee 50) and 250 for 5 wickets (K.E. Rigg 124). Drawn.

D.G. BRADMAN (capt.)   c. S. Quin b. E.H. Bromley                    357

The Victorian attack was very weak and H.I. Ebeling, their one bowler of class, was able to bowl only four overs; there was, therefore, little to prevent Bradman from making another huge score, though he was in relatively sedate form. He went to the wicket early on the first day, at 8 for 1, and when 17 completed 5,000 runs in Sheffield Shield matches; this was his 55th innings in Shield matches, W.H. Ponsford, the previous quickest to this landmark, having taken 62 innings to complete 5,000 runs.

His 50 was completed before lunch in 70 minutes, and his century took only two hours 32 minutes. Going rather faster thereafter, he reached 200 in four hours 27 minutes, and at the close of play was 229 not out, after batting for five hours ten minutes; he had put on 178 for the second wicket with Parker. Next morning he batted very brilliantly; after reaching 300 in two minutes under six and a half hours, he hit out ferociously and completed his century before lunch in 97 minutes, being 338 at lunchtime; then, after batting for a minute over seven hours, he threw his wicket away, being caught near square-leg by the wicket-keeper off a skier. The last 57 had taken him 33 minutes, while on the second day he added 128 in an hour and 51 minutes; the score was 510 for 8 when he was out. His runs were 71 per cent of the 502 added while he was in, and 63 per cent of the eventual South Australian total (the greatest proportion he ever achieved). His innings was chanceless and included 40 fours. It passed his own 340* in 1928–9 as the highest score ever made against Victoria, while the previous highest for South Australia *v* Victoria was 271 by G. Giffen in 1891–2, and in a Sheffield Shield match, 271 by C.E. Pellew in 1919–20; the next best, 325 by C.L. Badcock, later this season, is the only other score of 300 or over *v* Victoria in a Sheffield Shield match. It also passed Ponsford's 336 in 1927–8 as the highest score for either side in matches between Victoria and South Australia, and he came within 8 of C. Hill's record score for South Australia of 365* *v* New South Wales in 1900–1. More important, it showed that he had recovered his old stamina and concentration.

This was the fifth treble century of his career, one more than the previous world record, four by Ponsford; W.R. Hammond also made four, the last in 1939, but no other Australian has made more than one such score. Bradman added a sixth treble century later this season.

It was also the 54th century of his career, one more than the total scored by W. Bardsley, the most by any Australian until then; Bardsley played 374 innings, while this was Bradman's 181st innings in first-class cricket. It was also his 37th century in Australia, in his 118th innings in that country; A.F. Kippax, the previous best, had scored 36 centuries in Australia in 177 innings.

His time for reaching 300 in this match (six hours 28 minutes) is the fastest for South Australia in a Sheffield Shield match, Hill, till then the only other scorer of over 300, having taken seven and a half hours to reach this figure; in a non-Shield match *v* Tasmania later this season, Bradman improved considerably on this time.

The 40 fours and 160 runs he scored in boundaries in this innings were records for South Australia, the previous best being 153 (an eight, a five and 35 fours) by

Hill in his 365*, while Pellew in his 271 hit 37 fours. In his 369 *v* Tasmania later this season (a non-Shield match), Bradman scored 208 in boundaries (four sixes and 46 fours), while in 1939–40, in his 251* *v* New South Wales, he scored 164 in boundaries (two sixes and 38 fours).

For this third time, and the second time in Australia, he made two double centuries in successive innings; no one else up till then had ever done this more than twice, though Bradman did so four times in all. Ponsford is the only other Australian ever to do so, and he did so twice, but only once in Australia. It was also his third century in successive innings, the fifth time he had done this, thus equalling the record shared by W.G. Grace, J.B. Hobbs and Ponsford; Bradman did this ten times altogether.

He thus made 590 in two consecutive innings (233, 357), the most he ever made, and a South Australian record (previous best, 508 by Giffen, 1890–1–2). His 707 in three consecutive innings (117, 233, 357) was also the most he ever made, and a record for South Australia (previous best, 566 by Hill, 1909–10); while his 757 (50, 117, 233, 357) in four successive innings is also a record for South Australia, Hill's 609 in 1909–10 being the previous best.

Counting his last two innings of 253 and 128 for New South Wales in 1933–4, this was his fifth successive century in Sheffield Shield matches; in 1898–9–1900, M.A. Noble had made four hundreds in succession for New South Wales in Shield matches, while for South Australia only Hill, in 1909–10, had previously made as many as three in succession. In 1938–9, Bradman made five consecutive Shield centuries for South Australia.

## 123. SOUTH AUSTRALIA *v* QUEENSLAND, at Brisbane, 10, 11, 13 and 14 January 1936

SCORES: Queensland 205 and 163; South Australia 340 (A.J. Ryan 144, E. Gilbert 5 for 87) and 29 for no wicket. South Australia won by 10 wickets.

| | | |
|---|---|---|
| D.G. BRADMAN (capt.) | c. E.R.H. Wyeth b. E. Gilbert | 31 |
| | (did not bat) | – |

This was one of Bradman's least impressive displays; he went in at 38 for 2 on the second afternoon, gave a stumping chance off Wyeth when 5, and after being uncomfortable against Gilbert's great pace, he failed to get on top of a rising ball and gave gully an easy catch. He was in for 47 minutes and was out at 94 for 3; in his last five innings he had made 788 runs (50, 117, 233, 357, 31), then a South Australian record (previous best, 656 by C. Giffen, 1890–1–2), which Bradman beat in 1939–40 with 810.

He had won the toss and put Queensland in to bat.

### 124. SOUTH AUSTRALIA *v* NEW SOUTH WALES, at Sydney, 18 and 20 January 1936

SCORES: South Australia 94 (E.S. White 8 for 31); New South Wales 286 for 6 wickets (R.H. Robinson 94*, L. Fallowfield 53). Drawn (abandoned owing to the death of HM King George V).

D.G. BRADMAN (capt.)  c. R. Little b. L.C. Hynes                    0

Rain, which had washed out the first day's play, had seeped under the tarpaulin covers at one end of the wicket but not the other and made it curiously two-paced, the end towards which White bowled being very tricky. South Australia, sent in to bat when play started after lunch, found him most difficult; Bradman, coming in at 34 for 1, negotiated six balls from him at the 'sticky' end without trouble, but on getting to the other, which was perfect, was almost lbw. to Hynes' first ball, and was well caught at leg-slip off his second; Hynes was a fast-medium left-hander and Bradman failed to time his in-swinger properly in attempting a leg-glance. That made the score 39 for 2.

### 125. SOUTH AUSTRALIA *v* VICTORIA, at Adelaide, 21, 22, 24 and 25 February 1936

SCORES: Victoria 201 (A.L. Hassett 73, F.A. Ward 5 for 7) and 174; South Australia 565 for 6 wickets dec. (C.L. Badcock 325, R. Parker 88, A.J. Ryan 77). South Australia won by an innings and 190 runs.

D.G. BRADMAN (capt.)  c. J.A. Ledward b. H.I. Ebeling              1

Badcock and Parker had taken the score to 210 for the first wicket, and South Australia were already in the lead when Bradman batted on the second afternoon; one run and two minutes later, he was caught at second slip off a rising out-swinger, and Badcock went on to take the honours in an innings lasting nine hours 47 minutes.

### 126. SOUTH AUSTRALIA *v* TASMANIA, at Adelaide, 29 February, 2 and 3 March 1936

SCORES: Tasmania 158 (E.H. Smith 62) and 181 (A.W. Rushforth 73, F.A. Ward 6 for 47); South Australia 688 (D.G. Bradman 369, R.A. Hamence 121, T.T. O'Connell 53). South Australia won by an innings and 349 runs.

D.G. BRADMAN (capt.)  c. and b. R. Townley                        369

Bradman gave another overwhelming performance against weak opposition. He started at 23 for 1, and had 95 minutes' batting on the first evening, being 127 not out at the close of play; he had made 50 in 40 minutes (his first 40 taking only a quarter of an hour) and 100 in 70 minutes (the fastest of his career). Next morning he hit with such ferocity that he added 242 runs in two hours 38 minutes, 135 of them before lunch; he completed 200 in two hours 53 minutes, and 300 in three hours 33 minutes. Eventually, at 552 for 6 (529 while at the wicket), he gave a deliberate catch to the bowler.

He was batting for only four hours 13 minutes, gave only one hard chance (in the deep at 305), and hit four sixes and 46 fours; he and Hamence added 356 in one minute over three hours for the third wicket, and he and B.H. Leak (whose share was 19) put on 146 for the fourth. When 196 he completed his 1,000 runs for the season; and his 369 was 55 per cent of the South Australian score from the bat, scored at an average rate of 87 an hour.

Hs 369 remains the highest score ever made for South Australia and the highest ever made on the Adelaide ground, passing the 365* by C. Hill *v* New South Wales in 1900–1, which was, however, made in a Sheffield Shield match. The previous high score for South Australia *v* Tasmania (who had met only twice previously) was 120 by H.C. Nitschke in 1930–1; the previous highest partnership for the third wicket against Tasmania was 264, by F.E. Woolley and J.W. Hearne for MCC in 1911–2, while for South Australia the previous highest partnership for any wicket was 313 for the first *v* Western Australia, 1925–6, by A.J. Richardson and L.T. Gun, and for the third wicket, 253 by Hill and D.R.A. Gehrs, *v* New South Wales, 1909–10.

This was the sixth and last treble century of his career, four of them made in Australia and two in England; W.H. Ponsford, the previous record-holder, scored all four of his in Australia; Bradman is the only batsman to make two treble centuries for South Australia, Hill and C.L. Badcock being the only others to make even one such score. Ponsford had scored all his four triple centuries at Melbourne, while Bradman had now made them at Sydney (two), Melbourne and Adelaide. Of 16 first-class scores of over 350, Bradman and Ponsford have scored three each, B. Sutcliffe two and no one else more than one.

This time he took only nine innings to reach 1,000 runs, the previous best by a South Australian batsman being 15 innings, by Hill in 1897–8.

This was the 24th double century of his career, which equalled the number then to the credit of W.R. Hammond, both Bradman and Hammond having by then outstripped E. Hendren (then 21) and all other rivals. From 1936 until the end of their careers, Bradman and Hammond ran neck and neck in the matter of double centuries, sometimes one being in front and sometimes the other; but Bradman finished up with 37 against Hammond's 36.

This was the fourth and last occasion in Australia on which he added more than 100 runs to his score between the start of play and the lunch interval, and 135 is the most that has ever been made in Australia in that period of play (previous best, 131 by Bradman in 1933–4); no one else has added 100 before lunch more than

127

once in Australia, the rarity of the feat being due to the fact that playing time is normally only one and three-quarter hours at most.

His time for reaching 300 in this match, three hours 33 minutes, is the fastest ever achieved in Australia, the previous best being three hours 39 minutes, by Woolley for MCC *v* Tasmania, 1911–2, and, by an Australian, Ponsford's 300 in four hours 45 minutes in his 352 for Victoria *v* New South Wales, 1926–7, which remains the fastest in a Sheffield Shield match; for South Australia, his own six hours 28 minutes earlier this season was the previous fastest.

The four sixes and 46 fours were the most boundaries ever scored in an innings, and the 208 runs in boundaries were also a personal record; both are still records for South Australia, the previous best being his own 40 fours and 160 runs in his 357 earlier this season.

## SUMMARY, 1935–6

| | Matches | Innings | NO | HS | Runs | Average | Centuries |
|---|---|---|---|---|---|---|---|
| All First-class matches ⎫ | | | | | | | |
| All Matches for South ⎬ | 8 | 9 | 0 | 369 | 1173 | 130.33 | 4 |
| Australia ⎭ | | | | | | | |
| Sheffield Shield Matches | 6 | 6 | 0 | 357 | 739 | 123.16 | 3 |
| Match *v* MCC Team | 1 | 2 | 0 | 50 | 65 | 32.50 | 0 |

South Australia won the Sheffield Shield this season.

Bradman, for the seventh time, exceeded 1,000 runs and was the only batsman in Australia to do so this season; K.E. Rigg was second in aggregate with 773 runs, while C.L. Badcock's average of 86.75 was next best to Bradman's. In Sheffield Shield matches, indeed, Badcock's average was 124.40, a run better than Bradman's. Rigg hit three centuries, the next best to Bradman's four.

This was the third Australian season (out of five altogether) in which he made three double centuries, all for South Australia, two of these being in Sheffield Shield matches; no other South Australian batsman has ever made more than one in a season. He scored two treble centuries this season, a feat previously performed in Australia only by W.H. Ponsford (in 1927–8); in England, W.G. Grace (1876) is the only batsman to do this.

His total of 739 runs in Sheffield shield matches was then a record for a South Australian batsman, the previous best being 720 by G.W. Harris, 1928–9; Bradman passed this aggregate three times later, his highest being 1,062 in 1939–40. Six South Australian batsmen had made three centuries in a Sheffield Shield season, but no one else has made more than three, which Bradman made this season, except Bradman himself, who made four in 1937–8 and five in 1938–9.

Bradman's centuries in Shield matches were scored against all three of the other

States, Harris being the only other batsman to do this for South Australia since Queensland entered the competition in 1926–7. This was the second season in which Bradman had done this, Ponsford being the only other batsman to do this twice up till then; Bradman did so in four seasons altogether.

His total of 1,173 runs in all matches for South Australia was then a record (previous best, 873 by V.Y. Richardson, 1931–2); in 1939–40, Bradman beat this with a total of 1,448. In 1897–8, C. Hill made four centuries in all matches for South Australia; Bradman three times later scored five in a season.

This was the fifth time he had been top of the Australian batting averages, once more than the previous best, by M.A. Noble; he was top 11 times altogether. It was the fourth time that his average for a full Australian season exceeded 100; Bradman did this seven times altogether, the previous best being Ponsford, with a century-average in three full seasons.

# 1936–7

## AGED TWENTY-EIGHT

———◆◆✕◆●———

Bradman was appointed to the Australian Selection Committee and in due course was made captain of Australia in all the Test matches against the England team under G.O. Allen.

### 127. THE REST OF AUSTRALIA *v* AUSTRALIA (W. Bardsley and J.M. Gregory Testimonial), at Sydney, 9, 10, 12 and 13 October 1936

SCORES: Australia 363 (W.A. Brown 111, W.A. Oldfield 78, S.J. McCabe 76, F.A. Ward 7 for 127) and 180 (F.A. Ward 5 for 100); Rest of Australia 385 (D.G. Bradman 212, L.P. O'Brien 85) and 161 for 4 wickets (R.H. Robinson 57). Rest of Australia won by 6 wickets.

| | | |
|---|---|---|
| D.G. BRADMAN (capt.) | c. W.J. O'Reilly b. C.V. Grimmett | 212 |
| | c. J.H. Fingleton b. C.V. Grimmett | 13 |

The 11 representing Australia had all been members of V.Y. Richardson's team which had been so successful in South Africa the previous winter, their bowlers including E.L. McCormick, M.W. Sievers, W.J. O'Reilly and C.V. Grimmett; this was the first time that Bradman had faced O'Reilly in a first-class match, and he mastered him and the others in a brilliant innings. He went in ten minutes before lunch on the second day, with the score 51 for 4 and O'Reilly bowling at his best; however, he soon settled down, though at first his shots sometimes suffered from early-season mis-timing. He got to 50 in 56 minutes and at tea was 94; his century was registered in two hours ten minutes, and then he hit out so vigorously and so certainly that his second century took only 61 minutes. After seeing his side into a first-innings lead, he gave away his wicket; when 200, he was missed in the deep off O'Reilly, and soon afterwards he was caught at long-on, with the score 378 for 7. When he left, the rest of the side collapsed for seven more runs, his 212 thus being 56 per cent of his side's score from the bat.

He gave only the one chance, batted for three hours 22 minutes, and hit two sixes and 26 fours; he and O'Brien added 149 in 118 minutes for the fifth wicket, and he and A.D. McGilvray put on 177 in 78 minutes for the sixth wicket, the latter's share being 42.

130

This was the fourth and last time, and the third time in Australia, that he made two double centuries in successive innings; this has now been achieved 25 times altogether. W.R. Hammond has done so three times, no one else more than twice, and the only other Australian to do so, W.H. Ponsford, achieved the feat once in Australia and once in England. Hammond is the only other player to do this in Australia.

His team were set 159 to win in the last innings, and when he went in late on the third day the score was 63 for 1; this time, however, he failed, being caught at cover when mistiming an off-drive, at 76 for 2. He made his 13 in 13 minutes.

128. **SOUTH AUSTRALIA** *v* **VICTORIA**, at Melbourne, 13, 14, 16 and 17 November 1936

SCORES: Victoria 401 (K.E. Rigg 97, R.G. Gregory 85, M.W. Sievers 54, F.A. Ward 6 for 107) and 403 for 7 wickets (K.E. Rigg 105, L.S. Darling 102, I.S. Lee 93, B.A. Barnett 55); South Australia 386 (D.G. Bradman 192). Drawn.

D.G. BRADMAN (capt.)  c. L.P. O'Brien b. R.G. Gregory          192

Bradman, after winning the toss and putting Victoria in – a quite unsuccessful decision – did not field on the first day owing to an attack of gastroenteritis, and he had had nothing to eat, and was far from well when he went in on the second afternoon; nevertheless, he played another good innings, against bowlers who included E.L. McCormick, H.I. Ebeling, M.W. Sievers, J. Frederick and R.G. Gregory. Frederick had achieved considerable success the week before against the MCC team, taking 6 for 65 with his slow leg-spinners in the first innings, but Bradman, quick on his feet as ever, treated him very severely; McCormick, however, bowling very fast, caused him trouble at first.

In at 27 for 2, Bradman made 50 in 66 minutes and reached 103 in two hours 14 minutes, at 5.13 p.m., after some time in the nineties; then, in the next 46 minutes, he added another 89, the last 42 of them in 16 minutes. He was missed when 128 off Frederick, cover-point getting a hand to a hard stroke which went on to the boundary; and trying to hit a six, he was missed on the boundary the ball before he was out, caught at deep long-on just before the close of play. He was batting for exactly three hours, hit 32 fours, and gave only the two chances; he scored his 192 out of 268 while he was in (71 per cent), the total at his dismissal being 295 for 5, and out of 367 from the bat (52 per cent). His stand with R.A. Hamence (37) for the fifth wicket realised 108, in 48 minutes, Bradman's share being 99 and Hamence's 9.

This was the closest he ever got to 200 without reaching it.

### 129. AN AUSTRALIAN XI *v* MCC TEAM, at Sydney, 20, 21, 23 and 24 November 1936

SCORES: MCC Team 288 (M. Leyland 80, L.E.G. Ames 76, R.W.V. Robins 53, A.G. Chipperfield 8 for 66) and 245 for 8 wickets (M. Leyland 118*); An Australian XI 544 for 8 wickets dec. (C.L. Badcock 182, W.A. Brown 71, D.G. Bradman 63, J.H. Fingleton 56). Drawn.

| D.G. BRADMAN (capt.) b. T.S. Worthington | 63 |
|---|---|

Bradman went in on the second afternoon at 103 for 1, and played a smooth and confident innings, the only surprise being that he was dismissed when well set. On 31 not out at tea, he made his 50 in 73 minutes, and 63 in one minute under one and a half hours; he played on when trying to force a shortish ball to square-leg, the score being 194 for 2. He hit eight fours and passed his partner, Brown, at 59 despite having given him 38 runs and one hour and 41 minutes' start.

The MCC only just avoided an innings defeat.

### 130. AUSTRALIA *v* ENGLAND, First Test match, at Brisbane, 4, 5, 7, 8 and 9 December 1936

SCORES: England 358 (M. Leyland 126, C.J. Barnett 69, W.J. O'Reilly 5 for 102) and 256 (G.O. Allen 68, F.A. Ward 6 for 102); Australia 234 (J.H. Fingleton 100, S.J. McCabe 51, W. Voce 6 for 41) and 58 (G.O. Allen 5 for 36). Australia lost by 322 runs.

| D.G. BRADMAN (capt.) c. T.S. Worthington b. W. Voce | 38 |
|---|---|
| c. A.E. Fagg b. G.O. Allen | 0 |

Bradman's first innings started on the second afternoon, at 13 for 1, with two boundaries off Allen in his first over, and he continued to play brilliantly if rather streakily until tea-time, when he was 37 not out. He stayed for ten minutes after the interval, but did not settle down, being caught in the gully when trying to drive a going-away ball off his back foot; the score was then 89 for 2. He batted for 71 minutes and played 56 balls.

Australia were set to make 381 to win the match, a task which would probably have been too heavy in any event; but rain before the fifth day's play made the result a certainty for England, and Voce and Allen exploited a vicious wicket to run through the opposition. Bradman, going in soon after the start at 7 for 3, played one ball from Allen and was caught at third slip from his second; it pitched on a length, lifted sharply and hit the shoulder of his bat before he could withdraw it. Bradman's first experience of captaincy in a Test match was thus a melancholy one.

### 131. AUSTRALIA *v* ENGLAND, Second Test match, at Sydney, 18, 19, 21 and 22 December 1936

SCORES: England 426 for 6 wickets dec. (W.R. Hammond 231*, C.J. Barnett 57); Australia 80 and 324 (S.J. McCabe 93, D.G. Bradman 82, J.H. Fingleton 73). Australia lost by an innings and 22 runs.

D.G. BRADMAN (capt.)  c. G.O. Allen b. W. Voce          0
                          b. H. Verity                   82

After England had batted for the first two days, overnight rain presented Australia with their second sticky wicket in succession, and Bradman made his second successive 'duck'; on this occasion he went in at 1 for 1, early on the third morning, and played an indeterminate stroke to a good-length ball, to be easily caught at short-leg first ball.

Forced to follow on after lunch, 346 behind, Australia and Bradman did much better in the second innings, on a rapidly moving wicket. He went in at 38 for 1 and was 12 not out at the tea interval, by which time the vice had virtually disappeared from the wicket. He gave a hard chance to square-leg, off a full-blooded hook off Allen, when 24, but otherwise played very carefully in an endeavour to redeem the position; when 27, he passed C. Hill's aggregate of 2,660, the previous record for an Australian in Tests between England and Australia, this being his 34th innings against Hill's 76. He completed 50 in an hour and 52 minutes and was 57 not out at 6 p.m., after five minutes' further play.

Next morning he continued his careful progress, being obviously burdened with the weight of responsibility upon him. He lost Fingleton after 124 had been added for the second wicket in a minute over two and a half hours, and soon afterwards he himself was bowled by Verity. He was, in fact, guilty of lifting his head in attempting to hook a slow long hop, an unfortunate ending to an innings in which he had struggled hard to recover his form without ever quite succeeding. He batted for two hours 52 minutes and 139 balls for his 82, and hit six fours; his dismissal, at 186 for 3, meant the end of any slight hope that Australia might save the game.

### 132. AUSTRALIA *v* ENGLAND, Third Test match, at Melbourne, 1, 2, 4, 5, 6 and 7 January 1937

SCORES: Australia 200 for 9 wickets dec. (S.J. McCabe 63) and 564 (D.G. Bradman 270, J.H. Fingleton 136); England 76 for 9 wickets dec. (M.W. Sievers 5 for 21) and 323 (M. Leyland 111*, R.W.V. Robins 61, W.R. Hammond 51, L.O'B. Fleetwood-Smith 5 for 124). Australia won by 365 runs.

D.G. BRADMAN (capt.)  c. R.W.V. Robins b. H. Verity          13
                      c. G.O. Allen b. H. Verity          270

On this occasion the luck of the toss and the weather decisively favoured Australia, who were saved by rain from the effects of a first-innings batting failure on a good wicket. Bradman's first innings, early on the first day, began at 7 for 1 and lasted only 28 minutes and 22 balls before he put up an easy catch to square-leg to make the score 33 for 2; it was the first ball Verity bowled and Bradman apparently did not realise Robins' presence there – an unusual failure in his concentration. His first five Test innings this season had thus produced only 133 runs which, by a coincidence, was exactly the same as he had made in his first five Test innings in 1934.

After England had been dismissed on another 'glue-pot' wicket on the second day, the wicket had virtually recovered when Bradman joined Fingleton at 97 for 5 (he had put his tail-enders in early) at 2.50 p.m. on the third day, and he at once began to show his old mastery. Rain interrupted play on three occasions, without making the wicket more difficult; in fact, Bradman took advantage of the fact that the bowlers had trouble in gripping the slippery ball. He and Fingleton were still together at the close of play; Bradman had completed 50 in 85 minutes, and after an hour and 40 minutes was 56 not out. He reached 4,000 runs in all Test cricket when he was 18.

He then proceeded to bat the whole of the fourth day and, in fact, it was only 35 minutes before the close of play that he and Fingleton were separated. They started very slowly, only 58 being added in an hour and 31 minutes before lunch; Bradman's share of this was 40, making his score 96 at the interval. A snick through the slips for 4 off Voce seven minutes later gave him his century in three hours 18 minutes, and thereafter he began to score rather faster, without ever relaxing his concentration.

He was 164 not out at the tea interval, completed 200 at 5.15, after five hours 54 minutes, and was 206 when Fingelton was at last dismissed at 443 for 6; he and Bradman had added 346 for the sixth wicket in six hours four minutes.

In the last half-hour, Bradman increased the pace of his scoring and at the close, after six hours 39 minutes, he was 248 not out – his first double century *v* England in a Test match in Australia. During the day he scored 192 runs, thus breaking the record for an Australian in a Test match against England in Australia, previously held by C. Hill, who made 182 in one day in 1897–8.

His stand of 346 with Fingleton is still the highest for the sixth wicket in any first-class match in Australia (previous best, 323 by E. Hendren and J.W.H.T. Douglas, for MCC *v* Victoria, 1920–1; by Australians in Australia, 262 by A. Kenny and B.J. Kortlang, for Victoria *v* Queensland, 1909–10; by Australians *v* a touring team, 216 by V.S. Ransford and A.E. Liddicutt, *v* MCC, 1922-3). It is also still the sixth-wicket record for any Test match anywhere (previous best, 187 by W.W. Armstrong and C.E. Kelleway, for Australia *v* England, 1920–1).

At that time it was the highest for any wicket for any Test match in Australia (previous best, 323 for the first wicket, by J.B. Hobbs and W. Rhodes, England *v* Australia, 1911–2; by Australia, 274 for the second wicket by W.M. Woodfull and Bradman *v* South Africa, 1931–2; by Australia against England in Australia, 243 for the eighth wicket, by C. Hill and R.J. Hartigan, 1907–8). It was also the highest for any wicket against any touring team in Australia (previous best, 306 for the second wicket, by C.L. Badcock and W. Horrocks earlier in 1936–7). These records lasted until Bradman and S.G. Barnes added 405 for the fifth wicket *v* England, 1946–7.

Suffering from a chill on the fifth morning, Bradman batted rather listlessly for a further 59 minutes and his first aggressive stroke skied the ball wide of mid-on, where Allen took a good catch. His 270 in seven hours 38 minutes included 22 fours, and he was out to his 375th ball at 549 for 9; he gave no chance in an innings in which he took scarcely a single risk, and recovered his best form at the time when it was most needed to put Australia into an unassailable position. England's bowlers were W. Voce, G.O. Allen, J.M. Sims, H. Verity, R.W.V. Robins, W.R. Hammond and T.S. Worthington.

His time of seven hours 38 minutes was the longest he ever batted in a Test match and the second longest innings of his whole career; it was at that time the longest innings ever played by an Australian in a Test match in Australia, the previous longest being seven hours 28 minutes by A.C. Bannerman (for a score of 91) in 1891–2; Barnes stayed at the wicket for ten hours 42 minutes for his 234 in 1946–7.

His score of 270 is still the highest by an Australian against England in Australia (previous best, 201 by S.E. Gregory, 1894–5, and 201* by J.S. Ryder, 1924–5), and the highest in any Test match at Melbourne (previous best, 204 by G.A. Faulkner, 1910–1; in an England *v* Australia Test match, 200 by W.R. Hammond, 1928–9; by an Australian, 188 by C. Hill, 1897–8). It is equal to the highest Test match score against England outside England, 270* by G.A. Headley, in the West Indies, 1934–5.

It was then the highest score in the second innings of any Test match (previous best, 231 by A.D. Nourse, 1935–6; against England, 223 by Headley, 1929–30; by an Australian, 189* by S.J. McCabe, *v* South Africa, 1935–6; in Australia, and in an England *v* Australia Test match, 185* by V.T. Trumper, 1903–4). P.B.H. May made 285* in the second innings for England *v* West Indies, 1957, but Bradman's 270 remains the record for Australia, against England, in Australia, and in an England *v* Australia Test match.

It was also the highest 'captain's innings' ever played in a Test match (previous best, 211 by W.L. Murdoch, 1884), until May made his 285* in 1957; Bradman's 270 remains the highest score by a captain for Australia, against England, in Australia, and in an England *v* Australia Test match (next best, 240 by Hammond, 1938; previous best in Australia, 191 by C. Hill *v* South Africa, 1910–1; next best, 234 by Bradman in 1946–7).

In helping to increase the score by 452, he broke the record for an Australian in a Test match *v* England in Australia, 420 by C.E. Kelleway, in 1920–1; in 1946 S.G. Barnes helped to put on 564 before he was out.

### 133. SOUTH AUSTRALIA *v* MCC TEAM, at Adelaide, 22 and 23 January 1937

SCORES: MCC Team 301 (C.J. Barnett 78, G.O. Allen 60, R.E.S. Wyatt 53); South Australia 194 for 4 wickets (A.J. Ryan 71). Drawn.

D.G. BRADMAN (capt.)  c. L.E.G. Ames b. C.J. Barnett          38

Bradman went in at 109 for 2, just after tea on the second day, but was rather below his best form. He strained a leg muscle when he was 18 and thereafter had to have a runner; he batted altogether for 74 minutes, before being well caught at the wicket attempting a square-cut, at 167 for 4.

Owing to rain there was no play on the last two days.

### 134. AUSTRALIA *v* ENGLAND, Fourth Test match, at Adelaide, 29, 30 January, 1, 2, 3 and 4 February 1937

SCORES: Australia 288 (S.J. McCabe 88, A.G. Chipperfield 57*) and 433 (D.G. Bradman 212, S.J. McCabe 55, R.G. Gregory 50, W.R. Hammond 5 for 57); England 330 (C.J. Barnett 129, L.E.G. Ames 52) and 243 (R.E.S. Wyatt 50, L.O'B. Fleetwood-Smith 6 for 110). Australia won by 148 runs.

D.G. BRADMAN (capt.)  b. G.O. Allen                26
                      c. and b. W.R. Hammond       212

Australia on the first day again failed to take advantage of Bradman's fortune in winning the toss, he himself playing a subdued innings lasting 68 minutes (only 22 runs an hour). Going in just after lunch at 72 for 2, he reached an aggregate of 3,000 in England–Australia Tests with his first run and looked to have settled down for a big score when Allen bowled him; he tried to hook a ball (his 54th) which kept rather low, and played it on to his wicket, being out at 136 for 4.

Australia's first-innings deficit was only 42, though at one time it had looked as if it would be much more; and Bradman again set himself to win the match for Australia with another huge innings. Going in at 21 for 1 on the third evening, he made a solid 26 not out in exactly an hour before close of play; and again he batted all through the fourth day.

He completed 50 in one and three-quarter hours, was 70 at lunch, and at 3 p.m. reached his century by pulling Robins for 4, after three hours 16 minutes at the wicket. At 136 not out at the tea interval, he did not accelerate as he usually did in the evening, Verity keeping him quiet with some accurate if negative leg-theory to a deep-set field. The result was that he scored only 38 in an hour and 42 minutes after tea, and was 174 not out, after five hours 58 minutes' batting, when stumps were drawn; the wicket was, of course, becoming more worn the longer he batted, and he declined to be tempted by Verity's defensive bowling, again taking no risks, and even eschewing his hook-stroke. He and McCabe added 109 in 92 minutes for the third wicket.

When he was 53, he passed his season's 1,000 runs; in doing so on 2 February, he was 19 days earlier than his previous best by a South Australian batsman, C. Hill, who reached this total in 1897–8 on 21 February. Bradman reached his 1,000 for the season even sooner than this in 1937–8 and 1939–40, in the latter season on 13 January.

When he was 130, he passed Hill's aggregate of 11,129, previously the biggest total of runs ever scored in Australia; Hill had 233 innings in Australia, while this was Bradman's 135th innings in that country.

For the second consecutive Test match, and for the third time out of four altogether, Bradman's innings continued into a third day, when he and Gregory resumed their fifth-wicket partnership next morning; this they carried to 135 before Gregory was run out, having stayed for two hours 55 minutes. Bradman himself, after playing a maiden over of leg-theory from Verity when 199, completed 200 in two minutes over seven hours (the slowest of his career), and 19 minutes later, at 1.23 p.m., hit a catch very hard back to the bowler. He was out at 422 for 6, having batted for seven hours 21 minutes and 393 balls, and after he left the last four wickets fell for another 11 runs, his 212 thus being 52 per cent of his side's runs from the bat. Bradman hit only 14 fours and gave no chance; in fact, he scarcely made a false stroke or lifted the ball off the ground; but at 28 runs an hour, it was his slowest double century. Perhaps he revealed more clearly than ever the extent to which Australia depended on him in Test matches, and the concentration and self-discipline that enabled him to play an innings which virtually won the match for his side.

This was his first century v England on any Australian ground other than Melbourne, where so far he had made four; and England's bowlers included W. Voce, G.O. Allen, K. Farnes, W.R. Hammond, H. Verity and R.W.V. Robins. He is still the only Australian batsman to make more than one double century in Tests v England in Australia; up till then, only Bradman, S.E. Gregory and J.S. Ryder had made even one such score. His 212 is the highest in an England v Australia Test match at Adelaide (previous best, 201* by Ryder, 1924–5). This was the third time, all v England, that Bradman had made double centuries in two consecutive Test matches; Hammond, twice (v Australia and New Zealand), is the only other batsman ever to have done this.

This was the 17th Test century of Bradman's career, one more than the previous best, by H. Sutcliffe and Hammond; Hammond overhauled him again in 1939, and thus led Bradman during the war by 22 Test centuries to 21, but Bradman made eight more such scores after the war and thus finished easily ahead of all others.

Bradman out-scored the next highest scorer by 157 runs, the best by an Australian batsman in a Test match v England in Australia; in 1876–7, C.

Bannerman, with 165*, scored 147 more than his next rival, who made only 18 – an even more meritorious performance than Bradman's.

### 135. SOUTH AUSTRALIA *v* QUEENSLAND, at Brisbane, 12, 13 and 15 February 1937

SCORES: Queensland 137 (T. Allen 68) and 139; South Australia 257 (D.G. Bradman 123, C.L. Badcock 56) and 20 for no wicket. South Australia won by 10 wickets.

| D.G. BRADMAN (capt.) st. D. Tallon b. E.R.H. Wyeth | 123 |
|---|---|
| (did not bat) | – |

Bradman, displaying sound and watchful defence, was again much the most successful batsman. He had 65 minutes' batting at the end of the first day, starting at 59 for 3, and was 45 not out when bad light stopped play; next morning he completed 50 in the third over, in 71 minutes, and his century in two hours 22 minutes, being out at 235 for 5 just before lunch, after two and three-quarter hours at the wicket. He gave no chance and hit a six and ten fours; he and Badcock put on 109 for the fourth wicket, and after Bradman was out the last five wickets fell for 22 runs.

### 136. SOUTH AUSTRALIA *v* NEW SOUTH WALES, at Sydney, 19, 20, 22 and 23 February 1937

SCORES: New South Wales 355 (E.S. White 108*, W.A. Oldfield 63) and 242 (S.J. McCabe 68); South Australia 270 (C.L. Badcock 136) and 132 for 3 wickets. Drawn.

| D.G. BRADMAN (capt.) lbw. b. W.J. O'Reilly | 24 |
|---|---|
| not out | 38 |

Going in just after lunch on the second day at 23 for 2, Bradman batted in sedate fashion for an hour before being lbw. in trying to turn a well-pitched ball to leg, at 94 for 4.

There was never any chance of a result when he went in on the fourth day, just after lunch, at 62 for 2, and he took some batting practice for 72 minutes before rain stopped play.

### 137. AUSTRALIA *v* ENGLAND, Fifth Test match, at Melbourne, 26, 27 February, 1, 2 and 3 March 1937

SCORES: Australia 604 (D.G. Bradman 169, C.L. Badcock 118, S.J. McCabe 112, R.G. Gregory 80, K. Farnes 6 for 96); England 239 (J. Hardstaff 83, W.J. O'Reilly 5 for 51) and 165 (W.R. Hammond 56). Australia won by an innings and 200 runs, won the rubber and retained the Ashes.

D.G. BRADMAN (capt.)  b. K. Farnes      169

Having squared the rubber after being two games down, Australia emphasised her superiority in the Final Test match, and Bradman again played a big innings; whereas, however, in the previous Test matches he had been sedate and cautious, he now displayed his most aggressive and brilliant form.

He went in at 42 for 1, nine minutes after lunch on the first day, being 7 not out at the interval; he reached 50 in 69 minutes, had made 90 by tea-time, and at 4.33 pm. completed his century, after batting for five minutes over two hours. His only streaky stroke gave him 150, and at the close of play, after three hours 34 minutes' batting, he was 165 not out. He and McCabe added 249 for the third wicket in only two hours 43 minutes; while Bradman's display was chanceless, however, McCabe was missed three times. England's fast attack, G.O. Allen, W. Voce and K. Farnes, could make no impression on a perfect wicket, and in great heat, and Bradman off-drove them as though they were medium-pace; nor was Verity any more successful than they.

His partnership of 249 with McCabe was then the highest for the third wicket by Australia in any Test match (previous best, 242 by W. Bardsley and C.E. Kelleway, v South Africa, in England in 1912; against England, 299 by Bradman and A.F. Kippax, in England, 1930; in any Test in Australia and v England in Australia, 193 by J. Darling and J. Worrall, 1897–8); it was also then the highest third-wicket stand against England in any Test match anywhere, Bradman and Kippax's 229 being the previous highest; and the highest for the third wicket by Australians against any touring team in Australia, and the highest for the third wicket against any English touring team anywhere, the previous highest being 214 by A.J. Richardson and V.Y. Richardson v MCC, 1924–5. In company with A.L. Hassett, Bradman broke these records in 1946–7, with a partnership for the third wicket of 276.

Next morning, Bradman carried on for another nine minutes, but failed to settle down, and added only 4 runs before being bowled in Farnes' second over when trying to force the ball to the on. His faultless innings lasted three hours 43 minutes and included 15 fours; his wicket fell at 346 for 4 and he made his runs off 191 balls.

138. **SOUTH AUSTRALIA** v **VICTORIA**, at Adelaide, 12, 13 and 15 March 1937

SCORES: South Australia 182 (L.O'B. Fleetwood-Smith 6 for 66) and 79 (E.L. McCormick 9 for 40); Victoria 213 (I.S. Lee 109*) and 49 for 1 wicket. South Australia lost by 9 wickets.

| | | |
|---|---|---:|
| D.G. BRADMAN (capt.) | H.I. Ebeling b. L.O'B. Fleetwood-Smith | 31 |
| | c. A.L. Hassett b. E.L. McCormick | 8 |

Needing an outright win to retain the Sheffield Shield, South Australia failed badly. Bradman went in at 27 for 2 on the first morning, and batted brightly for 29 minutes before being caught at square-leg at 71 for 3; his 31 was the second-highest score.

The score was again 27 for 2 when he batted on the second afternoon, and after hitting two boundaries in five minutes, he gave an easy catch to square-leg in trying to hook, with the score 37 for 3. McCormick bowled at a great pace.

## SUMMARY, 1936–7

| | Matches | Innings | NO | HS | Runs | Average | Centuries |
|---|---|---|---|---|---|---|---|
| All First-class Matches | 12 | 19 | 1 | 270 | 1552 | 86.22 | 6 |
| Test Matches | 5 | 9 | 0 | 270 | 810 | 90.00 | 3 |
| All Matches v MCC | 7 | 11 | 0 | 270 | 911 | 82.81 | 3 |
| Sheffield Shield Matches | 4 | 6 | 1 | 192 | 416 | 83.20 | 2 |
| All Matches for South Australia | 5 | 7 | 1 | 192 | 454 | 75.66 | 2 |

Australia won the Test match series by three matches to two and retained the Ashes.

Bradman's aggregate of 810 for the Test match series was the highest by an Australian in any series in Australia (previous best, 806 by Bradman v South Africa, 1931–2; v England, 574 by V.T. Trumper, 1903–4); R.N. Harvey made 834 runs v South Africa in 1952–3, but Bradman's 810 remains the best by an Australian against England in a rubber in Australia, his own 680 in 1946–7 being the next best.

His average of 90.00 was also a record for Australia v England in Australia (previous best, 86.66 by C.G. Macartney, 1920–1); Bradman improved upon this in 1946–7 with an average of 97.14.

His three centuries in a series in Australia v England are a record for Australia which he shares with J. Darling (1897–8), W.W. Armstrong (1920–1), W.M. Woodfull (1928–9) and A.R. Morris (1946–7); no Australian has scored four centuries in a series v England in Australia.

Bradman, in scoring two double centuries in a series in Australia, did something which no other Australian has done against England; Bradman himself had done it against South Africa in 1931–2, and W.R. Hammond made two double centuries for England v Australia in 1928–9. Bradman is the only batsman of any country to make two double centuries in a season in all matches against an English touring team.

His aggregate of 1,552 is a record for an Australian season by a South Australian batsman (previous best, C. Hill's 1,196 in 1897–8); Hill made five centuries in 1897–8, the previous best by a South Australian batsman; Bradman, however, passed his own record with seven centuries in 1937–8, and then eight in 1947–8.

His total of 911 against the MCC team is the highest against an English touring team anywhere (previous best, 891 by G.A. Headley, in the West Indies, 1929–30; in Australia, 833 by Woodfull, 1928–9; next best in Australia, 870 by Bradman in 1946–7).

Bradman, for the eighth time, and for the second time in succession when playing for South Australia, exceeded 1,000 runs this season; Hill is the only other South Australian batsman to reach 1,000 runs in a season, and he did so twice, but not in consecutive seasons.

Bradman this season headed the Australian first-class averages and aggregates, A.L. Hassett being second in average with 71.85, and S.J. McCabe making the next most runs, with 956. C.L. Badcock, with four centuries, was second to Bradman in hundreds, among Australians, though for the MCC team W.R. Hammond and C.J. Barnett each hit five; these two also scored 1,242 and 1,375 respectively for averages of 59.14 and 55.00. For the fourth time, and for the second while playing for South Australia, Bradman scored three double centuries in an Australian season.

In the Test matches, McCabe was next to Bradman among Australians with 491 runs, average 54.55, while Hammond headed the England figures with 468 runs, average 58.50. J.H. Fingleton and M. Leyland, who each hit two hundreds, were the only players on either side, apart from Bradman, to score more than one century.

# 1937–8

## AGED TWENTY-NINE

---

The New Zealanders who had toured England in 1937 played three matches in Australia on their way home.

### 139. SOUTH AUSTRALIA *v* NEW ZEALANDERS, at Adelaide, 5, 6 and 8 November 1937

SCORES: New Zealanders 151 and 186 (H.G. Vivian 64, F.A. Ward 7 for 62); South Australia 331 (C.L. Badcock 114, R.A. Hamence 56) and 7 for no wicket. South Australia won by 10 wickets.

D.G. BRADMAN (capt.)  c. E.W. Tindill b. J.A. Cowie        11
                (did not bat)        –

Going in half an hour before the end of the first day, at 38 for 2, Bradman was 11 not out overnight, but was caught at the wicket off his first ball next morning, at 65 for 3.

### 140. D.G. BRADMAN'S XI *v* V.Y. RICHARDSON'S XI (V.Y Richardson and C.V. Grimmett Testimonial), at Adelaide, 26 and 27 November 1937

SCORES: D.G. Bradman's XI 184; V.Y. Richardson's XI 380 for 9 wickets (C. L. Badcock 102, S.J. McCabe 72). Drawn.

D.G. BRADMAN (capt.)  b. C.V. Grimmett        17

Bradman went in at 64 for 1 just after lunch on the first day, and Grimmett, in his own testimonial match, had the satisfaction of puzzling him completely for several overs, and then bowling him; he was well out of his crease when he was deceived and bowled by a ball which he was trying to force to leg, after he had helped raise the score to 87 for 2 in 33 minutes.

## 141. SOUTH AUSTRALIA *v* WESTERN AUSTRALIA, at Adelaide, 3, 4 and 6 December 1937

SCORES: Western Australia 100 and 185; South Australia 264 (D.G. Bradman 101, M.E. Mueller 56, G. Eyres 5 for 58) and 22 for no wicket. South Australia won by 10 wickets.

| | | |
|---|---|---|
| D.G. BRADMAN (capt.) | c. R.J. Wilberforce b. G. Eyres | 101 |
| | (did not bat) | – |

South Australia were already in the lead with 116 for 4 when Bradman went in to bat on the second morning, and he took the opportunity for some steady practice against a weak attack. He made 50 in 85 minutes before being caught in the deep one minute later, just before the tea interval, at 259 for 9; he was responsible for 70 per cent of the runs added while he was in. The outfield was very slow and he hit only three fours in a chanceless but subdued innings in which he attacked the bowling only towards the end.

## 142. SOUTH AUSTRALIA *v* NEW SOUTH WALES, at Adelaide, 17, 18, 20 and 21 December 1937

SCORES: New South Wales 337 (S.J. McCabe 106, J.H. Fingleton 81, S.G. Barnes 79, C.V. Grimmett 5 for 103) and 104; South Australia 217 (D.G. Bradman 91, R.S. Whitington 54, W.J. O'Reilly 9 for 41) and 191 (C.L. Badcock 77, D.G. Bradman 62, W.J. O'Reilly 5 for 57). South Australia lost by 33 runs.

| | | |
|---|---|---|
| D.G. BRADMAN (capt.) | c. L.J. O'Brien b. W.J. O'Reilly | 91 |
| | c. A.G. Chipperfield b. W.J. O'Reilly | 62 |

O'Reilly bowled at his very best in this match, and there was a tremendous duel between him and Bradman. The latter's first innings started ten minutes before lunch on the second day, at 4 for 1, and was one of his slowest; he took an hour and 43 minutes to reach 50, and his 91 lasted two minutes over three and a half hours, for all of which time he was troubled by O'Reilly's accuracy and spin. He and Whitington added 141 for the second wicket, raising the score to 145 before O'Reilly, in his 18th over, got his first wicket; but by the close of play the score was 163 for 6, O'Reilly had taken 5 wickets for 1 run, and his analysis was then 23–11–18–5. Bradman himself was out , caught at square-leg off a skier, at 152 for 4, to the first aggressive stroke he had played against O'Reilly; he hit only four fours.

South Australia were set 225 to win and Bradman went in at 32 for 3, three minutes before the end of the third day's play. Two not out overnight, he and Badcock stayed together until just after lunch on the last day, putting on 121 for the fourth wicket and giving South Australia a great chance of victory. However, Bradman was caught at short-leg the over after Badcock's dismissal, without addition to the score, and from 153 for 5 South Australia soon collapsed again to O'Reilly. Bradman, who took 95 minutes to reach 50, hit six fours in an innings lasting an hour and 52 minutes; and again O'Reilly was the only bowler to trouble him.

## 142. SOUTH AUSTRALIA *v* QUEENSLAND, at Adelaide, 25, 27, 28 and 29 December 1937

SCORES: Queensland 93 (R.G. Williams 6 for 21) and 426 (R.E. Rogers 181, W.A. Brown 132); South Australia 429 for 8 wickets dec. (D.G. Bradman 246, M.G. Waite 52*) and 93 for 2 wickets. South Australia won by 8 wickets.

| | | |
|---|---|---|
| D.G. BRADMAN (capt.) c. G. Baker b. P.L. Dixon | 246 |
| not out | 39 |

Bradman, going in at 15 for 1, was 28 not out at the end of the first day, after three-quarters of an hour's batting, and next morning, continuing soundly, he proceeded to make another huge score off the Queensland bowlers. He completed 50 in 95 minutes, 100 in three hours 14 minutes, and 200 in five hours 26 minutes; and he was eventually out ten minutes from time, caught in the deep after a brilliant burst of hitting, having batted for six hours four minutes. He hit 20 fours, gave no chance, and had carried the score to 414 for 8; he added 110 with R.H. Robinson (49) for the fifth wicket, and 161 in two hours with Waite for the eighth wicket. He was responsible for 59 per cent of his side's runs (apart from extras).

This score of 246 remains the highest ever made in matches between South Australia and Queensland, the previous best being the 233 made by Bradman two seasons earlier; in 1939–40, C.L. Badcock came close to it with 236.

Bradman's and Waite's eighth-wicket partnership of 161 is the highest for that wicket for South Australia (previous best, 124 by L.R. Hill and W.A. Hewer *v* New South Wales, 1910–1), and the highest in a Sheffield Shield match against Queensland (previous best, 156 by C.J. Hill and W. Howell, for New South Wales, 1932–3); the previous best partnership for the eighth wicket for South Australia *v* Queensland was 112, by W.C. Alexander and N.L. Williams in 1926–7.

On the fourth morning, Bradman went in at 1 for 1, and batted sedately for 85 minutes before his partner made the winning hit.

## 144. SOUTH AUSTRALIA *v* VICTORIA, at Melbourne, 31 December 1937, 1, 3 and 4 January 1938

SCORES: South Australia 304 (R.S. Whitington 81, D.G. Bradman 54, C.L. Badcock 50, L.O'B. Fleetwood-Smith 9 for 135) and 356 (R.A. Hamence

64, R.H. Robinson 62, M.G. Waite 51); Victoria 364 (K.E. Rigg 118, I.S Lee 67, R.G. Gregory 61, C.V. Grimmett 6 for 95) and 144 for 4 wickets (J.A. Ledward 58*). Drawn.

D.G. BRADMAN (capt.)   c. M.W. Sievers b. R.G. Gregory     54
                  c. M.W. Sievers b. R.G. Gregory     35

Bradman, in at 69 for 1, had half an hour's batting before lunch on the first day, in which time he made 25 not out and had settled down comfortably after lunch, reaching 50 in one and a quarter hours, when rather surprisingly he flicked at an off-break and was caught at slip; his was the only wicket not to be taken by Fleetwood-Smith. He was out at 149 for 2, after batting for an hour and 22 minutes, and he hit four fours. When he was 9, he passed C. Hill's aggregate of 17,160, the previous highest number of runs in first-class cricket by any Australian batsman; this was Bradman's 212th innings, against 413 by Hill. He also broke another record of Hill's when he had made 45; Hill made 6,270 runs in Sheffield Shield matches, the highest on record, in 126 innings, and Bradman now passed this landmark in his 69th innings in Shield matches.

This December he made 593 runs, equal to the most he ever made in one month in Australia (he also made 593 in December 1938), a total which is slightly more than half the 1,146 amassed by W.H. Ponsford in December 1927. It is, however, a record for a South Australian batsman (previous best, 473 by Hill in December 1910).

Bradman's second innings started at 0 for 1, just after lunch on the third day, and again he settled down steadily before being out in the same way as in the first innings, this time reaching over to try to chop a widish leg-break, and touching it to slip. He batted for one and a quarter hours and was out at 67 for 3.

## 145. SOUTH AUSTRALIA v QUEENSLAND, at Brisbane, 8, 10, 11 and 12 January 1938

SCORES: South Australia 398 (D.G. Bradman 107, R.G. Williams 75*) and 287 for 8 wickets dec. (D.G. Bradman 113, M.G. Waite 58); Queensland 192 (G. Baker 70*) and 155 for 8 wickets (T. Allen 55, F.A. Ward 5 for 66). Drawn.

D.G. BRADMAN (capt.)   c. D. Tallon b. P.L. Dixon     107
                  c. J. Hackett b. T. Allen     113

For the second time in a Sheffield Shield match and for the third time altogether, Bradman put together two centuries in a match. His first innings, starting at 61 for 1 on the first morning, was a very solid affair, characterised by shrewd placing. He completed 50 in 85 minutes, 100 in two hours 35 minutes, and batted altogether for two and three-quarter hours before being caught at the wicket at 264 for 6, just after tea; he hit nine fours and gave no chance. This was his 24th century in Sheffield Shield matches, in his 71st innings; A.F. Kippax, the previous record-holder, had scored 23 Shield centuries in 95 innings.

South Australia batted again with a first-innings lead of 206 and Bradman went in 40 minutes from the end of the second day at 2 for 1, a wicket having fallen in the first over. On 20 not out overnight, he reached 50 next morning after 89 minutes altogether, and then completed his century in a further 33 minutes. Altogether his chanceless 113 lasted two hours 23 minutes and included ten fours, before he was caught in the deep just before lunch, virtually throwing his wicket away, at 177 for 5; he and Waite added 103 for the fifth wicket in 73 minutes. Queensland was saved by rain.

Bradman was the first batsman to make a century in each innings of a Sheffield Shield match on more than one occasion, and is the only Australian to make a century in each innings of any first-class match more than twice; he is also the only batsman to perform this feat more than twice in Australia, this being the third time he had done so. He did a fourth time in 1947–8.

This was only the third time that a century in each innings had been made for South Australia in a Sheffield Shield match, and the fourth time in all matches; it has now been done eight times in Shield matches, including twice by C. Pinch (1956–7 and 1957–8), and 11 times altogether, including twice by R.A. Hamence.

## 146. SOUTH AUSTRALIA *v* NEW SOUTH WALES, at Sydney, 15, 17, 18 and 19 January 1938

SCORES: South Australia 187 and 334 (C.L. Badcock 132, D.G. Bradman 104*); New South Wales 295 (S.J. McCabe 83, V.E. Jackson 63) and 227 for 6 wickets (J.H. Fingleton 74). South Australia lost by 4 wickets.

| D.G. BRADMAN (capt.) c. S.J. McCabe b. L.J. O'Brien | 44 |
|---|---|
| not out | 104 |

Bradman went in at 10 for 1 on the first morning, and early in his innings had a collision with mid-on going for a quick single, as a result of which he was rather dazed and his lip was cut; but he continued batting and was out at 93 for 4 just before lunch, caught off an indecisive stroke at second slip after 81 minutes at the wicket.

Facing first innings arrears of 108, South Australia had almost cleared them off, with 106 for 1, when Bradman joined Badcock just after lunch on the third day. Badcock was batting well, and Bradman was content to let him be the dominant partner in a stand of 95. Badcock, however, was run out at 201 for 2, and after that South Australian wickets fell at regular intervals, despite solid resistance from

Bradman. He took 95 minutes for his 50, completed his 1,000 runs for the season when he was 80, and was 86 when the last man came in; by clever tactics, however, he completed his century after three hours 26 minutes, four minutes before the end of play, when he was 101 not out. It was not one of his best innings, a cut hand interfering with his timing; but W.J. O'Reilly was among the bowlers. The innings soon finished next morning and Bradman was left with 104*, after three hours 37 minutes; he hit 13 fours and gave no chance.

In completing his 1,000 runs on 18 January, he was 15 days earlier than the previous best by a South Australian batsman, he himself having reached this total in 1936–7 on 2 February; Bradman improved upon this by five days in 1939–40.

He showed his versatility by keeping wicket when C.W. Walker was injured, his record being five byes and a stumping in the first innings, and three byes and three good catches in the second.

## 147. SOUTH AUSTRALIA v VICTORIA, at Adelaide, 4, 5, 7 and 8 February 1938

SCORES: South Australia 157 (M.W. Sievers 6 for 43) and 340 (R.S. Whitington 86, D.G. Bradman 85); Victoria 195 and 177 (R.G. Williams 5 for 52). South Australia won by 125 runs.

| D.G. BRADMAN (capt.) | b. E.L. McCormick | 3 |
| | c. J.A. Ledward b. F. Thorn | 85 |

Bradman went in at 4 for 1, on the first morning, and was bowled by his fourth ball, a fast in-swinger, at 7 for 2. His second innings was much better; going in on the third afternoon at 95 for 1, he completed 50 in 53 minutes and batted for only 85 minutes for his 85. He and Whitington added 113 in 70 minutes for the second wicket, and Bradman was rather surprisingly caught at short fine-leg, off a medium-paced in-swinger, at 226 for 4; he hit nine fours.

## 148. AUSTRALIANS v TASMANIA, at Launceston, 26, 28 February, 1 March 1938

SCORES: Australians 477 (S.J. McCabe 83, D.G. Bradman 79, A.L. Hassett 75, J.H. Fingleton 66, S.G. Barnes 53*, D. Thollar 5 for 116) and 172 for 4 wickets dec. (S.G. Barnes 89); Tasmania 112 and 151. Australians won by 386 runs.

| D.G. BRADMAN (capt.) | c. C.J. Samkey b. R.V. Thomas | 79 |
| | (did not bat) | – |

The Australians enjoyed some lighthearted practice against weak bowling, and Bradman, coming in at 138 for 2 on the first afternoon, hit up a faultless 50 in 71 minutes before trying to get himself out, giving two deliberate chances in the deep, after passing 70, before finding a fieldsman who would catch him, at deep square-leg; he batted for 84 minutes, hit a six and five fours, and was out at 302 for 4. He and McCabe added 113 for the fourth wicket in 50 minutes.

## 149. AUSTRALIANS v TASMANIA, at Hobart, 3, 4 and 5 March 1938

SCORES: Australians 520 (C.L. Badcock 159, D.G. Bradman 144) and 240 for 3 wickets dec. (J.H. Fingleton 109, W.A. Brown 108); Tasmania 194 (W.J. O'Reilly 5 for 34) and 81 (W.J. O'Reilly 6 for 16). Australians won by 485 runs.

| D.G. BRADMAN (capt.) | b. C.L. Jeffrey | 144 |
| | (did not bat) | – |

Bradman was again in tremendous form against the weak Tasmanian attack; he went in at 111 for 2 on the first afternoon, and when he was out an hour and 38 minutes later, he and Badcock had carried the score to 352 for 3, Bradman's share of the third-wicket stand of 241 being 144 (an average of 88 and hour), including three sixes (off successive balls, soon after completing his century) and 19 fours. He took only 40 minutes to reach 50, one and a quarter hours for his century, and then added 44 on another 23 minutes. He gave a very hard chance to the bowler, C. Oakes, in the fifties, and in trying to throw his wicket away was missed by a skier at deep mid-off at 143; he then let himself be bowled just before the tea interval.

## 150. AUSTRALIANS v WESTERN AUSTRALIA, at Perth, 18, 19 and 21 March 1938

SCORES: Western Australia 192 and 73 (W.J. O'Reilly 5 for 12); Australians 391 (S.J. McCabe 122, D.G. Bradman 102). Australians won by an innings and 126 runs.

| D.G. BRADMAN (capt.) | st. O.I. Lovelock b. A.G. Zimbulis | 102 |

Bradman went in at 2 for 1, late on the first day, and again enjoyed himself against mediocre bowling, reaching 50 in 55 minutes, and being 68 not out at the close of play, after 85 minutes. Next morning he completed his century after a minute less than two hours' batting, and threw his wicket away next over, three minutes later; he was all but caught in the slips when 99, the ball just failing to carry, and his timing was not so perfect as usual. He and McCabe put on 121 for the third wicket in 72 minutes, and he hit ten fours; he was dismissed at 189 for 3 and gave no actual chance.

## SUMMARY, 1937–8

| | Matches | Innings | NO | HS | Runs | Average | Centuries |
|---|---|---|---|---|---|---|---|
| All First-class Matches | 12 | 18 | 2 | 246 | 1437 | 89.81 | 7 |
| Match v NZ Team | 1 | 1 | 0 | 11 | 11 | – | 0 |
| Sheffield Shield Matches | 6 | 12 | 2 | 246 | 983 | 98.30 | 4 |
| All Matches for South Australia | 8 | 14 | 2 | 246 | 1095 | 91.25 | 5 |

For the ninth time in successive Australian seasons (excluding 1934–5, when he did not play), Bradman exceeded 1,000 runs, this being the third successive season he had done so since transferring to South Australia; no other South Australian batsman has done so more than twice. For the third time he made seven centuries in a season in Australia, and he passed his own record, set up the previous season, for the number of hundreds in a season by a South Australian player; in 1947–8 he scored eight centuries.

Bradman's aggregate of 983 runs in Sheffield Shield matches was a record for South Australia, the previous best being his own 739 in 1935–6; his four centuries in a season in Shield matches were also a record for a South Australia batsman, the previous best being three, by seven players, including Bradman in 1935–6. Bradman broke both these records again later, with five Shield centuries in 1938–9 and 1,063 Shield runs in 1939–40.

With five centuries this season in all matches for South Australia, Bradman beat C. Hill's record of four in 1897–8, which he equalled in 1935–6; Bradman also made five in 1938–9 and 1939–40.

A.L. Hassett, with an average of 53.30, was second to Bradman this season in the Australian first-class averages, while C.L. Badcock, with 872 runs and four centuries, was second both in aggregate and in number of centuries.

# 1938

## AGED TWENTY-NINE

———————— ●━◆›◉‹◆━● ————————

Bradman was still a member of the Australian Selection Committee and was, of course, appointed captain of the team which toured England this season.

151. **AUSTRALIANS** *v* **WORCESTERSHIRE**, at Worcester, 30 April, 2 and 3 May 1938

SCORES: Australians 541 (D.G. Bradman 258, C.L. Badcock 67); Worcestershire 268 (E. Cooper 61, Hon. C.J. Lyttelton 50, L.O'B. Fleetwood-Smith 8 for 98) and 196 (C.H. Bull 69). Australians won by an innings and 77 runs.

D.G. BRADMAN (capt.)  c. S.H. Martin b. R. Howorth        258

Worcestershire, winning the toss, surprisingly put the Australians in to bat on a perfect wicket, and they took full advantage of this opportunity for some batting practice. Bradman went in at 9 for 1, 15 minutes after the start of the first day's play, and commenced with great care, taking an hour and three-quarters before lunch to score 37. After the interval he began to find his form and confidence; completing 50 in two hours seven minutes, he then raced to his century in another 38 minutes. After that he scored much as he pleased, adding 145 in two hours between lunch and tea; he reached 200 in four hours four minutes, and was at the wicket altogether for four hours 53 minutes for his 258. He was then caught in the slips, attempting to cut, with the score 428 for 5; he gave no chance, hit a five and 33 fours, and he and Badcock put on 277 for the fourth wicket in two hours 34 minutes.

This was the third successive tour in which he had started with a double century at Worcester in his first innings, a quite unprecedented achievement, and on this occasion the bowlers included R.J. Crisp and R.T.D. Perks, in addition to Howorth; he made 50 per cent of the Australian score (excluding extras), and his 258 is still the highest score *v* Worcestershire, and on the Worcester ground, by an Australian or any other touring batsman (previous best, 236 by Bradman in 1930).

In starting a first-class season in England with a double century in his first innings for the third time, Bradman did something which no other batsman,

English or visiting, had ever done more than once. His 258 was then the highest innings ever played by a visiting batsman in his first innings of an English tour, Bradman's 236 in 1930 being the previous best; K.R. Miller passed this record in 1956 with a score of 281* *v* Leicestershire.

It is also the highest score ever made on the opening day of first-class cricket in any English season, and the only double century; the previous highest was 176, by F.C. de Saram in 1934, while in 1951 J.T. Ikin made 192. Bradman is the only batsman, English or touring, ever to make centuries on the first days of two English seasons, he having reached 112 not out in 1934 before the end of the first day's play; the only other Australians to achieve this even once are C.G. Macartney (1921) and W.M. Woodfull (1930).

The total of 258 is also the highest score and the highest number of runs ever made in any April in England, the previous score being 181 by E.H.D. Sewell in 1904, and the most runs 190, in four innings, by W.G. Grace in 1902; for the Australians, Macartney made 140 not out *v* Leicestershire in April 1921. Ikin's 192 in 1951 was made in April and is now the next highest to Bradman's 258.

The partnership of 277 with Badcock was till then the highest ever made against Worcestershire for the fourth wicket, the previous highest being 263 by G. Lavis and C. Smart for Glamorgan, in 1934; however, A.V. Avery and R. Horsfall passed this in 1948 with a fourth-wicket stand of 298 for Essex.

This was the sixth time, out of ten altogether, that Bradman had made three (or more) centuries in successive innings, thus breaking the record he previously shared with W.G. Grace, J.B. Hobbs and W.H. Ponsford.


## 152. AUSTRALIANS *v* OXFORD UNIVERSITY, at Oxford (Christ Church ground), 4, 5 and 6 May 1938

SCORES: Australians 679 for 7 wickets dec. (A.L. Hassett 146, J.H. Fingleton 124, S.J. McCabe 110, W.A. Brown 72, D.G. Bradman 58, M.G. Waite 54, A.G. Chipperfield 53); Oxford University 117 (J.D. Eggar 51*, L.O'B. Fleetwood-Smith 5 for 28) and 75. Australians won by an innings and 487 runs.

D.G. BRADMAN (capt.)  lbw. b. G. Evans        58

All the first seven Australian batsmen reached 50 in this match, and Bradman's part in the butchery of the Oxford attack was a comparatively modest one. Going in at 140 for 1 soon after lunch on the first day, he all but gave a chance in the slips off D.H. Macindoe when 1; but thereafter he found no difficulty in the bowling. He reached 50 in 57 minutes, but five minutes later was rather surprisingly beaten by a straight ball which he tried to push to leg. Out at 245 for 2, he had helped Fingleton to add 105 for the second wicket; his strokes included eight fours.

## 153. AUSTRALIANS *v* CAMBRIDGE UNIVERSITY, at Cambridge, 11, 12 and 13 May 1938

SCORES: Cambridge University 120 (N.W.D. Yardley 67, M.G. Waite 5 for 23, W.J. O'Reilly 5 for 55) and 163 (P.A. Gibb 80*, F.A. Ward 6 for 64); Australians 708 for 5 wickets dec. (A.L. Hassett 220*, C.L. Badcock 186, D.G. Bradman 137, J.H. Fingleton 111). Australians won by an innings and 425 runs.

D.G. BRADMAN (capt.)  c. F.G. Mann b. J.V. Wild      137

There was nothing in the weak University bowling to prevent Bradman getting another century, and this he duly achieved. He went in on the first afternoon at 3 for 1 and completed his 50 in an hour; after tea, he advanced steadily to his century, which he reached in two hours 20 minutes. He was finally caught at cover, failing to get on top of a short ball, at 281 for 3, after batting for two hours 48 minutes. He was not, perhaps, at his best, but he gave no chance, hit 20 fours, and he and Fingleton put on 215 for the second wicket in two hours 23 minutes.

## 154. AUSTRALIANS *v* MCC, at Lord's, 14 and 16 May 1938

SCORES: Australians 502 (D.G. Bradman 278, A. L. Hassett 57, C.I.J. Smith 6 for 139); MCC 214 (R.E.S. Wyatt 84*) and 87 for 1 wicket (W.J. Edrich 53*). Drawn.

D.G. BRADMAN (capt.)  c. R.W.V. Robins b. C.I.J. Smith      278

MCC's strong bowling side included K. Farnes, C.I.J. Smith, J.W.A. Stephenson and R.W.V. Robins, but Bradman played one of his finest innings and put his side into a winning position before rain washed out the last day's play. He came in at 11 for 1, at 11.52 a.m. on the first day, and found at first that the wicket was helpful to the bowlers, Stephenson especially giving him trouble, and once hitting him painfully on the toe to have him nearly lbw. when he had scored only three. However, he soon got on top, reached 50 in 70 minutes, and was 68 at lunch; after the interval he was always the master and displayed sure defence as well as brilliant strokes. He completed his century in a minute under two and a half hours, and settled down again to achieve another double century, which he did after four hours 26 minutes at the wicket. By the close of play, after batting for five hours 26 minutes, he had made 257 not out; and he had never looked like getting out once he had settled down. He and Fingleton (44) put on 138 for the second wicket, and he and Hassett added 162 for the fifth wicket.

Next morning he carried his score to 278 before being well caught at cover in trying to square-cut a short ball. His innings lasted five hours 49 minutes, included a six and 35 fours, and concluded with the score 454 for 6; it was quite chanceless and scarcely included a false stroke, while his mastery on the leg side was particularly noticeable. The other batsmen contributed 209 and Bradman's share was 57 per cent.

This was his eighth successive innings of over 50, then a record for an Australian, beating the seven fifties he scored in succession in 1933–4 and 1934; in 1947–8 and 1948, Bradman made ten fifties in consecutive innings, which equalled E. Tyldesley's world record. This was also the 14th successive match in which Bradman made 50 in one innings or the other – the next best performance to his own record spell of 16 successive matches in 1932–3–4.

Including his 102 in his last innings in Australia in 1937–8, he had now scored 833 runs in five successive innings (102, 258, 58, 137, 278), the second highest of his career; and including his 132 in his last innings in 1934, he scored 863 in five consecutive innings in England (132, 258, 58, 137, 278), a record for an overseas player in England, the previous best being 788 by C.G. Macartney in 1921.

Bradman's highest score at Lord's was 278 and was only just short of the Australian record for the ground, 281* by W.H. Ponsford v MCC in 1934.

## 155. AUSTRALIANS v NORTHAMPTONSHIRE, at Northampton, 18, 19 and 20 May 1938

SCORES: Australians 406 for 6 wickets dec. (W.A. Brown 194*, C.L. Badcock 72); Northamptonshire 194 (R.P. Nelson 74, F.A. Ward 6 for 75) and 135. Australians won by an innings and 77 runs.

D.G. BRADMAN (capt.) c. K.C. James b. R.J. Partridge    2

Going in early on the second day on a damp but rather dead pitch, with the 131 for 1, Bradman gave an uninspiring display, batting for 22 minutes before being caught at the wicket at 143 for 2. This was a sharp reversal of form after his first four innings had realised 731 runs.

## 156. AUSTRALIANS v SURREY, at the Oval, 21, 23 and 24 May 1938

SCORES: Australians 528 (D.G. Bradman 143, A.L. Hassett 98, W.A. Brown 96) and 232 for 2 wickets dec. (B.A. Barnett 120*, C.L. Badcock 95); Surrey 271 (T.H. Barling 67, R.J. Gregory 60, W.J. O'Reilly 8 for 104) and 104 for 1 wicket (L.B. Fishlock 93). Drawn.

D.G. BRADMAN (capt.) c. E.W.J. Brooks b. E.A. Watts    143

Bradman went in on the first morning with the score 90 for 1 and, if he began none too certainly, he was soon playing as soundly as ever. It took him only 69 minutes to reach 50, and two and a quarter hours to reach 100; but thereafter, rather surprisingly, he slowed down and his innings lasted altogether for three hours 18 minutes. He was then well caught at the wicket on the leg side, with the score 349 for 4; he gave no chance and hit 11 fours off bowlers who included A.R. Gover and F.R. Brown. He and W.A. Brown added 120 for the second wicket; he had now scored 876 runs so far this season.

Bradman, did not enforce the follow-on, a course which met with some criticism; but by giving some of his later batsmen batting practice, he himself unselfishly missed a great opportunity for raising his aggregate towards his 1,000 runs by the end of May.

## 157. AUSTRALIANS v HAMPSHIRE, at Southampton, 26 and 27 May 1938

SCORES: Hampshire 157 (W.J. O'Reilly 6 for 65); Australians 320 for 1 wicket dec. (D.G. Bradman 145*, J.H. Fingleton 123*). Drawn.

D.G. BRADMAN (capt.)  not out                   145

Wednesday's play having been washed out, Bradman put Hampshire in to bat on a drying wicket, which was rather easier when the Australians began their innings. Bradman went in just before tea, at 78 for 1, and had scored 71 not out in an hour and 57 minutes by the end of the day, having reached 50 in 87 minutes; he was sometimes worried by the Hampshire spin bowlers, G.S. Boyes and G. Hill, who derived considerable help from the wicket.

Next morning the wicket was again affected by rain and was more difficult, though the Hampshire captain chose to rely mainly on his faster bowlers when it would probably have given more assistance to his spinners, as Boyes and Hill showed when they were eventually put on. Bradman and Fingleton were both uncomfortable at times but, showing sound defence, they stayed together until lunch-time, adding 242 for the second wicket without being separated. Bradman reached his century in a minute over two and a half hours, but when he was 109 rain interrupted play for 27 minutes. At 1.08 p.m., however, he carried his score past 124, and thereby reached his goal of 1,000 runs, this being the second time he had completed 1,000 runs before the end of May; he batted altogether for three hours 26 minutes without giving a chance, and hit 22 fours. He declared at lunch, but rain prevented any further play.

Only six batsmen altogether have completed 1,000 runs before the end of May; Bradman is the only one to do so twice, and the only Australian or touring batsman ever to perform this feat. Bradman is also the earliest to do so, on 27 May (previous best, 28 May, by W.R. Hammond, 1927); he reached his goal in his seventh innings of the season, the fewest on record by a batsman in England, the previous best being ten innings by W.G. Grace in 1985, though W.H. Ponsford, in Australia in 1927–8, reached 1,000 for the season in his fifth innings; the previous best in England by an Australian or other touring batsman was 11 innings by Bradman in 1930, and 13 innings by S.J. McCabe in 1934, while in 1948 Bradman reached 1,000 ahead of any English batsman, and he did so again in 1948; of touring players, only W.L. Murdoch, in 1882, and C.G. Macartney, in 1912, had done so before.

## 158. AUSTRALIANS v MIDDLESEX, at Lord's 30 and 31 May 1938

SCORES: Australians 132 and 114 for 2 wickets dec.; Middlesex 188 (D.C.S. Compton 65, E.L. McCormick 6 for 58) and 21 for no wicket. Drawn.

| | |
|---|---|
| D.G. BRADMAN (capt.) c. D.C.S. Compton b. W Nevell | 5 |
| not out | 30 |

After rain had prevented any play on Saturday, Bradman chose to bat on winning the toss on Monday morning and found that the damp wicket helped the bowlers more than he had anticipated; he himself, going in at 2 for 1, gave an uncharacteristic display, being missed at long-leg off Nevell when 0, off a wild heave, before being well caught off another crude stroke, Compton running across from slip to catch a nasty skier at short-leg. He was second out at 16, having survived uneasily for 21 minutes.

On the second afternoon he went in at 0 for 1, when the wicket was still taking spin, though only slowly, and after a hesitant start he displayed much better form, though this time he took no risks at all; his innings, which was twice interrupted by bad light, lasted an hour and 37 minutes altogether (an average of 18 an hour) and in making only 30 of the 114 added while he was in, he scored 26 per cent of the total added – the second-lowest proportion of his career; he hit no fours and as many as 22 singles. Although he himself wanted only another 19 runs for a record aggregate by the end of May, he generously declared 21 minutes before the close to give W.J. Edrich the opportunity of scoring the ten runs he needed to complete his 1,000, a feat which he duly accomplished.

Bradman's total by the end of May was thus 1,056, which is, of course, a record for an Australian or other visiting batsman, the previous being his own 1,001 in 1930.

## 159. AUSTRALIA v ENGLAND, First Test match, at Nottingham, 10, 11, 12 and 14 June 1938

SCORES: England 658 for 8 wickets dec. (E. Paynter 216*, C.J. Barnett 126, D.C.S. Compton 102, L. Hutton 100); Australia 411 (S.J. McCabe 232, D.G. Bradman 51) and 427 for 6 wickets dec. (D.G. Bradman 144*, W.A. Brown 133). Drawn.

| D.G. BRADMAN (capt.) c. L.E.G. Ames b. R.A. Sinfield | 51 |
| not out | 144 |

England's huge first-innings score left Australia nothing to play for except a draw, with about two and a half days' play remaining. Bradman went in for his first innings at 34 for 1 on the second afternoon and was soon in difficulties against D.V.P. Wright, who failed to take a hard return when he was 7, and frequently puzzled and beat him. He was 7 not out at the tea interval and afterwards gradually settled down, though he was again missed, in the gully off Farnes, when he was 47. He reached 50 in 85 minutes, but four minutes later was well caught at the wicket, off the inside edge of his bat and then his pads. He hit five fours and was out to his 95th ball at 111 for 2. He was replaced by McCabe, who next morning played one of the finest innings in cricket history, hitting 232 in three hours 55 minutes.

The chance of safety which this great innings gave Australia was seized by Bradman in his second innings. He went in at 89 for 1, 20 minutes before the close of the third day's play, and in that time he made 3 not out; and he then batted almost the whole of the last day, in an innings of dour defence and ruthless concentration which saved the game for Australia. The wicket was dry and beginning to break up, and both Verity and Wright made the ball spin unpleasantly at times; but, despite a strained leg, Bradman's defence was equal to all the demands put upon it. Being 44 not out at lunch, he completed his 50 soon afterwards in two and a half hours, his slowest in a Test match, and his century took four hours and 13 minutes, the slowest of his career; he reached it at 4.08 p.m. At 118 at the tea interval, he was 144 not out, after six hours five minutes' chanceless batting, when he declared at 15 minutes before the end of the match.

Scoring at only 23 runs an hour, his slowest century, he was at the wicket while 338 were added to the score, this 42 per cent being his lowest proportion in an innings of 100 and over – though in this case it was time, not runs, which mattered.

He received 376 balls. He hit five fours and he and Brown added 170 for the second wicket in three hours five minutes; this was his 13th century against England in Test matches, one more than the number scored by J.B. Hobbs against Australia, in 71 innings, while this was Bradman's 42nd innings against England. Bradman finished with 19 centuries in Tests between England and Australia.

This was the third occasion on which Bradman made over 50 in each innings of a Test match, all v England; up till then, only M.A. Noble had done this three times for Australia v England, and only Noble, W. Bardsley, C. Hill and J.S. Ryder had done so for Australia in all Tests. Bradman added a fourth occasion v India in 1947–8, and A.R. Morris has since also done so four times, all v England.

His 144* was his fourth successive Test innings of 50 and over, all v England; in Tests between England and Australia only four Australians (Hill, H.L. Collins,

J.M. Gregory and McCabe) and two Englishmen (Hobbs and H. Sutcliffe) had previously done this, though Morris later did so twice, and P.B.H. May, in 1954–5 and 1956, played five consecutive innings of 50 and over *v* Australia. In all Tests, the only Australians to achieve four successive fifties up till then were Hill, Collins, Gregory, McCabe, Bardsley and J.H. Fingleton; Bradman (1947–8 and 1948) and R.N. Harvey later made five fifties in consecutive Test innings.

## 160. AUSTRALIANS *v* GENTLEMEN OF ENGLAND, at Lord's, 15, 16 and 17 June 1938

SCORES: Australians 397 (D.G. Bradman 104, S.J. McCabe 79, A.G. Chipperfield 51, R.J.O. Meyer 5 for 66) and 335 for 4 wickets dec. (J.H. Fingleton 121, C.L. Badcock 112*); Gentlemen of England 301 (F.R. Brown 88, D.R. Wilcox 50, F.A. Ward 5 for 108) and 149 (P.A. Gibb 67, L.O'B. Fleetwood-Smith 7 for 44). Australians won by 282 runs.

| | | |
|---|---|---|
| D.G. BRADMAN (capt.) | c. B.H. Valentine b. R.J.O. Meyer | 104 |
| | (did not bat) | – |

Batting as low as sixth, Bradman went in on the first afternoon at 212 for 4 and played a gay innings against an attack which included J.W.A. Stephenson, D.H. Macindoe, R.J.O. Meyer and F.R. Brown. He reached 50 in 49 minutes and 100 in an hour and 48 minutes, before being caught at deep long-leg for a chanceless 104; he was out at 389 for 8, after batting for an hour and 54 minutes and hitting 13 fours.

## 161. AUSTRALIANS *v* LANCASHIRE, at Manchester, 18, 20 and 21 June 1938

SCORES: Australians 303 (A.L. Hassett 118, C.L. Badcock 96, W.E. Phillipson 5 for 93) and 284 for 2 wickets dec. (D.G. Bradman 101*, J.H. Fingleton 96, W.E. Phillipson 52) and 80 for 3 wickets. Drawn.

| | | |
|---|---|---|
| D.G. BRADMAN (capt.) | c. R. Pollard b. W.E. Phillipson | 12 |
| | not out | 101 |

Good bowling on the first morning by Phillipson on a green pitch accounted for three Australian wickets, including that of Bradman, falling for 35 in the first innings; Bradman went in at 14 for 1, and was caught at second slip in trying to drive, at 35 for 3. He batted for 29 minutes.

He was in his best form in his second innings; he went in at 153 for 1, on the third afternoon, and reached 50 in 40 minutes and 100 in 73 minutes, before declaring four minutes later. Despite the pace at which he scored (an average of 79 an hour), he gave no chance and, indeed, scarcely appeared ot be hurrying; yet he hit 15 fours – many of them powerful strokes off his back foot – and scored all but 30 of the runs added while he was in, or 77 per cent, this being the highest proportion he ever achieved in a century innings. Lancashire's bowlers included Phillipson, Pollard, A.E. Nutter, L.L. Wilkinson and J.L. Hopwood.

This was his first century at Old Trafford in his fourth match there.

162. **AUSTRALIA** *v* **ENGLAND**, Second Test match, at Lord's, 24, 25, 27 and 28 June 1938

SCORES: England 494 (W.R. Hammond 240, E. Paynter 99, L.E.G. Ames 83 ) and 242 for 8 wickets dec. (D.C.S. Compton 76*); Australia 422 (W.A. Brown 206*, A.L. Hassett 56) and 204 for 6 wickets (D.G. Bradman 102*). Drawn.

| D.G. BRADMAN (capt.) | b. Verity | 18 |
| | not out | 102 |

Going in on the second afternoon at 69 for 1, Bradman commenced in his best form, but at 101 for 2, after batting for 26 minutes, he was deceived by a ball (his 26th) from Verity which came in with the arm and, in attempting a cut, dragged it on to his wicket.

England's declaration, at 3.20 p.m. on the fourth day, set Australia 315 to win, an impossible task in the time available, and the only question was whether Australia could be dismissed by 6.30; Bradman, with another fine innings, soon answered that question. He went in at 8 for 1, 42 minutes before the tea interval, and had by then scored 38 not out. He completed 50 in 62 minutes, and after two hours 22 minutes reached his century, five minutes before play ended; he hit 15 fours, gave no chance, and again did not give the impression of scoring fast, though his forcing shots through the covers were particularly brilliant; he scored runs off 131 balls. England's bowlers were K. Farnes, A.W. Wellard, D.V.P. Wright, H. Verity and W.J. Edrich.

When Bradman was 18 he passed J.B. Hobbs' aggregate of 3,636, the previous record for Tests between England and Australia; this was the 44th innings, whereas Hobbs batted 71 times *v* Australia.

From the start of the third Test match, 1936–7, Bradman had now scored over 1,000 runs in five consecutive Test matches, all *v* England; Bradman (twice) and Hammond (once) had previously made 1,000 runs in six consecutive Tests, and one of Bradman's two such feats had been entirely against England bowling. On the earlier occasion, Bradman took eight innings to reach this total, whereas now it took him nine innings.

Hammond batted magnificently for England.

## 163. AUSTRALIANS *v* YORKSHIRE, at Sheffield, 2, 4 and 5 July 1938

SCORES: Australians 222 (A.L. Hassett 94, D.G. Bradman 59, T.F. Smailes 6 for 92) and 132; Yorkshire 205 (M.G. Waite 7 for 101) and 83 for 3 wickets. Drawn.

| | | |
|---|---|---|
| D.G. BRADMAN (capt.) | st. A. Wood b. T.F. Smailes | 59 |
| | c. W. Barber b. T.F. Smailes | 42 |

Yorkshire, winning the toss, put the Australians in to bat on a rain-affected wicket, which gave W.E. Bowes, T.F. Smailes, E.P. Robinson and H. Verity (probably the best bad-wicket combination in England) a great deal of assistance. Bradman went in at 6 for 1, and struggled to 48 by lunch-time; when 12, he might have been caught at second slip off Bowes, the ball just failing to go to hand. He reached 50 in 92 minutes, and batted altogether for an hour and 43 minutes for his 59; out at 101 for 4, he hit six fours in a solid innings in which, though often uncomfortable, he did well to master the difficult conditions.

The wicket was equally difficult when he came in at 10 for 1 on the second afternoon; cutting at his first ball, he was missed in the slips off Bowes, but thereafter he played another good innings on a bad wicket, though he was often in trouble against Bowes, who bowled splendidly. He was in for exactly two hours before being caught, via his pads, at short-leg; he made top score for the Australians, and after he left at 108 for 5, the remaining wickets fell for only 24.

Rain at lunch-time on the last day foiled Yorkshire when they wanted only another 67 runs for victory on an easy wicket.

\*\*\*

The third Test match was to have been played at Manchester on 8, 9, 11 and 12 July 1938, but was abandoned owing to rain without a ball being bowled.

## 164. AUSTRALIANS *v* WARWICKSHIRE, at Birmingham, 13 and 14 July 1938

SCORES: Warwickshire 179 (J.S. Ord 61) and 118; Australians 390 for 8 wickets dec. (D.G. Bradman 135, W.A. Brown 101, W.E. Hollies 5 for 130). Australians won by an innings and 93 runs.

| | | |
|---|---|---|
| D.G. BRADMAN (capt.) | c. K. Wilmot b. J.H. Mayer | 135 |

Bradman won the toss and put Warwickshire in on a soft wicket, a successful move; and he himself, going in at 17 for 1, had two and a half hours' batting on the first day, at the end of which he was 116 not out. Cautious at first on the slow wicket, he took one hour and 42 minutes to reach 50, but thereafter hit out brilliantly, completing his century in another 37 minutes (two hours 19 minutes altogether).

Next morning he lashed out at once, and after 13 minutes threw his wicket away, caught at short-leg. He was out at 223 for 2, he and Brown having added 206 for the second wicket; he batted for two hours 43 minutes, scoring his last 85 in 61 minutes. He gave no chance, and hit 14 fours. Warwickshire's best bowlers were W.E. Hollies and G.A.E. Paine.

### 165. AUSTRALIANS v NOTTINGHAMSHIRE, at Nottingham, 16, 18 and 19 July 1938

SCORES: Australians 243 (S.G. Barnes 58, D.G. Bradman 56) and 453 for 4 wickets dec (D.G. Bradman 144, A.L. lHassett 124, W.A. Brown 63, C.L. Badcock 54); Nottinghamshire 147 (G.V. Gunn 75, W.J. O'Reilly 5 for 39) and 137 (J. Hardstaff 67*, L.O'B. Fleetwood-Smith 5 for 39). Australians won by 142 runs.

| D.G. BRADMAN (capt.) | lbw. b. A. Jepson | 56 |
| | c. A. Jepson b. E.A. Marshall | 144 |

In at 8 for 1 early on the first day, Bradman soon settled down, despite poor light, and reached 50 in 83 minutes; and it was a surprise when, seven minutes later, he was lbw. in trying to turn a straight ball to leg. He was out just before lunch at 99 for 4; he hit three fours.

He committed no such error in his second innings; he went in at 121 for 1 and was 55 not out at the end of the second day, after batting for 94 minutes; his 50 took 84 minutes. Next morning he went steadily ahead, and reached his century in two hours 37 minutes; he then added another 44 in 22 minutes and finished by hitting a six off Marshall, being dropped in the covers next ball (when 139), hitting another four, and being caught at mid-off later in the over. Out at 404 for 4, he hit one six and 15 fours in an innings lasting a minute less than three hours, which included only the one chance; he and Hassett added 216 in two hours 24 minutes for the third wicket, off bowlers who included W. Voce.

When Bradman was 98, he completed 20,000 runs in first-class cricket, being the first Australian (and still the only one) to do so; this was his 243rd innings in first-class cricket, while the next quickest, K.S. Ranjitsinhji, took 401 innings to reach this landmark and, later, D.C.S. Compton took 385.

Bradman also completed 2,000 runs for the season when he was 120; this was on 19 July which, apart from his own achievement in 1930 of reaching this total on 11 July, is the earliest that any touring batsman has done so. He took only 21 innings to reach this aggregate, fewer than anyone else on record; the previous best was 23 innings, by T. Hayward in 1906, and by Bradman in 1930, while in 1950 E.D. Weekes required 22 innings.

Bradman beat W.R. Hammond to this aggregate by only two hours; this was the second time (the other being in 1930) that he was the first player, English or Australian, to reach 2,000 runs for the season; only V.T. Trumper (1902) and W. Bardsley (1912) among touring batsmen have, once each, done this before.

This was his 11th century of the season, the same number as Trumper hit in 1902; Trumper had 53 innings that season, while this was Bradman's 21st. It brought the number of centuries he had scored in England to 28, one more than the previous record of 27 hundreds, set up by Bardsley, on four tours and in 175 innings; this was Bradman's 84th innings in England.

166. **AUSTRALIA** *v* **ENGLAND**, Third Test match, at Leeds, 22, 23 and 25 July 1938

SCORES: England 223 (W.R. Hammond 76, W.J. O'Reilly 5 for 66) and 123 (W.J. O'Reilly 5 for 56); Australia 242 (D.G. Bradman 103, B.A. Barnett 57) and 107 for 5 wickets. Australia won by 5 wickets and retained the Ashes.

| D.G. BRADMAN (capt.) | b. W.E. Bowes | 103 |
| | c. H. Verity b. D.V.P. Wright | 16 |

Bradman's first innings was one of his greatest, and perhaps in no other was his superiority to his fellow-batsmen so pronounced. In at 87 for 2, at 12.55 p.m. on the second afternoon, he was 17 not out at lunch; thereafter, on a dampish wicket which always gave the bowlers, especially the faster ones (Farnes and Brown), some help, and in a light which got steadily worse, he batted easily and commandingly while wickets fell regularly at the other end. He completed 50 in 92 minutes, and when light eventually stopped play at 3.57 he was 71; after a 22-minute interval, he went on to reach 100 in two hours 50 minutes, and eight minutes later, at 4.58 p.m., lost his middle stump to a fine ball from Bowes. He gave no chance, hit nine fours, and despite bad light scarcely made a bad stroke; he was out at 240 for 8, having by astute nursing of his partners managed to get his side the first-innings lead, and he made his 103 off 187 balls out of 153 added while he was in, or 67 per cent, equal to the best proportion of his career for Test match innings of 100 and over.

This was his 12th century of the season, and he thereby broke V.T. Trumper's 36-year-old record for the most centuries scored in a season by an Australian or other touring batsman in England, which he had equalled in the previous match.

When he had made 26, he completed 5,000 runs in all Test matches; he was the third batsman and first Australian to do so, in his 56th innings; the only other batsmen to reach this landmark are all Englishmen: J.B. Hobbs (91 innings), W.R. Hammond (97 innings), L. Hutton (98 innings) and D.C.S. Compton (113 innings). At 29 years of age, he is the youngest to reach this aggregate, Hammond at 33 being the next best.

Australia had to work hard on the third afternoon to make 105 to win, again in bad light and with a storm threatening. Bradman came in at 17 for 1, and was out 35 minutes and 31 balls later at 50 for 3, caught at second slip in trying to cut a leg-break; Hassett then hit out and carried Australia almost to victory.

### 167. AUSTRALIANS *v* SOMERSET, at Taunton, 27, 28 and 29 July 1938

SCORES: Somerset 110 and 136 (L.O'B. Fleetwood-Smith 5 for 30); Australians 464 for 6 wickets dec. (D.G. Bradman 202, C.L. Badcock 110, S.J. McCabe 56*). Australians won by an innings and 218 runs.

D.G. BRADMAN (capt.)  b. W.H.R. Andrews          202

On a damp but easy wicket, Bradman went in at 108 for 1, very early on the second morning, and it was soon apparent that none of the Somerset bowlers (of whom only A.W. Wellard ever played for England) were likely to prevent him from getting another century. He reached 50 in 70 minutes and 100 in two hours 34 minutes; then forced the pace to reach 200 in three hours 43 minutes, after which he gave his wicket away two minutes later in the same over. He gave no chance and hit 32 fours, being out at 445 for 6; he and McCabe added 129 for the sixth wicket in 56 minutes.

This was his 13th century of the season and the 12th and last double century he ever made in England. It is also the highest score made for the Australians on the Taunton ground (previous best, 183 by R.A. Duff, 1902).

Somerset was the fourth English county against which he had scored a double century, one more than the previous record by W. Bardsley, who did so *v* three different counties.

### 168. AUSTRALIANS *v* GLAMORGAN, at Swansea, 30 July, 1 and 2 August 1938

SCORES: Glamorgan 148 for 5 wickets dec. (E. Davies 58); Australians 61 for 3 wickets. Drawn.

D.G. BRADMAN (capt.)  st. H. Davies b. J.C. Clay       17

This game was ruined by rain, and when the Australians batted on the third afternoon, the wicket was very wet indeed and scarcely fit for cricket. In at 3 for 1, Bradman stayed for 63 minutes; he found it difficult to score runs in such conditions, and he was considerably troubled by the bowling of J.C. Clay. He was third out at 43.

## 169. AUSTRALIANS *v* KENT, at Canterbury, 13, 15 and 16 August 1938

SCORES: Australians 479 (S.G. Barnes 94, C.L. Badcock 76, D.G. Bradman 67, B.A. Barnett 54, E.S. White 52) and 7 for no wicket; Kent 108 and 377 (L.E.G. Ames 139, F.E. Woolley 81, M.G. Waite 5 for 85). Australians won by 10 wickets.

| | | |
|---|---|---|
| D.G. BRADMAN (capt.) | c. L.J. Todd b. A.E. Watt | 67 |
| | (did not bat) | – |

Bradman went in at 31 for 1 on the first morning, and reached 50 in 50 minutes; he then slowed down until, after batting for one and a half hours, he was caught at cover, just before lunch, when failing to get over a forcing shot off his back foot. He hit ten fours and helped Badcock to add 107 for the third wicket; he was out at 145 for 3.

## 170. AUSTRALIA *v* ENGLAND, Fourth Test match, at the Oval, 20, 22, 23 and 24 August 1938

SCORES: England 903 for 7 wickets dec. (L. Hutton 364, M. Leyland 187, J. Hardstaff 169*, W.R. Hammond 59, A. Wood 53); Australia 201 (W.A. Brown 69, W.E. Bowes 5 for 49) and 123. Australia lost by an innings and 579 runs, the rubber being drawn.

| | | |
|---|---|---|
| D.G. BRADMAN (capt.) | absent hurt | – |
| | absent hurt | – |

Bradman had the misfortune to lose the toss for the fourth consecutive time in Test matches, and England took advantage of a perfect wicket and a timeless Test to bat until tea-time on the third day; Hutton, batting for 13 hours 17 minutes, made 364, thereby breaking Bradman's own record of 334, previously the highest in England *v* Australia Test matches, and Bradman himself was the first to congratulate Hutton when he had done so. Bradman had batted six hours 23 minutes for his 334, and Hutton took 12 hours 19 minutes to pass it.

Finally, with the score 887 for 7, at 4.25 p.m. Bradman slipped while bowling, and fractured a bone in his ankle; he had to be carried off the field and could not bat. In his absence and that of Fingleton, and against such a score, Australia did not take things too seriously, and were soon dismissed; but for over two and a half days Bradman fielded magnificently and set his side a splendid example.

***

Bradman was unable to take any further part in the tour owing to his injury, and in his absence the Australians suffered another defeat, by Mr H.D.G. Leveson-Gower's XI at Scarborough.

| | Matches | Innings | NO | HS | Runs | Average | Centuries |
|---|---|---|---|---|---|---|---|
| All First-class Matches | 20 | 26 | 5 | 278 | 2429 | 115.66 | 13 |
| Test Matches | 4 | 6 | 2 | 144* | 434 | 108.50 | 3 |

The Test match series was drawn, each side winning one match, with two drawn, and Australia retained the Ashes.

Bradman's batting average of 115.66 is still the highest on record for an English season, and the only time that any batsman has had a 'century-average' for a season in England; Bradman's 98.66 in 1930 was the previous best, and after that was 96.96 by H. Sutcliffe in 1931.

This was the third English season in which his average exceeded 80; previously only D.R. Jardine had twice had such an average. Bradman did it a fourth time in 1948.

In exceeding 2,000 runs for the third consecutive tour of England, he equalled the performance of W. Bardsley (in 1909, 1912 and 1921); Bradman made his 2,000 runs for a fourth time in 1948, so surpassing Bardsley's feat. Bradman's 13 centuries in a season remain a record for any Australian or other touring batsman in England, 11, by V.T. Trumper in 1902 and by Bradman in 1948, being the next best.

In scoring 13 centuries in 26 visits to the wicket, or 50 per cent, Bradman achieved a proportion of centuries to innings for an English season, much greater than anyone else has ever done. Among English batsmen, J.B. Hobbs in 1925 had a 33 per cent success (16 centuries in 48 innings), while W.R. Hammond this season had 35 per cent (15 in 42), and D.C.S. Compton in 1947 had 36 per cent (18 in 50); Bradman's 27 per cent in 1930 (ten in 36) was the previous best for a visiting batsman. In 1948, Bradman's proportion was 35 per cent (11 in 31).

His consistency this season was extraordinary, even for him, for not only did he make 13 centuries, but he also played five other innings of over 50; he was dismissed for under 50 only seven times. He made 50 in one innings or the other in 16 of the 19 matches in which he batted, and 100 in one innings or the other in 13 matches out of nineteen.

In all first-class matches this season, W.A. Brown came second to him among Australians, with 1,854 runs, average 57.93; he and A.L. Hassett each hit five centuries. Among Englishmen, W.R. Hammond was best, with 3.011 runs, average 75.27, including 15 centuries; eight Englishmen scored more than 2,000 runs.

In the Test matches, W.A. Brown, with 512, scored more runs than Bradman, and he came second to Bradman in the averages with 73.14. For England, L. Hutton, thanks mainly to his huge innings at the Oval, averaged 118.25 for 473 runs, and E. Paynter made 407 runs, average 101.75. Brown and Hutton each made two centuries, the next best to Bradman's three.

Bradman's achievement in having a century-average both in the Test series and in all first-class matches is, of course, unique so far as England is concerned, though he did so twice in Australia, in 1931–2 and 1947–8. No one else had ever done this anywhere, until E.D. Weekes also achieved it in the West Indies in 1952–3; G. Sobers again did so in the West Indies in 1957–8.

# 1938–9

## AGED THIRTY

―――●·▸◉◂·●―――

171. **D.G. BRADMAN'S XI** *v* **K.E. RIGG'S XI** (Melbourne Cricket Club Centenary match), at Melbourne, 9, 10, 12 and 13 December 1938

SCORES: K.E. Rigg's XI 215 (S.G. Barnes 63, W.J. O'Reilly 5 for 75) and 324 for 8 wickets (J.A. Ledward 85, K.E. Rigg 71); D.G. Bradman's XI 426 (D.G. Bradman 118, S.J. McCabe 105, W.A. Brown 67, V.C.L. Badcock 51*). Drawn.

D.G. BRADMAN (capt.)  b. L.E. Nagel       118

Bradman went in on the second afternoon at 48 for 1, and made a cautious start, taking two minutes less than two hours to complete his 50; at the close of play he was 83 not out, after two hours 36 minutes' careful batting.

Rain interrupted play on the third morning, but Bradman duly completed his century after another 44 minutes (three hours 20 minutes altogether), and he was bowled in going for a big hit soon after lunch, making 118 in three hours 38 minutes. He and McCabe added 163 for the third wicket in 125 minutes, Bradman being out at 301 for 3; he hit 12 fours and gave no chance. Rigg's side was not strong in bowling, but it included M.W. Sievers and L.E. Nagel.

172. **SOUTH AUSTRALIA** *v* **NEW SOUTH WALES**, at Adelaide, 16, 17, 19 and 20 December 1938

SCORES: South Australia 600 for 8 wickets dec. (C.L. Badcock 271*, D.G. Bradman 143, R.A. Hamence 90); New South Wales 389 (A.G. Chipperfield 154, S.G. Barnes 117, C.V. Grimmett 7 for 116) and 155. South Australia won by an innings and 54 runs.

D.G. BRADMAN (capt.)  b. J. Murphy       143

A wicket falling to the first ball of the match, Bradman was soon in and he made a very quiet start, scoring only 39 before lunch. He took an hour and 55 minutes to reach 50, and three hours five minutes for his 100, his 143 lasting altogether three hours 50 minutes; it included 11 fours and as many as 91 singles. In addition to Murphy, the New South Wales bowlers included A.G. Cheetham, W.J. O'Reilly and E.S. White; but Bradman gave no chance, and when he was out, soon after tea, at 242 for 3, playing a rather weary drive, he had helped Badcock add 175 for the third wicket. The match was played in great heat, but Badcock's innings lasted eight and a quarter hours.

## 173. SOUTH AUSTRALIA *v* QUEENSLAND, at Adelaide, 24, 26, 27 and 28 December 1938

SCORES: Queensland 131 (C.V. Grimmett 6 for 33) and 311 (W.A. Brown 174*); South Australia 462 (D.G. Bradman 225, C.L. Badcock 100, M.G. Waite 52). South Australia won by an innings and 20 runs.

D.G. BRADMAN (capt.)  c. G. Baker b. C. Christ        225

In at 17 for 1, Bradman had two hours and ten minutes' batting at the end of the first day's play and had scored 83 not out at the close; he reached 50 in 78 minutes. He took another 25 minutes to complete his century next morning, but good defensive bowling by Christ, a slow-medium left-hander, thereafter prevented him from quickening his scoring rate as usual, and it took him five hours four minutes to score 200, and five hours 29 minutes to reach 225; he was then caught at forward short-leg. He gave only one chance, a catch to mid-off when 147 off Christ's bowling, and he hit 14 fours; out of 405 for 5, he and Badcock put on 202 in two hours 31 minutes for the third wicket, while Waite helped him to add 131 for the fifth wicket.

This was his third century in succession, the seventh time that he had made three (or more) hundreds in consecutive innings.

## 174. SOUTH AUSTRALIA *v* VICTORIA, at Melbourne, 30, 31 December 1938, 2 and 3 January 1939.

SCORES: Victoria 499 (A.L. Hassett 211*, R.G. Gregory 71, D.T. Ring 51, B.A. Barnett 50) and 283 for 7 wickets dec. (F.W. Sides 61, A.L. Hassett 54, B.A. Barnett 54, I.S. Lee 51, F.A. Ward 5 for 126); South Australia 488 (D.G. Bradman 107, R.S. Whitington 100, R.A. Hamence 84, F.A. Ward 62, M.W. Sievers 6 for 95) and 50 for no wicket. Drawn.

D.G. BRADMAN (capt.)  c. A.L. Hassett b. M.W. Sievers        107

Bradman went in at 70 for 1 on the second afternoon, and had made only 6 when he was missed at square-leg off Sievers; thereafter, despite a sore throat, he batted very brightly, against bowlers who also included E.L. McCormick, D.T. Ring and L.O'B. Fleetwood-Smith. He reached 50 in 62 minutes and 100 in an hour and 41 minutes before being caught at cover. Out at 227 for 2, he and Whitington added 157 for the second wicket; he hit nine fours, gave no other chance and batted for only an hour and 46 minutes.

This December, as in December 1937, he made 593 runs, his highest in one month in Australia and still a record for a South Australian batsman.

This was his fourth century in successive innings, the second time he had done this in Australia; he later did so a third time, in England in 1948 and in Australia in 1948–9. C.G. Macartney, the only other Australian to do so, made four in succession in England in 1921, and the only other batsmen to achieve the feat in Australia are W.R. Hammond (1936–7) and D.C.S. Compton (1946–7).

He brought his aggregate for the year 1938 to 3,838 (in 40 innings), the second highest total by an Australian batsman for a year's cricket; his own 4,368 (52 innings) in 1930 is the highest. His 40 innings (six not-outs) this year included 22 centuries and seven other innings of over 50 – an extraordinary example of his consistency, for which even his own career provides no parallel. His average for the year was 113.88.

## 175. SOUTH AUSTRALIA *v* QUEENSLAND, at Brisbane, 7, 9, 10 and 11 January 1939

SCORES: Queensland 336 (D. Tallon 115, G. Baker 78, C. Stibe 58, H.J. Cotton 5 for 49) and 233 (W.A. Brown 81); South Australia 557 (D.G. Bradman 186, R.S. Whitington 125, K.L. Ridings 122) and 14 for no wicket. South Australia won by 10 wickets.

| | | |
|---|---|---|
| D.G. BRADMAN (capt.) c. C. Christ b. W. Tallon | 186 | |
| (did not bat) | – | |

When Bradman went in 72 minutes from the end of the second day's play, Whitington and Ridings had added 197 for the first wicket, and there was little in the bowling to prevent Bradman's scoring another century. On 42 not out overnight, he reached 50 next morning after 88 minutes' batting, and progressed slowly to his hundred; he was 92 not out at lunch, having taken the whole morning session of one and three-quarter hours to add 50 to his overnight score. However, he reached 100 soon after the interval, after three hours 12 minutes, and his 186 altogether took four hours 47 minutes; he gave no chance and hit 19 fours. He and Ridings added 109 for the second wicket, and E.J.R. Moyle (46) helped him add 132 for the fifth wicket; it was a catch at square-leg which dismissed him, at 530 for 6.

This was his fifth successive century, a record for Australia and for Australian batsmen. It was also his fourth century in successive innings against Queensland, which equalled the record of A.A. Jackson, who in 1926–7–8–9 made four centuries in successive innings *v* South Australia. Bradman's next innings *v* Queensland was another century, and he also next season completed a fourth in successive innings *v* New South Wales.

### 176. SOUTH AUSTRALIA *v* NEW SOUTH WALES, at Sydney, 14 and 18 January 1939

SCORES: New South Wales 246 (L.C. Hynes 63*) and 156 for 5 wickets (B. McCauley 76); South Australia 349 for 4 wickets dec. (D.G. Bradman 135*, C.L. Badcock 98, R.S. Whitington 59). Drawn.

D.G. BRADMAN (capt.)  not out      135

In 1901, seven years before Bradman was born, C.B. Fry made six centuries in successive innings, a feat which had hitherto stood unapproached, until in this match Bradman equalled it; no one else had ever made more than four in succession. On the first day – when incidentally he kept wicket throughout the New South Wales innings in stifling heat – he went in at 76 for 1 and scored 22 not out in 35 minutes' batting before the close of play; rain then prevented any play at all on 16 and 17 January. When the game resumed, he continued to bat soundly if rather cautiously; he completed 50 in one and a quarter hours, and finally reached his century in two hours 50 minutes. Just before that, when 87, he mis-hit a ball which luckily did not go to hand, but he gave no chance until he had reached 133, when a hard catch was dropped in the covers off A.G. Cheetham's bowling. He batted for three hours 20 minutes, hit seven fours, and in two hours six minutes added 186 with Badcock for the fourth wicket.

This was Bradman's fifth century in succession for South Australia and in Sheffield Shield matches, only C. Hill and Bradman having previously made as many as three in succession for South Australia, though in 1898–9–1900 M.A. Noble scored four successive Shield hundreds for New South Wales; and in 1933–4 and 1935–6, Bradman scored two centuries for New South Wales and three for South Australia in successive Shield innings.

This was Bradman's eighth successive hundred on Australian wickets.

Bradman's and Fry's record still stands, though in 1956, E.D. Weekes, for the West Indian team touring New Zealand, came very close to equalling it by scoring five consecutive centuries; this being the only time that any other player has made more than four in succession.

## 177. SOUTH AUSTRALIA *v* VICTORIA, at Adelaide, 24 and 25 February 1939

SCORES: Victoria 321 (A.S. Hassett 102, K.E. Rigg 78, B.A. Barnett 51); South Australia 207 for 7 wickets (M.G. Waite 63*). Drawn.

D.G. BRADMAN (capt.) c. L.O'B. Fleetwood-Smith b. F. Thorn     5

Bradman went in on the second afternoon at 30 for 1 and played cautiously for 22 minutes before a good catch at backward short-leg ended his chance of breaking C.B. Fry's record with a seventh century in succession; he was out at 38 for 2. Rain washed out the last two days' play and helped South Australia to win the Sheffield Shield.

### SUMMARY, 1938–9

| | Matches | Innings | NO | HS | Runs | Average | Centuries |
|---|---|---|---|---|---|---|---|
| All First-class Matches | 7 | 7 | 1 | 225 | 919 | 153.16 | 6 |
| Sheffield Shield Matches } All Matches for Australia | 6 | 6 | 1 | 225 | 801 | 160.20 | 5 |

South Australia won the Sheffield Shield this season.

For the first time since his first season of 1927–8, Bradman did not complete his 1,000 runs; but as he scored six centuries in seven innings, and averaged 153.16, his record can scarcely be described as one of failure.

His average of 153.16 is the highest on record for a full Australian season (five or more completed innings), the previous best being by W.H. Ponsford in 1927–8, who made 1,217 runs in eight innings, average 152.12; in 1922–3, Ponsford averaged 154.00 for four innings, while in 1909–10, C. Hill, in four innings for South Australia, averaged 152.25. Bradman was, of course, top of the Australian averages, C.L. Badcock being second with 108.00. Both W.A. Brown (1,057 runs, average 105.70) and A. L. Hassett (967 runs, average 74.38) scored more runs than Bradman, and Hassett, with five centuries, was next to Bradman's six.

Six centuries in seven innings, or 85 per cent, is the highest proportion ever achieved in an Australian season, the previous best being 60 per cent (six in ten) by Ponsford in 1926–7; Bradman had 66 per cent success (eight in 12) in 1947–8.

His five centuries (in successive innings) in Sheffield Shield matches remain a record for South Australia, beating the record of four which he himself had set up in 1937–8; this also equalled the most scored in a season for any State in Shield matches, five for Ponsford in 1926–7 and (later) by A.R. Morris, in 1948–9. No one has ever scored more than five in one season, though Bradman had scored five in all matches for South Australia in 1937–8.

For the third season he made a century against each of the other States in the Sheffield Shield competition, breaking Ponsford's record of having done so twice.

His average of 160.20 for Shield matches only and in all matches for South Australia is the highest on record for that State, 152.25 by C. Hill, in 1909–10, being the previous highest; in Shield matches for all States, it is second only to Bradman's 184.80 for New South Wales in 1933–4.

# 1939–40

## AGED THIRTY-ONE

——◆◆✕◆◆——

At the request of the Australian Government, first-class cricket, including the Sheffield Shield competition, was played normally in Australia this season, despite the outbreak of war.

**178. SOUTH AUSTRALIA *v* VICTORIA**, at Adelaide, 17, 18, 20 and 21 November 1939

SCORES: Victoria 207 (G.E. Tamblyn 67, B.A. Barnett 51) and 363 (A.L. Hassett 89, I.S. Lee 68, M.W. Sievers 56, C.V. Grimmett 5 for 118); South Australia 21 (T. Klose 80, D.G. Bradman 76, M.G. Waite 67) and 310 for 7 wickets (R.A. Hamence 99, D.G. Bradman 64). South Australia won by 3 wickets.

| | | |
|---|---|---|
| D.G. BRADMAN (capt.) | run out | 76 |
| | lbw. b. D.T. Ring | 64 |

Not since December 1929 had Bradman been run out in a first-class match, but in the first innings he went for a short single off a ball played to square-leg by his partner, who did not respond, leaving him helpless, and he was run out by the bowler. He had gone in at 28 for 3 on the first afternoon; he reached 50 in one and a quarter hours, and batted altogether for a minute more than two hours before being out at 137 for 5 just before the close of play. He hit six fours and his partnership with Klose for the fifth wicket added 102.

South Australia were set to make 310 in the fourth innings and Bradman went in, early on the fourth day, at 44 for 2. He was at first uncomfortable against the bowling of Ring and Fleetwood-Smith, but he later settled down to bat soundly, being at his best just before he was out. He and Hamence added 112 for the fourth wicket, the latter batting so well that he scored faster than Bradman and in no way suffered by comparison with him. Bradman reached 50 in 74 minutes, and, after surviving a confident appeal for lbw. by Fleetwood-Smith when 55, he was out at 64, made in an hour and 41 minutes; the score was then 182 for 4 and Bradman, who hit six fours, made a considerable contribution to his side's narrow victory.

## 179. SOUTH AUSTRALIA *v* NEW SOUTH WALES, at Adelaide, 15, 16 and 18 December 1939

SCORES: New South Wales 336 (C.M. Solomon 131) and 248 (A.G. Chipperfield 57, C.V. Grimmett 6 for 122); South Australia 430 (D.G. Bradman 251*, W.J. O'Reilly 5 for 108) and 156 for 3 wickets (D.G. Bradman 90*). South Australia won by 7 wickets.

| D.G. BRADMAN (capt.) | not out | 251 |
| | not out | 90 |

Bradman was in his most masterful form in this game and played two superb innings against bowlers who included W.J. O'Reilly, A.G. Cheetham, C.G. Pepper and J.E. Walsh. He started his first innings 40 minutes from the end of the first day's play, at 17 for 1, and in that time made 27 not out; next morning his 50 was achieved in an hour and 23 minutes, and his century, just before lunch, in two hours 19 minutes. Batting one short, South Australia were still only 317, or 19 runs behind on the first innings, when the seventh wicket fell, Bradman's score then being 164; thereafter he took complete control of the game and added 23 out of 32 with F.A. Ward for the eighth wicket, followed by 64 out of 81 with C.V. Grimmett for the ninth and last wicket in 32 minutes, before the latter was out shortly after the tea interval.

Bradman's 200 took four hours eight minutes and he then added a further 51 in 23 minutes, batting for four hours 31 minutes altogether for his 251 not out, which was 62 per cent of his side's total (apart from extras); he was dropped off Cheetham at short-leg when 177, but that was his only mistake, and he hit two sixes and 38 fours. M.G. Waite (46) had also helped him to add 147 for the fourth wicket at 87 minutes.

In scoring 164 in boundaries, Bradman broke his own Sheffield Shield record for South Australia, 160 (40 fours) in his 357 *v* Victoria in 1935–6.

This was Bradman's fourth century in successive innings *v* New South Wales; he had already made four in succession and was about to add a fifth *v* Queensland, while the only other Australian player to make as many as four in succession against another State was A.A. Jackson *v* South Australia in 1926–7–8–9. Against New South Wales, the previous best was three in succession by L.P. O'Connor in 1926–7, and by J.S. Ryder in 1926–7–8–9; no other South Australian batsman made more than two centuries in succession against any other State, until C. Pinch made three in succession *v* Western Australia in 1956–7.

Bradman again dominated the scene when South Australia required 155 to win on the third afternoon. In at 9 for 1, he reached 50 in 64 minutes and batted for an hour and 40 minutes for his 90 not out, the game being over just before the tea interval; he hit 14 fours and with a little more luck might have completed his second century of the match, for when 16 more runs were wanted for victory his score was 84.

## 180. SOUTH AUSTRALIA *v* QUEENSLAND, at Adelaide, 22, 23, 25 and 26 December 1939

SCORES: South Australia 821 for 7 wickets dec. (C.L. Badcock 236, K.L. Ridings 151, D.G. Bradman 138, M.G. Waite 137, R.S. Whitington 67); Queensland 222 (D. Tallon 70, F.A. Ward 5 for 62) and 377 (W.A. Brown 156, G. Baker 52, R. Rogers 50, C.V. Grimmett 6 for 124). South Australia won by an innings and 222 runs.

D.G. BRADMAN (capt.)   c. D. Hansen b. J. Ellis       138

Bradman, in brilliant form, started South Australia on the path to their highest score, though he himself was not the largest contributor to it. In at 36 for 1 on the first morning, he hit up 50 in 37 minutes and at the lunch interval was 80 not out after 70 minutes' batting. He completed his century only ten minutes after lunch and altogether made 138 in an hour and 55 minutes before being caught off a skier behind square-leg when mis-timing a hook; he gave no chance and this was his first false stroke. Out at 232 for 2, he added 1996 for the second wicket in company with K.L. Ridings, his share being 70 per cent; his strokes included 22 fours.

The 80 not out made before lunch on this occasion was the nearest he ever got to a century before lunch on the first morning of a match in Australia, though he twice achieved this feat in England; there is normally one and three-quarter hours' play, at most, before lunch in Australia, and no one has ever made 100 before lunch on the first morning of a Sheffield Shield match, though A.J. Richardson and J.M. Gregory both did so in Australia against touring teams when opening the innings. Bradman's 80 is the most ever made before lunch on the first day of a Shield match for South Australia (previous best, 79 by A.J. Richardson *v* New South Wales, 1923–4). His century in 80 minutes is also the fastest ever made for South Australia in a Shield match, the previous best being 93 minutes, by D.R.A. Gehrs *v* Victoria, 1910–1.

He thus scored 479 runs in successive innings before he was dismissed (251*, 90*, 138), a record for South Australia; the previous best was 411 by C. Hill (365*, 46) in 1900–1.

This was his fifth century in successive innings against Queensland; no one else has ever made five centuries in succession off another State's bowling in Australia, the previous best being four in succession by A.A. Jackson *v* South Australia in 1926–7–8–9, and by Bradman *v* New South Wales, finishing in the previous match. Against Queensland, the most centuries in succession were three by L.S. Darling in 1932–3–4, and three (all double centuries) by Bradman in 1933–4–5–6; three in succession (by C. Pinch in 1956–7) are the most that any other South Australian batsman has made against any other State.

181. **SOUTH AUSTRALIA** *v* **VICTORIA**, at Melbourne, 29, 30 December 1939, 1 and 2 January 1940

SCORES: Victoria 475 (K.R. Miller 108, P.J. Beames 104, A.L. Hassett 92, G. Burton 5 for 99) and 313 (A.L. Hassett 66); South Australia 610 (D.G. Bradman 267, M.G. Waite 64, C.L. Badcock 58, K.L. Ridings 56, T. Klose 54, D.T. Ring 5 for 123) and 60 for 1 wicket. Drawn.

D.G. BRADMAN (capt.)  c. I.W. Johnson b. L.O'B. Fleetwood-Smith          267
(did not bat)                                                            –

Bradman went in late on the second day at 108 for 1 and, completing 50 in 80 minutes just before 6 p.m., was 52 not out at the close. Next morning he played a bad stroke through the slips off the fast bowling of Scott, when 61, and he made another mis-hit soon after passing 150, though neither of these was a chance; otherwise he batted without the semblance of a mistake until just before 5 p.m., against the bowling of R.B. Scott, M.W. Sievers, D.T. Ring, L.O'B. Fleetwood-Smith and I.W. Johnson. He reached 100 in two hours 13 minutes, proceeding from 88 by hitting three fours of four balls from Ring; 142 not out at lunch, he reached 200 after batting for four hours 18 minutes and continued to bat soundly, his 267 taking five hours 40 minutes altogether. He was out, caught in the slips, at 556 for 7, having hit 27 fours and seen South Australia into the lead; he and Badcock added 137 for the third wicket, while he and Waite put on 126 for the seventh wicket. This was his 34th double century, passing W.R. Hammond's then total of 33; Bradman was thus in the lead for the duration of the war, though Hammond afterwards caught him up and passed him again before Bradman finally took the lead with 37 double centuries to Hammond's 36. This was also his 16th and last score of 250 and over, Hammond (13) and, among Australians, W.H. Ponsford (seven) being next best. His last five innings thus produced 810 runs (64, 251*, 90*, 138, 267), which is a South Australian record, the previous best being his own 788 in 1935–6.

182. **SOUTH AUSTRALIA** *v* **QUEENSLAND**, at Brisbane, 6, 8, 9 and 10 January 1940

SCORES: South Australia 230 (J. Stackpoole 6 for 72) and 252 (D.G. Bradman 97, M.G. Waite 62); Queensland 133 and 350 for 8 wickets (W.A. Brown 111, R. Rogers 74, D. Watts 59*, G.G. Cook 54). South Australia lost by 2 wickets.

D.G. BRADMAN (capt.)  c. P.L. Dixon b. J. Stackpoole           0
                      c. D. Tallon b. G.G. Cook                97

Having scored, so far this season, 886 runs in six innings, of which two were not out, Bradman now proceeded to get out first ball; in on the first morning at 53 for 1, he pushed an easy catch to short-leg off a fast ball, with the score unaltered.

His second innings was more successful; he had 50 minutes' batting at the end of the second day, after coming in at 8 for 2 and made 29 before stumps were drawn. Next morning he reached 50 in 72 minutes altogether, and by the lunch interval had taken his score to 97, only to be caught at the wicket off the first ball afterwards. He batted for two hours 37 minutes and was out at 173 for 7, having hit ten fours, mostly firm off-drives.

Queensland's performance in getting the 350 required for victory was a very fine one; it was South Australia's first defeat for two seasons.

## 183. SOUTH AUSTRALIA *v* NEW SOUTH WALES, at Sydney, 13, 15, 16 and 17 January 1940

SCORES: New South Wales 270 (M.B. Cohen 74, S.J. McCabe 59, C.V. Grimmett 6 for 118) and 311 (M.B. Cohen 70, H. Mudge 57, R.A. Saggers 57, S.J. McCabe 55, C.V. Grimmett 5 for 111); South Australia 211 (W.J. O'Reilly 6 for 77) and 133 (C.G. Pepper 5 for 49). South Australia lost by 237 runs.

| | | |
|---|---|---|
| D.G. BRADMAN (capt.) | lbw. b. W.J. O'Reilly | 39 |
| | c. D.K. Carmody b. C.G. Pepper | 40 |

On a wicket which took spin throughout, Bradman fought another duel with O'Reilly, this time with less success. His first innings started, at 8 for 2, on the first evening and he made 24 in 50 minutes before bad light put an end to the day's play; when 17, he completed 1,000 runs for the season, the only time he achieved this feat in Sheffield Shield matches only. In reaching this landmark on 13 January, he improved by five days upon the South Australian record he set up in 1937–8, and this remains the earliest for South Australia; and, as in 1935–6, he took only nine innings to reach 1,000, which is still also a South Australian record. This was the eighth and last season in which he was the first (or only) batsman in Australia to complete 1,000 runs; no one else has done this more than twice.

He batted for another 20 minutes next morning before playing across an off-break and being lbw., at 77 for 3; only R.A. Hamence and C.L. Badcock, with 43 and 40 respectively, scored more than he.

The light was again none too good when he went in half an hour before the end of the third day, at 22 for 2, with South Australia needing 371 to win; batting superbly, he made 35 not out, with seven fours, being especially severe upon O'Reilly.

Next morning two wickets fell quickly, and with his side in a hopeless position, he hit out and was caught at long-on, being sixth out at 85. His 40, made in 42 minutes, was top score; and he had batted on all four days.

This match virtually settled the result of the Sheffield Shield competition this season.

## 184. SOUTH AUSTRALIA *v* WESTERN AUSTRALIA, at Perth, 10, 12 and 13 February 1940

SCORES: South Australia 248 and 306 for 3 wickets dec. (D.G. Bradman 209*); Western Australia 275 (C. MacGill 78, M. Inverarity 57, F.A. Ward 6 for 105) and 121 for 3 wickets (D. Watt 52). Drawn.

| D.G. BRADMAN (capt.) c. O.I. Lovelock b. C. MacGill | 42 |
| not out | 209 |

Bradman went in on the first morning, and seemed to have played himself in comfortably, when he reached for a wide out-swinger and was caught at the wicket. He batted for 65 minutes, and helped to take the score from 28 for 2 to 97 for 3.

His second innings was a dazzling exhibition; going in on the third morning at 25 for 1, he completed his 50 in 45 minutes and his century in 99 minutes, while his 200 took him a further 56 minutes, or only two hours 35 minutes altogether. When he declared a the tea interval he had made 209 not out in two hours 41 minutes, and had hit one six and 30 fours. He gave very difficult chances when 161 (caught and bowled off G. Eyres), 183 (at mid-wicket off A. Barras) and 207 (on the boundary, again off Barras), but otherwise his display was chanceless; he and L. Michael (27*) added 171 unfinished for the fourth wicket in 100 minutes, and of the 281 added while he was in, his share was 74 per cent, the highest proportion he ever achieved in a double century innings. Bradman just failed to break the individual record for the Perth ground, which was then 211 (it is now 234*).

His time for reaching 200, two hours 35 minutes, was the fastest of his career, and the fastest by any Australian in Australia; the previous best was two hours 40 minutes by J.R.M. MacKay, for New South Wales *v* Queensland, 1905–6, and four South Australia, two hours 48 minutes, by Bradman *v* Queensland, 1935–6. His time was only a minute slower than the fastest ever achieved in Australia, two hours 34 minutes, by F.E. Woolley, for MCC *v* Tasmania, 1911–2.

## 185. SOUTH AUSTRALIA *v* WESTERN AUSTRALIA, at Perth, 16, 17 and 19 February 1940

SCORES: Western Australia 275 (A. Read 55, M. Inverarity 52, C.V. Grimmett 5 for 67) and 206 (C.V. Grimmett 6 for 57); South Australia 429 (D.G. Bradman 135, R.A. Hamence 63, T. Klose 60, F. Teisseire 56). Drawn.

D.G. BRADMAN (capt.) c. A.G. Zimbulis b. G. Eyres     135

Going in just after lunch on the second day at 79 for 1, Bradman batted easily, if rather sedately, for two hours 28 minutes before being caught on the leg-boundary for 135. He completed 50 in 79 minutes and 100 in two hours 12 minutes; he hit 14 fours, gave no chance, and helped to raise the score to 303 for 4, his stand for the third wicket with Hamence realising 150 in 98 minutes.

## 186. THE REST OF AUSTRALIA *v* NEW SOUTH WALES (Patriotic match), at Sydney, 8, 9 and 11 March 1940

SCORES: Rest of Australia 289 (A. L. Hassett 136) and 252 (W.A. Brown 97, A.L. Hassett 75); New South Wales 219 (S.J. McCabe 72, A.G. Cheetham 58, C.V. Grimmett 5 for 65) and 323 for 8 wickets (S.J. McCabe 96, M. Cohen 67, C.V. Grimmett 5 for 130). Rest of Australia lost by 2 wickets.

| | | |
|---|---|---|
| D.G. BRADMAN (capt.) | c. R.A. Saggers b. W.J. O'Reilly | 25 |
| | c. C.L. McCool b. A.G. Cheetham | 2 |

Going in early on the first day at 2 for 1, Bradman batted for 56 minutes, but he was never comfortable against O'Reilly, and after being twice beaten by good balls, was eventually caught at the wicket off that bowler, attempting a chop, at 64 for 3.

His second innings was even shorter; in at 31 for 1 on the second afternoon, he batted for five minutes before being well caught at first slip, a fast snick going high to the left of McCool, at 37 for 2.

## SUMMARY, 1939–40

| | Matches | Innings | NO | HS | Runs | Average | Centuries |
|---|---|---|---|---|---|---|---|
| All First-class Matches | 9 | 15 | 3 | 267 | 1475 | 122.91 | 5 |
| Sheffield Shield Matches | 6 | 10 | 2 | 267 | 1062 | 132.75 | 3 |
| All Matches for South Australia | 8 | 13 | 3 | 267 | 1448 | 144.80 | 5 |

A.L. Hassett's figures were second to Bradman's in all first-class matches this season, with 897 runs, including three centuries, for an average of 74.75.

W.H. Ponsford twice (in 1926–7 and 1927–8) scored over 1,000 runs in a season in Sheffield Shield matches only, his best being 1,217; no one else, except Bradman this season and N.C. O'Neill in 1957–8, has ever reached 1,000 runs in Shield matches only, and his total is a record for South Australia, beating the 983 he himself made in 1937–8. O'Neill, of course, also played two matches *v* Western Australia, who were admitted to the Shield competition in 1947–8; and in 1957–8 the best Australian bowlers were touring South Africa.

This was the tenth time, and the fourth while playing for South Australia, that he exceeded 1,000 runs in all first-class matches; and for the fifth and last time, and for the third while playing for South Australia, he hit three double centuries in a season (all for South Australia, two being in Sheffield Shield matches), a feat performed otherwise only by Ponsford and W.R. Hammond, once each.

For the fourth season, and for the second in succession, he scored centuries *v* all three other States in Sheffield Shield matches; and he also scored two centuries *v* Western Australia. A.R. Morris, in 1948–9, scored centuries in Shield matches against all four other States then taking part, and between 1926–7 (when Queensland entered the competition) and 1947–8 (when Western Australia first took part) only Bradman (once for New South Wales and three times for South Australia), Ponsford (twice in succession), A.F. Kippax, G.W. Harris and A.L. Hassett ever scored centuries in the same season against all other States in Shield matches.

His aggregate of 1,448 is the highest on record in all matches for South Australia, his own 1,173 in 1935–6 being the previous best. His five centuries in all matches for South Australia equalled his own record of 1937–8 and 1938–9.

This was the fifth consecutive season that he headed the Australian first-class batting average; the previous best was three times in succession by G. Giffen, from 1892–3 to 1894–5 inclusive. Kippax had had an average of over 50 in ten Australian seasons, which was a record; this was Bradman's 11th season with an average of over 50.

***

One of the tours which had to be cancelled owing to the war was an Australian visit to New Zealand early in 1940; it had been intended that Bradman should lead the side, which was to have played about a dozen matches, including a Test match *v* New Zealand at Christchurch in March 1940.

# 1940–1

## AGED THIRTY-TWO

———————◆◆◆◆◆———————

There was no competition for the Sheffield Shield this season, but there were altogether ten first-class matches played. Bradman, now a lieutenant in the army, obtained leave to play in two of them, but he was already beginning to suffer from the muscular trouble in his back which nearly put an end to his career.

### 187. SOUTH AUSTRALIA *v* VICTORIA, at Adelaide, 25, 26, 27 and 28 December 1940

SCORES: South Australia 191 (R.A. Hamence 85) and 421 (C.L. Badcock 172, P.L. Ridings 90, R.A. Hamence 62); Victoria 172 (D.T. Ring 72) and 265 (A.L. Hassett 113). South Australia won by 175 runs.

| | | |
|---|---|---|
| D.G. BRADMAN (capt.) | c. M.W. Sievers b. W. Dudley | 0 |
| | b. M.W. Sievers | 6 |

Bradman was out first ball in the first innings; in early on the first morning at 1 for 1, he groped for a ball on his off-stump and was caught in the slips. His second innings, starting at 30 for 1 on the second afternoon, was almost as brief, and he was as near as ever he was to making a 'pair of spectacles' when, to his first ball, from Sievers, he fell over and nearly sat on his wicket. He then made one hook for 4 in something of his old style, before being bowled, hitting across a straight ball, at 36 for 2. His unhappy display lasted ten minutes, long enough to make it obvious that his failures went beyond any mere matter of being out of form or practice, and that he simply was not 'seeing' the ball in his usual way.

This was the second and last time in his career that he was dismissed for single figures twice in a match.

### 188. D.G. BRADMAN'S XI *v* S.J. McCABE'S XI (Patriotic match), at Melbourne, 1, 3, and 4 January 1941

SCORES: S.J. McCabe's XI 449 for 9 wickets dec. (S.G. Barnes 137, C.L. Badcock 105, M.W. Sievers 55*); D.G. Bradman's XI 205 (R.A. Hamence 73, K.L. Ridings

50) and 141 (W.J. O'Reilly 5 for 53). Bradman's XI lost by an innings and 130 runs.

| | |
|---|---|
| D.G. BRADMAN (capt.) c. G.E. Tamblyn (sub.) b. J. Ellis | 0 |
| b. W.J. O'Reilly | 12 |

In at 25 for 1 after lunch on the second day, Bradman was again out first ball, trying to drive a swinging full-toss and snicking it to third slip. On the third afternoon he batted rather better, on a patchy wicket on which the rain had got through the covers; he started at 10 for 1, steered his first ball from K.R. Miller through the slips for a single, and batted for 18 minutes before playing on to an off-break which kept rather low, at 35 for 2. However, he still seemed to have difficulty in focusing on the ball.

## SUMMARY, 1940–1

| | Matches | Innings | NO | HS | Runs | Average | Centuries |
|---|---|---|---|---|---|---|---|
| All First-class matches | 2 | 4 | 0 | 12 | 18 | 4.50 | 0 |
| Matches for South Australia | 1 | 2 | 0 | 6 | 6 | 3.00 | 0 |

S.G. Barnes was the leading batsman in Australia this season; he made 1,050 runs, including six centuries, for an average of 75.00. Bradman found himself in the extremely unusual position, in the Australian averages, of equal 47th and last, both in aggregate and average; as he had only four innings, this was hidden in the obscurity of 'also batted'.

# 1945-6

## AGED THIRTY-SEVEN

———●▶✕◀●———

No further first-class cricket was played in Australia until after the end of the war, and Bradman himself, invalided out of the army in June 1941 as a result of fibrositis, was for some time in such poor health that it seemed unlikely that he would ever play cricket again. However, his back had recovered sufficiently, when first-class matches were resumed in 1945–6, to enable him to play in two matches, though he was not in practice and far from being really fit.

No Sheffield Shield matches were played this season, but the Australian Services team, after a heavy programme in England and India, played the five major States.

189. **SOUTH AUSTRALIA** *v* **QUEENSLAND**, at Adelaide, 24, 25, 26 and 27 December 1945

SCORES: South Australia 365 (R.J. Craig 84, D.G. Bradman 68, C. Webb 63, C.L. McCool 7 for 106) and 110 for 1 wicket (D.G. Bradman 52*); Queensland 573 for 8 wickets dec. (C.L. McCool 172, W.A. Brown 98, G.G. Cook 76, A. Carrigan 67). Drawn.

| | | |
|---|---|---|
| D.G. BRADMAN (capt.) | c. D. Tallon b. C.L. McCool | 68 |
| | not out | 52 |

Despite his lack of fitness and practice, as well as a strained leg, Bradman batted surprisingly well in this match, and his eyesight seemed to be again as good as ever. He was in after lunch on the first day, at 149 for 2, completed 50 in 54 minutes just before tea, and batted for an hour and 18 minutes altogether before being caught at the wicket in trying to cut. He hit ten fours and was fourth out at 268.

South Australia were left only two hours' batting on the last evening and, with a draw certain, Bradman used 78 minutes of it for some useful practice. In at 37 for 1, he reached 50 in 73 minutes and hit two fours.

190. **SOUTH AUSTRALIA** *v* **AUSTRALIAN SERVICES**, at Adelaide, 29, 31 December 1945, and 1 January 1946

SCORES: Australian Services 314 (R.S. Whitington 77, C.G. Pepper 63, R. Standford 59*, B. Dooland 5 for 104) and 255 (A.L. Hassett 92, D.R. Cristofani 58, R. Stanford 58); South Australia 319 (R.J. Craig 141, D.G. Bradman 112, R.S. Ellis 5 for 88) and 130 for 1 wicket (F.C. Bennett 56*, L. Michael 54). Drawn.

D.G. BRADMAN (capt.)  c. D.K. Carmody b. R.G. Williams       112
                      (did not bat)                           –

Going in on the second morning at 68 for 2, Bradman showed good form against bowlers who included A.G. Cheetham, R.G. Williams, C.G. Pepper, R.S. Ellis and D.R. Cristofani. He took only three-quarters of an hour to reach 50, and 95 minutes to complete his century, before throwing away his wicket, caught at long-on, after batting for an hour and 52 minutes. Out of 241 for 3, he and Craig added 173 for the third wicket; Bradman hit 11 fours and gave no chance.

## SUMMARY, 1945–6

| | Matches | Innings | NO | HS | Runs | Average | Centuries |
|---|---|---|---|---|---|---|---|
| All First-class Matches All Matches for South Australia | 2 | 3 | 1 | 112 | 232 | 116.00 | 1 |

S.G. Barnes, with 794 runs, average 88.22 and five centuries, was again the leading regular Australian batsman this season.

There was a short Australian tour of New Zealand early in 1946, under the captaincy of W.A. Brown, in which Australia won the only Test match played. Bradman, of course, was not considered for selection as a member of this team, though he himself was still one of the selectors.

# 1946–7

## AGED THIRTY-EIGHT

———•◆×◆•———

Bradman suffered a recurrence of the fibrositis in his back during the Australian winter, and he was still in very poor health when W.R. Hammond's MCC team arrived in Australia; he had, moreover, reached an age at which most Australian batsmen had retired from Test cricket. It was therefore for a long time in doubt whether he would be able to play in the Test matches. He was still a member of the Australian Selection Committee and when he finally decided that his health would allow him to play, he was naturally again selected as captain in all the Test matches.

**191. SOUTH AUSTRALIA _v_ MCC TEAM**, at Adelaide, 25, 26, 27 and 29 October 1946

SCORES: MCC Team 506 for 5 wickets dec. (L. Hutton 136, C. Washbrook 113, W.J. Edrich 71, D.C.S. Compton 71, N.W.D. Yardley 54*); South Australia 266 (D.G. Bradman 76, R. James 58, P.L. Ridings 57, T.P.B. Smith 5 for 93) and 276 for 8 wickets (R.J. Craig 111, J. Mann 62*). Drawn.

| D.G. BRADMAN (capt.) | c. and b. T.P.B. Smith | 76 |
| | c. W.J. Edrich b. R. Pollard | 3 |

Bradman played in this game although obviously very far from well, and he then had to field for two days against the big MCC score. In the circumstances, it was a considerable achievement on his part to score 76 in the first innings; he went in at 26 for 2 before lunch on the third day, and was soon in difficulties against Pollard, who had him missed at the wicket when 15. However, he gradually settled down and managed to attain better co-ordination and timing; he completed 50 in 97 minutes and was out to his first ball after the tea interval, having played an innings lasting two hours 33 minutes, which took considerable toll of his limited stamina. He hit six fours and was fourth out at 199.

In at 69 for 2 after lunch on the fourth day, he soon hit out wildly, to be caught at mid-off at 72 for 3; he stayed for only six minutes. South Australia did well to save the game.

## 192. AN AUSTRALIAN XI *v* MCC TEAM, at Melbourne, 9, 11 and 13 November 1946

SCORES: MCC Team 314 (L. Hutton 71, C. Washbrook 57, W.R. Hammond 51, C.L. McCool 7 for 106); An Australian XI 327 for 5 wickets (A.R. Morris 115, D.G. Bradman 106). Drawn.

D.G. BRADMAN (capt.)  c. R. Pollard b. D.C.S. Compton          106

In rather better health by this time, Bradman took the opportunity for further batting practice in a game much interfered with by rain. He had 56 minutes' batting at the close of the second day, starting at 39 for 1, and he made 28 not out overnight; on the last morning he completed 50 in 92 minutes, but soon afterwards strained his leg. However, after 25 minutes in the nineties, he reached 100 in three hours 35 minutes, and four minutes later threw his wicket away with a catch in the deep. He gave a stumping chance off Compton when 78, but otherwise batted in much better form; he hit five fours and, second out at 235, had helped Morris add 196 for the second wicket. The MCC bowling, though not at full strength, included W. Voce, R. Pollard and T.P.B. Smith.

## 193. SOUTH AUSTRALIA *v* VICTORIA, at Adelaide, 15, 16, 18 and 19 November 1946

SCORES: South Australia 270 (R. James 73, G.E. Tribe 7 for 85) and 356 (D.G. Bradman 119, R.A. Hamence 116, G.E. Tribe 6 for 68); Victoria 548 (K.R. Miller 188, A.L. Hassett 114, K. Meulemann 87, G.E. Tamblyn 75) and 79 for 1 wicket. South Australia lost by 9 wickets.

D.G. BRADMAN (capt.)  st. E.A. Baker b. I.W. Johnson          43
                 st. E.A. Baker b. G.E. Tribe          119

In his only Sheffield Shield match of the season, Bradman again showed improved form and fitness. In at 75 for 3 after lunch on the first day, he batted for one and a quarter hours before jumping out to drive, missing the ball and being unable to get back in time; he was fifth out at 159.

His strained leg prevented him from fielding during Victoria's big first innings, and it again bothered him when he went in to bat early on the fourth day. He joined Hamence at 62 for 2, and the pair added 195 for the third wicket in a great effort to save the game for South Australia, who were 278 behind on the first innings. He survived a stumping chance off Johnson when 26, reached 50 in two minutes over one and a half hours, and his century in two hours 48 minutes, despite having a pronounced limp. He batted altogether for three hours three minutes and hit eight fours; when he was out, stumped well down the pitch, at

284 for 4, at 3.30 p.m., the innings defeat had just been saved, but thereafter there was a collapse, the last six wickets falling for 72. Victoria had 35 minutes to make 79 to win and succeeded with two minutes to spare; their bowlers, in addition to Johnson and Tribe, included W.A. Johnston, F. Freer, K.R. Miller and D.T. Ring. Miller batted magnificently for Victoria.

194. **AUSTRALIA** *v* **ENGLAND**, First Test match, at Brisbane, 29, 30 November, 2, 3, 4 and 5 December 1946

SCORES: Australia 645 (D.G. Bradman 187, A.L. Hassett 128, C.L. McCool 95, K.R. Miller 79, D.V.P. Wright 5 for 167); England 141 (K.R. Miller 7 for 60) and 172 (E.R.H. Toshack 6 for 82). Australia won by an innings and 332 runs.

D.G. BRADMAN (capt.)  b. W.J. Edrich          187

Bradman, for the first time in a Test match, beat W.R. Hammond in the toss and in doing so virtually won the match for his side. Bradman himself went in at 9 for 1, at 12.15 p.m. on the first afternoon, and made one of the shakiest starts of his career; his first 7 runs took him 40 minutes, and in one and a quarter hours before lunch he managed to make 28, but at no time had he looked secure; just before the interval, when 28, he survived a very confident appeal for a catch at second slip off W. Voce.

Thereafter, in great heat, he and Hassett gradually mastered the bowling; Bradman's 50 came in an hour and 55 minutes, and by the tea interval, when he was 82, he was batting with much more of his old authority. He completed his first century against England at Brisbane (at 4.32 p.m., with a snick for 4 off Edrich which was almost a chance) after three hours 14 minutes, and after that began to increase his rate of scoring, so that at the close, after four hours 44 minutes, he was 162 not out; he had by then quite recovered his old confidence. When he had made 160, he reached 4,000 runs in Tests between England and Australia, the first and only batsman to do so.

He continued for a further 34 minutes next morning, adding 25 before Edrich bowled him off his pads with a good ball, at 322 for 3. He batted altogether for five hours 18 minutes and 305 balls, hit 19 fours, and gave no actual chance; he and Hassett added 276 for the third wicket in 278 minutes, against bowlers who included W. Voce, A.V. Bedser, D.V.P. Wright and W.J. Edrich. Torrential rain after the end of Australia's innings made the wicket impossible, and England had no chance.

His partnership of 276 with Hassett is still the highest for the third wicket by Australia *v* England, and the highest for that wicket against any touring team in Australia (previous best, 249 by Bradman and S.J. McCabe, 1936–7), as well as the highest Test match between England and Australia, and in any Test match in

Australia (previous best, 262 by W.R. Hammond and D.R. Jardine, 1928–9); and at that time it was also the highest for the third wicket in any Test match anywhere (previous best, 264 by L. Hutton and Hammond, for England *v* West Indies, 1939; against England in any Test match anywhere, 249 by Bradman and McCabe, 1936–7), until a few months later A. Melville and A.D. Nourse added 319 for South Africa *v* England, and then Edrich and D.C.S. Compton put on 370 for England *v* South Africa; it was also the highest for the third wicket by Australia in any Test anywhere, until in 1955 C.C. McDonald and R.N. Harvey put on 295 *v* the West Indies in the West Indies; and the highest for the third wicket against any English touring team anywhere, until E.D. Weekes and F.M. Worrell put on 338 for the West Indies, 1953–4.

His 187 is still the highest score in a Test match between England and Australia on the Brisbane Cricket Ground (previous best, 126 by M. Leyland, 1936–7; for Australia, 100 by J.H. Fingleton, 1936–7; E. Hendren scored 169 in 1928–9 at the Exhibition Ground, Brisbane).

## 195. AUSTRALIA *v* ENGLAND, Second Test match, at Sydney, 13, 14, 16, 17, 18 and 19 December 1946

SCORES: England 255 (W.J. Edrich 71, J.T. Ikin 60, I.W. Johnson 6 for 42) and 371 (W.J. Edrich 119, D.C.S. Compton 54, C.L. McCool 5 for 109); Australia 659 for 8 wickets dec. (S.G. Barnes 234, D.G. Bradman 234). Australia won by an innings and 33 runs.

D.G. BRADMAN (capt.) lbw. b. N.W.D. Yardley                234

Suffering both from a leg injury and gastric trouble, Bradman did not field on the second day, and batted sixth, joining Barnes at 159 for 4 at 3.50 p.m. on the third day; Barnes had a start of 71 runs and four hours five minutes. Five not out at the interval, he took 63 minutes to make 14, but thereafter batted well to be 52 not out overnight; he completed 50 four minutes before the close, in an hour and 51 minutes.

Next day, he and Barnes continued their fifth-wicket stand and were not separated until 17 minutes from the close of play, by which time they had added 405. Bradman, adding 34 in 88 minutes, was 86 at the lunch interval, and at 2.35 p.m. completed his century in two minutes under three and three-quarter hours; he had made 151 by tea, reached 200 at 5.21 p.m., after six hours 11 minutes at the wicket, and then hit out, adding a further 34 in 22 minutes, before being lbw. swinging wildly at Yardley. He batted altogether for three minutes longer than six and a half hours, hit 24 fours off 398 balls and gave no chance; his running between the wickets was hampered by his leg injury, but otherwise he batted soundly and well against bowlers who included A.V. Bedser, W.J. Edrich, D.V.P. Wright and T.P.B. Smith, in addition to Yardley. He was out at 564 for 5, and

Barnes, who batted ten hours 42 minutes for the same score of 234, was out four minutes later at the same total.

This was Bradman's eighth century in successive Test matches in which he batted, all against England, but his first against England at Sydney. He is the only batsman to make centuries in England v Australia Test matches in all four Australian cities, and the only one to make double centuries in all Test matches at Sydney, Melbourne, Adelaide and both grounds at Brisbane; no other Australian has scored more than one Test match double century in Australia, though W.R. Hammond for England reached 200 both at Sydney and Melbourne. It was also Bradman's 23rd century in all Test cricket, one more than the 22 with which Hammond finished his career; this was Bradman's 59th innings, while Hammond altogether played 140. Bradman had gone ahead of Hammond, and all other batsmen, in 1936–7, but in 1939 Hammond scored his 22nd century against Bradman's then total of 21; Bradman finished with 29 Test centuries, well ahead of any other player.

His partnership of 405 for the fifth wicket with Barnes broke numerous records, and it is still a world record for that wicket (previous best, 397 by W. Bardsley and C.E. Kelleway, for New South Wales v South Australia, 1920–1). It is a Test match record for the fifth wicket, the previous highest being 242 by Hammond and L.E.G. Ames for England v New Zealand, 1932–3; in an England v Australia Test, 206 by E. Paynter and D.C.S. Compton, 1938; in Australia, 192 by R.E. Foster and L.C. Braund, 1903–04; by Australian batsmen, 183 by Bradman and A.G. Fairfax, 1928–9. It remains a record for any wicket in a Test match in Australia, passing the 346 for the sixth wicket added by Bradman and J.H. Fingleton v England in 1936–7.

It is the highest for any wicket against any touring team in Australia, the previous highest being Bradman's and Fingleton's 346 for the sixth wicket, 1936–7, and for the fifth wicket, 197 by A.J. Richardson and E.L. Bowley v MCC, 1922-3; it is also the highest for the fifth wicket against any English touring team anywhere, Richardson's and Bowley's 197 being the previous best.

With this partnership, Bradman completed an extraordinary sequence, being concerned in the record partnerships in Test matches for the second, third, fourth, fifth and sixth wickets, all v England (second, 451 with W.H. Ponsford, 1934; third, 276 with A.L. Hassett, 1946–7; fourth, 388 with Ponsford, 1934; fifth, 405 with Barnes, 1946–7; sixth, 346 with Fingleton, 1936–47); only his figures for the third and fourth wickets have since been surpassed and these remain records for England v Australia Tests. (It is, of course, fair to add that he would normally have been associated with Ponsford, Barnes and Fingleton for the second wicket, and that it was the interposition of 'night-watchmen', injury and rain, respectively, which caused these partnerships to be for the fourth, fifth and sixth wickets.)

His and Barnes' scores of 234 remain a record for the Sydney ground by Australians in a Test match (previous best, 201 by S.E. Gregory, v England, 1894–5).

This was the eighth time that he had scored three (or more) centuries in successive innings in first-class cricket; it was the fifth time he had done so wholly in Australia, equal to Ponsford's record. Bradman did so ten times altogether, six times in Australia. This was also his third century in succession against the MCC team.

This was his fourth century in successive innings in Test matches in Australia – 212 and 169 (in 1936–7), and now 187 and 234, all against England; H. Sutcliffe had been the previous best, with three in succession in 1924–5. In making a century in one innings or the other of eight consecutive Test matches in which he batted (all *v* England), Bradman performed an unsurpassed feat; the previous best was by Bradman himself, five in all Tests (1931–3), and four *v* England (1928–30); no one else had made centuries in more than three successive Tests, until in 1935 J.H. Fingleton did so in four successive Tests *v* South Africa and England. This was the third time that Bradman had made a century in four (or more) successive Tests in which he batted.

Bradman is the oldest (as well as the youngest) player to make a double century in Tests between England and Australia; he was 38 years 112 days old, whereas E. Paynter, in 1938, when he made 216*, had been 36 years 218 days old, and the oldest Australian, J.S. Ryder, had been 35 years 162 days old when he made 201* in 1924–5. He also became the oldest to make a double century in any Test match for Australia, Ryder being the previous oldest; but Bradman himself scored another Test double century *v* India the next season.

196. **AUSTRALIA** *v* **ENGLAND**, Third Test match, at Melbourne, 1, 2, 3, 4, 6 and 7 January 1947

SCORES: Australia 365 (C.L. McCool 104*, D.G. Bradman 79) and 536 (A.R. Morris 155, R.R. Lindwall 100, D. Tallon 92); England 351 (W.J. Edrich 89, C. Washbrook 62, N.W.D. Yardley 61) and 319 for 7 wickets (C. Washbrook 112, N.W.D. Yardley 53*). Drawn.

| D.G. BRADMAN (capt.) | b. N.W.D. Yardley | 79 |
| | c. and b. N.W.D. Yardley | 49 |

This was Bradman's sixth Test match against England at Melbourne, and for the first time he failed to make a century there; in both innings he was dismissed by Yardley when well set and batting at his best. His first innings began at 32 for 1, 38 minutes before lunch on the first day; he started well, making 30 by the interval, but thereafter he went more sedately. He reached 50 in 79 minutes and was 73 by the tea interval, but soon afterwards played too late at an off-break and dragged it on to his wicket. Fourth out at 188, he batted for two hours 49 minutes and hit only two fours in a sound innings. He received 158 balls.

The score was 68 for 1 when he went in for his second innings on the fourth morning, and he again started very hesitantly, making 3 in half an hour and surviving some edgy strokes as well as an appeal for lbw. by Wright when he was 3. He was 19 at the lunch interval, and thereafter settled down in more confident style; he was missed at the wicket off Bedser when 44, but the mistake was not expensive, for soon afterwards he gave Yardley an easy return catch. He was second out at 159, having played an innings lasting an hour and 39 minutes and 88 balls.

This was the first drawn Test match in Australia for 65 years.

### 197. SOUTH AUSTRALIA *v* MCC TEAM, at Adelaide, 24, 25, 27 and 28 January 1947

SCORES: MCC Team 577 (W.R. Hammond 188, James Langridge 100, L. Hutton 88, L.B. Fishlock 57) and 152 for 2 wickets (L. Hutton 77*); South Australia 443 (R.A. Hamence 145, R. James 85, P.L. Ridings 77). Drawn.

D.G. BRADMAN (capt.)  c. James Langridge b. D.V.P. Wright          5

Going in on the third morning at 19 for 1, Bradman soon pushed an easy catch to silly mid-on, to make the score 25 for 2; he stayed for six minutes.

### 198. AUSTRALIA *v* ENGLAND, Fourth Test match, at Adelaide, 31 January, 1, 3, 4, 5 and 6 February 1947

SCORES: England 460 (D.C.S. Compton 147, L. Hutton 94, J. Hardstaff 67, C. Washbrook 65) and 340 for 8 wickets dec. (D.C.S. Compton 103*, L. Hutton 76); Australia 487 (K.R. Miller 141*, A.R. Morris 122, A.L. Hassett 78, I.W. Johnson 52) and 215 for 1 wicket (A.R. Morris 124*, D.G. Bradman 56*). Drawn; Australia won the rubber.

D.G. BRADMAN (capt.)  b. A.V. Bedser          0
                          not out               56

Bradman went in at 18 for 1, 18 minutes from the close of the second day, and played 7 balls from Bedser, in ten minutes before being completely beaten and bowled by the eighth, with the score still 18.

England's declaration left Australia three and a quarter hours to make 314 to win on the last day, and Australia did not accept the challenge. Bradman went in at 116 for 1 soon after tea, and nearly played his second ball from Yardley on to his wicket, going close to obtaining a 'pair of spectacles'. He reached 50 in 68 minutes and finished the game in very dull fashion with only 6 more in the last 23 minutes. He hit four fours and batted for 91 minutes and 99 balls.

The match was played in very hot, humid weather.

199. **AUSTRALIA** *v* **ENGLAND**, Fifth Test match, at Sydney, 28 February, 3, 4 and 5 March 1947

SCORES: England 280 (L. Hutton 122*, W.J. Edrich 60, R.R. Lindwall 7 for 63) and 186 (D.C.S. Compton 76, C.L. McCool 5 for 44); Australia 253 (S.G. Barnes 71, A.R. Morris 57, D.V.P. Wright 7 for 105) and 214 for 5 wickets (D.G. Bradman 63). Australia won by 5 wickets.

| | | |
|---|---|---|
| D.G. BRADMAN (capt.) | b. D.V.P. Wright | 12 |
| | c. D.C.S. Compton b. A.V. Bedser | 63 |

Having had no match practice for almost a month, Bradman was not at his best in his first innings; he went in after tea on the second day at 126 for 1 and batted for 27 minutes before going down the wicket to Wright. Hitting across and missing a full-pitch, he would have been stumped if he had not been bowled, being third out at 146 to his 23rd ball.

His second innings was a much better one and virtually won the match for his side. He went in after lunch on the fourth day, at 45 for 1, and found the wicket was worn and that Wright and Bedser were bowling splendidly with its assistance. Cutting at Wright when 2, he gave a sharp chance to slip, but thereafter he batted well, despite the difficult conditions. Reaching 32 by the tea interval, he completed 50 in 97 minutes and had been in for a hour and 57 minutes when he gave mid-off an easy catch in trying to drive. The score was then 149 for 3 and he had hit seven fours; he and Hassett added 98 for the third wicket; and when he was 31, he reached 1,000 runs for the season. He made his 63 off 117 balls.

Thereafter Australia always had the match in hand; but England might well have won had it not been for Bradman's innings – and the missed catch.

## SUMMARY, 1946–7

| | Matches | Innings | NO | HS | Runs | Average | Centuries |
|---|---|---|---|---|---|---|---|
| All First-class Matches | 9 | 14 | 1 | 234 | 1032 | 79.38 | 4 |
| Test Matches | 5 | 8 | 1 | 234 | 680 | 97.14 | 2 |
| All Matches *v* MCC Team | 8 | 12 | 1 | 234 | 870 | 79.09 | 3 |
| Sheffield Shield Matches | 1 | 2 | 0 | 119 | 162 | 81.00 | 1 |
| All Matches for South Australia | 3 | 5 | 0 | 119 2 | 46 | 49.20 | 1 |

Australia won the Test match series by three matches to nil, with two drawn, and retained the Ashes.

In all first-class matches, three Australians, A.R. Morris (1,234), A.L. Hassett (1,213) and K.R. Miller (1,202), and two Englishmen, D.C.S. Compton (1,432) and L. Hutton (1,267) scored more runs than Bradman, but Bradman had the highest average, Miller being next best with 75.12. Morris, Hassett and Compton each scored five centuries.

In the Test matches, Bradman scored more runs than anyone else on either side, Morris being second with 503; Miller's average of 76.80 was next to Bradman's, and Morris scored one more century than he. Bradman's average of 97.14 is still a record for an Australian against England in Australia, bettering his own 90.00 in 1936–7.

Although his health improved considerably during the season, his success was a remarkable achievement for one who was a sick man at its beginning. His consistency is shown by the fact that he played an innings of 50 or over in one innings or the other in all five Test matches; only W. Bardsley (1910–1) and S.J. McCabe (1936–7) had done this before among Australians, and only McCabe in an England *v* Australia Test series; up till then it had been achieved only six times in all Tests. It has now been done 11 times in all Tests, R.N. Harvey (1952–3) and K. Mackay (1957–8) being the only other Australians to do so, both *v* South Africa; Bradman and McCabe are still the only batsmen of either country to do so in an England *v* Australia Test series. Bradman had now scored 50 in one innings or the other in the last 12 Test matches in which he batted, all against England.

His aggregates of 680 in the Test matches and 870 in all matches *v* the MCC team are the next best to his own records, set up in 1936–7, of 810 (the highest by an Australian against England in a Test rubber in Australia) and 911 (the highest by an Australian against an English touring team).

# 1947–8

## AGED THIRTY-NINE

———◆◆◆◆◆———

In greatly improved health, Bradman played against the Indian team which toured Australia for the first time this season, under L. Amarnath, but he did not make up his mind until almost the end of it whether he would be available for the 1948 Australian tour of England.

200. **SOUTH AUSTRALIA** *v* **INDIANS**, at Adelaide, 24, 25, 27 and 28 October 1947

SCORES: South Australia 518 for 8 wickets dec. (D.G. Bradman 156, R.D. Niehuus 137, R.J. Craig 100) and 219 for 8 wickets dec. (G. Noblet 50*); Indians 451 (L. Amarnath 144, V.S. Hazare 95, V. Mankad 57) and 235 for 5 wickets (V. Mankad 116*, L. Amarnath 94*). Drawn.

| D.G. BRADMAN (capt.) | c. C.T. Sarwate b. V. Mankad | 156 |
| | st. P. Sen b. V. Mankad | 12 |

The Indian bowlers included D.G. Phadkar, L. Amarnath, C.S. Nayudu, C.T. Sarwate, V.S. Hazare and S.W. Sohoni, in addition to Mankad, but they had been punished in an opening stand of 226 before Bradman came to the wicket five minutes after tea on the first day. He gave a chance at deep square-leg off Sarwate, when 23, but was otherwise in his most brilliant form, taking only 47 minutes to reach 50, and he completed his century, in 98 minutes, in the last over of the day. Starting next morning at 102 not out, he hit out recklessly, carrying his score to 156 in another 54 minutes, before being caught off a skier at deep mid-on; he gave only the one chance, batted for two hours 32 minutes and hit 22 fours, being fifth out at 465.

He had also scored a century in his first match *v* English (1928–9) and South African (1931–2) touring teams, and now added the Indians to the list; no other Australian had done this against touring teams from three countries.

His second innings took place late on the third day, when he went in at 58 for 1, and lasted 17 minutes; he was stumped, reaching forward to Mankad, with the score 76 for 2.

## 201. SOUTH AUSTRALIA *v* VICTORIA, at Adelaide, 7, 8, 10 and 11 November 1947

SCORES: Victoria 440 (A.L. Hassett 118, D. Fothergill 102, M.R. Harvey 89) and 182; South Australia 536 (P.L. Ridings 151, D.G. Bradman 100, R.J. Craig 97, B. Dooland 62) and 87 for 1 wicket. South Australia won by 9 wickets.

| | | |
|---|---|---|
| D.G. BRADMAN (capt.) | lbw. b. I.W. Johnson | 100 |
| | (did not bat) | – |

Bradman went in at 17 for 1, soon after lunch on the second day, and played a sound and chanceless innings, against bowlers who included W.A. Johnston, F. Freer, S.J.E. Loxton, I.W. Johnson and D.T. Ring. He completed 50 in one and a quarter hours, and 100 in two hours 42 minutes, being lbw. two balls later, playing across a straight ball; second out at 190, he added 173 with Craig for the second wicket, and reached the boundary eight times. This was his 99th century in first-class cricket and his only Sheffield Shield appearance for South Australia this season.

## 202. AN AUSTRALIAN XI *v* INDIANS, at Sydney, 14, 15, 17 and 18 November 1947

SCORES: Indians 326 (Gul Mahomed 85, G. Kishenchand 75*) and 304 for 9 wickets dec. (G. Kishenchand 63*, C.T. Sarwate 58); an Australian XI 380 (D.G. Bradman 172, K.R. Miller 86) and 203 (R.N. Harvey 56*, V. Mankad 8 for 84). An Australian XI lost by 47 runs.

| | | |
|---|---|---|
| D.G. BRADMAN (capt.) | c. L. Amarnath b. V.S. Hazare | 172 |
| | c. C.T. Sarwate b. V. Mankad | 26 |

With his hundredth century in prospect, Bradman took this innings very seriously when he went in at 11 for 1 on the second morning, playing himself in with great care and taking no risks. He reached 50 in 78 minutes and thereafter hit out more freely, but as his century approached he again exercised great caution. He was 99 when the last over before tea was due, and Amarnath, the Indian captain, gave the ball to Kishenchand, who was no bowler and had not so far bowled a ball on the tour; Bradman pushed his second ball to leg for a single to complete his century after batting for two hours 12 minutes.

After tea, freed from the nervous tension, he added a further 72 runs in 45 minutes of glorious stroke-play before giving a catch to deep mid-off. He batted altogether for two hours and 57 minutes, gave no chance and hit a six (late in his innings) and 18 fours; he and Miller put on 252 for the third wicket in two hours

34 minutes, and Bradman was out soon after Miller, at 287 for 4, their partnership being still the highest for the third wicket against any Indian touring team anywhere (previous best, 171 by L. Hutton and J.V. Wilson in England, 1946). S.W. Sohoni, L. Amarnath, V. Mankad, C.T. Sarwate and V.S. Hazare were the main Indian bowlers.

This was his 295th innings in first-class cricket; W.R. Hammond, the previous best, took 679 innings to reach 100 hundreds, while D.C.S. Compton took 552. Bradman is the only one of the 14 batsmen to make 100 centuries who scored it at the first attempt, i.e. immediately after his 99th; the next best, E. Hendren, allowed only one innings (of 90) to elapse between his 99th and 100th hundreds. Bradman is the only Australian ever to make 100 centuries.

Set to make 251 to win in two and a half hours on the last day, the Australians accepted the challenge and were all out in two hours against good bowling by Mankad. Bradman went in at 60 for 1, and hit up 26 in 32 minutes before being caught at forward short-leg off a half-cock shot; the score had slumped to 120 for 5 by the time he was out.


203. **AUSTRALIA** _v_ **INDIA**, First Test match, at Brisbane, 28, 29 November, 1, 2 and 4 December 1947

SCORES: Australia 382 for 8 wickets dec. (D.G. Bradman 185, K.R. Miller 58)
India 58 (E.R.H. Toshack 5 for 2) and 98 (E.R.H. Toshack 6 for 29).
Australia won by an innings and 226 runs.

D.G. BRADMAN (capt.)  hit wicket b. L. Amarnath       185

Bradman's success in the toss at Brisbane in the first Test match ever played between Australia and India again virtually won his side the match, for after Australia had taken advantage of a perfect wicket, torrential rain made the conditions impossible for India. Bradman went in 35 minutes before lunch on the first day, at 38 for 1. and made 21 before the interval; he completed 50 in 83 minutes, as the sky gradually got darker, and had reached 86 by the tea interval, when a slight drizzle held up play for 20 minutes. When the game was resumed, he ran to his century in two hours 51 minutes, and thereafter hit out in devastating fashion, in light scarcely fit for cricket, adding a further 60 in 45 minutes before play ceased at 5.40 p.m. His stand with Hassett (48) added 101 in 89 minutes for the third wicket; and Bradman was 160 not out after three hours 36 minutes' batting. Of the 75 runs added in the last hour, Bradman scored 69 and Miller 6.

Next day no play was possible until 5 p.m. and Bradman carried his score to 179 in 59 minutes, the conditions being damp and unpleasant. On the third day, on a wicket which was rapidly becoming sticky, he stayed for a further 13 minutes before sacrificing his wicket in search of quick runs prior to declaring; he tried to cut a ball which kept low and hit his wicket down from behind. He batted for four hours 48 minutes in all, gave no chance, and hit 20 fours; he was out at 318 for 4, having scored 66 per cent of the runs added while he was in. He and Miller added 120 for the fourth wicket in two hours 12 minutes, Bradman's share being 94. The Indian bowlers included S.W. Sohoni, L. Amarnath, V. Mankad, C.T. Sarwate and V.S. Hazare, and Bradman's 185 remained the highest in Tests between Australia and India for less than two months until he himself made 201 in the fourth Test match.

This was the 13th successive Test match (in which he had batted) in which he played an innings of over 50 in one innings or the other; the previous best was eight successive Tests (in which he batted) *v* South Africa and England, by Bradman himself (1931–3), and *v* Australia and South Africa, by W.R. Hammond (1938–9). E.D. Weekes has since done so in nine successive Tests *v* England and India (1947–50).

Bradman is the only Australian to make a century in his first Test *v* India, and the only Australian to make a century in his first Test against two different countries (he also did so *v* South Africa). This was the fourth Test match innings in which Bradman batted on three different days, a feat which Hammond performed three times, and A.C. Bannerman twice, these being the next best. In 1956, I.D. Craig batted on four different days.

204. **AUSTRALIA** *v* **INDIA**, Second Test match, at Sydney, 12, 13 and 17 December 1947

SCORES: India 188 (D.G. Phadkar 51) and 61 for 7 wickets. Australia 107. Drawn.

D.G. BRADMAN (capt.) b. V.S. Hazare     13

Rain ruined this match, less than ten hours' cricket being played altogether. Bradman went in at 25 for 1, in the last over of the second day, and did not have to face the bowling that evening; after two blank days owing to rain, the wicket was very difficult when he resumed his innings on the third morning, but he stayed for 40 minutes, batting well under the tricky conditions, before playing a hesitant defensive stroke and being bowled at 48 for 4.

205. **AUSTRALIA** *v* **INDIA**, Third Test match, at Melbourne, 1, 2, 3 and 5 January 1948.

SCORES: Australia 394 (D.G. Bradman 132, A.L. Hassett 80) and 255 for 4 wickets dec. (D.G. Bradman 127*, A.R. Morris 100*); India 291 for 9 wickets dec. (V. Mankad 116, D.G Phadkar 55*) and 125. Australia won by 233 runs.

| D.G. BRADMAN (capt.) | lbw. b. D.G. Phadkar | 132 |
| | not out | 127 |

For the only time in his career Bradman scored a century in each innings of a Test match, and again dominated the unfortunate Indian bowlers, who this time included D.G. Phadkar, L. Amarnath, V.S. Hazare, V. Mankad and C.T. Sarwate.

His first innings commenced on the first morning at 29 for 1; 37 by lunch, he reached 50 in 84 minutes and had made 99 by the tea interval. He completed his century just afterwards, after two hours 39 minutes' batting, and carried his score to 132 before being attacked by cramp; he went on with his innings before properly recovering, swung wildly at the next ball and was lbw. His chanceless innings lasted three hours 17 minutes, ended at 280 for 4 and included eight fours; he and Hassett put on 169 in a minute under two hours for the third wicket, this being the highest for the third wicket in all Test matches against India (previous best, 127 by W.R. Hammond and T.S. Worthington, 1936), though in 1952–3 F.M. Worrell and E.D. Weekes broke this record with a stand of 197 for the West Indies, and then in 1955–6 B. Sutcliffe and J.R. Reid put on 222 for New Zealand. It remains a record for the third wicket for Tests between Australia and India (previous best, 101 by Bradman and Hassett in the first Test match).

Bradman's 29th run was his 6,000th in all Test matches.

When India declared on the third day after rain had made the wicket tricky, Bradman countered by putting in his tail-enders first; however, he had to go in himself when four batsmen were out for 32 soon after lunch, when he joined Morris in a long and unbroken stand. The wicket had by then lost much of its venom, and although Bradman had to exercise some caution early on, taking an hour over his first 23, he gradually opened out as the conditions became easier. Forty not out at the tea interval, he reached 50 in 86 minutes, and his century 42 minutes later, in two hours eight minutes; thereafter, he set himself to assist Morris to the same objective, which he achieved in the last over of the day. The pair added 223 for the fifth wicket and Bradman batted for two minutes under three hours; he gave no chance and hit 13 fours. More rain overnight making the wicket sticky again, Bradman declared at once next morning.

This was the fourth time he had made a century in each innings, the only Australian to do so more than twice and the only batsman to do so more than twice in Australia. Only W.R. Hammond (seven), J.B. Hobbs (six) and C.B. Fry (five) have made a century in each innings more often than Bradman; only Hammond, R.A, Hamence, Morris and C. Pinch have scored two hundreds in a match twice in Australia, while A.L. Hassett has done so once in Australia and once in India, and C.G. Macartney and A.F. Kippax once in Australia and once in England.

He was only the third Australian to do so in Test matches, and the first of any nationality to do so again against India; E.D. Weekes in 1948–9, for the West Indies, is the only batsman to do so since v India, and in 1949–50 v South Africa, J.A.R. Moroney joined Bradman, W. Bardsley and Morris to become the fourth Australians to perform this feat in all Test cricket.

This was the fourth occasion in all Tests in which he made a score of 50 or more in each innings, then a record for Australia; up till then, only Bradman, Bardsley, C. Hill, M.A. Noble and J.S. Ryder had done this three times in all Test matches. Morris has since done so four times, all *v* England.

The partnership of 223 between Bradman and Morris is still a record for the fifth wicket for all Test matches *v* India (previous best, 182 by J. Hardstaff and P.A. Gibb for England, 1946), and for all Test matches between Australia and India; it also remains a record for the fifth wicket against any Indian touring team anywhere (previous best, 201 by C. Washbrook and N. Oldfield, 1936).

206. **AUSTRALIA** *v* **INDIA**, Fourth Test match, at Adelaide, 23, 24, 26, 27 and 28 January 1948

SCORES: Australia 674 (D.G. Bradman 201, A.L. Hassett 198*, S.G. Barnes 112, K.R. Miller 67); India 381 (D.G. Phadkar 123, V.S. Hazare 116) and 277 (V.S. Hazare 145, H.R. Adhikari 51, R.R. Lindwall 7 for 38). Australia won by an innings and 16 runs and won the rubber.

D.G. BRADMAN (capt.)   b. V.S. Hazare          201

The Indian bowlers, D.G. Phadkar, L. Amarnath, C.R. Rangachari, V. Mankad, C.T. Sarwate and V.S. Hazare, came in for further heavy punishment when Bradman won the toss on a perfect wicket and he made the 37th and last double century of his career, thereby again passing W.R. Hammond, whose final total was 36; Hammond played 1,004 innings in first-class cricket, while this was Bradman's 301st innings.

He went in at 20 for 1 on the first morning and took an hour before lunch to score only 20; having completed 50 in an hour and 41 minutes, he was 94 not out at the tea interval, completing his century (his third successive innings, all in Test matches) soon afterwards in three hours 11 minutes. Thereafter he forced the pace brilliantly, taking only 79 minutes over his second century; he threw his wicket away two minutes later with a wild swing, having batted for four hours and 32 minutes and hit a six and 21 fours. Third out at 361, just before the end of the day, he and Barnes put on 236 in three and a half hours for the second wicket, while he and Hassett added 105 in an hour for the third; his innings was faultless and he reached his 1,000 runs for the season, for the 12th and last time when he was 77.

This was the sixth time that he had made 200 runs or more in a day's play in a Test match, three times in Australia and three times in England; W.R. Hammond has done this four times, and only eight other batsmen have done it once; the only other Australians in this list are V.T. Trumper, H.L. Collins, W.H. Ponsford and S.J. McCabe. Only Trumper and R.E. Foster have, apart from Bradman, achieved this feat in Australia, where there are usually only five hours of play each day.

For the ninth time he scored three (or more) successive centuries in first-class cricket, the next best being six times by Hammond; this was the sixth time that Bradman had done this wholly in Australia, one more than Ponsford's previous record of five. Bradman did this once more, in England. This was the first time that Bradman had achieved this feat in Test matches; the only other Australians to have done this in the same Test series are C.G. Macartney (*v* England, 1926), J.H. Fingleton (*v* South Africa, 1935–6) and A.R. Morris (*v* England, 1946–7), and only Morris and Bradman have done so in Australia, though for England H. Sutcliffe also did so. Fingleton made another century in his first innings in his next Test series, making four in successive Test innings, and E.D. Weekes made five in succession for the West Indies, one *v* England in 1947–8 and four *v* India in 1948–9.

At the age of 39 years 149 days, Bradman is the oldest batsman ever to score 200 for Australia in a Test match, he himself having previously been the oldest when he made 234 *v* England a year earlier. He had also been the youngest batsman to score 200 in a Test for Australia, and there was a period of 17 and a half years between his first and last Test double centuries, longer than anyone else has achieved, L. Hutton being next best with 15 and a half years. There was also 19 years between his first and last double centuries in first-class cricket, a record for Australians, W.W. Armstrong, 15 and a half years, being next best.

His 201 is the highest score in Australia *v* India Test matches, the previous best being his own 185 in the first Test match; he thus has made the highest score for Australia against four other countries, England, South Africa, West Indies and India – a unique achievement.

His second-wicket stand of 236 with Barnes is the highest for that wicket in any Test match against India (previous best, 134 by W.R. Hammond and A.E. Fagg, for England, 1936), and the highest for any wicket in Test matches between Australia and India (previous best, 223 for the fifth wicket, by Bradman and Morris in the third Test match).

He is the only batsman to make double centuries against four different countries in Test matches (*v* England, South Africa, West Indies and India); Hammond and Hutton, for England, scored over 200 *v* three different countries, while the next best for Australia, R.N. Harvey, has made scores of 200 or over *v* South Africa and the West Indies. Bradman is also the only batsman to score double centuries against touring teams from four different countries; Hammond and Hutton, made double centuries in England against teams from three different countries, but in Australia, A.J. Richardson, with two such scores *v* MCC, and V.T. Trumper (*v* New Zealanders and South Africans) are the only other batsmen to make more than one such score against any touring side. Indeed, largely because Australia, before the 1939–45 war, played Test matches mainly against England and South Africa, and apart from that had only one series against any other country (1930–1 *v* West Indies), up to 1948 no other Australian had scored even a single century against more than two different countries in Test matches, or against touring teams from more than two different countries; with the increase in

Australian Test cricket since 1945, however, A.R. Morris, A.L. Hassett and R.N. Harvey have all scored centuries against England, South Africa, West Indies and India in Test matches, and Hassett scored hundreds in Australia against touring teams from all these four countries.

***

The day before the start of the fifth Test match, Bradman announced that he would be available for the Australian tour of England, but that he would retire from cricket at its conclusion.

## 207. AUSTRALIA *v* INDIA, Fifth Test match, at Melbourne, 6, 7, 9 and 10 February 1948

SCORES: Australia 575 for 8 wickets dec. (R.N. Harvey 153, W.A. Brown 99, S.J.E. Loxton 80, D.G. Bradman 57*); India 331 (V. Mankad 111, V.S. Hazare 74, D.G. Phadkar 56*) and 67. Australia won by an innings and 177 runs.

D.G. BRADMAN (capt.)  retired hurt          57

Bradman went in at 48 for 1, three-quarters of an hour before lunch on the first day, and made 35 by the interval; he settled down in his best form afterwards, completed 50 in 73 minutes and was 57 after an hour and 25 minutes, when he tore a muscle in his left side and was compelled to retire; he had been batting so well that it seemed likely that he would complete his fifth century of the series. He gave no chance and hit four fours; the score when he left was 140 for 1, and K.R. Miller helped Brown to take the second-wicket partnership to 134. He was unable to resume his innings, but had recovered sufficiently after the weekend to field on the last two days, mainly in the slips.

## 208. AUSTRALIANS *v* WESTERN AUSTRALIA, at Perth, 13, 15 and 16 March 1948

SCORES: Western Australia 348 (W. Langdon 112, B. Rigg 65, A. Edwards 57) and 62 for 3 wickets; Australians 442 for 7 wickets dec. (A.R. Morris 115, D.G. Bradman 115, R.N. Harvey 79). Drawn.

D.G. BRADMAN (capt.)  c. T. Outridge b. T. O'Dwyer   115

Bradman went in at 48 for 1, on the second afternoon, and was soon scoring freely; he reached 50 in 47 minutes, and though he spent 40 minutes in the nineties, against the new ball, he reached 100 in a minute more than two hours. Just before the close, after two hours 21 minutes at the wicket, he was caught in the covers; second out at 249, he and Morris added 201 for the second wicket. Bradman hit 16 fours in a chanceless innings; this was his eighth century of the season, another record for Australian cricket.

## SUMMARY, 1947–8

| | Matches | Innings | NO | HS | Runs | Average | Centuries |
|---|---|---|---|---|---|---|---|
| All First-class Matches | 9 | 12 | 2 | 201 | 1296 | 129.60 | 8 |
| Test Matches | 5 | 6 | 2 | 201 | 715 | 178.75 | 4 |
| All Matches *v* Indians | 7 | 10 | 2 | 201 | 1081 | 135.12 | 6 |
| Sheffield Shield Matches | 1 | 1 | 0 | 100 | 100 | – | 1 |
| All matches for South Australia | 2 | 3 | 0 | 156 | 268 | 89.33 | 2 |

Australia won the Test match series by four matches to nil, with one drawn.

Bradman's recovery of health and form this season produced figures reminiscent of his best days, and in making as many as eight centuries he broke his own Australian and South Australian records for the number of centuries in an Australian season; in 1928–9 he and W.R. Hammond had scored seven hundreds, and in 1931–2 and 1937–8 he had again made seven, but no one else has ever made more than six in a season in Australia. His proportion of centuries, eight in 12 innings, or 66 per cent, is the next best on record for an Australian season, after his own 85 per cent (six in seven) in 1938–9.

For the 12th and last time, and for the sixth time since transferring to South Australia, he exceeded 1,000 runs for the season.

For the third time he made four centuries in a Test match rubber; up till then the only other batsmen to make four centuries in a rubber were H. Sutcliffe (twice), W.R. Hammond, G.A. Headley and D.C.S. Compton, no other Australian having ever done so. Since then, R.N. Harvey has made four centuries in a series *v* South Africa twice, and for the West Indies, C.L. Walcott made five centuries *v* Australia in 1955. Bradman is the only batsman to make four in a series twice in Australia, and was the only batsman to achieve this feat *v* India until E.D. Weekes also did so for the West Indies in 1948–9. Among Australians, only Harvey (two) and Bradman have scored more than one Test century *v* India, and until then only Hammond (two) and Bradman had scored more than one for any country *v* India; Weekes has since made seven.

For the second time Bradman played five innings of 50 or over in one Test match series; in fact, he did so in consecutive series, the previous occasion having been in 1946–7. Up till then, only J.B. Hobbs had done this in two Test rubbers, though five others have since achieved this performance twice; Harvey is the only other Australian to do so twice, Walcott and P.B.H. May are the only others to do so in successive series.

Bradman's aggregate of 715 for the series was also a Test record *v* India (previous best, 389 by Hammond in 1936), until Weekes amassed 779 for the West Indies in 1948–9. As only three more Test matches have since been played between the two countries, it remains, of course, the highest aggregate in all Tests between Australia and India by a batsman on either side.

His average of 178.75 is next to his own 201.50 in 1931–2, *v* South Africa, as the highest on record for any Test match rubber, and it is the highest against India (previous best, 73.66 by D.R. Jardine, for England, 1933–4; Hammond, in 1936, had only two completed innings when he averaged 194.50).

His total of 1,081 runs in all matches *v* the Indians is also the highest in one season by any batsman against any Indian touring team anywhere (previous best, 505 by Hammond, in England, 1936; next best, 969 by Weekes, in the West Indies, 1952–3). Only Bradman (twice), D.C.S. Compton and G. Sobers have made over 1,000 runs in a season against any touring team anywhere; only Bradman (twice) and Compton have scored six centuries in a season off a touring team's bowling.

Bradman was again easily top of the Australian batting figures this season with the highest aggregate and average; next to him among Australians was A.L. Hassett, with 893 runs, average 68.69. No Australian except Bradman scored more than three centuries. For the Indians, L. Amarnath and V.S. Hazare scored 1,162 and 1,056 runs respectively, the former scoring five centuries. This was the 11th season in which Bradman had headed the Australian batting averages, the seventh in which he had averaged over 100 and the 13th in which his average exceeded 50.

In the Test matches, Hazare's aggregate of 429 was the next highest on either side, while Hassett, for Australia, made 332 runs, average 110.66. No one else on either side made more than two centuries and no other Australian made more than one.

This was the second season in Australia that he had returned a century average both for the Test series and for all first-class matches, the other time being in 1931–2, and he also did so in England in 1938; no one else has ever done this, either in England or Australia, though E.D. Weekes and G. Sobers also did so in the West Indies in 1952–3 and 1957–8 respectively.

# 1948

## AGED THIRTY-NINE

———◆◆◆———

Bradman was, of course, again captain of the Australian team on his fourth and last tour of England, and he had helped to select one of the most powerful of all Australian sides. Nevertheless, his decision to undertake the tour was a courageous one, for he was, in effect, putting his reputation into jeopardy in a gamble upon his continued form and fitness. He must have had in mind the unhappy experience of W.R. Hammond who, after a very successful season in England in 1946, failed completely to recapture his form on Australian wickets in 1946–47, owing partly to muscular trouble of a nature similar to that from which Bradman had so recently recovered. Moreover, only W. Bardsley (42 in 1926), S.E. Gregory (42 in 1912), W.W. Armstrong (41 in 1921) and C.G. Macartney (39 in 1926), among Australian batsmen, had been older than Bradman was now when embarking upon an English tour.

### 209. AUSTRALIANS *v* WORCESTERSHIRE, at Worcester, 28, 29 and 30 April 1948

SCORES: Worcestershire 233 (C.H. Palmer 85, E. Cooper 51) and 212 (L. Outschoorn 54); Australians 462 for 8 wickets dec. (A.R. Morris 138, D.G. Bradman 107, K.R. Miller 50*, P.F. Jackson 6 for 135). Australians won by an innings and 17 runs.

D.G. BRADMAN (capt.)  b. P.F. Jackson      107

Although he did not on this occasion start the tour with a double century, Bradman for the fourth time made over 100 at Worcester in his first match and could probably have doubled his score had he wished. In cold and unpleasant weather, he went in on the second morning at 79 for 1, and in company with Morris raised the score by 186 to 265 for 2, before he threw his wicket away just after tea. He reached 50 in 71 minutes, and 100 in two hours 18 minutes, just before the interval, Morris (who had had one hour and 41 minutes' and 34 runs' start) narrowly winning the race for the century; Bradman batted altogether for two hours 32 minutes, gave no chance, and hit 15 fours. Jackson, who caused him to play on when going for a big hit, R.T.D. Perks, C.H. Palmer, R.O.

Jenkins and R. Howorth were among the opposing bowlers.

His record of commencing four successive English tours with innings of 236 (1930), 206 (1934), 258 (1938) and 107 (1948), all against Worcestershire, is quite unrivalled; but in this match Miller started a sequence which is the nearest approach to it. He began the 1948 tour with innings of 50* and 202*, and his first innings of the 1953 and 1956 tours were 220* and 281* respectively; moreover, Miller's first innings in any first-class match in England, in the Victory match in 1945, had been 105.

This was Bradman's second century in April, the first being his 258 in 1938; no other visiting batsman has done this more than once, and T. Hayward and E.H.D. Sewell are the only Englishmen to do so twice.

## 210. AUSTRALIANS v LEICESTERSHIRE, at Leicester, 1, 3 and 4 May 1948

SCORES: Australians 448 (K.R. Miller 202*, D.G. Bradman 81, S.G. Barnes 78, V.E. Jackson 5 for 91); Leicestershire 130 (D.T. Ring 5 for 45) and 147 (I.W. Johnson 7 for 42). Australians won by an innings and 171 runs.

D.G. BRADMAN (capt.) c. P. Corrall b. M.W. Etherington      81

For the only time on this tour Bradman forsook the number three position, and came in at 157 for 2, soon after lunch on the first day, on a soft by easy wicket; the weather was again bitterly cold. He was for some time in trouble against J.E. Walsh's spin, but otherwise he was at his best, reaching 50 in 53 minutes, and it was a surprise when he failed to cover a slower ball which moved away, and gave a catch to the wicket-keeper. He batted for an hour and 52 minutes, hit six fours and added 159 with Miller for the third wicket, being out at 316 for 3. Etherington, who dismissed him, took only 3 wickets for 59 runs each in his whole first-class career.

***

In Bradman's absence the Australians beat Yorkshire by 4 wickets, but came perilously close to defeat before they did so.

## 211. AUSTRALIANS v SURREY, at the Oval, 8, 10 and 11 May 1948

SCORES: Australians 632 (S.G. Barnes 176, D.G. Bradman 146, A.L. Hassett 110, A.R. Morris 65, D. Tallon 50*); Surrey 141 (L.B. Fishlock 81*, I.W. Johnson 5 for 53) and 195 (H.S. Squires 54). Australians won by an innings and 296 runs.

D.G. BRADMAN (capt.) b. A.V. Bedser      146

After the Surrey bowlers, who included A.V. Bedser and J.C. Laker, had been worn down on the first day in an opening stand of 136, which ended just before lunch, Bradman joined Barnes in a second-wicket partnership of 207 in two hours 18 minutes. Bradman made a most confident start and batted at his best; he reached 50 in 77 minutes and completed his century in two hours 16 minutes just before Barnes was out. When he was 137, he made his first mistake, putting up a catch to mid-wicket off Laker, and soon afterwards, at 403 for 3, he was bowled, playing a defensive stroke, by a fine ball from Bedser. He hit 15 fours in an innings lasting two hours 54 minutes.

Rain interfering with play on the last day, the Australians had only 22 minutes to spare at the end.

## 212. AUSTRALIANS v ESSEX, at Southend, 15 and 17 May 1948

SCORES: Australians 721 (D.G. Bradman 187, W.A. Brown 153, S.J.E. Loxton 120, R.A. Saggers 104*, S.G. Barnes 79); Essex 83 (E.R.H. Toshack 5 for 31) and 187 (T.N. Pearce 71, T.P.B. Smith 54, I.W. Johnson 6 for 37). Australians won by an innings and 451 runs.

D.G. BRADMAN (capt.)  b. T.P.B. Smith        187

Bradman went in to bat at 145 for 1, 22 minutes before lunch on the first day, and by the interval he had made 42 not out; he used his last over, from F.H. Vigar, to score 20 (five fours). From that extraordinary start he completed 50 after lunch in 34 minutes, 100 in 74 minutes and was at the wicket for only two hours four minutes altogether when he was bowled for 187, swinging across a straight ball; his last 87 came in 50 minutes. Between 50 and 80 he made two rather streaky strokes through the slips off T.P.B. Smith, and at 160 he gave a hard chance in the deep off E. Price, in an over in which he again hit five fours; otherwise, his display was faultless, and he hit a five and 32 fours (133 runs in boundaries, or 71 per cent). He and Brown added 219 in 94 minutes for the second wicket; he was himself out at 452 for 4, having put the Australians well on the way to their 721 in five hours 50 minutes, the highest day's total in history, and he had himself played the fastest innings of his career, averaging 90 runs an hour.

This was the second time that the Australians had played at Southend, and his 187 is the highest score made on the ground for them. Essex was the 12th English county against which he had made a century, thus passing W. Bardsley's record of centuries v 11 different counties; Bradman altogether made centuries v 13 different counties.

### 213. AUSTRALIANS *v* MCC, at Lord's, 22, 24 and 25 May 1948

SCORES: Australians 552 (K.R. Miller 163, D.G. Bradman 98, S.G. Barnes 81, I.W. Johnson 80, A.L. Hassett 51); MCC 189 (L. Hutton 52, E.R.H. Toshack 6 for 51) and 205 (L. Hutton 64). Australians won by an innings and 158 runs.

D.G. BRADMAN (capt.)  c. W.J. Edrich b. J.H.G. Deighton          98

Bradman came in early on the first day at 11 for 1 and was soon at his best, reaching 50 in 67 minutes. thereafter, though still batting well, he made slower progress against accurate bowling from J.A. Young and J.C. Laker, but it was a surprise when, at 98, he mistimed a cut and was caught, via the wicket-keeper's gloves, at slip. This was the closest he ever got to a century without reaching it; it was the sixth and last time he was dismissed in the nineties. He batted for two minutes under two and a half hours, and hit 11 fours; third out at 200, he and Barnes added 160 together for the second wicket.

W. Bardsley, in four tours and 175 innings, had made 7,866 runs for Australian teams in England (the highest on record), and when he had made 37, Bradman passed this total in his 94th innings in England.

This was Bradman's tenth successive innings of over 50, a feat of consistency previously achieved only by E. Tyldesley in 1926; the previous best by an Australian was eight successive fifties by Bradman in 1937–8 and 1938.

### 214. AUSTRALIANS *v* LANCASHIRE, at Manchester, 27 and 28 May 1948

SCORES: Australians 204 and 259 for 4 wickets (R.N. Harvey 76*, S.J.E. Loxton 52); Lancashire 182 (G.A. Edrich 55, W.A. Johnston 5 for 49). Drawn.

D.G. BRADMAN (capt.)  b. M.J. Hilton                        11
                      st. E.H. Edrich b. M.J. Hilton       43

Having so far scored 619 runs in five innings, the lowest of which was 81, Bradman was less successful in this match. The first day having been washed out, the Australians were put in to bat next morning on a drying wicket, and Bradman, at 37 for 1, appeared to have settled down comfortably; he was in for half an hour before being beaten by the 19-year-old Hilton at 58 for 2, chopping on to his wicket a ball which came in with the arm.

The wicket was a good deal easier, though still soft, when Bradman batted against at 25 for 1, on the last afternoon, but he was for some time in great trouble against R. Pollard; having mastered that bowler and settled down, he was then beaten by three successive balls from Hilton, before being stumped off the fourth; in trying an over-ambitious pull, he overbalanced and could not regain his ground

– a rather undignified exit. Third out at 125, he batted for 66 minutes; this was the only post-war match in which he was twice dismissed for less than 50 in either innings.

## 215. AUSTRALIANS *v* NOTTINGHAMSHIRE, at Nottingham, 29, 31 May, 1 June 1948

SCORES: Nottinghamshire 179 (R.T. Simpson 74, R.R. Lindwall 6 for 14) and 299 for 8 wickets (J. Hardstaff 107, R.T. Simpson 70); Australians 400 (W.A. Brown 122, D.G. Bradman 86, K.R. Miller 51). Drawn.

D.G. BRADMAN (capt.)   b. F.G. Woodhead   86

Bradman, having gone in at 32 for 1, was 22 not out after 41 minutes, when rain stopped the first day's play at 5.15 p.m. Next morning, on a slow but easy wicket, he reached 50 in 98 minutes, and soon afterwards, when 66, gave a sharp chance in the gully off H.J. Butler. In the first over after lunch, he was bowled, playing a forward defensive stroke, having batted for two hours 37 minutes; rather below his best form, he hit nine fours and helped Brown to add 165 before he was second out at 197. His total to the end of May was 759 in eight innings.

## 216. AUSTRALIANS *v* SUSSEX, at Hove, 5 and 7 June 1948

SCORES: Sussex 86 (R.R. Lindwall 6 for 34) and 138 (H.W. Parks 61, R.R. Lindwall 5 for 25); Australians 549 for 5 wickets dec. (A.R. Morris 184, D.G. Bradman 109, R.N. Harvey 100*, R.R. Lindwall 57). Australians won by an innings and 325 runs.

D.G. BRADMAN (capt.)  b. J. Cornford        109

Bradman went in at 153 for 1 on the first evening and after an escape at 2, when he was missed at the wicket off A.E. James, he made 43 not out in 74 minutes before the close of play in support of a fine innings by Morris. Next morning he took only six minutes to complete 50, himself hitting 20 of the first three overs of the day, and his century came up in two minutes under two hours. Six minutes later he threw his wicket away with a wild swing, having added 66 on the second morning in 50 minutes; third out at 360, he and Morris added 189 for the second wicket in one hour and 54 minutes, and he reached the boundary 12 times. He gave only the one chance.

This was his first century *v* Sussex, the 13th English county against which he had made at least 100.

217. **AUSTRALIA** *v* **ENGLAND**, First Test match, at Nottingham, 10, 11, 12, 14 and 15 June 1948

SCORES: England 165 (J.C. Laker 63, W.A. Johnston 5 for 36) and 441 (D.C.S. Compton 184, L. Hutton 74, T.G. Evans 50); Australia 509 (D.G. Bradman 138, A.L. Hassett 137, S.G. Barnes 62) and 98 for 2 wickets (S.G. Barnes 64*). Australia won by 8 wickets.

| | | |
|---|---|---|
| D.G. BRADMAN (capt.) | c. L. Hutton b. A.V. Bedser | 138 |
| | c. L. Hutton b. A.V. Bedser | 0 |

Bradman's first innings began at 73 for 1, at 12.50 p.m. on the second day, and he had scored 19 by the lunch interval. He was at first uncomfortable against both Bedser and Laker, but later he played very soundly, though always exercising great care. He reached 50 in an hour and 40 minutes, and was 78 at the tea interval, having failed to add to his score in the last 25 minutes; his last 32 runs to his century took him 86 minutes, and the 100 (at 5.21 p.m.) took him three hours 31 minutes, a slow rate of scoring, which was induced mainly by the defensive tactics and field-placing of the England bowlers. By the close of play, after four hours 40 minutes of watchful batting, he was 130 not out.

He lasted only another eight minutes next morning; when 132, he completed his 1,000 runs of the season (this being 12 June, and his tenth innings), but in the third over he played an in-swinger into the hands of backward short-leg, with the score 305 for 5. He hit ten fours, gave no chance, and, with Hassett, added 120 for the fifth wicket in two hours 43 minutes; the England bowlers included W.J. Edrich, A.V. Bedser, J.A. Young, J.C. Laker and N.W.D. Yardley. He made his runs off 321 balls.

His partnership of 120 with Hassett for the fifth wicket is a Test match record for Australia against England in England, the previous best being 118 by W. Bardsley and V.T. Trumper, 1909.

This was the third English season in which he had been the first batsman, English or Australian, to reach 1,000 runs; of overseas players, the only others to have done this are W.L. Murdoch and C.G. Macartney (once each). On this occasion he beat J.D. Robertson to this total by about an hour.

His 138 was his fifth successive Test match innings of over 50, a record for Australia; until then, only eight Australians, including Bradman himself in 1936–7 and 1938, had made as many as four fifties in consecutive innings in Test matches. R.N. Harvey equalled this record of Bradman's with five fifties in succession in 1952–3.

Despite a fighting recovery by England, Australia had ample time to make 98 to win on the last afternoon, but Bradman, who came in at 38 for 1, was out 13 minutes later to his tenth ball, at 48 for 2, in the same way as in the first innings, caught at backward short-leg, for his first 'duck' in a Test match in England, and the slowest 'duck' of his career. Australia then won without further loss.

## 218. AUSTRALIANS *v* YORKSHIRE, at Sheffield, 19, 21 and 22 June 1948

SCORES: Australians 249 (D.G. Bradman 54) and 285 for 5 wickets dec. (W.A. Brown 113, D.G. Bradman 86, R.N. Harvey 56); Yorkshire 206 (E.R.H. Toshack 7 for 81) and 85 for 4 wickets. Drawn.

| D.G. BRADMAN (capt.) | c. N.W.D. Yardley b. J.H. Wardle | 54 |
| | c. L. Hutton b. R. Aspinall | 86 |

The Australian first wicket fell to the third ball of the match and Bradman went in with the score 0 for 1, in poor light and on a pitch which gave the Yorkshire bowlers (who, in addition to Wardle and Aspinall, included A. Coxon, T.F. Smailes and E.P. Robinson) a good deal of help. Despite this, he completed his 50 in 78 minutes and had raised the score to 89 for 3 when he lifted a drive to extra-cover; he hit six fours and batted for 95 minutes altogether.

On the second evening, the Australian batted on a drying pitch and Bradman, after going in at 17 for 1, had to be at his best; though sometimes uncomfortable, he gave no actual chance and successfully overcame the difficult conditions in a long stand with Brown. He reached 50 in 75 minutes but then slowed down and was batting for an hour and 55 minutes for the 66 he had made by the close of play. Next morning, on an easier wicket, he carried his score to 86 before again falling victim to Hutton at backward short-leg; second out at 171, he and Brown added 154. His innings lasted two hours 35 minutes and included eight fours.

## 219. AUSTRALIA *v* ENGLAND, Second Test match, at Lord's, 24, 25, 26, 28 and 29 June 1948

SCORES: Australia 350 (A.R. Morris 105, D. Tallon 53) and 460 for 7 wickets dec. (S.G. Barnes 141, D.G. Bradman 89, K.R. Miller 74, A.R. Morris 62); England 215 (D.C.S. Compton 53, R.R. Lindwall 5 for 70) and 186 (E.R.H. Toshack 5 for 40). Australia won by 409 runs.

| D.G. BRADMAN (capt.) | c. L. Hutton b. A.V. Bedser | 38 |
| | c. W.J. Edrich b. A.V. Bedser | 89 |

Bradman's first innings began at 3 for 1, soon after the start of play, on a rather damp and green wicket and in a heavy atmosphere, and for the first hour he was as uncertain as he ever was. He nearly played on to his first ball, from A. Coxon, and survived a confident lbw. appeal in the same over; while not long afterwards two very streaky shots only just avoided the leg-trap. However, after making 35 in an hour and 48 minutes before lunch, he appeared to have settled down; but soon afterwards he gave yet another catch to Hutton at backward short-leg off Bedser's in-swinger – the third time in successive innings in Test matches that he had failed to time his leg-glance properly against Bedser's bowling. He made 38 in an hour and 55 minutes (an average of 19 runs an hour) off 104 balls and helped to raise the score to 87 for 2.

His second innings was much better; he went in at 2.52 p.m. on the third afternoon, at 122 for 1, and though he was not comfortable at first against Laker or Bedser, he soon settled down to a long partnership with Barnes. He resisted the temptation to glance Bedser's in-swingers, playing them mainly with his pads, and this checked his rate of scoring; however, he was 50 at the tea interval, having reached 50 in the last over after 98 minutes' batting, and looked certain to reach his century when Bedser took his wicket for the sixth time in six successive innings, and for the fifth time in successive Test match innings. This time he was caught in the slips, Edrich taking a brilliant diving catch; he was out at 6.12 p.m., after 162 balls and three hours five minutes' batting, and he hit 13 fours. He and Barnes put on 174 in two hours 35 minutes for the second wicket, and Bradman was fourth out at 329.

This was the 14th successive Test match *v* England (in which he batted) in which he made at least 50 in one innings or the other – an achievement of extraordinary consistency. The next best performance of this nature in Tests between England and Australia was by S.J. McCabe who in 1934–8 made at least 50 in one innings or the other in seven successive Tests against England; before that, Bradman, six successive Tests against England in 1928–30, had held the record, no one else before that having scored over 50 in more than four consecutive Tests between England and Australia.

This was the nearest he ever got to a Test match century without attaining it.


## 220. AUSTRALIANS *v* SURREY, at the Oval, 30 June, 1 and 2 July 1948

SCORES: Surrey 221 (J.F. Parker 76) and 289 (J.F. Parker 81, L.B. Fishlock 61, E.R.T. Holmes 54, C.L. McCool 6 for 113); Australians 389 (A.L. Hassett 139, D.G. Bradman 128) and 122 for no wicket (R.N. Harvey 73*). Australians won by 10 wickets.

| | | |
|---|---|---|
| D.G. BRADMAN (capt.) c. M.R. Barton b. H.S. Squires | 128 |
| (did not bat) | – |

There was little in Surrey's weakened attack to prevent Bradman from scoring his sixth century of the season. He went in at 6 for 1 on the first evening and had 91 minutes' batting before the close, hitting up 84 not out; his 50 took 56 minutes. Next morning he completed his century in a further 20 minutes, and threw his wicket away half an hour later, caught at mid-on off a wild heave; he was in altogether for two hours 21 minutes, gave no chance and hit 15 fours, being second out at 237 after he and Hassett had added 231 for the second wicket.

Bradman had previously won the toss and put Surrey in to bat.

## 221. ENGLAND *v* AUSTRALIA, Third Test match, at Manchester, 8, 9, 10 and 13 July 1948

SCORES: England 363 (D.C.S. Compton 145*) and 174 for 3 wickets dec. (C. Washbrook 85*, W.J. Edrich 53); Australia 221 (A.R. Morris 51) and 92 for 1 wicket (A.R. Morris 54*). Drawn; Australia retained the Ashes.

D.G. BRADMAN (capt.) lbw. b. R. Pollard     7
               not out            30

Going in at 3 for 1 on the second afternoon, Bradman had his first innings ended after nine minutes and seven balls by an in-swinger at 13 for 2. By the end of the third day, England had played themselves into an encouraging position, but rain prevented any further play until 2.15 p.m. on the last day, and though Yardley declared at once, Australia had little difficulty in forcing a draw. On a very soft wet wicket, which was too slow and lifeless to give much help to the bowlers, Bradman and Morris defended grimly; the former, coming in at 2.49 p.m. with the score at 10 for 1, took 35 balls and 28 minutes before opening his score (the longest of his career), and neither made any real effort to score runs. Further rain interrupted the game for four minutes during the afternoon, and again at 4.10 p.m., when Bradman was 24; this shower prevented further play until 5.45 p.m., after which there was only 45 minutes left. Bradman scored only six more runs in these 45 minutes; indeed, he scored on 2 in the last 42 minutes, but time was what mattered, not runs. He survived 146 balls.

At the close, Bradman had been in for two minutes over two hours. At 14 runs an hour this was the slowest innings he ever played, and he scored only 36 per cent of the runs added while he was at the wicket, the lowest proportion of his career in Test matches. He hit as many as six fours; play had been in progress for 99 minutes and Bradman had been in for 65 minutes before the batsmen changed ends.

This was his 50th Test match.

## 222. AUSTRALIANS *v* MIDDLESEX, at Lord's, 19 and 20 July 1948

SCORES: Middlesex 203 (D.C.S. Compton 62) and 135 (J.G. Dewes 51); Australians 317 (S.J.E. Loxton 123, A.R. Morris 109, J.M. Sims 6 for 65) and 22 for no wicket. Australians won by 10 wickets.

D.G. BRADMAN (capt.) c. D.C.S. Compton b. P.A. Whitcombe     6
               (did not bat)            –

Bradman, in at 14 for 1 early on the second day, gave backward short-leg another catch off an in-swinger; he was second out at 38, after batting for 24 minutes.

### 223. AUSTRALIA *v* ENGLAND, Fourth Test match, at Leeds, 22, 23, 24, 26 and 27 July 1948

SCORES: England 496 (C. Washbrook 143, W.J. Edrich 111, L. Hutton 81, A.V. Bedser 79) and 365 for 8 wickets dec. (D.C.S. Compton 66, C. Washbrook 65, L. Hutton 57, W.J. Edrich 54); Australia 458 (R.N. Harvey 112, S.J.E. Loxton 93, R.R. Lindwall 77, K.R. Miller 58) and 404 for 3 wickets (A.R. Morris 182, D.G. Bradman 173*). Australia won by 7 wickets and won the rubber.

| | | |
|---|---|---|
| D.G. BRADMAN (capt.) | b. R. Pollard | 33 |
| | not out | 173 |

Bradman went in for his first innings at 13 for 1, 51 minutes from the end of the second day, and, thanks to some explosive hooking, reached 31 overnight. Next morning a shower had livened the pitch and Bradman, after being hit on the thigh by a lifting ball from Bedser, was out in the second over after another eight minutes; he was late in playing back to Pollard and lost his off-stump, with the score 68 for 3. He received 56 balls.

On the fifth day, Yardley's declaration set Australia 404 to win in five hours 44 minutes (70 runs an hour) on a worn wicket which took spin, but Bradman and Morris, assisted by indifferent bowling and fielding, had a huge partnership which won the match against all the odds. Bradman came in at 1 p.m. with the score 57 for 1 and had some unhappy moments against Compton's bowling, being missed off that bowler in the slips when 22 and 30, the latter a relatively easy chance; he was 35 at lunchtime after half an hour, and afterwards reached 50 in an hour, before giving another hard chance when 59, at square-cover off K. Cranston. He completed his century at 4.10 p.m. in two hours 25 minutes, and just before tea, when 108, he might have been stumped off Laker.

By the tea interval, when he was still 108, Australia needed 116 in one and three-quarter hours, and they eventually won with 15 minutes to spare; Bradman and Morris added 301 for the second wicket in three hours 37 minutes, Bradman's share being 143 and Morris's 148. Bradman's 173 not out (his fourth century in four Test matches at Leeds) took him four and a quarter hours and 292 balls, and included 29 fours; this was his last Test match century, his 19th *v* England and his 29th in all Tests. When he was 145 he completed 5,000 runs against England, the only batsman ever to do so, and the only batsman of either country ever to make 5,000 runs in Tests between England and Australia.

There were over 19 and a half years between his first and last Test centuries, a greater span than anyone else has achieved; the next best are 19 years by J.B. Hobbs, and, by an Australian, 18 years by W.W. Armstrong.

**224. AUSTRALIANS** *v* **DERBYSHIRE**, at Derby, 28, 29 and 30 July 1948

SCORES: Australians 456 (W.A. Brown 140, D.G. Bradman 62, K.R. Miller 57, S.J.E. Loxton 51); Derbyshire 240 (C.S. Elliott 57) and 182 (D. Smith 88, C.L. McCool 6 for 77). Australians won by an innings and 34 runs.

D.G. BRADMAN (capt.)  b. E.J. Gothard        62

Bradman went in on the first morning at 29 for 1 and, on a rather green wicket, started slowly with only 5 in his first half-hour; however, he completed 50 in 102 minutes just after lunch and batted for two hours four minutes altogether before being bowled, trying to hook an off-spinner which kept rather low, at 134 for 2. He and Brow added 105 for the second wicket and he hit five fours.

**225. AUSTRALIANS** *v* **WARWICKSHIRE**, at Birmingham, 4, 5 and 6 August 1948

SCORES: Warwickshire 138 and 155; Australians 254 (A.L. Hassett 68, W.E. Hollies 8 for 107) and 41 for 1 wicket. Australians won by 9 wickets.

D.G. BRADMAN (capt.)  b. W.E. Hollies        31
                      not out                13

Bradman, having won the toss, put Warwickshire in on a wet wicket, which gave the bowlers help throughout the match; he himself made 20 not out in 40 minutes at the end of the first day, after going in at 50 for 1, but next morning, after another 33 minutes, he played outside a top-spinner, and was bowled out 116 for 3.

On the third morning, going in at 18 for 1, he had 15 minutes' batting practice before the winning hit was made.

**226. AUSTRALIANS** *v* **LANCASHIRE** (C. Washbrook's benefit), at Manchester, 7, 9 and 10 August 1948

SCORES: Australians 321 (S.G. Barnes 67, W.B. Roberts 6 for 73) and 265 for 3 wickets dec. (D.G. Bradman 133*, S.G. Barnes 90); Lancashire 130 and 199 for 7 wickets (J.T. Ikin 99). Drawn.

D.G. BRADMAN (capt.)  c. A.E. Wilson b. W.B. Roberts    28
                      not out                          133

Bradman's first innings, on a green wicket, was one of his least impressive; he went in on the first afternoon at 123 for 1, and took 40 minutes for his first 4 runs, before giving a stumping chance of Roberts. He then tried to force the pace, but after giving another stumping chance off Roberts when 27, was soon afterwards caught at the wicket off that bowler, at 175 for 3; he was in for an hour and 13 minutes.

He had 66 minutes' batting at the end of the second day, when he went in at 21 for 1, and reached 50 by the close, steady bowling keeping him on the defensive; next morning he batted much more confidently, and, after 23 minutes in the forties, ran to 50 in an hour and 56 minutes. He completed his century in three hours six minutes, and by the lunch interval, when he declared, he had made 133 in three hours 36 minutes, having added 108 in two and a half hours before lunch. He hit 17 fours, gave no chance and helped Barnes put on 167 for the second wicket. His declaration left Lancashire only two and three-quarter hours' batting.

This was the eighth occasion altogether, and the fourth in England, on which he added over 100 runs before lunch, though his three previous such performances in England (in 1930 and 1934) were more meritorious, in that the period of play was only two hours, and two of them took place on the first morning of the matches. However, no one else has done this anywhere more than four times (J.B. Hobbs being the next best; V.T. Trumper, the next best Australian, did so thrice).

### 227. **AUSTRALIA** *v* **ENGLAND,** Fifth Test match, at the Oval, 14, 16, 17 and 18 August 1948

SCORES: England 52 (R.R. Lindwall 6 for 20) and 188 (L. Hutton 64); Australia 389 (A.R. Morris 196, S.G. Barnes 61, W.E. Hollies 5 for 131). Australia won by an innings and 149 runs.

D.G. BRADMAN (capt.)  b. W.E. Hollies          0

After England's lamentable first innings on a wet but easy pitch, Barnes and Morris added 117 for Australia's first wicket, and set the stage for a big score by Bradman in his last Test match; he went in at 5.50 p.m. on the first evening, and the England team, led by Yardley, greeted him by giving him three cheers. Possibly affected by this reception, Bradman played his first ball, a leg-break, hesitantly to silly mid-off, and tried to play the same stroke, equally hesitantly, to his second; this time it was a googly, which turned back just enough to beat his bat and dislodge his off-bail. His Test match career thus ended on a note of anti-climax and disappointment, so far as his personal performance was concerned; but Australia's easy victory was some consolation. Had he scored 4 runs, he would have completed an aggregate of 7,000 runs in all Test matches, and would have had a career Test average of 100.

**228. AUSTRALIANS *v* KENT**, at Canterbury, 21 and 23 August 1948
SCORES: Australians 361 (W.A. Brown 106, D.G. Bradman 65, R.N. Harvey 60);
Kent 51 and 124. Australians won by an innings and 186 runs.

D.G. BRADMAN (capt.)  c. B.H. Valentine b. E. Crush   65

Bradman went in on the first morning at 64 for 1, and helped Brown to add 104 for the second wicket before he was second out at 168. He reached 50 just after lunch in 90 minutes, and 17 minutes later was caught off a skier at mid-off in trying to drive the new ball; he hit six fours.

**229. AUSTRALIANS *v* GENTLEMEN OF ENGLAND**, at Lord's, 25, 26 and 27 August 1948

SCORES: Australians 610 for 5 wickets dec. (A.L. Hassett 200*, D.G. Bradman 150, W.A. Brown 120, K.R. Miller 69); Gentlemen of England 245 (R.T. Simpson 60) and 284 (W.J. Edrich 128, D.T. Ring 5 for 70). Australians won by an innings and 81 runs.

D.G. BRADMAN (capt.)  c. M.P. Donelly b. F.R. Brown      150

Bradman's last innings at Lord's was one of his best and most assured; starting at 40 for 1 on the first morning, he soon made the 18 he required to complete an aggregate of 2,000 runs for the tour, this being the fourth occasion he had done so. He reached 50 just after lunch in 82 minutes, and 100 in two and a half hours; but after batting for three hours 32 minutes, he threw away his wicket, being caught off a skier at wide mid-on. The Gentlemen's bowlers included T.E. Bailey, W. Wooller, C.H. Palmer, W.J. Edrich, N.W.D. Yardley and F.R. Brown, but Bradman was in no trouble and hit 19 fours in a chanceless innings. He and W.A. Brown put on 181 for the second wicket in one hour and 57 minutes, while he and Hassett added 110 before Bradman was third out at 331.

He celebrated his 40th birthday on the last day of the match, and he thus became the oldest (as he had been the youngest) touring batsman to make 2,000 runs in an English season; the previous oldest had been B. Mitchell, the South African (38 in 1947), while the previous oldest Australian was W. Bardsley (37 in 1921).

**230. AUSTRALIANS *v* SOUTH OF ENGLAND**, at Hastings, 1, 2 and 3 September 1948

SCORES: Australians 522 for 7 wickets dec. (A.L. Hassett 151, D.G. Bradman 143,

R.N. Harvey 110, S.J.E. Loxton 67*); South of England 298 (D.C.S. Compton 82, W.J. Edrich 52). Drawn.

D.G. BRADMAN (capt.) c. F.G. Mann b. T.E. Bailey    143

With a wicket falling to the first ball of the match, Bradman went in at 0 for 1, and was again at his best, reaching 50 in exactly an hour and 100 in two hours 13 minutes, before being caught at mid-on after three hours five minutes at the wicket; he gave no chance and hit a six and 17 fours. He and Hassett added 188 for the third wicket, off bowlers who included T.E. Bailey, R.T.D. Perks, A.W.H. Mallett and C. Cook; the score when he was out was 237 for 3.

## 231. AUSTRALIANS *v* Mr H.D.G. LEVESON-GOWER'S XI, at Scarborough, 8, 9 and 10 September 1948

SCORES: Mr H.D.G. Leveson-Gower's XI 177 (R.R Lindwall 6 for 59) and 75 for 2 wickets; Australians 489 for 8 wickets dec. (D.G. Bradman 153, S.G. Barnes 151, A.R. Morris 62). Drawn.

D.G. BRADMAN (capt.) c. L. Hutton b. A.V. Bedser    153

Bradman ended his cricket career in England with another triumph, hitting his 11th century of the season and his third in successive innings, and also ensuring that his team retained their unbeaten record – the only Australian team to do so. In a match interfered with by rain, he went in late on the second evening, at 102 for 1, and made 30 not out in 36 minutes before the close, on a wicket which took a certain amount of spin.

Next morning, on an easier wicket, he started slowly and completed 50 in 91 minutes and 100 in two hours 20 minutes shortly before lunch; after the interval, when he was 109, he hit out and added 44 in 38 minutes before giving his wicket away to Bedser, being caught off a skier in the covers from a wild swing. He batted faultlessly for three hours 14 minutes altogether, and hit two sixes (off consecutive balls from Laker, when 130) and 19 fours; he and Barnes added 225 for the second wicket in two hours 36 minutes, and Bradman had just passed Barnes' score when he was out at 407 for 3. The opposing bowlers, in addition to Bedser and Laker, included T.L. Pritchard and F.R. Brown.

For the tenth and last time, and for the second time in England, Bradman made three (or more) centuries in successive innings; the next best in this respect are W.R. Hammond (six times) and, among Australians, W.H. Ponsford (five times). C.G. Macartney and A.L. Hassett are the only Australians to do this twice in England.

The tour finished with Bradman bowling the last over of the match.

| | Matches | Innings | NO | HS | Runs | Average | Centuries |
|---|---|---|---|---|---|---|---|
| All First-class Matches | 23 | 31 | 4 | 187 | 2428 | 89.92 | 11 |
| Test Matches | 5 | 9 | 2 | 173* | 508 | 72.57 | 2 |

Australia won the Test match series by four matches to nil, with one drawn, and retained the Ashes.

In exceeding 2,000 runs for the fourth consecutive Australian tour of England, Bradman surpassed the performance of W. Bardsley, who had done so in 1909, 1912 and 1921, and his form throughout the season, at the age of nearly 40, was a remarkable tribute both to his ability to avoid injury and his judgement of his own capabilities.

Sometimes he was more uncertain than hitherto at the start of an innings, and this was so especially in the Test matches, where he was only third in the Australian batting averages, the lowest of his career; A.R. Morris, 696 runs, average 87.00, was first, and S.G. Barnes, average 82.25, was second, while the best Englishman was D.C.S. Compton with 562 runs, average 62.44.

In all first-class matches, however, Bradman headed the Australian averages, scored most runs and hit the most centuries, A.L. Hassett, with an average of 74.22, Morris with 1,922 runs and W.A. Brown with eight centuries, being the next best in each case. C. Washbrook was the top Englishman in the averages, with 70.37; six Englishmen exceeded 2,000 runs, L. Hutton's 2,654 (average 64.73) being the highest. Hutton scored ten centuries, more than any other Englishman. This was the fourth English season in which Bradman's average exceeded 80.

Bradman scored 11 centuries in 31 innings this season, or 35 per cent, the next best proportion among touring batsmen to his 50 per cent in 1938. He also played eight other innings of 50 and over, and was dismissed for less than 50 in only ten of his innings. He made 50 in one innings or the other in 18 of his 23 matches,

Bradman became, incidentally, only the third batsman to make 1,000 runs in Test cricket in a calendar year, his total for 1948 being 1,025 (13 innings); in 1902, C. Hill made 1,060 runs (21 innings), and in 1947 Compton amassed 1,159 runs (15 innings) in all Tests. Bradman's previous best was 978 in 1930, and it was an exceptional feat to achieve at such a late stage of his career; altogether he made 1,223 runs in Test matches in the year between 1 November 1947 and 31 October 1948, which compares favourably with his record total of 1,421 runs made in a year in 1930 and 1930–1.

# 1948–9

## AGED FORTY

———◆➤❉◆———

Bradman played in three more matches on his return to Australia, his own and two other testimonial matches.

**232. D.G. BRADMAN'S XI** *v* **A.L. HASSETT'S XI** (D.G. Bradman Testimonial), at Melbourne, 3, 4, 6 and 7 December 1948

SCORES: A.L. Hassett's XI 406 (R.R. Lindwall 104, W. Langdon 60, R.A. Saggers 52) and 430 (A.L. Hassett 102, S.G. Barnes 89, L. Johnson 53*); D.G. Bradman's XI 434 (D.G. Bradman 123, K. Meulemann 100, R.A. Hamence 58, C.L. McCool 5 for 101) and 402 for 9 wickets (D. Tallon 146*, A.R. Morris 108). A tie.

| | |
|---|---|
| D.G. BRADMAN (capt.)  c. R.N. Harvey b. B. Dooland | 123 |
| c. R.A. Saggers b. W.A. Johnston | 10 |

Bradman's testimonial match proved to be a brilliant success, and produced some splendid cricket; while in the first innings, Bradman himself went in at 3 p.m. on the second day (Saturday) and made his 117th and last century in first-class cricket. Starting at 138 for 2 with a single off his first ball, he played himself in carefully, but nevertheless reached his 50 in an hour just before tea, and after the interval carried on majestically towards his hundred. However, when he was 97, he tried to force Johnston to leg and sent up a skier off the edge of his bat to wide mid-on, where McCool, perhaps tactfully, dropped the catch and enabled him to run 3 to complete his century. He had then been in for two hours 17 minutes, and had scored his runs against Lindwall, L. Johnson, McCool, W.A. Johnston and Dooland; he played Lindwall, who was at his fastest, particularly well, though he was sometimes troubled by that bowler when he took the new ball just after the tea interval. After completing his century, he lashed out and gave two stumping chances, as well as a chance at slip off a skier from Dooland when 108, before finally throwing his wicket away, caught at deep square-leg off a full-pitch, ten minutes from the close of play. He was in for two hours 34 minutes, hit 13 fours, and with Meulemann added 112 for the third wicket; he was himself sixth out at 348. V.T. Trumper, W.M. Woodfull and Hassett are the only Australian batsmen apart from Bradman who have scored centuries in their own testimonial matches.

His last three innings in England having been centuries, this was his fourth century in succession; this was the third time that he had made four or more centuries in successive innings. The only other batsmen to do this as often as twice are C.B. Fry, W.R. Hammond, J.B. Hobbs and H. Sutcliffe; and C.G. Macartney is the only other Australian to do so even once. It has been achieved only 25 times altogether.

Bradman took the last two wickets with the last ball he ever bowled in Hassett's XI's second innings for 12 runs, thus taking a wicket with the last ball he ever bowled. Set 403 to win on the last day, his XI made a great effort, though he himself did not succeed again. He went in at 12 for 1, before lunch, and after batting well for 29 minutes, he was caught at the wicket at 29 for 2 off a ball which lifted and went away.

The final stages were remarkable for a magnificent innings by Tallon who, after 9 wickets had fallen for 302, helped to add 100, of which his own share was 91, in the last hour and, scoring 12 off the last over, levelled the scores off the last ball.

As a result of the match Bradman received a cheque for £A 9,342.

## 233. A.R. MORRIS'S XI *v* A.L. HASSETT'S XI (A.F. Kippax and W.A. Oldfield Testimonial), at Sydney, 25, 26, 28 February, and 1 March 1949.

SCORES: A.L. Hassett's XI 204 (A.L. Hassett 73, D.T. Ring 5 for 49) and 437 (A.L. Hassett 159, S.J.E. Loxton 93, R.N. Harvey 87); A.R. Morris's XI 581 (J.A.R. Moroney 217, R.R. Lindwall 73, A.R. Morris 66, D.G. Bradman 53) and 62 for 2 wickets. A.R. Morris's XI won by 8 wickets.

D.G. BRADMAN  c. K. Meulemann b. K.R. Miller        53
            (did not bat)                            –

Bradman played under Morris's captaincy in this game, the first time for over 14 years that he did not captain his side. He went in at 111 for 1, at 2.48 p.m. on the second day (Saturday), on a slow, easy wicket and, despite being completely out of practice, at once settled down confidently. He had to face a strong bowling side, including three fast bowlers in Miller, A.K. Walker and W.A. Johnston, and he played them as though he were years younger; the way he hooked bumpers from Miller was thrilling to watch, and without appearing to hit hard or to force the pace, he reached 50 in 63 minutes, mainly by skilful placing. Just afterwards, he mis-timed Miller's slower ball, spooning it to mid-on, where Meulemann took a brilliant catch, one-handed, when running at full speed. Bradman hit only three fours, batted for 65 minutes and was out at 194 for 2.

## 234. SOUTH AUSTRALIA *v* VICTORIA (A.J. Richardson Testimonial), at Adelaide, 4, 5, 7 and 8 March 1949

SCORES: Victoria 229 (K. O'Neill 5 for 45) and 328 (S.J.E. Loxton 135); South Australia 154 and 132. South Australia lost by 271 runs.

| | | |
|---|---|---|
| D.G. BRADMAN b. W.A. Johnston | | 30 |
| absent hurt | | – |

Bradman played under the captaincy of P.L. Ridings on his last appearance in a first-class match. He went in at 26 for 2, 37 minutes from the close of the first day's play, and defended rather anxiously to make 18 not out; Loxton had him missed at backward short-leg. Next morning, he stayed for another three-quarters of an hour, but was well below his best form, and never really timed the ball properly, until he chopped on to his stumps a ball which kept low; he was out at 84 for 4, having batted for 82 minutes, and his 30 was top score for his side.

Later that day he trod on a ball while fielding, turned his right ankle over, and had to be helped off the field; with his ankle very swollen and painful, he was unable to bat in the second innings and his last appearance was thus something of an anti-climax.

## SUMMARY, 1948–9

| | Matches | Innings | NO | HS | Runs | Average | Centuries |
|---|---|---|---|---|---|---|---|
| All first-class Matches | 3 | 4 | 0 | 123 | 216 | 54.00 | 1 |
| Sheffield Shield Matches | | | | | | | |
| Match for South Australia | 1 | 1 | 0 | 30 | 30 | – | 0 |

A.R. Morris scored most runs this season (1,069) and hit most centuries (six), while J.A.R. Moroney had the highest average (81.54) among Australian batsmen. These two and A.L. Hassett were the only three with averages higher than Bradman's.

*** 

It was announced on 1 January 1949, in the New Year's Honours List, that Bradman was to be knighted 'in recognition of his services over many years as a cricketer and captain of the Australian Test team and for public services in several directions'. On 15 March 1949 he received the accolade of knighthood from the Governor-General of Australia (Mr W.J. McKell) at an investiture held in Queen's Hall, Parliament House, Melbourne. He is the only Australian to be knighted for services to cricket, and his was the first knighthood to be conferred mainly for work actively on the cricket field rather than in the administration of the game.

# PART II

## Summary and Statistics of Bradman's Career in First-Class Cricket

# 1927–49

SECTION 1

# BATTING AVERAGES

## (a) CAREER SUMMARY, 1927–49

| | Matches | Innings | NO | HS | Runs | Average | Centuries |
|---|---|---|---|---|---|---|---|
| All First-class Matches | 234 | 338 | 43 | 452* | 28067 | 95.14 | 117 |
| All Matches in Australia | 142 | 218 | 25 | 452* | 18230 | 94.45 | 76 |
| All Matches in England | 92 | 120 | 18 | 334 | 9837 | 96.44 | 41 |
| All Test Matches | 52 | 80 | 10 | 334 | 6996 | 99.94 | 29 |
| Test Matches v England | 37 | 63 | 7 | 334 | 5028 | 89.78 | 19 |
| v England in England | 19 | 30 | 4 | 334 | 2674 | 102.84 | 11 |
| v England in Australia | 18 | 33 | 3 | 270 | 2354 | 78.46 | 8 |
| All Tests in Australia | 33 | 50 | 6 | 299* | 4322 | 98.22 | 18 |
| All Sheffield Shield Matches | 62 | 96 | 15 | 452* | 8926 | 110.19 | 36 |
| Shield Matches for New South Wales | 31 | 52 | 9 | 452* | 4633 | 107.74 | 17 |
| Shield Matches for South Australia | 31 | 44 | 6 | 357 | 4293 | 112.97 | 19 |
| All Matches for New South Wales | 41 | 69 | 10 | 452* | 5813 | 98.52 | 21 |
| All Matches for South Australia | 44 | 63 | 8 | 369 | 5753 | 104.60 | 25 |
| All Matches v Touring Teams | 54 | 84 | 8 | 299* | 6259 | 82.35 | 25 |
| Matches v MCC Teams | 32 | 55 | 5 | 270 | 3352 | 67.04 | 11 |

## (b) SEASON-BY-SEASON RECORD IN ALL FIRST-CLASS MATCHES

| | Matches | Innings | NO | HS | Runs | Average | Centuries |
|---|---|---|---|---|---|---|---|
| 1927–8 | 5 | 10 | 1 | 134* | 416 | 46.22 | 2 |
| 1928–9 | 13 | 24 | 6 | 340* | 1690 | 93.88 | 7 |
| 1929–30 | 11 | 16 | 2 | 452* | 1586 | 113.28 | 5 |
| 1930 | 27 | 36 | 6 | 334 | 2960 | 98.66 | 10 |
| 1930–1 | 12 | 18 | 0 | 258 | 1422 | 79.00 | 5 |
| 1931–2 | 10 | 13 | 1 | 299* | 1403 | 116.91 | 7 |
| 1932–3 | 11 | 21 | 2 | 238 | 1171 | 61.63 | 3 |
| 1933–4 | 7 | 11 | 2 | 253 | 1192 | 132.44 | 5 |
| 1934 | 22 | 27 | 3 | 304 | 2020 | 84.16 | 7 |
| 1934–5 | – | – | – | – | – | – | – |
| 1935–6 | 8 | 9 | 0 | 369 | 1173 | 130.33 | 4 |

| | Matches | Innings | NO | HS | Runs | Average | Centuries |
|---|---|---|---|---|---|---|---|
| 1936–7 | 12 | 19 | 1 | 270 | 1552 | 86.22 | 6 |
| 1937–8 | 12 | 18 | 2 | 246 | 1437 | 89.81 | 7 |
| 1938 | 20 | 26 | 5 | 278 | 2429 | 115.66 | 13 |
| 1938–9 | 7 | 7 | 1 | 225 | 919 | 153.16 | 6 |
| 1939–40 | 9 | 15 | 3 | 267 | 1475 | 122.91 | 5 |
| 1940–1 | 2 | 4 | 0 | 12 | 18 | 4.50 | 0 |
| 1945–6 | 2 | 3 | 1 | 112 | 232 | 116.00 | 1 |
| 1946–7 | 9 | 14 | 1 | 234 | 1032 | 79.38 | 4 |
| 1947–8 | 9 | 12 | 2 | 201 | 1296 | 129.60 | 8 |
| 1948 | 23 | 31 | 4 | 187 | 2428 | 89.92 | 11 |
| 1948–9 | 3 | 4 | 0 | 123 | 216 | 54.00 | 1 |
| | | | | | | | |
| In Australia | 142 | 218 | 25 | 452* | 18230 | 94.55 | 76 |
| In England | 92 | 120 | 18 | 334 | 9837 | 96.44 | 41 |
| | | | | | | | |
| *Total:* | 234 | 338 | 43 | 452* | 28067 | 95.14 | 117 |

## Career Figures

*All First-class Cricket*

Bradman's career average of 95.14 is easily the highest by any batsman in history; the next best is 72.74 by the Indian batsman, V.M. Merchant, while the next best Australian is W.H. Ponsford with 65.18. Only Bradman, Merchant, G.A. Headley, Ponsford and W.M. Woodfull have career averages of over 60, and only 24 others, including eight Australians, have averages between 50 and 60.

His career aggregate of 28,067 is the highest by any Australian, the next best being 17,160 by C. Hill. Only 20 Australians have career aggregates over 10,000 runs.

His career total of 117 centuries is the highest by any Australian, the next best being 53 by W. Bardsley; A.L. Hassett has since also passed Bardsley's total and had made 59 hundreds – just over half as many as Bradman. These and R.N. Harvey are the only three other Australians to have made 50 centuries.

His career total of 37 double centuries is the most by any batsman in history; the next best are 36 by W.R. Hammond and 22 by E. Hendren, he being the only other with more than 20 to his credit. The best by any other Australian is 13 by Ponsford; no other Australian has made more than eight scores of 200 and over.

His career total of six treble centuries is two more than the next best, four each by Ponsford and Hammond; apart from Bradman and Ponsford, only nine other Australians have made even one such score each.

He made 186 scores of 50 or over during his career; the next best by an Australian batsman is 129 by V.T. Trumper.

## In Australia

His average of 94.45 for all matches in Australia is again easily the highest on record, W.H. Ponsford being next best with 71.20, and after that the only Australian to average 60 in Australia is W.M. Woodfull, though four Englishmen have also done so.

His total of 18,230 runs in Australia is the most ever scored by any batsman in that country, C. Hill's 11,129 being the previous best; A.L. Hassett is the only other batsman to reach 10,000 runs on Australian wickets.

His 76 centuries in Australia are the most by any batsman, the previous best being A.F. Kippax, who scored 36 of his centuries in Australia. Ponsford and Hassett are the only others to have made 320 or more centuries in that country.

He scored 25 of his double centuries in Australia, Ponsford being second best with nine.

His four treble centuries in Australia equal the number which Ponsford put together in that country; apart from Bradman's four and Ponsford's four, only seven treble centuries altogether have been made in Australia, no one else having scored more than one.

He made 121 scores of 50 or over in Australia; C. Hill, the next best, made 87.

## In England

Bradman's average of 96.44 for all matches in England is also easily the highest on record; his nearest rival is the West Indian, G.A. Headley, whose average on English wickets is 68.61 (for 74 innings). The batsman with the highest average among those who played most of their cricket in England is K.S. Ranjitsinhji, with 56.15, followed by W.R. Hammond, with 55.02, and five other Englishmen with averages in this country of over 50. Among Australians, W.M. Woodfull, with 56.07, and W.H. Ponsford with 55.54, have the best figures; of overseas batsmen who have toured England more than once, only Bradman, seven other Australians, three West Indians and one Indian have averages on English wickets of over 50.

Bradman, W. Bardsley, W.A. Brown and R.N. Harvey are the only major Australian batsmen who have a higher average on English wickets than on Australian.

His total of 9,837 runs in England is the highest by any Australian or other batsman from overseas; Bardsley, 7,866 runs in England, is the next best, and nine other Australians and one South African have exceeded 5,000. Bardsley altogether made 9,488 runs outside Australia, and Bradman's 9,837 are thus also the most runs scored by any Australian outside his own country.

His 41 centuries on English wickets are the most by any Australian or other overseas player; and C.G. Macartney is the only other touring batsman to have made as many as 20 hundreds.

His 12 double centuries in England are also the most by any Australian or other overseas batsman; the next best are five by E.D. Weekes, and four by W.H. Ponsford and K.R. Miller. Only nine Englishmen have scored more than 12 double centuries in England.

His two treble centuries in England are the most by any Australian or other overseas batsman; only four other overseas batsmen, three Australians and one West Indian, have even one such score, and only W.G. Grace and W.R. Hammond, three each, have made more than two such scores in England.

He made 65 scores of 50 or over in England, W. Bardsley being next best among Australians with 57.

## Season-by-Season Figures

### In Australia

He batted in 17 seasons in Australia, and missed another (1934–5) entirely, owing to illness; in three of these 17 seasons (1940–1, 1945–6 and 1948–9) he played less than five completed innings. Of the remaining 14 seasons, he completed 1,000 runs on 12 occasions, the seasons he did not do so being 1927–8 (his first) and 1938–9 (when he made 919 runs, including six centuries, in seven innings); he reached 1,000 runs for nine seasons in succession, 1928–9 to 1937–8 inclusive, apart from 1934–5, when he did not play. Only E. Hendren, on three consecutive MCC tours, and A.R. Morris have reached this aggregate for an Australian season as often as three times, and only W.H. Ponsford and Morris have done so two seasons in succession. Only 15 other Australian batsmen have ever scored 1,000 in an Australian season, a feat which has been performed by Australians only 36 times altogether, of which Bradman was responsible for 12.

In two of the 12 Australian seasons in which he made 1,000 runs there was no visiting team to increase his batting opportunities (1933–4 and 1939–40); the only other Australians to make 1,000 runs in a purely domestic season are Ponsford (twice), A.F. Kippax, W.A. Brown, S.G. Barnes, A.R. Morris and N.C. O'Neill. Moreover, in three other season (1929–30, 1935–6 and 1937–8), Bradman played in only one match against the visitors and made over 1,000 runs in domestic cricket only, without counting the runs he made against the tourists.

During the 18 seasons spanned by his career, the only other Australian batsmen to reach four figures were Ponsford (1927–8), Kippax and J.S. Ryder (1928–9), Brown (1938–9), Barnes (1940–1), Morris (1946–7 and 1948–9) and A.L. Hassett and K.R. Miller (1946–7).

Bradman was top of the Australian batting averages 11 times in his 14 full seasons; the other three occasions were 1927–8 (his first season), when he was 14th, 1930–1, when he was second, F.C. Thompson beating him by 0.16 of a run, and in 1932–3, when he was the leading Australian batsman, but second to H. Sutcliffe, for the MCC team. Otherwise he was always top of the Australian averages, including the five seasons 1935–6 to 1939–40 in succession. No other batsman has ever been top of the Australian batting averages more often than four times (M.A. Noble being the previous best); G. Giffen was top three seasons in succession from 1892–3 to 1894–5.

Bradman had an average of over 100 in seven of his 14 full seasons in Australia; W.H. Ponsford, three times, was the previous best in this respect.

He had an average of over 50 in 13 of his 14 full seasons (the exception being 1927–8 when it was 46.22); A.F. Kippax's average exceeded 50 in ten different Australian seasons, that being the previous best.

He made at least one century in 16 of his 17 seasons (the exception being 1940–1).

He made five or more centuries in ten different seasons in Australia; W.W. Armstrong had previously been the only player to have done this even twice, though A.R. Morris now has done so three times.

He made seven or more centuries in four different Australian seasons; W.R. Hammond is the only other batsman to do so even once.

He made at least one double century in 13 different seasons in Australia, including 11 in succession; A.F. Kippax and W.H. Ponsford both made at least one score of 200 or more in six different seasons, Kippax having done so in six successive seasons.

He made three double centuries in each of five different Australian seasons; Ponsford and W.R. Hammond, once each, are the only other batsmen to do this.

He made at least one treble century in three different Australian seasons; Ponsford also did so thrice.

## In England

Bradman made four tours of England and exceeded 2,000 runs on all of them; W. Bardsley, who made over 2,000 runs in 1909, 1912 and 1921, and 1,424 and 1,926, has the next best record among touring batsmen. No overseas player has exceeded even 1,000 runs on more than four different English tours, and only 13 overseas players have reached 2,000 in an English season; this includes Bradman (four times), Bardsley (three times), C.G. Macartney (twice), and four other Australians and six others once each.

He headed the English batting averages in all four seasons in which he played in this country; the only other touring batsmen to have headed the English averages are W. Bardsley (1909), G.A. Headley (1939), E.D. Weekes (1950), R.N. Harvey (1953), D.J. McGlew (1955) and K. Mackay (1956), once each.

W.L. Murdoch had headed the Australian first-class averages on the tours of 1882, 1884 and 1890; Bradman improved upon that by doing so on all his four tours.

Bradman's average exceeded 80 on all his four tours. The only batsmen to have achieved such an average in an English season are Bradman (four times), D.R. Jardine (twice, on each occasion in less than 20 innings), and (once each) H. Sutcliffe, R.M. Poore, D.C.S. Compton, K.S. Ranjitsinhji, W.R. Hammond, J.B. Hobbs, C.C. Fry and W.J. Edrich; Bradman's record, therefore, is quite without parallel. W.M. Woodfull is the only other overseas batsman who returned an average for the season of over 50 for as many as three different tours of England.

He made ten or more centuries on three of his four tours, V.T. Trumper and R.N. Harvey (once each) being the only other visiting batsmen to do this.

He made at least three double centuries in 1930, 1934 and 1938; W.H. Ponsford is the only other Australian to make as many as three scores of over 200 in one season, in 1934, and among Englishmen, W.R. Hammond, four times, is the only one to do so more often than Bradman. K.R. Miller is the only other touring batsman to make at least one score of 200 or over in three different English seasons.

He made at least one treble century in two different English seasons; no other Australian has made more than one such score in England.

### (c) SEASON-BY-SEASON RECORD IN TEST MATCHES

|         | Opponents    | Matches | Innings | NO | HS   | Runs | Average | Centuries |
|---------|--------------|---------|---------|----|------|------|---------|-----------|
| 1928–9  | England      | 4       | 8       | 1  | 123  | 468  | 66.85   | 2         |
| 1930    | England      | 5       | 7       | 0  | 334  | 974  | 139.14  | 4         |
| 1930–1  | West Indies  | 5       | 6       | 0  | 223  | 447  | 74.50   | 2         |
| 1931–2  | South Africa | 5       | 5       | 1  | 299* | 806  | 201.50  | 4         |
| 1932–3  | England      | 4       | 8       | 1  | 103* | 396  | 56.57   | 1         |
| 1934    | England      | 5       | 8       | 0  | 304  | 758  | 94.75   | 2         |
| 1936–7  | England      | 5       | 9       | 0  | 270  | 810  | 90.00   | 3         |
| 1938    | England      | 4       | 6       | 2  | 144* | 434  | 108.50  | 3         |
| 1946–7  | England      | 5       | 8       | 1  | 234  | 680  | 97.14   | 2         |
| 1947–8  | India        | 5       | 6       | 2  | 201  | 715  | 178.75  | 4         |
| 1948    | England      | 5       | 9       | 2  | 173* | 508  | 72.57   | 2         |
| *Totals:* |            |         |         |    |      |      |         |           |
| *v* England in Australia |  | 18 | 33 | 3 | 270  | 2354 | 78.46   | 8         |
| *v* England in England   |  | 19 | 30 | 4 | 334  | 2674 | 102.84  | 11        |
| Total *v* England        |  | 37 | 63 | 7 | 334  | 5028 | 89.78   | 19        |
| All Tests in Australia   |  | 33 | 50 | 6 | 299* | 4322 | 98.22   | 18        |
| TOTAL:                   |  | 52 | 80 | 10| 334  | 6996 | 99.64   | 29        |

# Career Figures

*All Test Matches*

His career average of 99.94 is easily the highest by any batsman, the next best being 65.72 by C.S. Dempster (New Zealand); the next best by an Australian is 63.05 by S.G. Barnes, and the previous best, 51.62 by J.S. Ryder. R.N. Harvey is the only other Australian to have a Test average of over 50, a record achieved by only 21 batsmen in history, only five of these exceeding 60.

When Bradman went in to bat in his last Test match, he needed to score four runs to have a century-average in all Test matches; instead, he failed to score.

His average of 98.22 in all Test matches in Australia is the highest on record; the previous best was 73.20 by G.A. Faulkner, and, for more than one series, 63.70 by H. Sutcliffe; for Australia, the previous best was 47.26 by W.M. Woodfull, and the next best, 61.50 by S.G. Barnes.

His average of 102.84 for all Test matches in England is over 40 runs an innings better than his nearest rivals, H. Sutcliffe for England (62.60) and W.H. Ponsford for Australia (62.40).

His career aggregate of 6,996 in all Test matches is the largest by any Australian, the previous best being 3,412 by C. Hill; R.N. Harvey and A.R. Morris have both since passed Hill's total, Harvey now being second to Bradman with 4,353 runs in all Tests. (Although only 29 years of age, Harvey has played in 52 Test matches and has had 89 Test innings – already nine more innings than Bradman in his whole career.) W.R. Hammond scored 7,249 runs for England, the highest aggregate by any batsman, though he took 85 Test matches and 140 innings to do so; and Bradman's total is second to his. Only Hammond, Bradman, L. Hutton, D.C.S. Compton and J.B. Hobbs have reached an aggregate of 5,000 runs in Test matches, and only six Australians altogether have scored more than 3,000 Test runs.

Bradman's aggregate of 4,322 runs for all Test matches in Australia is the largest on record, the previous best being 2,493 by J.B. Hobbs, and by an Australian, 2.308 by C. Hill.

His aggregate of 2,674 runs in Test matches in England is the highest by any overseas batsman, and more than double the next best, 1,336 by B. Mitchell for South Africa, and by an Australian, 1,300 by W. Bardsley (959 *v* England and 341 *v* South Africa).

His total of 29 centuries in all Tests is easily the best, W.R. Hammond being the next best with 22; no one else has reached 20 hundreds. V.T. Trumper, with eight, was the previous best among Australians, though Harvey has now scored 16.

His total of 18 centuries in all Tests in Australia is twice as many as the next best, nine by J.B. Hobbs; the next best by an Australian in Australia is six by Trumper, Harvey and Morris.

His total of 18 centuries in Test matches in England was at one time the highest on record by any batsman, W.R. Hammond and H. Sutcliffe both having made nine centuries for England in England; L. Hutton and D.C.S. Compton have now made 13 centuries each in Test matches in England, but Bradman's 11 is still easily the highest by any overseas player, W. Bardsley being next with five.

His total of 12 double centuries is the most by any batsman, Hammond being second with seven; no one else has made more than four, and no Australian except Bradman had made more than one double century in Test cricket until Harvey scored his second in 1955. Only 24 double centuries have been scored for Australia in Test matches, including Bradman's 12.

His total of seven Test match double centuries in Australia is also the most by any batsman, Hammond being second with three. No other Australian has scored more than one double century in Test cricket in Australia.

His total of five double centuries in Test matches in England is the highest by any batsman, Hutton being second with three such scores.

He made a double century against four other countries; Hutton and Hammond, with double centuries *v* three other countries, are the next best, Harvey with two being the next best Australian. Harvey, A.R. Morris and A.L. Hassett are the only other Australians to make a century against four other countries.

Only seven treble centuries have been scored in Tests, Bradman having scored two of them, both in England, and five other players one each. No other Australian has made 300 in a Test match, and no innings of 300 has been played in a Test match in Australia, Bradman having got closest thereto when he made 299* *v* South Africa in 1931–2. Hutton is the only other batsman to make a score of 300 and over in a Test match in England.

Bradman made 42 scores of 50 and over in all Tests, the most by any Australian (previous best, 26 by C. Hill; next best, 32 by R.N. Harvey).

## *Test Matches between Australia and England, and all Tests against England*

Bradman's career average of 89.78 is the highest on record. For England, E. Paynter had an average of 82.42 for 11 innings, H. Sutcliffe averaged 66.85 for 46 innings, and seven others averaged over 50; while for Australia, S.G. Barnes, in 14 innings averaged 70.50, and A.R. Morris, in 43 innings, averaged 50.73, these being the next best to Bradman's figures among Australians; the next best among batsmen of any country against English bowling is 71.23 by G.A. Headley. Only three Australians and seven others have averages of over 50 *v* England.

His average of 78.46 *v* England in Australia is the highest on record, the next best being 63.70 by H. Sutcliffe (for England), and by an Australian, 48.66 by S.J. McCabe.

His average of 102.84 *v* England in England is the highest on record; H. Sutcliffe (71.29) and, for Australia, W.H. Ponsford (62.40) are his nearest rivals. Ponsford's 62.40 is the next best by any touring batsman in Tests in England.

His career aggregate of 5,028 runs is easily the best, J.B. Hobbs with 3,636, and for Australia, C. Hill, with 2,660, being the next; for South Africa, B. Mitchell made 2,732 runs off English bowling, the next best by any batsman. Four Englishmen have made over 2,000 runs *v* Australia, while six Australians and three South Africans have reached 2,000 against England.

His aggregate of 2,354 runs in Australia is the highest by any Australian (previous best, 1,883 by C. Hill); for England, J.B. Hobbs scored 2,493 runs *v* Australia in Australia, though he had five series, 24 Tests and 45 innings in which to do so.

His aggregate of 2,674 runs *v* England in England is the highest on record, the next best being 1,415 by Hon. F.S. Jackson (for England), and by an Australian, 1,055 by S.J. McCabe; B. Mitchell made 1,336 for South Africa *v* England in England.

Bradman is the only player of either country to make over 2,000 runs in these matches both in England and in Australia; indeed, A.R. Morris for Australia, and J.B. Hobbs, H. Sutcliffe and L. Hutton for England, are the only other batsmen to make even 1,000 runs in each country in England *v* Australia Tests.

His total of 19 centuries is the most on record; the previous best were 12 by Hobbs, and by an Australian, six by V.T. Trumper and W.M. Woodfull. A.R. Morris has now scored eight centuries for Australia *v* England, while G.A. Headley has made eight for the West Indies *v* England.

His total of eight centuries *v* England in Australia is the most by any Australian, four by W.W. Armstrong and Trumper being the previous best; Morris scored five altogether. For England, Hobbs made as many as nine centuries *v* Australia in Australia.

His total of 11 centuries *v* England in England is much the highest on either side; for England, the Hon. F.S. Jackson made five centuries *v* Australia in England, and for Australia C.G. Macartney made four, while B. Mitchell also made four for South Africa *v* England in England.

Only 23 double centuries have been made in 173 Test matches between England and Australia, of which 16 have been scored for Australia and seven for England; Bradman has scored eight of them, Hammond four, and no one else more than one. G.A. Headley, for the West Indies, who made two double centuries, is the only other batsman to make more than one such score *v* England.

Bradman scored three of his double centuries in Australia; no other Australian has scored more than one, but Hammond also made three such scores on Australian wickets.

His five double centuries *v* England in England are easily a record, no one else having made more than one such score, either in England *v* Australia Tests in England or for any country against England in England.

He made two treble centuries *v* England, both in England; L. Hutton, for England, made the only other score of 300 and over in Test matches between England and Australia. No one else has made 300 *v* England.

He played 31 innings of 50 and over in Tests between England and Australia, the most on record (previous best, 27 by J.B. Hobbs; by an Australian, 20 by C. Hill; B. Mitchell made 23 fifties for South Africa *v* England).

*Test Matches between Australia and South Africa, and all Tests against South Africa*

Bradman's average of 201.50 is the highest on record by any batsman against any other country, the next best being his own 178.75 *v* India. After that came W.R. Hammond *v* New Zealand, 112.7, and for Australia, J.S. Ryder's 111.33 *v* South Africa, that also being the next best by any batsman against South African bowling. The next highest average *v* South Africa in Australia is 94.42 by V.T. Trumper.

Bradman and R.N. Harvey are the only Australians to score as many as four centuries *v* South Africa on Australian wickets.

Bradman scored two double centuries *v* South Africa; only seven other double centuries have been made *v* South Africa, four by Englishmen and three by Australians (Trumper, Harvey and H.L. Collins), no one else having made more than one.

*Test Matches between Australia and West Indies*

Bradman, W.H. Ponsford and A.L. Hassett are the only Australians to score two centuries *v* West Indies in Australia, and G.A. Headley is the only West Indian to do so *v* Australia in that country.

Bradman scored the only double century *v* West Indies in Australia, R.N. Harvey being the only other Australian to do so *v* West Indies.

*Test Matches between Australia and India, and all Test Matches against India*

Bradman's average of 178.75 is the highest ever achieved against India, the next best being A.L. Hassett's 110.66.

His aggregate of 715 is the highest by any Australian *v* India, R.N. Harvey with 419 being the next; on Australian wickets, Hassett with 322, is second to Bradman. For India, V.S. Hazare scored 429 runs *v* Australia, all in Australia, this being the best for India.

His four centuries *v* India is the record for an Australian batsman, Harvey, with one in Australia and one in India, being next; no one else has scored more than one for Australia in Australia, though Hazare and V. Mankad each scored two for India.

He is the only Australian to score a double century *v* India; two Englishmen and two West Indians are the only others to do so, also one each. No Indian has scored a double century *v* Australia.

## Season-by-Season Figures

In his 11 Test match series (eight *v* England) he never failed to average over 50, a demonstration of his extraordinary consistency against the best bowling. In all Test matches, L. Hutton had an average for England of over 50 in 11 of his 21 series, and, before that, W.R. Hammond did so in ten of the 16 series in which he batted often enough to have three completed innings; for Australia, C. Hill, five times in 11 series, averaged 50 most frequently. In Test matches between England and Australia, J.B. Hobbs averaged over 50 in six of the nine series in which he batted, and H. Sutcliffe did so in six series out of six against Australia. No one else has done this for Australia *v* England more than three times, by C. Hill (out of nine series) and W.M. Woodfull (out of five series).

He had an average of over 100 for a series four times (twice against England); this has been done only 21 times altogether, and apart from Bradman, only R.N. Harvey, E. Hendren and E.D. Weekes (twice each) have done so more than once. No other batsman has ever done this against England, and only Hammond, Hutton and E. Paynter (once each) have averaged 100 and over for a series *v* Australia.

In his 11 Test match series he was top of the combined averages for both sides on five occasions, including three times *v* England (1930, 1931–2, 1936–7, 1946–7 and 1947–8); and in addition he was second four times and third twice; he was never lower than third in the combined averages for a series, which makes his record outstanding by comparison with every other batsman of any country; unlike every other player, he never had an unsuccessful Test match series. So far as the combined averages of both sides are concerned, Hobbs and Hammond each were top in four different series, Hobbs being so twice in England *v* Australia rubbers; the best Australians were C.G. Macartney, V.T. Trumper and W.H. Ponsford, twice each, Macartney being so twice in an England *v* Australia series; Ponsford's successes were the more noteworthy in that the second batsman on each occasion was Bradman himself. Hutton has now headed the combined averages for a series seven times in 21 series, including three times in six England *v* Australia series.

In addition to the five times he headed the combined averages for a series, he headed the Australian averages, but was second to an English batsman, in 1932–3 and 1938. His positions in the Australian Test averages were therefore: in all Test matches, first seven times, second three times, and third once; against England, first five times, second twice and third once. This compares with R.N. Harvey, who has four times headed the Australian averages for a series, though never against England; and W.W. Armstrong and C.G. Macartney, who have each three times headed the Australian averages in a series against England. For England, Hobbs and Hutton have each been top of the averages in four series against Australia, and Hutton was first in the England averages in ten of his 21 series against all countries.

In seven different series, including five against England, Bradman's aggregate of runs exceeded 500; this aggregate has been reached only 14 times altogether by Australian batsmen in a series against England, Bradman being responsible for five, and A.R. Morris (twice) being the only other batsman to do so more than once. For England, J.B. Hobbs three times exceeded 500 in a rubber against Australia, and once against South Africa, while W.R. Hammond also did so four times, though only once *v* Australia; R.N. Harvey has done so for Australia three times, though never against England; and for South Africa H.W. Taylor twice made over 500 runs in a series *v* England.

Of the six aggregates for a series exceeding 800 runs, Bradman was responsible for three, two of them against England; Hammond (*v* Australia), Harvey (*v* South Africa) and G. Sobers (*v* Pakistan) are the other players concerned.

Bradman made three or more centuries in a series on five occasions, three of them in series against England; A.R. Morris and J.B. Hobbs are the only batsmen to do this as often as twice each in Tests between England and Australia, and in all Tests no one else has done so more than twice; R.N. Harvey is the only other Australian besides Morris to have achieved this twice, both times *v* South Africa.

C.L. Walcott in 1955 made five centuries in a series for West Indies *v* Australia, and after him comes a short list of batsmen who have scored four centuries in one series; this has been done 11 times, three times by Bradman, and twice each by H. Sutcliffe and Harvey. Bradman, Hammond and Sutcliffe are the only ones to do this in a series between England and Australia, and G.A. Headley (West Indies) is the only other batsman to achieve the feat off English bowling.

Bradman scored at least one century in every one of his 11 Test match series; indeed, in ten of them he scored at least two hundreds. There is again no real comparison in this respect between him and any other player, for no one else has a 100 per cent record, or anything near it, in this respect. Hammond, for England, made at least one century in 13 of the 23 series in which he took part, though he did so in only five series out of seven against Australia, and Hobbs made at least one such score in six of his nine series (in which he batted) against Australia; for Australia, Harvey has done so in eight series out of 13 against all countries, while against England V.T. Trumper has the next best record with a century in five series out of eight in which he took part. In consistency, his nearest rival is the Hon. F.S. Jackson, who played at least one three-figure innings in four of his five Test match series, all against Australia.

He made two or more double centuries in four different series, including three series against England. For England, Hammond did this twice (once against Australia), and V. Mankad did so for India *v* New Zealand, 1955–6, but no one else has ever done so.

He made at least one double century in seven of his 11 series, including four series against England); Hammond did this in five different series, including three against Australia. Harvey is the only other Australian to have made more than one Test double century; he has made two.

He made five fifties in a Test match series on two occasions; he and R.N. Harvey are the only Australians to do this twice, and the only others to score five or more fifties in two different series are J.B. Hobbs, L. Hutton, P.B.H. May, E.D. Weekes and C.L. Walcott.

## Record in Matches other than Test Matches

|  | Matches | Innings | NO | HS | Runs | Average | Centuries |
|---|---|---|---|---|---|---|---|
| In Australia | 109 | 168 | 19 | 452* | 13908 | 93.34 | 58 |
| In England | 73 | 90 | 14 | 278 | 7163 | 94.25 | 30 |
| *Total:* | 182 | 258 | 33 | 452* | 21071 | 93.64 | 88 |

S.G. Barnes is the only other major Australian batsman with a higher average in Test matches than in other first-class matches; but among Englishmen, this proof of 'Test match temperament' has been given by J.B. Hobbs, H. Sutcliffe, W.R. Hammond, M. Leyland, the Hon. F.S. Jackson, L. Hutton and E. Paynter – a very distinguished company.

## (d) SEASON-BY-SEASON RECORD IN SHEFFIELD SHIELD MATCHES

|  | Matches | Innings | NO | HS | Runs | Average | Centuries |
|---|---|---|---|---|---|---|---|
| **For New South Wales** | | | | | | | |
| 1927–8 | 5 | 10 | 1 | 134* | 416 | 46.22 | 2 |
| 1928–9 | 5 | 9 | 3 | 340* | 893 | 148.83 | 4 |
| 1929–30 | 6 | 10 | 2 | 452* | 894 | 111.75 | 1 |
| 1930–1 | 4 | 6 | 0 | 258 | 695 | 115.83 | 3 |
| 1931–2 | 3 | 5 | 0 | 167 | 213 | 42.60 | 1 |
| 1932–3 | 3 | 5 | 1 | 238 | 600 | 150.00 | 2 |
| 1933–4 | 5 | 7 | 2 | 253 | 922 | 184.40 | 4 |
| **For South Australia** | | | | | | | |
| 1935–6 | 6 | 6 | 0 | 357 | 739 | 123.16 | 3 |
| 1936–7 | 4 | 6 | 1 | 192 | 416 | 83.20 | 2 |
| 1937–8 | 6 | 12 | 2 | 246 | 983 | 98.30 | 4 |
| 1938–9 | 6 | 6 | 1 | 225 | 801 | 160.20 | 5 |
| 1939–40 | 6 | 10 | 2 | 267 | 1062 | 132.75 | 3 |
| 1946–7 | 1 | 2 | 0 | 119 | 162 | 81.00 | 1 |
| 1947–8 | 1 | 1 | 0 | 100 | 100 | – | 1 |
| 1948–9 | 1 | 1 | 0 | 30 | 30 | – | 0 |
| **For New South Wales** | 31 | 52 | 9 | 452* | 4633 | 107.74 | 17 |
| **For South Australia** | 31 | 44 | 6 | 357 | 4293 | 112.97 | 19 |
| *Total:* | 62 | 96 | 15 | 452* | 8926 | 110.19 | 36 |

Bradman's average in all Sheffield Shield matches of 110.19 is the highest on record, the next best being 85.57 by W.H. Ponsford.

His average for New South Wales of 107.74 is the highest on record, the next best being 70.88 by A.F. Kippax.

His average for South Australia of 112.97 is the highest on record, the next best being 58.88 by C.L. Badcock.

His aggregate of 8,926 is easily the highest on record, the next best being 6,270 by C. Hill, all for South Australia.

His total of 36 centuries is the most on record, A.F. Kippax with 23 (all for New South Wales) being the next best.

His total of 19 centuries for South Australia is the most ever made for South Australia in Shield matches, C. Hill and V.Y. Richardson, the previous best, having each made 18.

His total of 13 double centuries is the most on record, Ponsford being next with seven. Bradman made seven double centuries for New South Wales in Sheffield Shield matches, one more than the next best, six by A.F. Kippax; he made six double centuries for South Australia in Shield matches, the next best being three each by C.L. Badcock and C. Hill.

Only nine treble centuries have been made in the whole history of the competition, and Bradman and Ponsford have each scored three of these. Bradman scored two of his treble centuries for New South Wales, Kippax being the only other batsman to make even one such score in a Shield match for that State; Bradman made one score of 300 and over for South Australia in a Shield match as did Hill and Badcock.

## Sheffield Shield Matches – Record *v* other States

| | Matches | Innings | NO | HS | Runs | Average | Centuries |
|---|---|---|---|---|---|---|---|
| *For New South Wales* | | | | | | | |
| *v* Victoria | 13 | 21 | 7 | 340* | 2065 | 147.50 | 8 |
| *v* South Australia | 11 | 20 | 0 | 258 | 1269 | 63.45 | 4 |
| *v* Queensland | 7 | 11 | 2 | 452* | 1299 | 144.33 | 5 |
| *Total for New South Wales:* | 31 | 52 | 9 | 452* | 4633 | 107.74 | 17 |
| *For South Australia* | | | | | | | |
| *v* Victoria | 13 | 18 | 0 | 357 | 1577 | 87.61 | 6 |
| *v* New South Wales | 9 | 14 | 5 | 251* | 1178 | 130.88 | 5 |
| *v* Queensland | 9 | 12 | 1 | 246 | 1538 | 139.81 | 8 |
| *Total for South Australia:* | 31 | 44 | 6 | 357 | 4293 | 112.97 | 19 |
| *Total in all Sheffield Shield Matches* | | | | | | | |
| *v* Victoria | 26 | 39 | 7 | 357 | 3642 | 113.81 | 14 |

| | Matches | Innings | NO | HS | Runs | Average | Centuries |
|---|---|---|---|---|---|---|---|
| *v* New South Wales | 9 | 14 | 5 | 251* | 1178 | 130.88 | 5 |
| *v* South Australia | 11 | 20 | 0 | 258 | 1269 | 63.45 | 4 |
| *v* Queensland | 16 | 23 | 3 | 452* | 2837 | 141.85 | 13 |
| *Total:* | 62 | 96 | 15 | 452* | 8926 | 110.19 | 36 |

## All Sheffield Shield Matches

His aggregate of 3,642 is the highest ever scored against Victoria (previous best, 2,985 by C. Hill).

His 14 centuries *v* Victoria are a record (previous best, 12 by M.A. Noble).

His five double centuries *v* Victoria are a record (previous best, four by A.F. Kippax).

His two treble centuries *v* Victoria are a record, the only other such score being by C.L. Badcock.

His 2,837 runs *v* Queensland are the most ever scored against that State (previous best, 1,637 by Kippax).

His 13 centuries *v* Queensland are a record (previous best, eight by Kippax).

His six double centuries *v* Queensland are a record (previous best, two by W.H. Ponsford; next best, three by A.L. Hassett).

No one else has scored over 1,000 runs *v* four other States in Sheffield Shield matches, nor has anyone else scored over 1,000 runs for two different States against three other States in such matches.

Bradman made at least one double century *v* all four other States against which he played in the Shield competition; he is the only batsman to do so.

## For New South Wales

Queensland only came into the competition in 1926–7, and Bradman and Kippax are the only batsmen to make over 1,000 runs for New South Wales against Victoria, South Australia and Queensland in Shield matches.

Only Bradman and Kippax have made double centuries for New South Wales *v* the other three States in Shield matches, though V.T. Trumper did so *v* Victoria and South Australia, and also *v* Queensland before that State entered the competition.

Bradman's three double centuries *v* Queensland are a record, no other New South Wales batsman having made more than one such score.

## For South Australia

Bradman, V.Y. Richardson and P.L. Ridings are the only batsmen to make over 1,000 runs for South Australia *v* Victoria, New South Wales and Queensland in Shield matches.

His eight centuries *v* Queensland are a South Australian record (previous best, six by V.Y. Richardson).

His three double centuries *v* Queensland are a record; no one else has made more than one such score for South Australia *v* Queensland.

His two double centuries *v* Victoria are a record; no other South Australian batsman had made more than one such score *v* Victoria in Shield matches, though G. Giffen made two before the start of the competition.

Only Bradman and C.L. Badcock have made double centuries for South Australia *v* the other three States in Shield matches.

### (e) SEASON-BY-SEASON RECORD IN ALL MATCHES FOR NEW SOUTH WALES

|  | Matches | Innings | NO | HS | Runs | Average | Centuries |
|---|---|---|---|---|---|---|---|
| 1927–8 | 5 | 10 | 1 | 134* | 416 | 46.22 | 2 |
| 1928–9 | 7 | 12 | 4 | 340* | 1127 | 140.87 | 5 |
| 1929–30 | 7 | 11 | 2 | 452* | 1051 | 116.77 | 2 |
| 1930–1 | 6 | 10 | 0 | 258 | 873 | 87.30 | 3 |
| 1931-2 | 5 | 8 | 0 | 219 | 597 | 74.62 | 3 |
| 1932-3 | 5 | 9 | 1 | 238 | 713 | 89.12 | 2 |
| 1933–4 | 6 | 9 | 2 | 253 | 1036 | 148.00 | 4 |
| *Total:* | 41 | 69 | 10 | 452* | 5813 | 98.52 | 21 |

Bradman's average of 98.52 in all matches for New South Wales is the highest on record, the next best being 67.85 by A.F. Kippax.

His total for eight double centuries is the most on record, Kippax with six being the next best.

His two treble centuries are the most on record, the only others to make even one such score for New South Wales being W.L. Murdoch, C.W. Gregory and Kippax.

Bradman made over 1,000 runs in all matches for New South Wales in three different seasons; N.C. O'Neill (1957–8) is the only other batsman to reach this total.

### (f) SEASON-BY-SEASON RECORD IN ALL MATCHES FOR SOUTH AUSTRALIA

|  | Matches | Innings | NO | HS | Runs | Average | Centuries |
|---|---|---|---|---|---|---|---|
| 1935–6 | 8 | 9 | 0 | 369 | 1173 | 130.33 | 4 |
| 1936–7 | 5 | 7 | 1 | 192 | 454 | 75.66 | 2 |
| 1937–8 | 8 | 14 | 2 | 246 | 1095 | 91.25 | 5 |
| 1938–9 | 6 | 6 | 1 | 225 | 801 | 160.20 | 5 |
| 1939–40 | 8 | 13 | 3 | 267 | 1448 | 144.80 | 5 |
| 1940–1 | 1 | 2 | 0 | 6 | 6 | 3.00 | 0 |
| 1945–46 | 2 | 3 | 1 | 112 | 232 | 116.00 | 1 |

| | Matches | Innings | NO | HS | Runs | Average | Centuries |
|---|---|---|---|---|---|---|---|
| 1946–7 | 3 | 5 | 0 | 119 | 246 | 49.20 | 1 |
| 1947–8 | 2 | 3 | 0 | 156 | 268 | 89.33 | 2 |
| 1948–9 | 1 | 1 | 0 | 30 | 30 | – | 0 |
| Total: | 44 | 63 | 8 | 369 | 5753 | 104.60 | 25 |

Bradman's average of 104.60 in all matches for South Australia is the highest on record, C.L. Badcock being second with 56.58.

His total of 25 centuries is a record for South Australia, C. Hill being second with 24.

His total of eight double centuries is a record for South Australia, G. Giffen, C. Hill and A.J. Richardson being next with four each.

His two treble centuries are a record for South Australia, Hill and Badcock (once each) being the only other batsmen to make 300 or over for that State.

He made over 1,000 runs in all matches for South Australia in three different seasons; no one else has ever reached this total, the next best being 873 by V.Y. Richardson, 1931–2.

## (g) SEASON-BY-SEASON RECORD IN ALL MATCHES AGAINST TOURING TEAMS IN AUSTRALIA

| | Opponents | Matches | Innings | NO | HS | Runs | Average | Centuries |
|---|---|---|---|---|---|---|---|---|
| 1928–9 | MCC | 7 | 13 | 3 | 132* | 778 | 77.80 | 3 |
| 1929–30 | MCC | 1 | 1 | 0 | 157 | 157 | – | 1 |
| 1930–1 | West Indians | 7 | 10 | 0 | 223 | 625 | 62.50 | 2 |
| 1931–2 | South Africans | 7 | 8 | 1 | 299* | 1190 | 170.00 | 6 |
| 1932–3 | MCC | 8 | 16 | 1 | 103* | 571 | 38.06 | 1 |
| 1935–6 | MCC | 1 | 2 | 0 | 50 | 65 | 32.50 | 0 |
| 1936–7 | MCC | 7 | 11 | 0 | 270 | 911 | 82.81 | 3 |
| 1937–8 | New Zealanders | 1 | 1 | 0 | 11 | 11 | – | 0 |
| 1946–7 | MCC | 8 | 12 | 1 | 234 | 870 | 79.09 | 3 |
| 1947–8 | Indians | 7 | 10 | 2 | 201 | 1081 | 135.12 | 6 |
| | | | | | | | | |
| Total v MCC and England: | | 32 | 55 | 5 | 270 | 3352 | 67.04 | 11 |
| Total v all Touring Teams: | | 54 | 84 | 8 | 299* | 6259 | 82.35 | 25 |

Bradman's average of 82.35 against all touring teams in Australia is the highest on record, A.J. Richardson being second with 63.45.

His average of 67.04 against English touring teams in Australia, though relatively small for him, is also the highest on record by any Australian, A.J. Richardson again being second with 61.00.

His average of 170.00 against the South Africans is the highest against South African touring teams anywhere, 78.50 by R.N. Harvey being next best.

His average of 135.12 against the Indians is the highest against Indian touring teams anywhere, E.D. Weekes being next best with 121.12; A.L. Hassett, 100.00, is the next best Australian.

Bradman's aggregate of 6,259 against all touring teams in Australia is the largest on record, C. Hill being next best with 3,885.

His aggregate of 3,352 against English touring teams is the largest on record against English teams on tour anywhere, Hill again being second with 3,279.

His aggregate of 1,190 against the South Africans is the biggest by any Australian, R.N. Harvey being next best with 942.

His aggregate of 1,081 against the Indians is the biggest against Indian teams on tour anywhere, E.D. Weekes being second with 969; A.L. Hassett, 400, is the next best Australian.

Bradman's total of 25 centuries against all touring teams in Australia is more than twice as many as the next best, 11 by A.R. Morris.

His total of 11 centuries against English teams in Australia is a record, A.R. Morris being second with nine. In the West Indies, G.A. Headley also made 11 centuries *v* English bowling, thus sharing with Bradman the record against all English teams anywhere; but only six of Headley's centuries were scored against official MCC teams, the other five being made against unofficial, and sometimes weaker, sides.

His total of six centuries against South African teams in Australia is a record for Australians, R.N. Harvey being next with four.

His total of six centuries against the Indians is the most against Indian touring sides anywhere, E.D. Weekes again being second with four; A.R. Morris is the next best Australian with two.

Bradman made eight double centuries against all touring teams in Australia; A.J. Richardson and V.T. Trumper (two each) are the only other Australians to make more than one such score.

Bradman made three double centuries against English teams in Australia, all in Test matches; A.J. Richardson (two) is the only other Australian to make more than one such score. In the West Indies, G.A. Headley made two double hundreds against official MCC teams and two more against unofficial English XIs.

Bradman made three double centuries against the South Africans in Australia; no one else has made more than one such score against South African teams on tour anywhere.

He made one double century against the West Indians; no batsman from any country has made more than one against West Indian touring sides, and no other Australian has made even one such score.

He made one double century against the Indians, being the only Australian to do so.

He made at least one double century against touring teams from four different countries; W.R. Hammond and L. Hutton, in England, made 200 or more against teams from three different countries, and in Australia, V.T. Trumper (*v* the New Zealanders and South Africans) is the only other batsman to do so against teams from more than one country. A.L. Hassett is the only other Australian to make even a single century in Australia against teams from four different countries.

Bradman twice exceeded 1,000 runs against a touring team; this has only been done twice more by any batsman against any touring team anywhere (by D.C.S. Compton in England in 1947 *v* the South Africans, and by G. Sobers in the West Indies in 1957–8 *v* the Pakistanis). The next highest aggregate against a touring team in Australia is 942 by R.N. Harvey *v* the South Africans, 1952–3.

## (h) SUMMARY OF FIRST-CLASS CRICKET

*Sides for which he scored his runs (in Australia)*

| | Matches | Innings | NO | HS | Runs | Average | Centuries |
|---|---|---|---|---|---|---|---|
| For Australia (Tests) | 33 | 50 | 6 | 299* | 4322 | 98.22 | 18 |
| For New South Wales | 41 | 69 | 10 | 452* | 5813 | 98.52 | 21 |
| For South Australia | 44 | 63 | 8 | 369 | 5753 | 104.60 | 25 |
| For an Australian XI (*v* Touring Teams) | 5 | 8 | 1 | 172 | 492 | 70.28 | 2 |
| For Australian Touring Teams (en route to England) | 7 | 7 | 0 | 144 | 626 | 89.42 | 4 |
| For Combined XI | 1 | 2 | 0 | 10 | 13 | 6.50 | 0 |
| Other Trial and Testimonial Matches etc. not incl. in above | 11 | 19 | 0 | 225 | 1211 | 63.73 | 6 |
| *Total:* | 142 | 218 | 25 | 452* | 18230 | 94.45 | 76 |

*Sides against which he scored his runs (in Australia)*

| | Matches | Innings | NO | HS | Runs | Average | Centuries |
|---|---|---|---|---|---|---|---|
| *v* MCC (and England) | 32 | 55 | 5 | 270 | 3352 | 67.04 | 11 |
| *v* South Africans | 7 | 8 | 1 | 299* | 1190 | 170.00 | 6 |
| *v* West Indians | 7 | 10 | 0 | 223 | 625 | 62.50 | 2 |
| *v* Indians | 7 | 10 | 2 | 201 | 1081 | 135.12 | 6 |
| *v* New Zealanders | 1 | 1 | 0 | 11 | 11 | – | 0 |
| *v* Victoria | 27 | 41 | 7 | 357 | 3648 | 107.29 | 14 |
| *v* New South Wales | 10 | 16 | 5 | 251* | 1205 | 109.54 | 5 |
| *v* South Australia | 11 | 20 | 0 | 258 | 1269 | 63.45 | 4 |
| *v* Queensland | 17 | 25 | 4 | 452* | 2957 | 140.80 | 13 |
| *v* Western Australia | 6 | 7 | 1 | 209* | 731 | 121.83 | 5 |
| *v* Tasmania | 5 | 5 | 0 | 369 | 751 | 150.20 | 3 |
| *v* Australian Services | 1 | 1 | 0 | 112 | 112 | – | 1 |
| Other Trial and Testimonial Matches etc. not incl. in above | 11 | 19 | 0 | 225 | 1298 | 68.31 | 6 |
| *Total:* | 142 | 218 | 25 | 452* | 18230 | 94.45 | 76 |

He made at least one double century *v* each of the six first-class States in Australia; W.H. Ponsford and V.T. Trumper each scored double centuries *v* four different States, and Ponsford also had a score of 158 *v* a fifth, those being the next best feats of this nature. W.A. Brown and K.R. Miller are the only others to score even a single century against all six States.

*Sides against which he scored his runs (in England)*

| | Matches | Innings | NO | HS | Runs | Average | Centuries |
|---|---|---|---|---|---|---|---|
| *v* England (Tests) | 19 | 30 | 4 | 334 | 2674 | 102.84 | 11 |
| *v* MCC | 4 | 5 | 0 | 278 | 451 | 90.20 | 1 |
| *v* Derbyshire | 3 | 4 | 1 | 71 | 183 | 61.00 | 0 |
| *v* Essex | 1 | 1 | 0 | 187 | 187 | – | 1 |
| *v* Glamorgan | 2 | 3 | 1 | 58 | 94 | 47.00 | 0 |
| *v* Gloucestershire | 1 | 2 | 0 | 42 | 56 | 28.00 | 0 |
| *v* Hampshire | 3 | 3 | 1 | 191 | 336 | 168.00 | 2 |
| *v* Kent | 4 | 4 | 1 | 205* | 355 | 118.33 | 1 |
| *v* Lancashire | 5 | 10 | 4 | 133* | 446 | 74.33 | 2 |
| *v* Leicestershire | 3 | 3 | 1 | 185* | 331 | 165.50 | 1 |
| *v* Middlesex | 4 | 6 | 1 | 160 | 254 | 50.80 | 1 |
| *v* Northamptonshire | 3 | 5 | 0 | 65 | 149 | 29.80 | 0 |
| *v* Nottinghamshire | 2 | 3 | 0 | 144 | 286 | 95.33 | 1 |
| *v* Somerset | 3 | 3 | 0 | 202 | 336 | 112.00 | 2 |
| *v* Surrey | 7 | 8 | 2 | 252* | 839 | 139.83 | 4 |
| *v* Sussex | 2 | 2 | 0 | 109 | 128 | 64.00 | 1 |
| *v* Warwickshire | 2 | 3 | 1 | 135 | 179 | 89.50 | 1 |
| *v* Worcestershire | 4 | 4 | 0 | 258 | 807 | 201.75 | 4 |
| *v* Yorkshire | 5 | 7 | 0 | 140 | 460 | 65.71 | 1 |
| *v* Oxford University | 3 | 3 | 0 | 58 | 127 | 42.33 | 0 |
| *v* Cambridge University | 3 | 3 | 0 | 137 | 169 | 56.33 | 1 |
| *v* Scotland | 1 | 0 | – | – | – | – | – |
| *v* An England XI | 2 | 2 | 1 | 149* | 212 | – | 1 |
| *v* Gentlemen of England | 2 | 2 | 0 | 150 | 254 | 127.00 | 2 |
| *v* South of England | 1 | 1 | 0 | 143 | 143 | – | 1 |
| *v* Leveson-Gower's XI | 3 | 3 | 0 | 153 | 381 | 127.00 | 2 |
| | | | | | | | |
| *Total v counties:* | 54 | 71 | 13 | 258 | 5426 | 93.55 | 22 |
| *Total, all matches except Tests:* | 73 | 90 | 14 | 278 | 7163 | 94.25 | 30 |
| *Total:* | 92 | 120 | 18 | 334 | 9837 | 96.44 | 41 |

He made at least one century against 13 of the 17 first-class counties; W. Bardsley, the previous best Australian, scored centuries *v* 11 different counties. He made a double century *v* four different counties (previous best, three by Bardsley; E.D. Weekes, for the West Indians, also did so *v* four counties).

## All First-class Matches

*Australia*

|  | Matches | Innings | NO | HS | Runs | Average | Centuries |
|---|---|---|---|---|---|---|---|
| Adelaide | 40 | 60 | 6 | 369 | 4840 | 89.62 | 18 |
| Brisbane | 12 | 16 | 0 | 226 | 1593 | 99.56 | 8 |
| Brisbane (Exhibition Ground) | 4 | 7 | 1 | 223 | 620 | 103.33 | 3 |
| Hobart | 2 | 2 | 0 | 144 | 283 | 141.50 | 2 |
| Launceston | 2 | 2 | 0 | 79 | 99 | 49.50 | 0 |
| Melbourne | 30 | 47 | 8 | 357 | 4024 | 103.17 | 19 |
| Perth | 6 | 8 | 1 | 209 | 643 | 91.85 | 4 |
| Sydney | 46 | 76 | 9 | 452* | 6128 | 91.46 | 22 |
| *Total:* | 142 | 218 | 25 | 452* | 18230 | 94.45 | 76 |

He made at least one century on every Australian ground except Launceston, a double century on all except Launceston and Hobart, and a treble century at Adelaide, Melbourne and Sydney. A.F. Kippax also made centuries on seven different Australian grounds; W.H. Ponsford, W. Bardsley, M.A. Noble and W.R. Hammond are next best with double centuries on three different Australian grounds; and Ponsford, the only other player to score more than one treble century in Australia, made all his on one ground.

*England*

|  | Matches | Innings | NO | HS | Runs | Average | Centuries |
|---|---|---|---|---|---|---|---|
| Birmingham | 2 | 3 | 1 | 135 | 179 | 89.50 | 1 |
| Bradford | 1 | 1 | 0 | 1 | 1 | – | 0 |
| Bristol | 1 | 2 | 0 | 42 | 56 | 28.00 | 0 |
| Cambridge | 3 | 3 | 0 | 137 | 169 | 56.33 | 1 |
| Canterbury | 4 | 4 | 1 | 205* | 355 | 118.33 | 1 |
| Chesterfield | 2 | 3 | 1 | 71 | 121 | 60.50 | 0 |
| Derby | 1 | 1 | 0 | 62 | 62 | – | 0 |
| Edinburgh | 1 | 0 | – | – | – | – | – |
| Folkestone | 2 | 2 | 1 | 149* | 212 | – | 1 |
| Hastings | 1 | 1 | 0 | 143 | 143 | – | 1 |
| Hove | 2 | 2 | 0 | 109 | 128 | 64.00 | 1 |
| Leeds | 4 | 6 | 1 | 334 | 963 | 192.60 | 4 |
| Leicester | 3 | 3 | 1 | 185* | 331 | 165.50 | 1 |
| Liverpool | 1 | 2 | 1 | 48* | 57 | – | 0 |

| | Matches | Innings | NO | HS | Runs | Average | Centuries |
|---|---|---|---|---|---|---|---|
| Lord's | 14 | 21 | 2 | 278 | 1510 | 79.47 | 6 |
| Manchester | 7 | 12 | 4 | 133* | 470 | 58.75 | 2 |
| Northampton | 3 | 5 | 0 | 65 | 149 | 29.80 | 0 |
| Nottingham | 6 | 11 | 1 | 144* | 812 | 81.20 | 4 |
| Oval | 11 | 12 | 2 | 252* | 1392 | 139.20 | 6 |
| Oxford (Christ Church) | 3 | 3 | 0 | 58 | 127 | 42.33 | 0 |
| Scarborough | 3 | 3 | 0 | 153 | 381 | 127.00 | 2 |
| Sheffield | 4 | 6 | 0 | 140 | 459 | 76.50 | 1 |
| Southampton | 3 | 3 | 1 | 191 | 336 | 168.00 | 2 |
| Southend | 1 | 1 | 0 | 187 | 187 | – | 1 |
| Swansea | 2 | 3 | 1 | 58 | 94 | 47.00 | 0 |
| Taunton | 3 | 3 | 0 | 202 | 336 | 112.00 | 2 |
| Worcester | 4 | 4 | 0 | 258 | 807 | 201.75 | 4 |
| *Total:* | 92 | 120 | 18 | 334 | 9837 | 96.44 | 41 |

Bradman batted on 26 different grounds in England; he made at least one century on 18 of them, a double century on six of them, and a score of at least 50 on 23. W. Bardsley also hit centuries on 18 different English grounds, while W.H. Ponsford made a double century on four different grounds, and E.D. Weekes for the West Indians did so on five.

## Test Matches

*In Australia – All Test Matches*

| | Matches | Innings | NO | HS | Runs | Average | Centuries |
|---|---|---|---|---|---|---|---|
| Adelaide | 7 | 11 | 2 | 299* | 970 | 107.77 | 3 |
| Brisbane | 5 | 7 | 0 | 226 | 736 | 105.14 | 3 |
| Brisbane (Exhibition Ground) | 2 | 3 | 0 | 223 | 242 | 80.66 | 1 |
| Melbourne | 11 | 17 | 4 | 279 | 1671 | 128.53 | 9 |
| Sydney | 8 | 12 | 0 | 234 | 703 | 58.58 | 2 |
| *Total:* | 33 | 50 | 6 | 299* | 4322 | 98.22 | 18 |

Bradman made a double century on every ground in Australia on which Tests are or have been played. His relative lack of success at Sydney is noteworthy; he had to wait until 1946–7 before scoring a double century there. No other Australian has scored more than one Test match double century in Australia, though W.R. Hammond for England reached 200 both at Sydney and Melbourne. A.L. Hassett and R.N. Harvey are the only other batsmen to make Test hundreds at Adelaide, Brisbane, Melbourne and Sydney.

*In Australia – Test Matches v England*

|  | Matches | Innings | NO | HS | Runs | Average | Centuries |
|---|---|---|---|---|---|---|---|
| Adelaide | 4 | 8 | 1 | 212 | 466 | 66.57 | 1 |
| Brisbane | 3 | 5 | 0 | 187 | 325 | 65.00 | 1 |
| Brisbane (Exhibition Ground) | 1 | 2 | 0 | 18 | 19 | 9.50 | 0 |
| Melbourne | 6 | 11 | 2 | 270 | 1034 | 114.88 | 5 |
| Sydney | 4 | 7 | 0 | 234 | 510 | 72.85 | 1 |
| *Total:* | 18 | 33 | 3 | 270 | 2354 | 78.46 | 8 |

Bradman made a double century *v* England at Adelaide, Melbourne and Sydney, and a century in all the four Australian cities in which Tests are played; however, he had to wait until 1946–7 before he did so at Brisbane or Sydney, and until 1936–7 before he did so anywhere except Melbourne. No other Australian has scored more than one Test double century in Australia, though W.R. Hammond scored 200 or more on two different Australian grounds. Only three Englishmen and two other Australians (W.W. Armstrong and A.R. Morris) have scored centuries in England *v* Australia Tests on as many as three different Australian grounds.

*In England*

|  | Matches | Innings | NO | HS | Runs | Average | Centuries |
|---|---|---|---|---|---|---|---|
| Leeds | 4 | 6 | 1 | 334 | 963 | 192.60 | 4 |
| Lord's | 4 | 8 | 1 | 254 | 551 | 78.71 | 2 |
| Manchester | 3 | 4 | 1 | 30* | 81 | 27.00 | 0 |
| Nottingham | 4 | 8 | 1 | 144* | 526 | 75.14 | 3 |
| Oval | 4 | 4 | 0 | 244 | 553 | 138.25 | 2 |
| *Total:* | 19 | 30 | 4 | 334 | 2674 | 102.84 | 11 |

His scores at Leeds were: 334, 304, 103 and 16, 33 and 173*; on the other hand, his record at Manchester was very disappointing.

He made a double century in Tests at Leeds, Lord's and the Oval, and centuries on four of the five Test grounds in England. W.R. Hammond (at Lord's and the Oval) is the only other batsman to make a double century in all Test cricket on more than one ground in England; no one except Bradman has scored more than one double century in England in Tests between England and Australia. Only four Englishmen and three other Australians (C.G. Macartney, W.M. Woodfull and A.R. Morris) have made centuries in Tests between England and Australia on as many as three different English grounds.

In England and Australia together, Bradman made a double century in all Test cricket on eight different grounds, and in Tests *v* England on six different grounds. Hammond scored double centuries on six different grounds in all Tests (two in England, two in Australia and two in New Zealand), and on three different grounds in Tests *v* Australia (one in England and two in Australia); R.N. Harvey is the only other Australian to make more than one Test double century in all Tests (one in Australia and one in the West Indies).

In England and Australia together, Bradman made centuries on nine different grounds in all Test matches, and on eight different grounds in Test matches against England. In all Tests, Hammond scored centuries on eight different grounds in England and Australia, and for Australia, A.R. Morris, R.N. Harvey and A.L. Hassett have done so on six. In Tests between England and Australia, Morris is next best to Bradman with centuries on six different grounds (three in England and three in Australia).

## (j) STATE OF WHOLE CAREER AT END OF EACH SEASON

### All First-class Matches

|  | Matches | Innings | NO | HS | Runs | Average | Centuries |
|---|---|---|---|---|---|---|---|
| 1927–8 | 5 | 10 | 1 | 134* | 416 | 46.22 | 2 |
| 1928–9 | 18 | 34 | 7 | 340* | 2106 | 78.00 | 9 |
| 1929–30 | 29 | 50 | 9 | 452* | 3692 | 90.04 | 14 |
| 1930 | 56 | 86 | 15 | 452* | 6652 | 93.69 | 24 |
| 1930–1 | 68 | 104 | 15 | 452* | 8074 | 90.72 | 29 |
| 1931–2 | 78 | 117 | 16 | 452* | 9477 | 93.83 | 36 |
| 1932–3 | 89 | 138 | 18 | 452* | 10648 | 88.73 | 39 |
| 1933–4 | 96 | 149 | 20 | 452* | 11840 | 91.78 | 44 |
| 1934 | 118 | 176 | 23 | 452* | 13860 | 90.58 | 51 |
| 1935–6 | 126 | 185 | 23 | 452* | 15033 | 92.79 | 55 |
| 1936–7 | 138 | 204 | 24 | 452* | 16585 | 92.13 | 61 |
| 1937–8 | 150 | 222 | 26 | 452* | 18022 | 91.94 | 68 |
| 1938 | 170 | 248 | 31 | 452* | 20451 | 94.24 | 81 |
| 1938–9 | 177 | 255 | 32 | 452* | 21370 | 95.86 | 87 |
| 1939–40 | 186 | 270 | 35 | 452* | 22845 | 97.21 | 92 |
| 1940–1 | 188 | 274 | 35 | 452* | 22863 | 95.66 | 92 |
| 1945–6 | 190 | 277 | 36 | 452* | 23095 | 95.82 | 93 |
| 1946–7 | 199 | 291 | 37 | 452* | 24127 | 94.98 | 97 |
| 1947–8 | 208 | 303 | 39 | 452* | 25423 | 96.29 | 105 |
| 1948 | 231 | 334 | 43 | 452* | 27851 | 95.70 | 116 |
| 1948–9 } Total: } | 234 | 338 | 43 | 452* | 28067 | 95.14 | 117 |

The highest point his career average ever reached was 98.04 half-way through the 1939–40 season, after his innings of 267 for South Australia *v* Victoria (match no. 181); it had fallen to 97.21 by the end of that season.

## All Test Matches

|  | Matches | Innings | NO | HS | Runs | Average | Centuries |
|---|---|---|---|---|---|---|---|
| 1928–9 | 4 | 8 | 1 | 123 | 468 | 66.85 | 2 |
| 1930 | 9 | 15 | 1 | 334 | 1442 | 193.00 | 6 |
| 1930–1 | 14 | 21 | 1 | 334 | 1889 | 94.45 | 8 |
| 1931–2 | 19 | 26 | 2 | 334 | 2695 | 112.29 | 12 |
| 1932–3 | 23 | 34 | 3 | 334 | 3091 | 99.70 | 13 |
| 1934 | 28 | 42 | 3 | 334 | 3849 | 98.69 | 15 |
| 1936–7 | 33 | 51 | 3 | 334 | 4659 | 97.06 | 18 |
| 1938 | 37 | 57 | 5 | 334 | 5093 | 97.94 | 21 |
| 1946–7 | 42 | 65 | 6 | 334 | 5773 | 97.84 | 23 |
| 1947–8 | 47 | 71 | 8 | 334 | 6488 | 102.98 | 27 |
| 1948 } Total: } | 52 | 80 | 10 | 334 | 6996 | 99.94 | 29 |

Immediately before he went in to bat in his last Test match, his average was 101.39; his 'duck' then reduced it to below 100.

## Test Matches against England

|  | Matches | Innings | NO | HS | Runs | Average | Centuries |
|---|---|---|---|---|---|---|---|
| 1928–9 | 4 | 8 | 1 | 123 | 468 | 66.85 | 2 |
| 1930 | 9 | 15 | 1 | 334 | 1442 | 103.00 | 6 |
| 1932–3 | 13 | 23 | 2 | 334 | 1838 | 87.52 | 7 |
| 1934 | 18 | 31 | 2 | 334 | 2596 | 89.51 | 9 |
| 1936–7 | 23 | 40 | 2 | 334 | 3406 | 89.63 | 12 |
| 1938 | 27 | 46 | 4 | 334 | 3840 | 91.42 | 15 |
| 1946–7 | 32 | 54 | 5 | 334 | 4520 | 92.94 | 17 |
| 1948 } Total: } | 37 | 63 | 7 | 334 | 5028 | 89.78 | 19 |

## First and Second Innings

Bradman was equally successful in the first or second innings, though his averages for the second innings were rather higher owing to the greater number of 'not outs'.

### All First-class Matches

|  | Matches | Innings | NO | HS | Runs | Average | Centuries |
|---|---|---|---|---|---|---|---|
| In Australia – First Innings | 142 | 141 | 7 | 369 | 12417 | 92.66 | 55 |
| In Australia – Second Innings | 142 | 77 | 18 | 452* | 5813 | 98.52 | 21 |
| In England – First Innings | 92 | 89 | 4 | 334 | 7986 | 93.95 | 33 |
| In England – Second Innings | 92 | 31 | 14 | 205* | 1851 | 108.88 | 8 |
| *Total – First Innings* | 234 | 230 | 11 | 369 | 20403 | 93.16 | 88 |
| *Total – Second Innings* | 234 | 108 | 32 | 452* | 7664 | 100.84 | 29 |
| *Total:* | 234 | 338 | 43 | 452* | 28067 | 95.14 | 117 |

He had two innings in 108 of his matches (77 in Australia and 31 in England); he had only a first innings in 122 matches (64 in Australia and 58 in England); and in four matches (one in Australia and three in England) he did not bat at all, twice owing to rain and twice owing to injury, while in one match (his last) he missed his second innings 'absent hurt'.

He had a second innings in England comparatively rarely; 12 of the 31 innings were in Test matches, and in eight of the 31 he was not out after having only a limited time in which to bat.

He never made a century in each innings in England (a feat performed by only five Australian batsmen); of the 33 matches in which he made a century in the first innings, in only one did he have the time and opportunity to make another in the second; he then made 77.

In his 230 first innings he made 129 scores of 50 and over, including 88 centuries, while in his 108 second innings he made 57 scores of 50 and over, including 29 centuries. In 19 matches he made over 50 in each innings (including a century in each innings four times), while in 22 matches he redeemed a first-innings failure (under 20) with a score of at least 50 in his second innings. Against that he was dismissed twice in the same match for scores under 50 in each innings in a further 22 matches.

# Test Matches

| | Matches | Innings | NO | HS | Runs | Average | Centuries |
|---|---|---|---|---|---|---|---|
| All Tests – First Innings | 52 | 50 | 2 | 334 | 4697 | 97.85 | 19 |
| All Tests – Second Innings | 52 | 30 | 8 | 270 | 2299 | 104.50 | 10 |
| *Total* | 52 | 80 | 10 | 334 | 6996 | 99.94 | 29 |
| Tests *v* England – First Innings | 37 | 36 | 0 | 334 | 3023 | 83.97 | 11 |
| Tests *v* England – Second Innings | 37 | 27 | 7 | 270 | 2005 | 100.25 | 8 |
| *Total:* | 37 | 63 | 7 | 334 | 5028 | 89.78 | 19 |

Bradman had two innings in 30 of his Test matches (27 *v* England, but only one each *v* West Indies, South Africa and India); he had only one innings in 20 of his Test matches (nine *v* England, four *v* West Indies, three *v* South Africa and four *v* India); and in two Test matches (one *v* England and one *v* South Africa) he did not bat at all owing to injury.

In 23 of his 50 first innings he made a score of 50 and over, including 19 centuries, while 19 of his 30 second innings exceeded 50, including ten centuries. In four matches he made over 50 in each innings (including a century in each innings once), while in ten matches he redeemed a first-innings failure (under 20) with a score of at least 50 in his second innings, and in five Tests he was twice dismissed for scores of under 50 in each innings.

## Before and After the War

### All First-class Cricket

| | Matches | Innings | NO | HS | Runs | Average | Centuries |
|---|---|---|---|---|---|---|---|
| 1927–41 | 188 | 274 | 35 | 452 | 22863 | 95.66 | 92 |
| 1945–9 | 46 | 64 | 8 | 234 | 5204 | 92.92 | 25 |
| *Total:* | 234 | 338 | 43 | 452* | 28067 | 95.14 | 117 |

One of the most commendable achievements of his career was to return to first-class cricket, after an interval of five years, and notwithstanding a severe illness, and then to score another 5,204 runs with an average of 92.92, including 25 centuries. He scored only two double centuries after the war, but 41 of his 64 innings exceeded 50.

## All Test Matches

|  | Matches | Innings | NO | HS | Runs | Average | Centuries |
|---|---|---|---|---|---|---|---|
| 1928–38 | 37 | 57 | 5 | 334 | 5093 | 97.94 | 21 |
| 1946–8 | 15 | 23 | 5 | 234 | 1903 | 105.72 | 8 |
| *Total:* | 52 | 80 | 10 | 334 | 6996 | 99.94 | 29 |

## Test Matches against England

|  | Matches | Innings | NO | HS | Runs | Average | Centuries |
|---|---|---|---|---|---|---|---|
| 1928–38 | 27 | 46 | 4 | 334 | 3840 | 91.42 | 15 |
| 1946–8 | 10 | 17 | 3 | 234 | 1188 | 84.85 | 4 |
| *Total:* | 37 | 63 | 7 | 334 | 5028 | 89.78 | 19 |

SECTION 2

# CENTURIES AND DOUBLE CENTURIES

## (a) DOUBLE CENTURIES (37) IN ALL FIRST-CLASS MATCHES

| Score | Match | Season | Match No. |
|---|---|---|---|
| 452* | New South Wales *v* Queensland, Sydney | 1929–30 | 24 |
| 369 | South Australia *v* Tasmania, Adelaide | 1935–6 | 126 |
| 357 | South Australia *v* Victoria, Melbourne | 1935–6 | 122 |
| 340* | New South Wales *v* Victoria, Sydney | 1928–9 | 14 |
| 334 | Australia *v* England, Leeds | 1930 | 46 |
| 304 | Australia *v* England, Leeds | 1934 | 113 |
| 299* | Australia *v* South Africa, Adelaide | 1931–2 | 76 |
| 278 | Australians *v* MCC, Lord's | 1938 | 154 |
| 270 | Australia *v* England, Melbourne | 1936–7 | 132 |
| 267 | South Australia *v* Victoria, Melbourne | 1939–40 | 181 |
| 258 | New South Wales *v* South Australia, Adelaide | 1930–1 | 61 |
| 258 | Australians *v* Worcestershire, Worcester | 1938 | 151 |
| 254 | Australia *v* England, Lord's | 1930 | 44 |
| 253 | New South Wales *v* Queensland, Sydney | 1933–4 | 95 |
| 252* | Australians *v* Surrey, Oval | 1930 | 36 |
| 251* | South Australia *v* New South Wales, Adelaide | 1939–40 | 179 |
| 246 | South Australia *v* Queensland, Adelaide | 1937–8 | 143 |
| 244 | Australia *v* England, Oval | 1934 | 114 |
| 238 | New South Wales *v* Victoria, Sydney | 1932–3 | 80 |
| 236 | Australians *v* Worcestershire, Worcester | 1930 | 30 |
| 234 | Australia *v* England, Sydney | 1946–7 | 195 |
| 233 | South Australia *v* Queensland, Adelaide | 1935–6 | 121 |
| 232 | Australia *v* England, Oval | 1930 | 52 |
| 226 | Australia *v* South Africa, Brisbane | 1931–2 | 71 |
| 225 | Woodfull's XI *v* Ryder's XI, Sydney | 1929–30 | 21 |
| 225 | South Australia *v* Queensland, Adelaide | 1938–9 | 173 |
| 223 | Australia *v* West Indies, Brisbane | 1930–1 | 64 |
| 220 | New South Wales *v* Victoria, Sydney | 1930–1 | 65 |
| 219 | New South Wales *v* South Africans, Sydney | 1931–2 | 72 |
| 212 | Bradman's XI *v* Richardson's XI, Sydney | 1936–7 | 127 |
| 212 | Australia *v* England, Adelaide | 1936–7 | 134 |

251

| 209* | South Australia *v* Western Australia, Perth | 1939–40 | 184 |
| 206 | Australians *v* Worcestershire, Worcester | 1934 | 97 |
| 205* | Australians *v* Kent, Canterbury | 1930 | 54 |
| 202 | Australians *v* Somerset, Taunton | 1938 | 167 |
| 201 | Australia *v* India, Adelaide | 1947–8 | 206 |
| 200 | New South Wales *v* Queensland, Brisbane | 1933–4 | 90 |

## (b) DOUBLE CENTURIES (12) IN TEST MATCHES

| Score | Match | Season | Match No. |
|---|---|---|---|
| 334 | *v* England, Leeds (Third Test) | 1930 | 46 |
| 304 | *v* England, Leeds (Fourth Test) | 1934 | 113 |
| 299* | *v* South Africa, Adelaide (Fourth Test) | 1931–2 | 76 |
| 270 | *v* England, Melbourne (Third Test) | 1936–7 | 132 |
| 254 | *v* England, Lord's (Second Test) | 1930 | 44 |
| 244 | *v* England, Oval (Fifth Test) | 1934 | 114 |
| 234 | *v* England, Sydney (Second Test) | 1946–7 | 195 |
| 232 | *v* England, Oval (Fifth Test) | 1930 | 52 |
| 226 | *v* South Africa, Brisbane (First Test) | 1931–2 | 71 |
| 223 | *v* West Indies, Brisbane (Third Test) | 1930–1 | 64 |
| 212 | *v* England, Adelaide (Fourth Test) | 1936–7 | 134 |
| 201 | *v* India, Adelaide (Fourth Test) | 1947–8 | 206 |

## (c) CENTURIES (117) IN FIRST-CLASS CRICKET

| Season | Match No. | Score | Match |
|---|---|---|---|
| 1927–8 (two) | 1 | 118 | New South Wales *v* South Australia, Adelaide |
| | 5 | 134* | New South Wales *v* Victoria, Sydney |
| 1928–9 (seven) | 7 | 131 } 133* } | New South Wales *v* Queensland, Brisbane |
| | 8 | 132* | New South Wales *v* MCC, Sydney |
| | 12 | 112 | Australia *v* England, Melbourne |
| | 14 | 340* | New South Wales *v* Victoria, Sydney |
| | 17 | 175 | New South Wales *v* South Australia, Sydney |
| | 18 | 123 | Australia *v* England, Melbourne |
| 1929–30 (five) | 20 | 157 | New South Wales *v* MCC, Sydney |
| | 21 | 124 } 225 } | Woodfull's XI *v* Ryder's XI, Sydney |
| | 24 | 452* | New South Wales *v* Queensland, Sydney |
| | 28 | 139 | Australians *v* Tasmania, Hobart |
| 1930 (ten) | 30 | 236 | Australians *v* Worcestershire, Worcester |
| | 31 | 185* | Australians *v* Leicestershire, Leicester |

| Season | Match No. | Score | Match |
|--------|-----------|-------|-------|
| | 36 | 252* | Australians *v* Surrey, Oval |
| | 38 | 191 | Australians *v* Hampshire, Southampton |
| | 41 | 131 | Australia *v* England, Nottingham |
| | 44 | 254 | Australia *v* England, Lord's |
| | 46 | 334 | Australia *v* England, Leeds |
| | 49 | 117 | Australians *v* Somerset, Taunton |
| | 52 | 232 | Australia *v* England, Oval |
| | 54 | 205* | Australians *v* Kent, Canterbury |
| 1930–1 (five) | 57 | 121 | New South Wales *v* South Australia, Sydney |
| | 61 | 258 | New South Wales *v* South Australia, Adelaide |
| | 64 | 223 | Australia *v* West Indies, Brisbane |
| | 65 | 220 | New South Wales *v* Victoria, Sydney |
| | 66 | 152 | Australia *v* West Indies, Melbourne |
| 1931–2 (seven) | 70 | 135 | New South Wales *v* South Africans, Sydney |
| | 71 | 226 | Australia *v* South Africa, Brisbane |
| | 72 | 219 | New South Wales *v* South Africans, Sydney |
| | 73 | 112 | Australia *v* South Africa, Sydney |
| | 74 | 167 | Australia *v* South Africa, Melbourne |
| | 75 | 167 | New South Wales *v* Victoria, Sydney |
| | 76 | 299* | Australia *v* South Africa, Adelaide |
| 1932–3 (three) | 80 | 238 | New South Wales *v* Victoria, Sydney |
| | 83 | 157 | New South Wales *v* Victoria, Melbourne |
| | 84 | 103* | Australia *v* England, Melbourne |
| 1933–4 (five) | 90 | 200 | New South Wales *v* Queensland, Brisbane |
| | 91 | 101 | Richardson's XI *v* Woodfull's XI, Melbourne |
| | 94 | 187* | New South Wales *v* Victoria, Melbourne |
| | 95 | 253 | New South Wales *v* Queensland, Sydney |
| | 96 | 128 | New South Wales *v* Victoria, Sydney |
| 1934 (seven) | 97 | 206 | Australians *v* Worcestershire, Worcester |
| | 103 | 160 | Australians *v* Middlesex, Lord's |
| | 112 | 140 | Australians *v* Yorkshire, Sheffield |
| | 113 | 304 | Australia *v* England, Leeds |
| | 114 | 244 | Australia *v* England, Oval |
| | 117 | 149* | Australians *v* An England XI, Folkestone |
| | 118 | 132 | Australians *v* Leveson-Gower's XI, Scarborough |
| 1935–6 (four) | 120 | 117 | South Australia *v* New South Wales, Adelaide |
| | 121 | 233 | South Australia *v* Queensland, Adelaide |
| | 122 | 357 | South Australia *v* Victoria, Melbourne |
| | 126 | 369 | South Australia *v* Tasmania, Adelaide |
| 1936–7 (six) | 127 | 212 | Rest of Australia *v* Australia, Sydney |
| | 128 | 192 | South Australia *v* Victoria, Melbourne |
| | 132 | 270 | Australia *v* England, Melbourne |
| | 134 | 212 | Australia *v* England, Adelaide |

| *Season* | *Match No.* | *Score* | *Match* |
|---|---|---|---|
| | 135 | 123 | South Australia *v* Queensland, Brisbane |
| | 137 | 169 | Australia *v* England, Melbourne |
| 1937–8 (seven) | 141 | 101 | South Australia *v* Western Australia, Adelaide |
| | 143 | 246 | South Australia *v* Queensland, Adelaide |
| | 145 | 107 107 }<br>113 } | South Australia *v* Queensland, Brisbane |
| | 146 | 104* | South Australia *v* New South Wales, Sydney |
| | 149 | 144 | Australians *v* Tasmania, Hobart |
| | 150 | 102 | Australians *v* Western Australia, Perth |
| 1938 (13) | 151 | 258 | Australians *v* Worcestershire, Worcester |
| | 153 | 137 | Australians *v* Cambridge University, Cambridge |
| | 154 | 278 | Australians *v* MCC, Lord's |
| | 156 | 143 | Australians *v* Surrey, Oval |
| | 157 | 145* | Australians *v* Hampshire, Southampton |
| | 159 | 144* | Australia *v* England, Nottingham |
| | 160 | 104 | Australians *v* Gentlemen of England, Lord's |
| | 161 | 101* | Australians *v* Lancashire, Manchester |
| | 162 | 102* | Australia *v* England, Lord's |
| | 164 | 135 | Australians *v* Warwickshire, Birmingham |
| | 165 | 144 | Australians *v* Nottinghamshire, Nottingham |
| | 166 | 103 | Australia *v* England, Leeds |
| | 167 | 202 | Australians *v* Somerset, Taunton |
| 1938–9 (six) | 171 | 118 | Bradman's XI *v* Rigg's XI, Melbourne |
| | 172 | 143 | South Australia *v* New South Wales, Adelaide |
| | 173 | 225 | South Australia *v* Queensland, Adelaide |
| | 174 | 107 | South Australia *v* Victoria, Melbourne |
| | 175 | 186 | South Australia *v* Queensland, Brisbane |
| | 176 | 135* | South Australia *v* New South Wales, Sydney |
| 1939–40 (five) | 179 | 251* | South Australia *v* New South Wales, Adelaide |
| | 180 | 138 | South Australia *v* Queensland, Adelaide |
| | 181 | 267 | South Australia *v* Victoria, Melbourne |
| | 184 | 209* | South Australia *v* Western Australia, Perth |
| | 185 | 135 | South Australia *v* Western Australia, Perth |
| 1945–6 (one) | 190 | 112 | South Australia *v* Australian Services, Adelaide |
| 1946–7 (four) | 192 | 106 | Australian XI *v* MCC, Melbourne |
| | 193 | 119 | South Australia *v* Victoria, Adelaide |
| | 194 | 187 | Australia *v* England, Brisbane |
| | 195 | 234 | Australia *v* England, Sydney |
| 1947–8 (eight) | 200 | 156 | South Australia *v* Indians, Adelaide |
| | 201 | 100 | South Australia *v* Victoria, Adelaide |
| | 202 | 172 | Australian XI *v* Indians, Sydney |
| | 203 | 185 | Australia *v* India, Brisbane |

| Season | Match No. | Score | Match |
|--------|-----------|-------|-------|
| | 205 | 132 } 127* } | Australia *v* India, Melbourne |
| | 206 | 201 | Australia *v* India, Adelaide |
| | 208 | 115 | Australians *v* Western Australia, Perth |
| 1948 (eleven) | 209 | 107 | Australians *v* Worcestershire, Worcester |
| | 211 | 146 | Australians *v* Surrey, Oval |
| | 212 | 187 | Australians *v* Essex, Southend |
| | 216 | 109 | Australians *v* Sussex, Hove |
| | 217 | 138 | Australia *v* England, Nottingham |
| | 220 | 128 | Australians *v* Surrey, Oval |
| | 223 | 173* | Australia *v* England, Leeds |
| | 226 | 133* | Australians *v* Lancashire, Manchester |
| | 229 | 150 | Australians *v* Gentlemen of England, Lord's |
| | 230 | 143 | Australians *v* South of England, Hastings |
| | 231 | 153 | Australians *v* Leveson-Gower's XI, Scarborough |
| 1948–9 (one) | 232 | 123 | Bradman's XI *v* Hassett's XI, Melbourne |

He made a century in each innings on four occasions.

In the 234 matches in which he played, 300 centuries were scored for the side for which he was playing, of which he scored 117 and the other batsmen 183.

## (d) CENTURIES (29) IN ALL TEST MATCHES

| Season | Match No. | Score | Match |
|--------|-----------|-------|-------|
| 1928–9 (two) | 12 | 112 | *v* England, Melbourne (Third Test) |
| | 18 | 123 | *v* England, Melbourne (Fifth Test) |
| 1930 (four) | 41 | 131 | *v* England, Nottingham (First Test) |
| | 44 | 254 | *v* England, Lord's (Second Test) |
| | 46 | 334 | *v* England, Leeds (Third Test) |
| | 52 | 232 | *v* England, Oval (Fifth Test) |
| 1930–1 (two) | 64 | 233 | *v* West Indies, Brisbane (Third Test) |
| | 66 | 152 | *v* West Indies, Melbourne (Fourth Test) |
| 1931–2 (four) | 71 | 226 | *v* South Africa, Brisbane (First Test) |
| | 73 | 112 | *v* South Africa, Sydney (Second Test) |
| | 74 | 167 | *v* South Africa, Melbourne (Third Test) |
| | 76 | 299* | *v* South Africa, Adelaide (Fourth Test) |
| 1932–3 (one) | 84 | 103* | *v* England, Melbourne (Second Test) |
| 1934 (two) | 113 | 304 | *v* England, Leeds (Fourth Test) |
| | 114 | 244 | *v* England, Oval (Fifth Test) |
| 1936–7 (three) | 132 | 270 | *v* England, Melbourne (Third Test) |
| | 134 | 212 | *v* England, Adelaide (Fourth Test) |
| | 137 | 169 | *v* England, Melbourne (Fifth Test) |

| Season | Match No. | Score | Match |
|--------|-----------|-------|-------|
| 1938 (three) | 159 | 144* | v England, Nottingham (First Test) |
| | 162 | 102* | v England, Lord's (Second Test) |
| | 166 | 103 | v England, Leeds (Third Test) |
| 1946–7 (two) | 194 | 187 | v England, Brisbane (First Test) |
| | 195 | 234 | v England, Sydney (Second Test) |
| 1947–8 (four) | 103 | 185 | v India, Brisbane (First Test) |
| | 205 | 132 } 127* } | v India, Melbourne (Third Test) |
| | 206 | 201 | v India, Adelaide (Fourth Test) |
| 1948 (two) | 217 | 138 | v England, Nottingham (First Test) |
| | 223 | 173* | v England, Leeds (Fourth Test) |

In his 52 Test matches, 70 centuries were scored for Australia, of which he made 29 and the other batsmen 41. In his 37 Tests v England, his share was 19 out of 51.

## PERCENTAGES OF SIDE'S TOTAL RUNS
### (Excluding Extras)

Bradman, over his whole first-class career, scored 25.47 per cent of the total runs (excluding extras) scored (in innings in which he batted) by the sides for which he was playing; in Test matches, he scored 26.03 per cent of the runs scored by Australian batsmen.

### (a) CAREER SUMMARY, 1927–49

| | Matches | Innings | Runs | Side's Total (excluding extras) | Percentage |
|---|---|---|---|---|---|
| All First-class Matches | 234 | 338 | 28067 | 110171 | 25.47 |
| All Matches in Australia | 142 | 218 | 18230 | 69828 | 26.10 |
| All Matches in England | 92 | 120 | 9837 | 40343 | 24.38 |
| All Test Matches | 52 | 80 | 6996 | 26871 | 26.03 |
| Test Matches *v* England | 37 | 63 | 5028 | 20427 | 24.61 |
| *v* England in England | 19 | 30 | 2674 | 10282 | 26.00 |
| *v* England in Australia | 18 | 33 | 2354 | 10145 | 23.20 |
| All Tests in Australia | 33 | 50 | 4322 | 16589 | 26.05 |
| All Sheffield Shield Matches | 62 | 96 | 8926 | 31723 | 28.13 |
| Shield Matches for New South Wales | 31 | 52 | 4633 | 17484 | 26.49 |
| Shield Matches for South Australia | 31 | 44 | 4293 | 14239 | 30.14 |
| All Matches for New South Wales | 41 | 69 | 5813 | 22381 | 25.97 |
| All Matches for South Australia | 44 | 63 | 5753 | 21107 | 27.25 |
| All Matches *v* Touring Teams | 54 | 84 | 3352 | 15688 | 21.36 |
| Matches *v* MCC Teams | 32 | 55 | 3352 | 15688 | 21.36 |

### (b) SEASON-BY-SEASON RECORD, 1927–49, IN ALL FIRST-CLASS MATCHES

| | Matches | Innings | Runs | Side's Total (excluding extras) | Percentage |
|---|---|---|---|---|---|
| 1927–8 | 5 | 10 | 416 | 3306 | 12.58 |
| 1928–9 | 13 | 24 | 1690 | 7219 | 23.41 |

| | Matches | Innings | Runs | Side's Total (excluding extras) | Percentage |
|---|---|---|---|---|---|
| 1929–30 | 11 | 16 | 1586 | 6038 | 26.26 |
| 1930 | 27 | 36 | 2960 | 10497 | 28.19 |
| 1930–1 | 12 | 18 | 1422 | 5376 | 26.45 |
| 1931–2 | 10 | 13 | 1403 | 4594 | 30.53 |
| 1932–3 | 11 | 21 | 1171 | 4472 | 26.18 |
| 1933–4 | 7 | 11 | 1192 | 3891 | 30.63 |
| 1934 | 22 | 27 | 2020 | 9611 | 21.01 |
| 1935–6 | 8 | 9 | 1173 | 3863 | 30.36 |
| 1936–7 | 12 | 19 | 1552 | 5145 | 30.16 |
| 1937–8 | 12 | 18 | 1437 | 5287 | 27.17 |
| 1938 | 20 | 26 | 2429 | 8809 | 27.57 |
| 1938–9 | 7 | 7 | 919 | 2987 | 30.77 |
| 1939–40 | 9 | 15 | 1475 | 4755 | 31.01 |
| 1940–1 | 2 | 4 | 18 | 934 | 1.92 |
| 1945–6 | 2 | 3 | 232 | 763 | 30.40 |
| 1946–7 | 9 | 14 | 1032 | 5114 | 20.17 |
| 1947–8 | 9 | 12 | 1296 | 4558 | 28.43 |
| 1948 | 23 | 31 | 2428 | 11426 | 21.24 |
| 1948–9 | 3 | 4 | 216 | 1526 | 14.15 |
| | | | | | |
| In Australia | 142 | 218 | 18230 | 69828 | 26.10 |
| In England | 92 | 120 | 9837 | 40343 | 24.38 |
| *Total:* | 234 | 338 | 28067 | 110171 | 25.47 |

(Extras in his 338 innings amounted to 4,222, and the total runs including extras were 114,393; his percentage of his side's total inclusive of extras was therefore 24.53.)

(c) SEASON-BY-SEASON RECORD, 1928–48, IN TEST MATCHES

| | Opponents | Matches | Innings | Runs | Side's Total (excluding extras) | Percentage |
|---|---|---|---|---|---|---|
| 1928–9 | England | 4 | 8 | 468 | 2343 | 19.97 |
| 1930 | England | 5 | 7 | 974 | 2743 | 35.50 |
| 1930–1 | West Indies | 5 | 6 | 447 | 1988 | 22.48 |
| 1931–2 | South Africa | 5 | 5 | 806 | 2107 | 38.25 |
| 1932–3 | England | 4 | 8 | 396 | 1861 | 21.27 |
| 1934 | England | 4 | 8 | 758 | 2951 | 25.68 |
| 1936–7 | England | 5 | 9 | 810 | 2687 | 30.14 |
| 1938 | England | 4 | 6 | 434 | 1730 | 25.08 |
| 1946–7 | England | 5 | 8 | 680 | 3254 | 20.89 |

| | Opponents | Matches | Innings | Runs | Side's Total (excluding extras) | Percentage |
|---|---|---|---|---|---|---|
| 1947–8 | India | 5 | 6 | 715 | 2349 | 30.43 |
| 1948 | England | 5 | 9 | 508 | 2858 | 17.77 |

*Totals:*

| | Matches | Innings | Runs | Side's Total (excluding extras) | Percentage |
|---|---|---|---|---|---|
| *v* England in Australia | 18 | 33 | 2354 | 10145 | 23.20 |
| *v* England in England | 19 | 30 | 2674 | 10282 | 26.00 |
| Total *v* England | 37 | 63 | 5028 | 20427 | 24.61 |
| All Tests in Australia | 33 | 50 | 4322 | 16589 | 26.05 |
| TOTAL: | 52 | 80 | 6996 | 26871 | 26.03 |

(Extras in his 80 innings in all Tests amounted to 1,151, and the total runs including extras were 28,022; his percentage of his side's total inclusive of extras was therefore 24.96. For his 63 innings against England, the figures were 949 extras and 21,376 total runs; and his percentage of his side's total inclusive of extras was therefore 23.52.)

## (d) INDIVIDUAL INNINGS

In the following 20 matches he scored 50 per cent or more of his side's total runs from the bat in a completed innings.

| Match No. | Match | Score | Side's Total (excl. extras) | Percentage |
|---|---|---|---|---|
| 122 | South Australia *v* Victoria, 1935–6 | 357 | 563 | 63 |
| 179 | South Australia *v* New South Wales, 1939–40 | 251* | 399 | 62 |
| 76 | Australia *v* South Africa, 1931–2 | 299* | 490 | 61 |
| 46 | Australia *v* England, 1930 | 334 | 552 | 60 |
| 143 | South Australia *v* Queensland, 1937–8 | 246 | 415 | 59 |
| 38 | Australians *v* Hampshire, 1930 | 191 | 325 | 58 |
| 154 | Australians *v* MCC, 1938 | 278 | 487 | 57 |
| 84 | Australia *v* England, 1932–3 | 103* | 182 | 56 |
| 86 | New South Wales *v* MCC, 1932–3 | 71 | 126 | 56 |
| 127 | Rest of Australia *v* Australia, 1936–7 | 212 | 374 | 56 |
| 126 | South Australia *v* Tasmania, 1935–6 | 369 | 668 | 55 |
| 7 | New South Wales *v* Queensland, 1928–9 | 131 | 240 | 54 |
| 94 | New South Wales *v* Victoria, 1933–4 | 187* | 343 | 54 |
| 113 | Australia *v* England, 1934 | 304 | 567 | 53 |
| 87 | New South Wales *v* South Australia, 1932–3 | 56 | 106 | 52 |

| Match No. | Match | Score | Side's Total (excl. extras) | Percentage |
|---|---|---|---|---|
| 128 | South Australia *v* Victoria, 1936–7 | 192 | 367 | 52 |
| 134 | Australia *v* England, 1936–7 | 212 | 406 | 52 |
| 71 | Australia *v* South Africa, 1931–2 | 226 | 442 | 51 |
| 79 | New South Wales *v* Victoria, 1932–3 | 238 | 461 | 51 |
| 151 | Australians *v* Worcestershire, 1938 | 258 | 509 | 50 |

All these 20 innings were played prior to 1940. Fifteen of them were played in Australia and five in England, and six of them were played in Test matches (four *v* England and two *v* South Africa).

# ANALYSIS OF BRADMAN'S SCORES

## (a) ALL FIRST-CLASS CRICKET

| Scores | | Number of Times | Not Out | Runs |
|---|---|---|---|---|
| 0 | | 16 | 0 | 0 |
| 1–9 | | 37 | 1 | 146 |
| 10–19 | | 33 | 2 | 476 |
| 20–29 | | 22 | 2 | 544 |
| 30–39 | | 29 | 5 | 991 |
| 40–49 | | 15 | 1 | 663 |
| 50–59 | | 17 | 5 | 937 |
| 60–69 | | 16 | 1 | 1027 |
| 70–79 | | 20 | 2 | 1503 |
| 80–89 | | 9 | 0 | 859 |
| 90–99 | | 7 | 1 | 571 |
| 100–109 | | 15 | 4 | 1557 |
| 110–119 | | 10 | 0 | 1153 |
| 120–129 | | 8 | 1 | 997 |
| 130–139 | | 16 | 5 | 2150 |
| 140–149 | | 10 | 3 | 1441 |
| 150–199 | | 21 | 3 | 3608 |
| 200–249 | | 21 | 2 | 4648 |
| 250–299 | | 10 | 3 | 2640 |
| 300 and over | | 6 | 2 | 2156 |
| *Total:* | | 338 | 43 | 28067 |
| | Australia | 97 | 4 | 1707 |
| 0–49 | England | 55 | 7 | 1113 |
| | *Total:* | 152 | 11 | 2820 |
| | Australia | 45 | 8 | 3208 |
| 50–99 | England | 24 | 1 | 1689 |
| | *Total:* | 69 | 9 | 4897 |

| Scores | | Number of Times | Not Out | Runs |
|---|---|---|---|---|
| | Australia | 51 | 8 | 6876 |
| 100–199 | England | 29 | 8 | 4030 |
| | *Total:* | 80 | 16 | 10906 |
| | Australia | 25 | 5 | 6439 |
| 200 and over | England | 12 | 2 | 3005 |
| | *Total:* | 37 | 7 | 9444 |
| | Australia | 121 | 21 | 16523 |
| 50 and over | England | 65 | 11 | 8724 |
| | *Total:* | 186 | 32 | 25247 |
| | Australia | 76 | 13 | 13315 |
| 100 and over | England | 41 | 10 | 7035 |
| | *Total:* | 117 | 23 | 20350 |
| *Total (Australia):* | | 218 | 25 | 18230 |
| *Total (England):* | | 120 | 18 | 9837 |
| TOTAL: | | 338 | 43 | 28067 |

The lowest scores he never made were 21, 34, 41, 45, 46, 60, 69, 70, 72, 74, 75, 80, 83, 93, 94, 95 and 99.

Apart from his 16 noughts, the score he made most often was 5 (eight times); 1, 2 and 13 he made seven times, and 18 six times.

Of his 338 innings, 37 were double centuries (10 per cent); 117 were a century or more (34 per cent); 186 were 50 or more (55 per cent); on the other hand, 16 were 'ducks', or over 4 per cent – a relatively high proportion.

His percentage of centuries, 34 per cent, or about one in every three visits to the wicket, is very high indeed; G.A. Headley, W.M. Woodfull and W.H. Ponsford (20 per cent) are his nearest rivals. Bradman's percentage is the same both in Australia and in England.

His percentage of double centuries (ten) is twice as high a proportion as that of any other batsman; Headley and Ponsford are next best, five per cent of their innings having reached 200.

His percentage of innings of 50 and over (55) is also the highest on record; the next best is Headley, who reached 50 in 46 per cent of his innings, and the next best Australian is W.M. Woodfull with 43 per cent.

He was dismissed for less than 100 in 201 of his 338 innings (59 per cent); for less than 50 in 141 (41 per cent); for less than 20 in 83 (24 per cent); for single figures in 52 (15 per cent).

He was dismissed 118 times between 20 and 99, and 60 times between 50 and 99.

He was dismissed in the nineties only six times, his scores being 98, 97, 97, 96, 92 and 91. He made two scores between 190 and 199 (192 and 191).

He was dismissed twice in the same match for single figures on only two occasions: match no. 13, New South Wales v South Australia, 1928–9, when he made 5 and 2; and match no. 187, South Australia v Victoria, 1940–1, when he made 0 and 6. The only time he was dismissed twice in a day was in match no. 79, Combined XI v MCC, 1932–3, for 3 and 10.

He was dismissed twice in the same match for scores of under 50 in each innings in only 22 matches of the 108 in which he had two innings; from the beginning of the 1935–6 season, he failed for less than 50 twice in a match on only seven occasions, and in only one match after the end of the war.

He made 50 in one innings of the other in 167 of the 230 matches in which he batted at least once, and failed to do so in 63 (this including the 122 matches in which he had only one innings). He made a century in one innings or the other in 113 of these 230 matches – 117 centuries in 234 matches altogether. After the war he played in 46 matches and made at least 50 in one innings or the other in 38 of them.

He made 50 or over in each innings in 19 of the 108 matches in which he batted twice – 15 out of 77 in Australia and four out of 31 in England; this includes the four occasions in which he made a century in each innings, all in Australia.

In his 117 innings of 100 and over, he scored 20,350 runs, his 'average-per-century' thus being 173; i.e. once he had reached his century he added, on the average, another 73 runs before his innings ended.

If he had been 'compulsorily retired' at 100 in all his innings, he would still have had an average of 61.06:

$$338-20-100-19,417-61.06$$

i.e. 8,650 of his 28,067 runs (30 per cent) were scored after he had completed his century.

The longest spell he ever had without an innings of 50 or over was six innings; in his first season (1927–8), after starting his career with an innings of 118, he made 33, 31, 5, 0, 13 and 2 before playing an innings of 73; and, after finishing the 1939–40 season with innings of 135, 25 and 2, he made 0, 6, 0 and 12 in 1940–1 (when he was ill), starting thereafter with 68 when he next played first-class cricket in 1945–6. Apart from that, his scores of 65, 25, 36, 13, 17, 27 and 61* in 1934 included his longest spell without reaching at least 50.

The longest spell he ever had without a century was 13 innings in 1934 when, after his innings of 160 v Middlesex, he made 7, 29, 25, 65, 25, 36, 13, 17, 27, 61*, 30, 71 and 6*, before making 140 v Yorkshire; as, however, these 13 innings produced 482 runs for an average of 43.81, it was only in relation to his own standards that he could be regarded as out of form. The next longest spell was in 1932–3 when he made 103*, 8, 66, 1, 71, 56, 97, 76, 24, 48 and 71, then commencing 1933–4 with 200; in these ten consecutive innings without a century he scored 518 runs, average 51.80. The worst shorter spell he had was also in 1934 when, just before the 160 *v* Middlesex, he made 0, 5, 37 and 0.

Apart from the above, his performance in 1932–3 against the MCC team's 'body-line' attack was the nearest he came to being out of form: 3, 10, 36, 13, 18, 23, 0, 103*, 8, 66, 1, 71, 76, 24, 48 and 71 – 571 runs, average 38.06, and interspersed with scores of 238, 52*, 157, 56 and 97 in Sheffield Shield matches

Eighty-nine of 338 innings were interrupted by his being not out overnight, four of them (all in Test matches) lasting into a third day. Of these 93 occasions, he was already past his century in 29; in 35 he was not out overnight with less than 100, and went on to complete a century; and in 29 he was dismissed next day for less than 100.

## (b) TEST MATCHES

| Scores | ALL TESTS | | | v ENGLAND | | |
|---|---|---|---|---|---|---|
| | Number of Times | Not Out | Runs | Number of Times | Not Out | Runs |
| 0 | 7 | | 0 | 6 | | 0 |
| 1–9 | 7 | | 31 | 5 | | 25 |
| 10–19 | 8 | | 117 | 7 | | 104 |
| 20–29 | 5 | | 129 | 4 | | 104 |
| 30–39 | 7 | 2 | 242 | 7 | 2 | 242 |
| 40–49 | 4 | | 180 | 3 | | 137 |
| 50–59 | 4 | 2 | 222 | 3 | 1 | 165 |
| 60–69 | 2 | | 129 | 2 | | 129 |
| 70–79 | 5 | | 382 | 5 | | 382 |
| 80–89 | 2 | | 171 | 2 | | 171 |
| 90–99 | 0 | | – | 0 | | – |
| 100–149 | 11 | 4 | 1327 | 8 | 3 | 956 |
| 150–199 | 6 | 1 | 1033 | 3 | 1 | 529 |
| 200–249 | 7 | | 1572 | 4 | | 922 |
| 250–299 | 3 | 1 | 823 | 2 | | 524 |
| 300 and over | 2 | | 638 | 2 | | 638 |
| *Total:* | 80 | 10 | 6996 | 63 | 7 | 5028 |
| 0–49 | 38 | 2 | 699 | 32 | 2 | 612 |
| 50–99 | 13 | 2 | 904 | 12 | 1 | 847 |
| 100–199 | 17 | 5 | 2360 | 11 | 4 | 1485 |
| 200 and over | 12 | 1 | 3033 | 8 | 0 | 2084 |
| 50 and over | 42 | 8 | 6297 | 31 | 5 | 4416 |
| 100 and over | 29 | 6 | 5393 | 19 | 4 | 3569 |
| *Total:* | 80 | 10 | 6996 | 63 | 7 | 5028 |

The lowest scores he never made in all Tests were 3, 5, 6 and 9; *v* England he did not make 2 or 4 either.

Apart from his seven noughts, the score he made most often was 13 (three times); against England, he did not make any individual score, other than 0, more than twice. His only single-figure scores (apart from 0) were 1, 1, 7, 8 and 8 *v* England, 2 *v* South Africa and 4 *v* West Indies.

Of his 80 innings in all Tests, 12 were double centuries (15 per cent); 29 were a century or more (36 per cent); 42 were over 50 (52 per cent); seven (or 8 per cent) were 'ducks'.

Of his 63 innings in Tests *v* England, eight were double centuries (12 per cent); 19 were over 100 (30 per cent); 31 were over 50 (49 per cent); and on the other hand, six, or as many as 9 per cent, were 'ducks'.

His percentages of centuries, 36 in all Tests and 30 *v* England, are easily the highest on record; in all Tests, 25 per cent by G.A. Headley is the next best, with R.N. Harvey, at 17 per cent, the next best Australian; in Tests between England and Australia, A.R. Morris is his nearest rival with 18 per cent.

His percentages of double centuries, 15 in all Tests and 12 *v* England, are also easily the largest; W.R. Hammond, who reached 200 in five per cent of his innings in all Tests and in six per cent of his innings *v* Australia, and Headley, also five per cent in all Tests, are the next best, while R.N. Harvey, the only other Australian to score more than one Test double century, has two per cent. No one except Bradman and Hammond has scored more than one double century in Tests between England and Australia.

His percentage of innings of 50 and over in all Tests, 52, is the highest on record, H. Sutcliffe being next best with 46 per cent, and R.N. Harvey being the next best Australian with 37 per cent. In Tests between England and Australia, however, Sutcliffe's performance is slightly superior in this respect to Bradman's, for he made 24 fifties in 46 visits to the wicket (52 per cent), compared with Bradman's 49 per cent. The latter is the best in this respect among Australians, A.R. Morris being next with 37 per cent.

Bradman was dismissed, in all Tests, for less than 100 in 47 of his 80 innings (58 per cent); for less than 50 in 36, or 45 per cent; for less than 20 in 22, or 27 per cent; for single figures in 14 (17 per cent). Against England, his figures were: for less than 100, in 41 of his 63 innings (65 per cent); for less than 50 in 30 (47 per cent); for less than 20 in 18 innings or 28 per cent; for single figures, in 11 or 17 per cent.

He was never dismissed in the nineties and only twice in the eighties (89 and 82 *v* England).

He was dismissed 25 times between 20 and 99 in all Tests, 23 of these occasions being against England; and in 11 innings, all *v* England, he was dismissed between 50 and 99.

He was never dismissed twice in the same Test match for single figures.

He had two innings in 30 of his Test matches, of which 27 were against England; and he was dismissed twice in the same match for scores of under 50 in each innings in only five of his Tests against small countries (four times *v* England and once *v* West Indies).

He made 50 in one innings or the other in 38 of the 50 Tests in which he had at least one innings, and failed to do so in only 12 (this including 20 Tests in which he had only one innings); in 28 of these 50 Tests he made a century in one innings or the other – 29 centuries in 52 Tests altogether. Against England he made 50 in one innings or the other in 28 of the 36 Tests in which he batted at least once, and failed to do so in only eight; there were nine Tests *v* England in which he got only one innings. In 19 of his 37 Tests *v* England (in one of which he did not bat) he scored a century in one innings or the other.

He made 50 or over in each innings on four occasions in the 30 Tests in which he batted twice – three times out of 27 *v* England and once *v* India, when he made a century in each innings.

In his 29 innings of 100 and over in all Tests, he scored 5,393 runs, his 'average-per-century' thus being 185; *v* England, in his 19 innings of 100 and over, he scored 3,569 runs, his 'average-per-century' being 187.

If he had been 'compulsorily retired' at 100 in all his innings, his record would have been:

| | |
|---|---|
| *v* England... | 63–3–100–3,359–55.98 |
| All Tests... | 80–4–100–4,503–59.25 |

i.e. 1,669 of his 5,028 runs *v* England (33 per cent) and 2,493 of his 6,996 runs in all Tests (35 per cent) were scored after he had completed his century.

The longest spell he ever had in Test matches without an innings of 50 or over was five innings, all *v* England; after finishing 1932–3 with 71, his first five innings in the 1934 series were 29, 25, 36, 13 and 30 (a total of 133), followed by 304 at Leeds and 244 and 77 at the Oval. His first five innings in 1936–7 also added up to only 133 (38, 0, 0, 82 and 13), followed by 270, 26, 212 and 169.

The longest spell he ever had in Test matches without a century was 11 innings, all *v* England: after his 103* in 1932–3, he had innings in that season and 1934 of 8, 66, 76, 24, 48, 71, 29, 25, 36, 13 and 30 – 426 runs, average 38.72.

In 14 consecutive Test matches in which he batted, *v* England, from 1936–7 to 1948, he made at least 50 in one innings or the other. Included in this spell were eight consecutive Test matches *v* England in which he made a century in one innings or the other: 0 and 82, 13 and 270, 26 and 212, 169, 51 and 144*, 18 and 102*, 103 and 16, (did not bat), 187, 234, 79 and 49, 0 and 56*, 12 and 63, 138 and 0, 38 and 89.

Twenty-five of his 80 Test match innings were interrupted by his being not out overnight, four of them (three *v* England and one *v* India) lasting into a third day. Of these 29 occasions, he was already past his century in 15; in eight he was not out overnight with less than 100 and went on to complete his century; and in six he was dismissed next day for less than 100.

## (c) TOP SCORE

Bradman made the highest score for his side (all innings included, whether completed or not) in 128 of his 338 innings.

In all Test matches he made top score 30 times in his 80 innings.

In Test matches *v* England, he did so 21 times in his 63 innings.

He made the top score in both innings in nine different matches, including one Test match *v* India.

## (d) BRADMAN'S 'DUCKS'

| Match No. | Match | Remarks |
|---|---|---|
| 3 | New South Wales *v* Queensland, 1927–8 | First ball |
| 68 | Australia *v* West Indies, 1930–1 | After 10 minutes |
| 69 | New South Wales *v* Queensland, 1931–2 | Fifth ball |
| 78 | New South Wales *v* South Australia, 1931–2 | Fifth ball |
| 84 | Australia *v* England, 1932–3 | First ball |
| 99 | Australians *v* Cambridge, 1934 | Fourth ball |
| 102 | Australians *v* Hampshire, 1934 | Second ball |
| 124 | South Australia *v* New South Wales, 1935–6 | Eighth ball |
| 130 | Australia *v* England, 1936–7 | Second Ball |
| 131 | Australia *v* England, 1936–7 | First ball |
| 182 | South Australia *v* Queensland, 1939–40 | First ball |
| 187 | South Australia *v* Victoria, 1940–1 | First ball |
| 188 | Bradman's XI *v* McCabe's XI, 1940–1 | First ball |
| 198 | Australia *v* England, 1946–7 | Eighth ball, after 10 minutes |
| 217 | Australia *v* England, 1948 | Tenth ball, after 13 minutes |
| 227 | Australia *v* England, 1948 | Second ball |

Of his 16 'ducks' six were 'first balls' and three were 'second balls'.

Twelve were made in Australia and four in England; he went through the 1930 and 1938 tours without a nought.

Seven were made in Test matches, six of them *v* England.

He never made 'spectacles', though he twice made two noughts in the successive innings in different matches (in 1930–1–2 and 1936–7).

Of his 16 'ducks', 12 were in the first innings and four in the second; but he only 'bustled for a pair', i.e. batted in the second innings after making 0 in the first, on seven occasions, making 13, 103*, 82, 97, 6, 12 and 56* respectively. Three of these occasions were in Tests *v* England.

The longest he ever took to open his score was 28 minutes (match no. 221, Australia *v* England, 1948); the next longest, 18 minutes (match no. 49, Australians *v* Somerset, 1930); he usually succeeded in getting off the mark with as little delay as possible.

## SECTION 5

## BRADMAN IN PARTNERSHIP

### (a) HIGHEST PARTNERSHIP FOR EACH WICKET IN ALL FIRST-CLASS CRICKET

| Wicket | Runs added | Partner | Match | Match No. |
|---|---|---|---|---|
| 1st | 172 | W.A. Brown | New South Wales *v* Victoria, 1933–4 | 96 |

(He batted No. 3 in this match, replacing J.H. Fingleton, one of the openers, when he retired hurt, and contributing to a first-wicket partnership which totalled 340; his only century partnership for the first wicket as opening batsman was:

| | | | | |
|---|---|---|---|---|
| | 172 | A.A. Jackson | New South Wales *v* South Australia, 1929–30 | 22) |
| 2nd | 451 | W.H. Ponsford | Australia *v* England, 1934 | 114 |
| 3rd | 363 | A.F. Kippax | New South Wales *v* Queensland, 1933–4 | 95 |
| 4th | 388 | W.H. Ponsford | Australia *v* England, 1934 | 113 |
| 5th | 405 | S.G. Barnes | Australia *v* England, 1946–7 | 195 |
| 6th | 346 | J.H. Fingleton | Australia *v* England, 1936–7 | 132 |
| 7th | 126 | M.G. Waite | South Australia *v* Victoria, 1938–9 | 181 |
| 8th | 161 | M.G. Waite | South Australia *v* Queensland, 1937–8 | 143 |
| 9th | 81 | C.V. Grimmett | South Australia *v* New South Wales, 1939–40 | 179 |
| 10th | 39 | W. Howell | New South Wales *v* Victoria, 1933–4 | 94 |

### (b) HIGHEST PARTNERSHIP FOR EACH WICKET IN TEST MATCHES

| Wicket | Runs added | Partner | Opponents | Match No. |
|---|---|---|---|---|
| 1st | – | – | – | – |
| 2nd | 451 | W.H. Ponsford | England, 1934 | 114 |
| 3rd | 276 | A.L. Hassett | England, 1946–7 | 194 |
| 4th | 388 | W.H. Ponsford | England, 1934 | 113 |
| 5th | 405 | S.G. Barnes | England, 1946–7 | 195 |
| 6th | 346 | J.H. Fingleton | England, 1936–7 | 132 |
| 7th | 86 | E.L. a'Beckett | England, 1928–9 | 12 |

| Wicket | Runs added | Partner | Opponents | Match No. |
|---|---|---|---|---|
| 8th | 93 | R.K. Oxenham | England, 1928–9 | 12 |
| 9th | 78 | W.J. O'Reilly | South Africa, 1931–2 | 76 |
| (His best *v* England for the ninth wickets was: | | | | |
| | 38 | F.A. Ward | England, 1936–7 | 132) |
| 10th | 14 | H.M. Thurlow | South Africa, 1931–2 | 76 |
| (His best *v* England for the 10th wicket was: | | | | |
| | 5 | H. Ironmonger | England, 1932–3 | 84) |

## (c) DOUBLE CENTURY PARTNERSHIPS (41) IN ALL FIRST-CLASS CRICKET

| Wicket | Runs added | Partner | Match | Match No. |
|---|---|---|---|---|
| 4th | 249* | A.F. Kippax | New South Wales *v* MCC, 1928–9 | 8 |
| 3rd | 218 | A.F. Kippax | Woodfull's XI *v* Ryder's XI, 1929–30 | 21 |
| 3rd | 272 | A.F. Kippax | New South Wales *v* Queensland, 1929–30 | 24 |
| 2nd | 296 | W.H. Ponsford | Australians *v* Tasmania, 1929–30 | 28 |
| 2nd | 208 | W.M. Woodfull | Australians *v* Worcestershire, 1930 | 30 |
| 2nd | 231 | W.M. Woodfull | Australia *v* England, 1930 | 44 |
| 3rd | 229 | A.F. Kippax | Australia *v* England, 1930 | 46 |
| 2nd | 231 | A.A. Jackson | Australians *v* Somerset, 1930 | 49 |
| 4th | 243 | A.A. Jackson | Australia *v* England, 1930 | 52 |
| 3rd | 219 | A.F. Kippax | New South Wales *v* South Australia, 1930–1 | 57 |
| 2nd | 334 | A.A. Jackson | New South Wales *v* South Australia, 1930–1 | 61 |
| 2nd | 229 | W.H. Ponsford | Australia *v* West Indies, 1930–1 | 64 |
| 5th | 234 | O.W. Bill | New South Wales *v* Victoria, 1930–1 | 65 |
| 2nd | 216 | J.H. Fingleton | New South Wales *v* South Africans, 1931–2 | 70 |
| 2nd | 274 | W.M. Woodfull | Australia *v* South Africa, 1931–2 | 74 |
| 2nd | 294 | W.A. Brown | New South Wales *v* Queensland, 1933–4 | 90 |
| 3rd | 363 | A.F. Kippax | New South Wales *v* Queensland, 1933–4 | 95 |
| 4th | 388 | W.H. Ponsford | Australia *v* England, 1934 | 113 |
| 2nd | 451 | W.H. Ponsford | Australia *v* England, 1934 | 114 |
| 2nd | 202 | C.L. Badcock | South Australia *v* New South Wales, 1935–6 | 120 |
| 3rd | 356 | R.A. Hamence | South Australia *v* Tasmania, 1935–6 | 126 |
| 6th | 346 | J.H. Fingleton | Australia *v* England, 1936–7 | 132 |
| 3rd | 249 | S.J. McCabe | Australia *v* England, 1936–7 | 137 |
| 3rd | 241 | C.L. Badcock | Australians *v* Tasmania, 1937–8 | 149 |
| 4th | 277 | C.L. Badcock | Australians *v* Worcestershire, 1938 | 151 |
| 2nd | 215 | J.H. Fingleton | Australians *v* Cambridge, 1938 | 153 |
| 2nd | 242* | J.H. Fingleton | Australians *v* Hampshire, 1938 | 157 |
| 2nd | 206 | W.A. Brown | Australians *v* Warwickshire, 1938 | 164 |
| 3rd | 216 | A.L. Hassett | Australians *v* Nottinghamshire, 1938 | 165 |

| Wicket | Runs added | Partner | Match | Match No. |
|--------|-----------|---------|-------|-----------|
| 3rd | 202 | C.L. Badcock | South Australia v Queensland, 1938–9 | 173 |
| 3rd | 276 | A.L. Hassett | Australia v England, 1946–7 | 194 |
| 5th | 405 | S.G. Barnes | Australia v England, 1946–7 | 195 |
| 3rd | 252 | K.R. Miller | Australian XI v Indians, 1947–8 | 202 |
| 5th | 223* | A.R. Morris | Australia v India, 1947–8 | 205 |
| 2nd | 236 | S.G. Barnes | Australia v India, 1947–8 | 206 |
| 2nd | 201 | A.R. Morris | Australians v Western Australia, 1947–8 | 208 |
| 2nd | 207 | S.G. Barnes | Australians v Surrey, 1948 | 211 |
| 2nd | 219 | W.A. Brown | Australians v Essex, 1948 | 212 |
| 2nd | 231 | A.L. Hassett | Australians v Surrey, 1948 | 220 |
| 2nd | 301 | A.R. Morris | Australia v England, 1948 | 223 |
| 2nd | 225 | S.G. Barnes | Australians v L.-Gower's XI, 1948 | 231 |

He took part in 41 stands of 200 and upwards, 21 for the second wicket, 12 for the third wicket, four for the fourth wicket, three for the fifth wicket and one for the sixth wicket.

Of the 41 double-century partnerships eight were in excess of 300 and two also exceeded 400.

Although he never had two partnerships both over 200 in the same innings, he three times had one partnership of over 200 and another of over 190 in the same innings, all in Test matches (match nos. 44 and 46, v England, 1930, and no. 64 v West Indies, 1930–1). In match no. 24 (New South Wales v Queensland, 1929–30), he had one stand of over 200, and two other stands of over 100. In addition to these matches, there were two other occasions when he had partnerships of over 200 and over 100 in the same innings.

In match no. 14 (New South Wales v Victoria, 1928–9) he had four separate century partnerships in the same innings, and in match nos. 24 (New South Wales v Queensland, 1929–30) and 36 (Australians v Surrey, 1930) he took part in three separate three-figure partnerships in the same innings.

In 19 matches, he took part in two century partnerships in the same innings.

### (d) CENTURY PARTNERSHIPS (35) IN TEST MATCHES

| Wicket | Runs added | Partner | Opponents | Match No. |
|--------|-----------|---------|-----------|-----------|
| 5th | 183 | A.G. Fairfax | England, 1928–9 | 18 |
| { 2nd | 231 | W.M. Woodfull | England, 1930 ⎫ | 44 |
| { 3rd | 192 | A.F. Kippax | England, 1930 ⎭ | |
| { 2nd | 192 | W.M. Woodfull | England, 1930 ⎫ | 46 |
| { 3rd | 229 | A.F. Kippax | England, 1930 ⎭ | |
| 4th | 243 | A.A. Jackson | England, 1930 | 52 |

| Wicket | Runs added | Partner | Opponents | Match No. |
|--------|-----------|---------|-----------|-----------|
| { 2nd | 229 | W.H. Ponsford | West Indies, 1930–1 | |
| { 3rd | 193 | A.F. Kippax | West Indies, 1930–1 } | 64 |
| 2nd | 156 | W.M. Woodfull | West Indies, 1930–1 | 66 |
| 2nd | 163 | W.M. Woodfull | South Africa, 1931–2 | 71 |
| 3rd | 111 | K.E. Rigg | South Africa, 1931–2 | 73 |
| 2nd | 274 | W.M. Woodfull | South Africa, 1931–2 | 74 |
| { 2nd | 176 | W.M. Woodfull | South Africa, 1931–2 | 76 |
| { 5th | 114 | K.E. Rigg | South Africa, 1931–2 } | |
| 2nd | 115 | W.M. Woodfull | England, 1932–3 | 89 |
| 4th | 388 | W.H. Ponsford | England, 1934 | 113 |
| { 2nd | 451 | W.H. Ponsford | England, 1934 } | 114 |
| { 3rd | 150 | S.J. McCabe | England, 1934 | |
| 2nd | 124 | J.H. Fingleton | England, 1936–7 | 131 |
| 6th | 346 | J.H. Fingleton | England, 1936–7 | 132 |
| 3rd | 109 | S.J. McCabe | England, 1936–7 | |
| { 5th | 135 | R.G. Gregory | England, 1936–7 } | 134 |
| { 3rd | 249 | S.J. McCabe | England, 1936–7 | |
| 137 | | | | |
| 2nd | 170 | W.A. Brown | England, 1938 | 159 |
| 3rd | 276 | A.L. Hassett | England, 1946–7 | 194 |
| 5th | 405 | S.G. Barnes | England, 1946–7 | 195 |
| { 3rd | 101 | A.L. Hassett | India, 1947–8 | 203 |
| { 4th | 120 | K.R. Miller | India, 1947–8 } | |
| { 3rd | 169 | A.L. Hassett | India, 1947–8 | 205 |
| { 5th | 223 | A.R. Morris | India, 1947–8 } | |
| { 2nd | 236 | S.G. Barnes | India, 1947–8 | 206 |
| { 3rd | 105 | A.L. Hassett | India, 1947–8 } | |
| 5th | 120 | A.L. Hassett | England, 1948 | 217 |
| 2nd | 174 | S.G. Barnes | England, 1948 | 219 |
| 2nd | 301 | A.R. Morris | England, 1948 | 223 |

(In addition, he and K.R. Miller between them helped W.A. Brown to add 134 for the second wicket v India, 1947–8, in match no. 207; Bradman retired hurt after helping Brown to add 92 of them.)

He took part in 35 century stands in all Test cricket, 21 of them being v England, three v West Indies, five v South Africa and six v India.

Of these 35 partnerships, 14 were for the second wicket, 11 for the third wicket, three for the fourth wicket, six for the fifth wicket, and one for the sixth wicket.

Of these 35 partnerships, 14 exceeded 200, five also exceeded 300, and two also exceeded 400.

Seven times he had two different partnerships in excess of 100 in the same innings; on four of these occasions one of the partnerships was of over 200.

His partners were: W.M. Woodfull (seven times), A.L. Hassett (five times), S.G. Barnes, A.F. Kippax, S.J. McCabe and W.H. Ponsford (three times each), J.H. Fingleton, A.R. Morris and K.E. Rigg (twice each), and W.A. Brown, A.G. Fairfax, R.G. Gregory, A.A. Jackson and K.R. Miller (once each).

## (e) CENTURY PARTNERSHIPS

| Wicket | All First-class Cricket | All Tests | Tests v England |
|---|---|---|---|
| 1st | 2 | – | – |
| 2nd | 65 | 14 | 8 |
| 3rd | 45 | 11 | 6 |
| 4th | 19 | 3 | 2 |
| 5th | 20 | 6 | 4 |
| 6th | 8 | 1 | 1 |
| 7th | 3 | – | – |
| 8th | 2 | – | – |
| 9th | – | – | – |
| 10th | – | – | – |
| *Total:* | 164 | 35 | 21 |

## (f) PARTNERS IN CENTURY STANDS IN ALL FIRST-CLASS CRICKET

17 – A.F. Kippax

15 – S.J. McCabe, W.M. Woodfull

12 – W.A. Brown

11 – C.L. Badcock

10 – A.L. Hassett

9 – J.H. Fingleton

8 – A.A. Jackson

7 – S.G. Barnes

6 – W.H. Ponsford, A.R. Morris

5 – R.A. Hamence, M.G. Waite

4 – A.G. Fairfax

3 – K.E. Rigg, K.R. Miller, R.S. Whitington

2 – V.Y. Richardson, L.P. O'Brien, K.L. Ridings, R.J. Craig

Seventeen other batsmen shared one century partnership with him.

## (g) CENTURY PARTNERSHIPS – SEASON-BY-SEASON DETAILS

| | *All First-class Cricket* | *All Test Matches* | *Tests v England* |
|---|---|---|---|
| 1927–8 | 2 | – | – |
| 1928–9 | 9 | 1 | 1 |
| 1929–30 | 10 | – | – |
| 1930 | 21 | 5 | 5 |
| 1930–1 | 7 | 3 | – |
| 1931–2 | 7 | 5 | – |
| 1932–3 | 5 | 1 | 1 |
| 1933–4 | 6 | – | – |
| 1934 | 11 | 3 | 3 |
| 1935–6 | 6 | – | – |
| 1936–7 | 9 | 5 | 5 |
| 1937–8 | 9 | – | – |
| 1938 | 12 | 1 | 1 |
| 1938–9 | 8 | – | – |
| 1939–40 | 8 | – | – |
| 1940–1 | – | – | – |
| 1945–6 | 1 | – | – |
| 1946–7 | 4 | 2 | 2 |
| 1947–8 | 9 | 6 | – |
| 1948 | 19 | 3 | 3 |
| 1948–9 | 1 | – | – |
| | | | |
| In Australia | 101 | 23 | 9 |
| In England | 63 | 12 | 12 |
| | | | |
| *Total:* | 164 | 35 | 21 |

## (h) RUNS ADDED WHILE BRADMAN WAS BATTING – ALL FIRST-CLASS CRICKET

| | *Innings* | *Runs* | *Total added while in* | *Average runs added while in* | *Percentage of runs added while in* |
|---|---|---|---|---|---|
| 1927–8 | 10 | 416 | 853 | 85 | 48 |
| 1928–9 | 24 | 1690 | 3134 | 130 | 53 |
| 1929–30 | 16 | 1586 | 2817 | 176 | 56 |
| 1930 | 36 | 2960 | 5183 | 143 | 57 |
| 1930–1 | 18 | 1422 | 2466 | 137 | 57 |
| 1931–2 | 13 | 1403 | 2355 | 181 | 59 |
| 1932–3 | 21 | 1171 | 1865 | 88 | 62 |
| 1933–4 | 11 | 1192 | 1889 | 171 | 63 |

| | Innings | Runs | Total added while in | Average runs added while in | Percentage of runs added while in |
|---|---|---|---|---|---|
| 1934 | 27 | 2020 | 3432 | 127 | 58 |
| 1935–6 | 9 | 1173 | 1778 | 197 | 65 |
| 1936–7 | 19 | 1552 | 2599 | 136 | 59 |
| 1937–8 | 18 | 1437 | 2515 | 139 | 57 |
| 1938 | 26 | 2429 | 4308 | 165 | 56 |
| 1938–9 | 7 | 919 | 1654 | 236 | 55 |
| 1939–40 | 15 | 1475 | 2390 | 159 | 61 |
| 1940–1 | 4 | 18 | 31 | 7 | 58 |
| 1945–6 | 3 | 232 | 365 | 121 | 63 |
| 1946–7 | 14 | 1032 | 1873 | 133 | 55 |
| 1947–8 | 12 | 1296 | 2177 | 181 | 59 |
| 1948 | 31 | 2428 | 4543 | 146 | 53 |
| 1948–9 | 4 | 216 | 368 | 92 | 58 |
| | | | | | |
| In Australia | 218 | 18230 | 31129 | 142 | 53 |
| In England | 120 | 9837 | 17466 | 145 | 56 |
| | | | | | |
| *Total:* | 338 | 28067 | 48595 | 143 | 57 |

On the average, therefore, over his whole career, Bradman in every innings helped to add 143 to his side's score from the time he went in until his innings finished. His proportion was 57 per cent, the remainder being supplied by the batsmen at the other end (39 per cent) and extras (4 per cent); i.e. he scored almost half as fast again as his partners. The only season in which he failed to out-score his partners and extras combined was 1927–8, his first.

In 175 of his innings (112 in Australia and 63 in England), Bradman helped to raise his side's score by 100 and over before his innings ended.

In 98 of his innings (63 in Australia and 35 in England), he helped to raise his side's score by 200 or over before his innings ended.

In 44 of his innings (27 in Australia and 17 in England), he helped raise his side's score by 300 or over before his innings ended.

In 21 of his innings (13 in Australia and eight in England) he helped to raise his side's score by 400 or over before his innings ended.

In the following seven innings he helped to raise his side's score by 500 or over:

| Match No. | Match | Bradman's score | Score when in | Score when out | Increase |
|---|---|---|---|---|---|
| 24 | New South Wales *v* Queensland, 1929–30 | 452* | 22/1 | 761/8 | 739 |
| 14 | New South Wales *v* Victoria, 1928–9 | 340* | 76/1 | 713/6 | 637 |
| 126 | South Australia *v* Tasmania, 1935–6 | 369 | 23/1 | 552/6 | 529 |
| 113 | Australia *v* England, 1934 | 304 | 39/3 | 550/6 | 511 |
| 46 | Australia *v* England, 1930 | 334 | 2/1 | 508/6 | 506 |

| Match No. | Match | Bradman's score | Score when in | Score when out | Increase |
|---|---|---|---|---|---|
| 76 | Australia *v* South Africa, 1931–2 | 299* | 9/1 | 513/10 | 504 |
| 122 | South Australia *v* Victoria, 1935–6 | 357 | 8/1 | 510/8 | 502 |

He played altogether 252 innings of 20 and over, and scored 50 per cent or more of the runs added while he was at the wicket in 207 of them; in Australia, 138 out of 162; in England, 69 out of 90.

He played altogether 186 innings of 50 and over, and scored 50 per cent or more of the runs added while he was at the wicket in 166 of them; in Australia, 108 out of 121; in England, 58 out of 65.

Of his 117 centuries, he scored 50 per cent or more of the runs added while he was in, in 108; in Australia, 70 out of 76; in England, 38 out of 41.

In all his 37 double centuries, he scored more than 50 per cent of the runs added while he was batting.

In 22 of his 252 innings of 20 and over (15 in Australia and seven in England), he scored over 70 per cent of the runs added while he was at the wicket. The highest proportions were:

| Match No. | Match | Bradman's score | Score when in | Score when out | Increase | Percentage |
|---|---|---|---|---|---|---|
| 29 | Australians *v* Western Australia, 1929–30 | 27 | 52/1 | 83/3 | 31 | 87 |
| 80 | New South Wales *v* Victoria, 1932–3 | 52* | 19/1 | 82/1 | 63 | 82 |
| 105 | Australia *v* England, 1934 | 29 | 88/2 | 125/3 | 37 | 78 |
| 39 | Australians *v* Middlesex, 1930 | 35 | 13/1 | 58/2 | 45 | 77 |
| 161 | Australians *v* Lancashire, 1938 | 101* | 153/1 | 284/2 | 131 | 77 |
| 85 | Australia *v* England, 1932–3 | 66 | 12/2 | 100/3 | 88 | 75 |
| 89 | Australia *v* England, 1932–3 | 48 | 0/1 | 64/3 | 64 | 75 |

The only double centuries in which he scored 70 per cent of the runs added were:

| Match No. | Match | Bradman's score | Score when in | Score when out | Increase | Percentage |
|---|---|---|---|---|---|---|
| 184 | South Australia *v* Western Australia, 1939–40 | 209* | 25/1 | 306/3 | 281 | 74 |
| 122 | South Australia *v* Victoria, 1935–6 | 357 | 8/1 | 510/8 | 502 | 71 |
| 80 | New South Wales *v* Victoria, 1932–3 | 238 | 16/1 | 355/4 | 339 | 70 |

In 11 of his 252 innings of 20 and over (five in Australia and six in England), he scored less than 40 per cent of the runs added while he was at the wicket. The lowest proportions were:

| Match No. | Match | Bradman's score | Score when in | Score when out | Increase | Per-centage |
|---|---|---|---|---|---|---|
| 115 | Australians v Sussex, 1934 | 19 | 436/5 | 519/7 | 83 | 22 |
| 158 | Australians v Middlesex, 1938 | 30* | 0/1 | 114/2 | 114 | 26 |
| 70 | NSW v South Africans, 1931–2 | 30 | 1/1 | 98/3 | 97 | 30 |
| 82 | New South Wales v MCC, 1932–3 | 23 | 90/4 | 161/6 | 71 | 32 |
| 136 | South Australia v NSW, 1936–7 | 24 | 23/2 | 94/4 | 71 | 33 |
| 35 | Australians v Derbyshire, 1930 | 44* | 127/1 | 253/3 | 126 | 34 |
| 37 | Australians v Oxford, 1930 | 32 | 172/1 | 261/2 | 89 | 35 |
| 221 | Australia v England, 1948 | 30* | 10/1 | 92/1 | 82 | 36 |

The lowest proportions for centuries and double centuries respectively were:

| Match No. | Match | Bradman's score | Score when in | Score when out | Increase | Per-centage |
|---|---|---|---|---|---|---|
| 159 | Australia v England, 1938 | 144* | 89/1 | 427/6 | 338 | 42 |
| 1 | NSW v South Australia, 1927–8 | 118 | 250/4 | 519/10 | 269 | 43 |
| 64 | Australia v West Indies, 1930–1 | 223 | 1/1 | 434/4 | 433 | 51 |
| 134 | Australia v England, 1936–7 | 212 | 21/1 | 422/6 | 401 | 52 |

## (i) RUNS ADDED WHILE BRADMAN WAS BATTING – TEST MATCHES

| | Opponents | Innings | Runs | Total added while in | Average runs added while in | Percentage of runs added while in |
|---|---|---|---|---|---|---|
| 1928–9 | England | 8 | 468 | 846 | 105 | 55 |
| 1930 | England | 7 | 974 | 1638 | 234 | 59 |
| 1930–1 | West Indies | 6 | 447 | 781 | 130 | 57 |
| 1931–2 | South Africa | 5 | 806 | 1435 | 287 | 60 |
| 1932–3 | England | 8 | 396 | 612 | 76 | 64 |
| 1934 | England | 8 | 758 | 1360 | 170 | 55 |
| 1936–7 | England | 9 | 810 | 1471 | 163 | 55 |
| 1938 | England | 6 | 434 | 829 | 138 | 52 |
| 1946–7 | England | 8 | 680 | 1188 | 148 | 57 |
| 1947–8 | India | 6 | 715 | 1210 | 201 | 59 |
| 1948 | England | 9 | 508 | 1027 | 114 | 49 |
| Totals: | | | | | | |
| v England in Australia | | 33 | 2354 | 4117 | 124 | 57 |
| v England in England | | 30 | 2674 | 4854 | 161 | 55 |
| Total v England | | 63 | 5028 | 8971 | 142 | 56 |
| all Tests in Australia | | 50 | 4322 | 7543 | 150 | 57 |
| all Tests | | 80 | 6996 | 12397 | 154 | 56 |

Over his whole career, Bradman helped to add 154 to Australia's score in all Tests, and 142 in Tests *v* England, from the time he went in until the end of his innings, his share being in each case 56 per cent of the runs added while he was at the wicket; extras contributed about 4 per cent and the batsmen at the other end 40 per cent.

In 38 of his innings, including 28 in Tests *v* England, he helped to raise Australia's score by 200 or over before his innings ended.

In 26 of his innings, including 16 in Tests *v* England, he helped to raise Australia's score by 200 or over before his innings ended.

In 16 of his innings, including 12 in Tests *v* England, he helped raise Australia's score by 300 or over before his innings ended.

In ten of his innings, including eight in Tests *v* England, he helped to raise Australia's score by 400 or over before his innings ended.

In three of his innings, including two Tests *v* England, he helped to raise Australia's score by 500 or over before his innings ended.

He played altogether 58 innings of 20 and over in all Test matches, and in 48 of them scored 50 per cent or more of the runs added while he was in; *v* England, he did so in 35 out of 45 innings of 20 and over.

He played 42 innings of 50 and over in all Test matches, and in 38 of them scored 50 per cent or more of the runs added while he was in; *v* England, he did so in 27 of his 31 innings of 50 and over.

Of his 29 centuries, he scored 50 per cent or more of the runs added while he was batting in 27; the only two in which he failed to do so were both *v* England. All his double centuries represented more than 50 per cent of the runs added while he was at the wicket.

In five of his 58 Test match innings of 20 and over, he scored over 70 per cent of the runs added while he was in:

| Match No. | Opponents | Bradman's score | Score when in | Score when out | Increase | Percentage |
|---|---|---|---|---|---|---|
| 105 | England, 1934 | 29 | 88/2 | 125/3 | 37 | 78 |
| 85 | England, 1932–3 | 66 | 12/2 | 100/3 | 88 | 75 |
| 89 | England, 1932–3 | 48 | 0/1 | 64/3 | 64 | 75 |
| 68 | West Indies, 1930–1 | 43 | 7/1 | 66/2 | 59 | 72 |
| 88 | England, 1932–3 | 24 | 46/1 | 79/2 | 33 | 72 |

The biggest proportions in his innings of 100 and over were:

| Match No. | Opponents | Bradman's score | Score when in | Score when out | Increase | Percentage |
|---|---|---|---|---|---|---|
| 18 | England, 1928–9 | 123 | 203/3 | 386/5 | 183 | 67 |
| 166 | England, 1938 | 103 | 87/2 | 240/8 | 153 | 67 |
| 46 | England, 1930 | 334 | 2/1 | 508/9 | 506 | 66 |
| 203 | India, 1947–8 | 185 | 38/1 | 318/4 | 280 | 66 |

In six of his 58 Test match innings of 20 and over, he scored less than 45 per cent of the runs scored while he was batting:

| Match No. | Opponents | Bradman's score | Score when in | Score when out | Increase | Percentage |
|---|---|---|---|---|---|---|
| 221 | England, 1948 | 30* | 10/1 | 92/1 | 82 | 36 |
| 134 | England, 1936–7 | 26 | 72/2 | 136/4 | 64 | 40 |
| 159 | England, 1938 | 144* | 89/1 | 427/6 | 338 | 42 |
| 219 | England, 1948 | 89 | 122/1 | 329/4 | 208 | 42 |
| 114 | England, 1934 | 77 | 13/1 | 192/3 | 179 | 43 |
| 18 | England, 1928–9 | 37* | 204/5 | 287/5 | 83 | 44 |

### (j) POSITION IN BATTING ORDER – ALL FIRST-CLASS CRICKET

Bradman's normal position in the batting order was no. 3; he went in at the fall of the first wicket in 243 of his 338 innings.

In the others, he opened the innings on nine occasions, batted no. 4 on 39, no. 5 on 17, no. 6 on 22, no. 7 on six, and no. 8 on two occasions.

In 1927–8, his first season, he never batted higher than no. 6, and in 1928–9 he batted 16 times (out of 24) at no. 5, 6 or 7. After that he batted lower than no. 4 on only 21 occasions; usually either because of injury, because the order was altered owing to weather conditions, or because of the interposition of a 'nightwatchman'.

His nine innings as an opening batsman realised 836 runs, including three centuries, for an average of 104.50. He only once went in first in England (Australians v Hampshire, 1930, match no. 38), and that was to give him a chance of reaching 1,000 runs before the end of May. The last time he opened the innings was in 1933–4; he never put himself in first when he was captain.

When he batted no. 3, the opening batsmen had paved the way for him with a century partnership for the first wicket on 34 occasions; on 18 of such occasions he himself made a century.

On the other hand, 16 of his centuries were made when the score was still in single figures when he went in to bat, out of 63 such occasions (apart from the innings in which he was himself one of the opening batsmen).

The highest score he found on the board was 476/6 (match no. 3, New South Wales v Queensland, 1927–8), when he made 0; the next highest was 436/5 (Match no. 115, Australians v Sussex, 1934), when he made an indifferent 19.

The highest score for the opening stand when he went in at no. 3 was 239/1 (match no. 104, Australians v Surrey, 1934), when he made 77; the next highest was 226/1 (match no. 200, South Australia v Indians, 1947–8), when he made 156.

Three of his 117 first-class centuries were made when opening the innings, 91 when no. 3, nine when no. 4, five when no. 5, seven when no. 6, and two when no. 7.

Bradman batted no. 3 for Australia in 56 of his 80 Test match innings, ten times no. 4, three times no. 5, eight times no. 6 and three times no. 7. He never opened the innings for Australia in a Test match.

In 1928–9, he never batted higher than no. 5, and that only once. Thereafter he went in lower than no. 4 on only six occasions in Test matches.

When he batted no. 3, the opening batsman had put over 100 on the board for the first wicket in eight innings, and in two of these he himself made a century. Five of his Test match centuries were made after he had come to the wicket before the score had reached 10; he faced such a poor start in 15 of his Test match innings.

The highest score when he went in to bat in a Test match was 320/4 (match no. 110, 1934), when he batted as low as no. 6 owing to illness and made 30.

The highest scores for the opening stand when he went in no. 3 were 162/1 (match no. 44, 1930), when he made 254, and 159/1 (match no. 52, 1930), when he made 232.

Twenty of his 29 Test centuries were scored when he went in no. 3, three at no. 4, two at no. 5, three at no. 6 and one at no. 7.

# SPEED OF SCORING

## (a) ALL FIRST-CLASS MATCHES

### Average Runs per Hour and Average Length of Innings

Over his whole career, Bradman maintained an average rate of scoring of 42 runs
per hour, and the average length of each of his completed innings was two hours
14 minutes.

| | Innings | NO | Runs | Time hrs min. | Average runs per hour | Average length of innings hrs min. |
|---|---|---|---|---|---|---|
| 1927–8 | 10 | 1 | 416 | 11 51 | 35 | 1 19 |
| 1928–9 | 24 | 6 | 1690 | 48 51 | 34 | 2 42 |
| 1929-30 | 16 | 2 | 1586 | 32 35 | 48 | 2 19 |
| 1930 | 36 | 6 | 2960 | 75 28 | 39 | 2 30 |
| 1930–1 | 18 | 0 | 1422 | 30 57 | 45 | 1 43 |
| 1931–2 | 13 | 1 | 1403 | 29 54 | 46 | 2 29 |
| 1932–3 | 21 | 2 | 1171 | 27 46 | 42 | 1 27 |
| 1933-4 | 11 | 2 | 1192 | 23 34 | 50 | 2 37 |
| 1934 | 27 | 3 | 2020 | 40 13 | 50 | 1 40 |
| 1935–6 | 9 | 0 | 1173 | 20 3 | 58 | 2 13 |
| 1936–7 | 19 | 1 | 1552 | 39 13 | 39 | 2 10 |
| 1937–8 | 18 | 2 | 1437 | 35 50 | 40 | 2 14 |
| 1938 | 26 | 5 | 2429 | 58 29 | 41 | 2 46 |
| 1938–9 | 7 | 1 | 919 | 23 12 | 39 | 3 52 |
| 1939–40 | 15 | 3 | 1475 | 29 13 | 50 | 2 26 |
| 1940–1 | 4 | 0 | 18 | – 30 | 36 | – 7 |
| 1945–6 | 3 | 1 | 232 | 4 28 | 51 | 2 14 |
| 1946–7 | 14 | 1 | 1032 | 31 6 | 33 | 2 23 |
| 1947–8 | 12 | 2 | 1296 | 29 1 | 44 | 2 54 |
| 1948 | 31 | 4 | 2428 | 62 28 | 38 | 2 18 |
| 1948–9 | 4 | 0 | 216 | 5 30 | 39 | 1 22 |

| | Innings | NO | Runs | Time hrs min. | Average runs per hour | Average length of innings hrs min. |
|---|---|---|---|---|---|---|
| In Australia | 218 | 25 | 18230 | 423 34 | 43 | 2 11 |
| In England | 120 | 18 | 9837 | 236 38 | 41 | 2 19 |
| *Total:* | 338 | 43 | 28067 | 660 12 | 42 | 2 14 |

For his 186 innings of 50 and over, his average was 44 runs per hour (25,247 runs in 567 hours 23 minutes). It was 44 runs per hour both in England (8,724 runs in 196 hours 46 minutes) and in Australia (16,523 runs in 370 hours 37 minutes).

For his 117 centuries, his average was 46 runs per hour (20,350 runs in 435 hours 36 minutes). It was 47 runs per hour in Australia in 435 hours 36 minutes). It was 47 runs per hour in Australia in 13,315 runs in 283 hours 11 minutes) and 46 runs per hour in England (7,035 runs in 152 hours 25 minutes).

For his 37 double centuries, his average was 49 runs per hour (9,444 runs in 190 hours 55 minutes). It was 50 runs per hour in Australia (6,439 runs in 127 hours 20 minutes) and 47 runs per hour in England (3,005 runs in 63 hours 35 minutes).

He made 12,120 runs in the 'playing-in' period before reaching 50 (including innings which ended before 50) at an average rate of 36 an hour, and 15,947 runs after reaching 50 at an average rate of 48 runs an hour.

He made 19,417 runs before reaching 100 (including innings which ended before 100) at an average rate of 38 runs an hour, while the 8,650 runs he made after passing 100 were scored at an average rate of 55 runs an hour.

In all first-class matches excluding Test matches, he averaged 44 runs per hour (21,071 runs in 470 hours 41 minutes).

While Bradman was at the wicket, 48,595 runs were scored, at an average rate of 73 runs per hour.

## Average Scoring Rate for Individual Innings

| | Centuries | 50–99 | 20–49 | Total (20 and over) |
|---|---|---|---|---|
| 80 runs per hour and over | 6 | 0 | 0 | 6 |
| 70–79 runs per hour | 8 | 1 | 1 | 10 |
| 60–69 runs per hour | 8 | 2 | 2 | 12 |
| 50–59 runs per hour | 25 | 9 | 7 | 41 |
| 40–49 runs per hour | 39 | 17 | 10 | 66 |
| 30–39 runs per hour | 25 | 28 | 22 | 75 |
| 20–29 runs per hour | 6 | 10 | 20 | 36 |
| under 20 runs per hour | 0 | 2 | 4 | 6 |
| *Total:* | 117 | 69 | 66 | 252 |

Twenty-two of his centuries were scored at a rate of 60 or more runs per hour. His fastest innings were:

90 runs per hour – 187, Australians *v* Essex, 1948 (match no. 212).

88 runs per hour – 132, Australians *v* Leveson-Gower's XI, 1934 (match no. 118).

88 runs per hour – 144, Australians *v* Tasmania, 1937–8 (match no. 149).

87 runs per hour – 369, South Australia *v* Tasmania, 1935–6 (match no. 126).

85 runs per hour – 149*, Australians *v* an England XI, 1934 (match no. 117).

80 runs per hour – 128, New South Wales *v* Victoria, 1933–4 (match no. 96).

79 runs per hour – 101*, Australians *v* Lancashire, 1938 (match no. 161).

His slowest innings were:

14 runs per hour – 30*, Australia *v* England, 1948 (match no. 221).

18 runs per hour – 58*, Australian XI *v* MCC, 1928–9 (match no. 9).

18 runs per hour – 66, New South Wales *v* South Australia, 1929–30 (match no. 19).

18 runs per hour – 30*, Australians *v* Middlesex, 1938 (match no. 158).

19 runs per hour – 38, Australians *v* Lancashire, 1930 (match no. 43).

19 runs per hour – 38, Australia *v* England, 1948 (match no. 219).

His slowest century was 144*, at 23 runs per hour, for Australia *v* England, 1938 (match no. 159). His slowest double century was 212, at 28 runs an hour, for Australia *v* England, 1936–7 (match no. 134).

Thirty-eight of the 41 double-century partnerships in which he shared were scored at the rate of a run a minute or faster – many of them very much faster.

## Average Time Taken to Reach 50, 100 and 200

|  | Innings of 50 and over | Average time to reach 50 hrs min. | Innings of 100 and over | Average time to reach 100 hrs min. | Innings of 200 and over | Average time to reach 200 hrs min. |
|---|---|---|---|---|---|---|
| 1927–8 | 3 | 1 11 | 2 | 2 59 | 0 | – – |
| 1928–9 | 12 | 1 38 | 7 | 2 53 | 1 | 5 57 |
| 1929–30 | 9 | 1 17 | 5 | 1 58 | 2 | 3 19 |
| 1930 | 15 | 1 19 | 10 | 2 40 | 6 | 4 26 |
| 1930–1 | 9 | 1 12 | 5 | 2 14 | 3 | 4 15 |
| 1931–2 | 7 | 1 6 | 7 | 2 10 | 3 | 4 10 |
| 1932–3 | 10 | 1 13 | 3 | 2 17 | 1 | 2 52 |
| 1933–4 | 9 | 1 7 | 5 | 2 1 | 2 | 3 4 |
| 1934 | 13 | 1 9 | 7 | 1 55 | 3 | 4 25 |
| 1935–6 | 5 | 1 9 | 4 | 1 54 | 3 | 3 32 |
| 1936–7 | 8 | 1 19 | 6 | 2 34 | 3 | 5 22 |
| 1937–8 | 12 | 1 18 | 7 | 2 27 | 1 | 5 26 |
| 1938 | 18 | 1 19 | 13 | 2 28 | 3 | 4 4 |
| 1938–9 | 6 | 1 29 | 6 | 2 47 | 1 | 5 4 |

283

| | Innings of 50 and over | Average time to reach 50 hrs min. | Innings of 100 and over | Average time to reach 100 hrs min. | Innings of 200 and over | Average time to reach 200 hrs min. |
|---|---|---|---|---|---|---|
| 1939–40 | 9 | 1 7 | 5 | 1 56 | 3 | 3 40 |
| 1940–1 | 0 | – – | 0 | – – | 0 | – – |
| 1945–6 | 3 | – 57 | 1 | 1 35 | 0 | – – |
| 1946–7 | 8 | 1 33 | 4 | 3 20 | 1 | 6 9 |
| 1947–8 | 9 | 1 14 | 8 | 2 25 | 1 | 4 30 |
| 1948 | 19 | 1 18 | 11 | 2 20 | 0 | – – |
| 1948–9 | 2 | 1 1 | 1 | 2 17 | 0 | – – |
| In Australia | 121 | 1 17 | 76 | 2 24 | 25 | 4 12 |
| In England | 65 | 1 17 | 41 | 2 23 | 12 | 4 20 |
| *Total:* | 186 | 1 17 | 117 | 2 24 | 37 | 4 15 |

(50 runs in an hour and 17 minutes = 39 runs an hour)
(100 runs in two hours and 24 minutes = 41 runs an hour)
(200 runs in four hours 15 minutes = 47 runs an hour)

## Time for Reaching 50 – Individual Innings

| Time | Number of innings |
|---|---|
| 1 hour or less | 45 |
| 1 hour to 1¼ hours | 50 |
| 1¼ to 1½ hours | 44 |
| 1½ to 2 hours | 41 |
| 2 to 2½ hours | 4 |
| 2½ to 3 hours | 2 |
| *Total:* | 186 |

His fastest times for reaching 50 were:

30 minutes – 238, New South Wales *v* Victoria, 1932–3 (Match no. 80).
34 minutes – 200, New South Wales *v* Queensland, 1933–4 (Match no. 90).
34 minutes – 187, Australians *v* Essex, 1948 (Match no. 212).
37 minutes – 135, New South Wales *v* South Africans, 1931–2 (Match no. 70).
37 minutes – 138, South Australia *v* Queensland, 1939–40 (Match no. 180).
40 minutes – 132, Australians *v* Leveson-Gower's XI, 1934 (Match no. 118).
40 minutes – 369, South Australia *v* Tasmania, 1935–6 (Match no. 126).
40 minutes – 144, Australians *v* Tasmania, 1937–8 (Match no. 149).
40 minutes – 101*, Australians *v* Lancashire, 1938 (Match no. 161).

Despite the speed at which he started, he completed his century in all these matches.

His slowest times for reaching 50, and the only occasions on which he took longer than two hours, were:

Two hours 45 minutes – 58*, Australian XI *v* MCC, 1928–9 (Match no. 9).
Two hours 35 minutes – 66, New South Wales *v* Queensland, 1929–30 (Match no. 19).
Two hours 30 minutes – 144*, Australia *v* England, 1938 (Match no. 159).
Two hours 23 minutes – 112, Australia *v* England, 1928–9 (Match no. 12).
Two hours 15 minutes – 185*, Australians *v* Leicestershire, 1930 (Match no. 31).
Two hours seven minutes – 258, Australians *v* Worcestershire, 1938 (Match no. 151).

## Time for Reaching 100 – Individual Innings

| Time | Number of innings |
|---|---|
| 1½ hours or less | 11 |
| 1½ to 2 hours | 20 |
| 2 to 2½ hours | 38 |
| 2½ to 3 hours | 23 |
| 3 to 3½ hours | 17 |
| over 3½ hours | 8 |
| *Total:* | 117 |

His fastest times for reaching 100 were:
70 minutes – 369, South Australia *v* Tasmania, 1935–6 (Match no. 126).
73 minutes – 238, New South Wales *v* Victoria, 1932–3 (Match no. 80).
73 minutes – 101*, Australians *v* Lancashire, 1938 (Match no. 161).
74 minutes – 187, Australians *v* Essex, 1948 (Match no. 212).
75 minutes – 144, Australians *v* Tasmania, 1937–8 (Match no. 149).
77 minutes – 160, Australians *v* Middlesex, 1934 (Match no. 103).
80 minutes – 138, South Australia *v* Queensland, 1939–40 (Match no. 180).
His slowest times for reaching 100, and the only occasions on which he took more than three and a half hours, were:
Four hours 13 minutes – 144*, Australia *v* England, 1938 (Match no. 159).
Three hours 46 minutes – 112, Australia *v* England, 1928–9 (Match no. 12).
Three hours 45 minutes – 185*, Australians *v* Leicestershire, 1930 (Match no. 195).
Three hours 43 minutes – 234, Australia *v* England, 1946–7 (Match no. 195).
Three hours 35 minutes – 131, Australia *v* England, 1930 (Match no. 41).
Three hours 35 minutes – 106, Australian XI *v* MCC, 1946–7 (Match no. 192).
Three hours 31 minutes – 133*, New South Wales *v* Queensland, 1928–9 (Match no. 7).
Three hours 31 minutes – 138, Australia *v* England, 1948 (Match no. 217).
In 49 of his 117 centuries he took longer over his second 50 than over his first. His fastest time from 50 to 100 was 26 minutes (in his 140 for Australians *v* Yorkshire, 1934, match no. 112); his slowest was two hours 14 minutes (in his 205* for Australians *v* Kent, 1930, match no. 54).

# Time for Reaching 200 – Individual Innings

| Time | Number of innings |
|------|-------------------|
| 3 hours or less | 4 |
| 3 to 4 hours | 11 |
| 4 to 5 hours | 14 |
| 5 to 6 hours | 5 |
| over 6 hours | 3 |
| *Total:* | 37 |

His fastest times for reaching 200 were:

Two hours 35 minutes – 209*, South Australia *v* W. Australia, 1939–40 (Match no. 184).

Two hours 48 minutes – 233, South Australia *v* Queensland, 1935–6 (Match no. 121).

Two hours 52 minutes – 238, New South Wales *v* Victoria, 1932–3 (Match no. 80).

Two hours 53 minutes – 369, South Australia *v* Tasmania, 1935–6 (Match no. 126).

His slowest times for reaching 200, and the only occasions on which he exceeded five and a half hours, were:

Seven hours two minutes – 212, Australia *v* England, 1936–7 (Match no. 134).

Six hours 23 minutes – 232, Australia *v* England, 1930 (Match no. 52).

Six hours 11 minutes – 234, Australia *v* England, 1946–7 (Match no. 195).

Five hours 57 minutes – 340*, New South Wales *v* Victoria, 1928–9 (Match no. 14).

Five hours 54 minutes – 270, Australia *v* England, 1936–7 (Match no. 132).

In nine of his 37 double centuries he took longer over his second century than over his first. His quickest time from 100 to 200 was 56 minutes (in his 209* for South Australia *v* W. Australia, 1939–40, match no. 184); his slowest was three hours 46 minutes (in his 212 for Australia *v* England, 1936–7, match no. 134).

# Length of Innings

| Time | Number of innings |
|------|-------------------|
| over 7 hours | 6 |
| 6–7 hours | 6 |
| 5–6 hours | 8 |
| 4–5 hours | 19 |
| 3–4 hours | 38 |

| Time | Number of innings |
|------|-------------------|
| 2–3 hours | 55 |
| 1–2 hours | 88 |
| under 1 hour | 118 |
| *Total:* | 338 |

His longest innings were:

Eight hours eight minutes – 340*, New South Wales *v* Victoria, 1928–9 (match no. 14).

Seven hours 38 minutes – 270, Australia *v* England, 1936–7 (Match no. 132).

Seven hours 21 minutes – 212, Australia *v* England, 1936–7 (Match no. 134).

Seven hours 18 minutes – 232, Australia *v* England, 1930 (Match no. 52).

Seven hours ten minutes – 304, Australia *v* England, 1934 (Match no. 113).

Seven hours one minute – 357, South Australia *v* Victoria, 1936–7 (Match no. 122).

Six hours 55 minutes – 452*, New South Wales *v* Queensland, 1929–30 (Match no. 24).

Six hours 36 minutes – 299*, Australia *v* South Africa, 1931–2 (Match no. 76).

Six hours 33 minutes – 234, Australia *v* England, 1946–7 (Match no. 195).

Six hours 23 minutes – 334, Australia *v* England, 1930 (Match no. 46).

Six hours five minutes – 144*, Australia *v* England, 1938 (Match no. 159).

Six hours four minutes – 246, South Australia *v* Queensland, 1937–8 (Match no. 143).

His longest stay at the wicket without reaching 200 was six hours five minutes, in his 144* for Australia *v* England, 1938 (match no. 159); only three times did he play an innings lasting longer than five hours without completing his second century, and in only eight of his 37 double centuries did he take longer than five hours to reach 200.

The longest innings he played without reaching 100 were three hours 32 minutes (91, South Australia *v* New South Wales, 1937–8, match no. 142), and three hours 29 minutes (66, New South Wales *v* South Australia, 1929–30, match no. 19). In only eight of his 117 centuries did he take longer than three and a half hours to reach three figures.

The longest innings he played without reaching 50 were two hours two minutes (30*, Australia *v* England, 1948, match no. 221), two hours (42, Australians *v* Yorkshire, 1938, match no. 163), and an hour and 55 minutes (38, Australia *v* England, 1948, match no. 219). In only six of his 186 fifties did he take longer than two hours to reach 50.

## (b) TEST MATCHES

### Average Runs per Hour and Average Length of Innings

Bradman's average rate of scoring in all Tests was 36 runs per hour, and *v* England 34 runs per hour. The average length of each of his completed innings was two hours 43 minutes in all Tests and two hours 35 minutes *v* England.

| | Opponents | Innings | NO | Runs | Time hrs min. | Average runs per hour | Av. length of innings hrs min. |
|---|---|---|---|---|---|---|---|
| 1928–9 | England | 8 | 1 | 468 | 16 25 | 28 | 2 20 |
| 1930 | England | 7 | 0 | 974 | 24 8 | 40 | 3 26 |
| 1930–1 | W. Indies | 6 | 0 | 447 | 9 27 | 47 | 1 34 |
| 1931–2 | S. Africa | 5 | 1 | 806 | 17 5 | 47 | 4 16 |
| 1932–3 | England | 8 | 1 | 396 | 10 33 | 37 | 1 30 |
| 1934 | England | 8 | 0 | 758 | 17 58 | 42 | 2 14 |
| 1936–7 | England | 9 | 0 | 810 | 24 24 | 33 | 2 42 |
| 1938 | England | 6 | 2 | 434 | 14 0 | 31 | 3 30 |
| 1946–7 | England | 8 | 1 | 680 | 20 24 | 33 | 2 54 |
| 1947–8 | India | 6 | 2 | 715 | 17 40 | 40 | 4 25 |
| 1948 | England | 9 | 2 | 508 | 17 27 | 29 | 2 29 |
| | | | | | | | |
| *v* England in Australia | | 33 | 3 | 2354 | 71 46 | 32 | 2 23 |
| *v* England in England | | 30 | 4 | 2674 | 73 33 | 36 | 2 49 |
| Total *v* England | | 63 | 7 | 5028 | 145 19 | 34 | 2 35 |
| All Tests in Australia | | 50 | 6 | 4322 | 115 58 | 37 | 2 38 |
| | | | | | | | |
| *Total:* | | 80 | 10 | 6996 | 189 31 | 36 | 2 43 |

For his 42 innings of 50 and over in all Tests, his average per hour was 38 (6,297 runs in 165 hours 41 minutes). For his 31 innings of 50 and over in Tests against England, his average per hour was 35 (4,416 runs in 124 hours 19 minutes).

For his 29 innings of 100 and over in all Tests, his average per hour was 39 (5,393 runs in 137 hours 39 minutes). For his 19 centuries against England his average was 36 runs an hour (3,569 runs in 97 hours 42 minutes).

For his 12 innings of 200 and over in all Tests, his average per hour was 41 (3,033 runs in 73 hours 39 minutes). For his eight double centuries against England, his average was 39 runs an hour (2,084 runs in 52 hours 59 minutes).

In all Test matches he made 2,799 runs in the 'playing-in' period before reaching 50 (including innings which ended before 50) at an average rate of 33 runs an hour, and 4,197 runs after reaching 50 at an average rate of 39 runs an hour. In Tests against England, his figures were: before reaching 50, 2,162 runs at an average rate of 31 runs an hour; after reaching 50, 2,866 runs at an average rate of 36 runs an hour.

In all Test matches, he made 4,503 runs before reaching 100 (including innings which ended before 100) at an average of 34 runs an hour, and 2,493 runs after reaching 100 at an average rate of 43 runs an hour. In Tests against England, his figures were: before reaching 100, 3,359 runs at an average rate of 32 runs an hour; after reaching 100, 1,669 runs at an average rate of 40 runs an hour.

Australia scored 12,397 runs in all Tests and 8,971 runs in Tests $v$ England, while Bradman was batting, at average rates of 65 and 62 runs per hour respectively.

In Tests against England, he scored 5,028 runs off 8,586 balls bowled to him, an average of 58 runs per 100 balls.

## Average Scoring Rate for Individual Innings

*All Tests*

|  | Centuries | 50–99 | 20–49 | Total (20 and over) |
|---|---|---|---|---|
| 50 runs per hour and over | 3 | 1 | 2 | 6 |
| 40–49 runs per hour | 13 | 2 | 3 | 18 |
| 30–39 runs per hour | 8 | 4 | 6 | 19 |
| 20–29 runs per hour | 4 | 6 | 3 | 13 |
| under 20 runs per hour | 0 | 0 | 2 | 2 |
| *Total:* | 29 | 13 | 16 | 58 |

*Tests against England*

|  | Centuries | 50–99 | 20–49 | Total (20 and over) |
|---|---|---|---|---|
| 50 runs per hour and over | 1 | 1 | 1 | 3 |
| 40–49 runs per hour | 6 | 1 | 3 | 10 |
| 30–39 runs per hour | 8 | 4 | 5 | 17 |
| 20–29 runs per hour | 4 | 6 | 3 | 13 |
| under 20 runs per hour | 0 | 0 | 2 | 2 |
| *Total:* | 19 | 12 | 14 | 45 |

His fastest innings in Test matches were:
60 runs per hour – 29 $v$ England, 1934 (Match no. 105).
59 runs per hour – 152 $v$ West Indies, 1930–1 (Match no. 66).
54 runs per hour – 167 $v$ South Africa, 1931–2 (Match no. 74).

54 runs per hour – 66 *v* England, 1932–3 (Match no. 85).
52 runs per hour – 334 *v* England, 1930 (Match no. 46).
50 runs per hour – 43 *v* West Indies, 1930–1 (Match no. 68).

His slowest innings in Test matches were:
14 runs per hour – 30* *v* England, 1948 (Match no. 221).
19 runs per hour – 38 *v* England, 1948 (Match no. 219).
22 runs per hour – 26 *v* England, 1936–7 (Match no. 134).
23 runs per hour – 144* *v* England, 1938 (Match no. 159).
24 runs per hour – 79 *v* England, 1928–9 (Match no. 12).
25 runs per hour – 58 *v* England, 1928–9 (Match no. 15).

His slowest double century in a Test match was his 212 *v* England, 1936–7, at 28 runs an hour (match no. 134).

Twenty-six of the 35 century partnerships in which he shared were scored at the rate of a run a minute or faster.

## Average Time Taken to Reach 50, 100 and 200

| | Opponents | Innings of 50 and over | Average time to reach 50 hrs min. | Innings of 100 and over | Average time to reach 100 hrs min. | Innings of 200 and over | Average time to reach 200 hrs min. |
|---|---|---|---|---|---|---|---|
| 1928–9 | England | 4 | 1 47 | 2 | 3 19 | 0 | – – |
| 1930 | England | 4 | 1 13 | 4 | 2 31 | 3 | 4 40 |
| 1930–1 | W. Indies | 2 | 1 2 | 2 | 2 2 | 1 | 4 11 |
| 1931–2 | S. Africa | 4 | 1 8 | 4 | 2 10 | 2 | 4 28 |
| 1932–3 | England | 4 | 1 20 | 1 | 3 2 | 0 | – – |
| 1934 | England | 3 | 1 28 | 2 | 2 59 | 2 | 4 54 |
| 1936–7 | England | 4 | 1 32 | 3 | 2 53 | 2 | 6 28 |
| 1938 | England | 4 | 1 37 | 3 | 3 8 | 0 | – – |
| 1946–7 | England | 5 | 1 34 | 2 | 3 28 | 1 | 6 11 |
| 1947–8 | India | 5 | 1 25 | 4 | 2 42 | 1 | 4 30 |
| | | | | | | | |
| *Totals* | | | | | | | |
| *v* England in Australia | | 17 | 1 33 | 8 | 3 9 | 3 | 6 22 |
| *v* England in England | | 14 | 1 26 | 11 | 2 51 | 5 | 4 46 |
| Total *v* England | | 31 | 1 30 | 19 | 2 58 | 8 | 5 22 |
| All Tests in Australia | | 28 | 1 26 | 18 | 2 42 | 7 | 5 15 |
| *Total:* | | 42 | 1 26 | 29 | 2 46 | 12 | 5 2 |

(50 runs in an hour and 26 minutes = 34 runs an hour)
(100 runs in two hours and 46 minutes = 36 runs an hour)
(200 runs in five hours two minutes = 39 runs an hour)

## Time for Reaching 50 – Individual Innings

| Time | Number of innings all Tests | Number of innings Tests v England |
|---|---|---|
| 1 hour or less | 4 | 3 |
| 1 hour to 1¼ hours | 9 | 5 |
| 1¼ to 1½ hours | 11 | 6 |
| 1½ to 2 hours | 16 | 15 |
| over 2 hours | 2 | 2 |
| Total: | 42 | 31 |

His fastest times for reaching 50 were:

45 minutes – 254 *v* England, 1930 (Match no. 44).
45 minutes – 152 *v* West Indies, 1930–1 (Match no. 66).
49 minutes – 334 *v* England, 1930 (Match no. 46).
60 minutes – 173* *v* England, 1948 (Match no. 223).
62 minutes – 226 *v* South Africa, 1931–2 (Match no. 71).
62 minutes – 299* *v* South Africa, 1931–2 (Match no. 76).
62 minutes – 102* *v* England, 1938 (Match no. 162).
64 minutes – 167 *v* South Africa, 1931–2 (Match no. 74).
64 minutes – 66 *v* England, 1932–3 (Match no. 85).

His slowest times for reaching 50 were:

Two hours 30 minutes – 144* *v* England, 1938 (Match no. 159).
Two hours 23 minutes – 112 *v* England, 1928–9 (Match no. 12).
One hour 55 minutes – 187 *v* England, 1946–7 (Match no. 194).
One hour 52 minutes – 82 *v* England, 1936–7 (Match no. 131).
One hour 51 minutes – 58 *v* England, 1928–9 (Match no. 15).
One hour 51 minutes – 234 *v* England, 1946–7 (Match no. 195).

## Time for Reaching 100 – Individual Innings

| Time | Number of innings all Tests | Number of innings Tests v England |
|---|---|---|
| 2 hours or less | 4 | 2 |
| 2 to 2½ hours | 8 | 3 |
| 2½ to 3 hours | 5 | 3 |
| 3 to 3½ hours | 7 | 6 |
| 3½ to 4 hours | 4 | 4 |
| over 4 hours | 1 | 1 |
| Total: | 29 | 19 |

His fastest times for reaching 100 were:

One hour 38 minutes – 167 *v* South Africa, 1931–2 (Match no. 74).

One hour 39 minutes – 334 *v* England, 1930 (Match no. 46).

One hour 42 minutes – 152 *v* West Indies, 1930–1 (Match no. 66).

One hour 45 minutes – 254 *v* England, 1930 (Match no. 44).

Two hours five minutes – 169 *v* England, 1936–7 (Match no. 137).

Two hours eight minutes – 127* *v* India, 1947–8 (Match no. 205).

Two hours 13 minutes – 299* *v* South Africa, 1931–2 (Match no. 76).

His slowest times for reaching 100 were:

Four hours 13 minutes – 144* *v* England, 1938 (Match no. 159).

Three hours 46 minutes – 112 *v* England, 1928–9 (Match no. 12).

Three hours 43 minutes – 234 *v* England, 1946–7 (Match no. 195).

Three hours 35 minutes – 131 *v* England, 1930 (Match no. 41).

Three hours 31 minutes – 138 *v* England, 1948 (Match no. 217).

Three hours 18 minutes – 270 *v* England, 1936–7 (Match no. 132).

Three hours 16 minutes – 212 *v* England, 1936–7 (Match no. 134).

In 14 of his 29 centuries, Bradman took longer over his second 50 than over his first. His fastest time from 50 to 100 was 34 minutes (in his 167 *v* South Africa, 1931–2, match no. 74); his slowest was an hour and 55 minutes (in his 131 *v* England, 1930, match no. 41).

## Time for Reaching 200 – Individual Innings

| Time | Number of innings all Tests | Number of innings Tests v England |
|---|---|---|
| 4 hours or less | 1 | 1 |
| 4 to 5 hours | 6 | 2 |
| 5 to 6 hours | 2 | 2 |
| over 6 hours | 3 | 3 |
| *Total:* | 12 | 8 |

His fastest times for reaching 200 were:

Three hours 34 minutes – 334 *v* England, 1930 (Match no. 46).

Four hours five minutes – 254 *v* England, 1930 (Match no. 44).

Four hours 11 minutes – 233 *v* West Indies, 1930–1 (Match no. 64).

Four hours 13 minutes – 226 *v* South Africa, 1931–2 (Match no. 71).

His slowest times for reaching 200 were:

Seven hours two minutes – 212 *v* England, 1936–7 (Match no. 134).

Six hours 23 minutes – 232 *v* England, 1930 (Match no. 52).

Six hours 11 minutes – 234 *v* England, 1946–7 (Match no. 195).

Five hours 54 minutes – 270 *v* England, 1936–7 (Match no. 132).

In five of his 12 double centuries he took longer over his second century than over his first. His quickest time from 100 to 200 was 79 minutes (in his 201 *v*

India, 1947–8, match no. 206); his slowest was three hours 46 minutes (in his 212 *v* England, 1936–7, match no. 134).

## Length of Innings

| Number of innings–<br>Time | Number of innings–<br>all Tests | Tests v England |
|---|---|---|
| over 7 hours | 4 | 4 |
| 5–6 hours | 3 | 3 |
| 4–5 hours | 8 | 4 |
| 3–4 hours | 7 | 5 |
| 2–3 hours | 10 | 7 |
| 1–2 hours | 15 | 14 |
| under 1 hour | 29 | 23 |
| *Total:* | 80 | 63 |

His longest Test match innings were:

Seven hours 38 minutes – 270 *v* England, 1936–7 (match no. 132).
Seven hours 21 minutes – 212 *v* England, 1936–7 (match no. 134).
Seven hours 18 minutes – 232 *v* England, 1930 (match no. 52).
Seven hours ten minutes – 304 *v* England, 1934 (match no. 113).
Six hours 36 minutes – 299* *v* South Africa, 1931–2 (match no. 76).
Six hours 33 minutes – 234 *v* England, 1946–7 (match no. 195).
Six hours 23 minutes – 334 *v* England, 1930 (match no. 46).
Six hours five minutes – 144* *v* England, 1938 (match no. 159).

His longest stay at the wicket without reaching 200 was six hours five minutes in his 144* *v* England, 1938 (match no. 159). That was the only time that he batted longer than five hours in a Test match without completing his second century, but in five of his 12 double centuries he took over five hours to complete 200.

The longest innings he played without reaching 100 was three hours 14 minutes, for his 79 *v* England, 1928–9 (match no. 12). This was the only time he batted for longer than three hours in a Test match without reaching his century, but in 12 of his 29 centuries he took over three hours to reach three figures.

The longest innings he played without reaching 50 were two hours two minutes (30* *v* England, 1948, match no. 221) and an hour and 55 minutes (38 *v* England, 1948, match no. 219). In only two of his 42 fifties did he take longer than two hours to reach 50.

# BOUNDARIES

## (a) ALL FIRST-CLASS CRICKET

In Bradman's 186 innings of 50 and over, in which he scored 25,247 of his runs, he hit 44 sixes, seven fives and 2,586 fours – 10,643 runs in boundaries (42 per cent). (This includes also, of course, a small number of fives and fours 'all-run', which did not reach the boundary, as well as overthrows.)

| Score | Innings | Runs | Sixes | Fives | Fours | Total in boundaries | Percentage |
|---|---|---|---|---|---|---|---|
| 50–99 | 69 | 4897 | 3 | 2 | 471 | 1912 | 39 |
| 100–199 | 80 | 10906 | 22 | 4 | 1055 | 4372 | 40 |
| 200 and over | 37 | 9444 | 19 | 1 | 1060 | 4359 | 46 |
| In Australia | 121 | 16523 | 26 | 3 | 1544 | 6347 | 38 |
| In England | 65 | 8724 | 18 | 4 | 1042 | 4296 | 49 |
| | | | | | | | |
| *Total* (*innings of* 50 *and over*): | 186 | 25247 | 44 | 7 | 2586 | 10643 | 42 |

It is, perhaps, surprising that the proportion of runs he scored in boundary strokes was so much higher in England than in Australia.

## (b) ALL TEST CRICKET

| Score | Innings | Runs | Sixes | Fives | Fours | Total in boundaries | Percentage |
|---|---|---|---|---|---|---|---|
| 50–99 | 13 | 904 | 2 | – | 90 | 372 | 41 |
| 100–199 | 17 | 2360 | – | 2 | 216 | 874 | 37 |
| 200 and over | 12 | 3033 | 4 | – | 312 | 1272 | 41 |
| | | | | | | | |
| *Total* (*innings of* 50 *and over*): | 42 | 6297 | 6 | 2 | 618 | 2518 | 39 |

## (c) TEST MATCHES *v* ENGLAND

| Score | Innings | Runs | Sixes | Fives | Fours | Total in boundaries | Percentage |
|---|---|---|---|---|---|---|---|
| 50–99 | 12 | 847 | 3 | – | 86 | 356 | 42 |
| 100–199 | 11 | 1485 | – | – | 134 | 536 | 36 |
| 200 and over | 8 | 2084 | 3 | – | 222 | 906 | 43 |
| Total (*innings of* 50 *and over*): | 31 | 4416 | 5 | – | 442 | 1798 | 40 |

## (d) MOST BOUNDARIES IN AN INNINGS

| Match No. | Match | Runs | Boundaries Sixes | Boundaries Fours |
|---|---|---|---|---|
| 126 | South Australia *v* Tasmania, 1935–6 | 369 | 4 | 46 |
| 24 | New South Wales *v* Queensland, 1929–30 | 452* | | 49 |
| 46 | Australia *v* England, 1930 | 334 | | 46 |
| 113 | Australia *v* England, 1934 | 304 | 2 | 43 |
| 122 | South Australia *v* Victoria, 1935–6 | 357 | | 40 |
| 179 | South Australia *v* New South Wales, 1939–40 | 251* | 2 | 38 |
| 14 | New South Wales *v* Victoria, 1928–9 | 340* | | 38 |
| 61 | New South Wales *v* South Australia, 1930–1 | 258 | | 37 |
| 154 | Australians *v* MCC, 1938 | 278 | 1 | 35 |

## (e) INNINGS WITH HIGHEST PROPORTION OF BOUNDARY HITS

| Match No. | Match | Runs | Boundaries Sixes | Boundaries Fives | Boundaries Fours | Percentage |
|---|---|---|---|---|---|---|
| 118 | Australians *v* L.-Gower's XI, 1934 | 132 | 1 | | 24 | 77 |
| 103 | Australians *v* Middlesex, 1934 | 160 | 1 | 1 | 27 | 74 |
| 112 | Australians *v* Yorkshire, 1934 | 140 | 2 | | 22 | 71 |
| 212 | Australians *v* Essex, 1948 | 187 | | 1 | 32 | 71 |
| 96 | New South Wales *v* Victoria, 1933–4 | 128 | 4 | | 17 | 71 |

| Size of innings | Match No. | Match | Runs | Boundaries (fours) | Percentage |
|---|---|---|---|---|---|
| 50–99 | 119 | South Australia *v* MCC, 1935–6 | 50 | 0 | – |
| | 19 | New South Wales *v* Queensland, 1929–30 | 66 | 1 | 6 |
| 100-199 | 141 | South Australia *v* West Australia, 1937–8 | 101 | 3 | 11 |
| | 159 | Australia *v* England, 1938 | 144* | 5 | 13 |
| 200 and over | 65 | New South Wales *v* Victoria, 1930–1 | 220 | 13 | 23 |
| | 173 | South Australia v Queensland, 1938–9 | 225 | 14 | 24 |

## (g) SIXES

Bradman was not a great hitter of sixes, preferring to keep the ball on the ground. The first he ever hit was off a no-ball (in his innings of 32 for Australians *v* Oxford, 1930, match no. 37), this being the only six he hit in an innings of under 50. Most of the other 44 sixes he hit in the course of his career were scored late in his innings, after he had completed his century or double century, and when he was hitting out without worrying overmuch whether he got out or not.

Oddly enough, of the three sixes he hit in innings between 50 and 99, two were in Test matches *v* England, though both were in the second innings, at a time when the result of the match was almost a foregone conclusion (in his innings of 66, 1932–3, match no. 85, when Australia had to make 532 on a worn wicket; and in his innings of 77, 1934, match no. 114, when Australia batted again with a lead of 380 on the first innings).

He hit only six sixes in Test matches, five *v* England and one *v* India.

SECTION 8

## DISMISSALS AND CHANCES

### (a) HOW BRADMAN WAS OUT

|  | *All First-class Cricket* | *All Tests* | *Tests v England* |
|---|---|---|---|
| Bowled | 78 | 23 | 20 |
| Caught | 174 | 39 | 32 |
| Lbw. | 27 | 6 | 3 |
| Stumped | 11 | 0 | 0 |
| Hit wicket | 1 | 1 | 0 |
| Run out | 4 | 1 | 1 |
| *Total:* | 295 | 70 | 56 |

His 174 catches and about 76 missed chances in all first-class matches were given to the following parts of the field:

|  | Caught | Missed |
|---|---|---|
| Wicket-keeper | 40 | 11 |
| Slips | 28 | 16 |
| Gully | 5 | 4 |
| Cover | 11 | 5 |
| Extra-cover | 2 | 0 |
| Silly point | 2 | 2 |
| Mid-off | 4 | 2 |
| Bowler | 13 | 10 |
| Mid-on | 6 | 3 |
| Mid-wicket | 1 | 2 |
| Short-leg | 26 | 5 |
| Deep | 21 | 11 |
| Square-leg | 11 | 3 |
| Deep square-leg | 3 | 1 |
| Long-leg | 1 | 1 |
| *Total:* | 174 | 76 |

He also gave about 17 stumping chances.

Almost all the catches he gave in the deep, whether caught or dropped, were given when he was past his century and not worrying about losing his wicket; the only exceptions were: match no. 59, New South Wales v West Indians, 1930–1, when he made 22; match no. 148, Australians v Tasmania, 1937–8, when he made 79, and then gave his wicket away; and match no. 183, South Australia v New South Wales, 1939–40, when his side was in a hopeless position and he was out for 40.

He appears to have given his wicket away, having made enough runs, on about 43 occasions; once when he had made 22; Match no. 148, Australians v Tasmania, 1937–8, when he made 79 (match no. 148), 28 times when he made between 100 and 200, 12 times between 200 and 300, and twice when over 300. He did so only four times in Test matches: match no. 73, v South Africa, 1931–2, when he had made 112; match no. 195, v England, 1946–7, when he had made 234; and matches nos. 205 and 206, v India, 1947–8, when he had made 132 and 201 respectively.

At the start of his career, he was a somewhat uncertain runner between wickets, but he soon developed into a very good one; and after being run out three times in his first three seasons, he was dismissed in this way only once more in his career.

He was 'not out' 43 times, for the following reasons: retired hurt once, innings ended six times (five times after he had completed his century), innings declared closed 13 times, match won nine times, match drawn 11 times, rain stopped play three times. On one other occasion he retired hurt but resumed batting later.

He was bowled for under 100 in only 58 of his innings.


## (b) MISSED CHANCES


### All First-class Cricket

Bradman gave some 93 unaccepted chances during his career; in 53 innings he gave only one chance, in ten he gave two chances, in four he gave three chances, and in two he gave as many as four chances. All but 69 of his 388 innings were therefore chanceless.

Thirty-two of these 93 chances were given after he had passed 100 – mostly when hitting out recklessly, not caring whether he lost his wicket or not.

Of his 186 innings of 50 and over, 54 included at least one escape.

Of his 117 centuries, 43 included at least one escape, but of these innings, 20 were chanceless until after he had reached the century. Thus, 74 of his centuries were completely free from fault, and another 20 were chanceless up to at least 100. Only in 23 of his 117 centuries would he have failed to make 100, had every possible chance been taken.

Approximately 4,400 (15 per cent) of his 28,067 runs were scored after he had been let off in the field, and ten of his 43 not-out innings included chances. Had every chance he gave been accepted, his career record would have been approximately: innings 338, not out 33, highest score 452*, runs 23,667, average 77.92.

## Test Matches

Bradman gave 24 unaccepted chances in Test matches, including 18 against England. In 13 innings, he gave only one chance, in two innings he gave two chances, in one he gave three and in one he gave four chances.

Four of these 24 chances (including three *v* England) were given after he had passed 100.

Of his 42 innings of 50 and over, 13 included at least one chance; of his 31 innings of 50 and over against England, nine included at least one chance.

Of his 29 centuries, ten included at least one chance, and of these ten, two were chanceless until after he had reached 100. Only in eight of his 29 centuries would he have failed to make 100, had every possible chance been taken.

Of his 19 centuries *v* England, six included at least one chance, and of these six, one was chanceless until after he had reached 100. Only in five of his 19 centuries against England would he have failed to make 100 had every possible chance been taken.

Of his 6,996 runs in all Tests, 1,558 (22 per cent) were scored after he had been let off in the field; *v* England, the figures were 950 (18 per cent) out of 5,028. Had every chance he gave been accepted, his career record would have been: all tests, innings 80, not out 7, highest score 273, runs 5,438, average 74.79; *v* England, innings 63, not out 5, highest score 273, runs 4,078, average 70.31.

### (c) SUCCESSFUL BOWLERS

Bradman was dismissed by bowlers in 291 of his innings, approximately as follows: fast bowlers (right/left) 44, fast-medium and medium (right/left) 132, 'googly' (right/ left) 45, slow right-arm off-spinners 27, slow left-arm 'natural' spinners 43.

The following six great bowlers were the only ones to dismiss him more than five times:

*C.V. Grimmett* dismissed him ten times and also induced Bradman to offer nine chances which the fielders missed, in six innings, in three of which he later got him out and in three of which he fell to other bowlers. Bradman played 27 innings against sides in which Grimmett was playing, and made 1,709 runs, average 63.29, including six centuries. Grimmett was always a better bowler in England than in Australia, and his impressive record on Australian wickets against Bradman shows what a very great bowler he was.

*H. Verity* dismissed him ten times, including eight times in Test matches; he three times bowled him for less than 100. He was among the bowlers in 41 of Bradman's innings, in which he scored 2,895 runs, average 74.23, including ten centuries. In Test matches, Bradman scored 401 runs off 932 balls bowled by Verity.

*A. V. Bedser* dismissed him eight times, including six times in Test matches, and on another occasion made him give a chance at the wicket. Bradman played 19 innings against him, in which he scored 1,487 runs, average 92.83, including six centuries. The eight dismissals include six in six successive innings in which he faced Bradman, including five Test matches, and including three in succession caught at short-leg off in-swingers. He got his wicket six times in 1948, including four times in Tests; but perhaps it was not entirely a coincidence that in his first two Test series *v* Australia (1946–7 and 1948), in which Bradman was playing, he took 34 wickets for 46 runs each, while in 1950–1 and 1953, after Bradman had retired, he took 69 wickets at 16 runs each. In Test matches, Bedser bowled 509 balls to Bradman, who scored 263 runs off them.

*H. Larwood* dismissed him seven times, including five times in Test matches. Bradman's record against his bowling was 27 innings, 2,009 runs, average 87.34, including seven centuries. Larwood bowled for almost two seasons without taking his wicket, or even inducing him to give a chance; and then, using 'body-line' methods, dismissed him six times in 1932–3, including four times in Tests, bowling him for under 100 on three occasions. In Test matches, Bradman scored 325 runs off 434 balls bowled by Larwood.

*M. W. Tate* dismissed him seven times, including five times in Test matches. He bowled to him in 26 innings, in which Bradman scored 2,024 runs, average 88.00, including seven centuries. In Test matches, Tate bowled 746 balls to Bradman, who scored 357 runs off him.

*W. J. O'Reilly* dismissed him six times in 18 innings, in which Bradman scored 1,207 runs, average 86.21, including four centuries. He also had Bradman missed in another innings in which Grimmett later dismissed him.

In addition to the above, T.W. Wall dismissed him five times in 18 innings, in which Bradman scored 1,092 runs, average 60.66, including three centuries; he dismissed him for scores of 5, 2, 0, 56 and 55. W.E. Bowes also had his wicket five times in 18 innings, in which Bradman made 1,468 runs, average 86.35, including six centuries.

The following dismissed him twice in a match:

T.W. Wall (5 and 2), C.W.L. Parker (42 and 14), C.S. Deverson (61 and 121), A.A. Mailey (73 and 29), H. Larwood (36 and 13), H. Larwood (76 and 24), A.D.G. Matthews (65 and 25), H. Verity (36 and 13), W.E. Bowes (244 and 77), C.V. Grimmett (212 and 13), H. Verity (13 and 270), W.J. O'Reilly (91 and 62), R.G. Gregory (54 and 35), T.F. Smailes (59 and 42), N.W.D. Yardley (79 and 49), V. Mankad (156 and 12), M.J. Hilton (11 and 43), A.V. Bedser (138 and 0), A.V. Bedser (38 and 89).

Larwood, Verity and Bedser performed this feat twice.

The following dismissed him for 0:

F.J. Gough, H.C. Griffith, E. Gilbert, T.W. Wall, W.E. Bowes, J.G.W. Davies, A.E.G. Baring, L.C. Hynes, G.O. Allen, W. Voce, J. Stackpole, W. Dudley, J. Ellis, A.V. Bedser (twice), W.E. Hollies.

The following bowled him twice or more for less than 100:

Three times: H. Larwood, H. Verity.

Twice: C.V. Grimmett, W.E. Bowes, C.W. L. Parker, T.W. Wall, W.E. Hollies.

The following dismissed him in Test matches:

H. Verity (eight times), A.V. Bedser (six times), W.E. Bowes, H. Larwood and M.W. Tate (five times), G. Geary, W.R. Hammond, N.W.D. Yardley (three times).

Twice: G.O. Allen, K. Farnes, H.C. Griffith, V.S. Hazare, F.R. Martin, R. Pollard, C.L. Vincent, W. Voce, J.C. White, D.V.P. Wright.

Once: L. Amarnath, L.N. Constantine, W.J. Edrich, G.N. Francis, W.E. Hollies, D.P.B. Morkel, I.A.R. Peebles, D.G. Phadkar, N.A. Quinn, R.W.V. Robins, R.A. Sinfield.

# SECTION 9

## BRADMAN ON RAIN-AFFECTED WICKETS

Bradman had some spectacular failures on rain-affected wickets, but it would not by any means be accurate to say that he was only a fair-weather batsman, or that he never succeeded in making runs save on plumb wickets. The following is his record on wickets affected by rain.

### (a) IN AUSTRALIA

| Year | Match No. | Ground | Opponents | Total | Bradman's full score | Bradman's runs on wet wicket |
|------|-----------|--------|-----------|-------|----------------------|------------------------------|
| 1927–8 | 3 | Sydney | Queensland | 100(8) | 13 | 13 |
| 1928–9 | 10 | Brisbane | England | 66 | 1 | 1 |
| 1928–9 | 16 | Sydney | MCC | 128 | 15 | 15 |
| 1929–30 | 26 | Sydney | Victoria | 330 | 77 | 77 |
| 1930–1 | 62 | Melbourne | Victoria | 97(6) | 2 | 2 |
| 1930–1 | 64 | Brisbane | West Indies | 558 | 223 | 0 |
| 1930–1 | 66 | Melbourne | West Indies | 328(8) | 152 | last 60 |
| 1930–1 | 68 | Sydney | West Indies | 224 | 43 | 43 |
|  |  |  |  | 220 | 0 | 0 |
| 1932–3 | 79 | Perth | MCC | 159 | 3 | 3 |
|  |  |  |  | 139(4) | 10 | 10 |
| 1932–3 | 81 | Melbourne | MCC | 19(2) | 13 | 13 |
| 1932–3 | 86 | Sydney | MCC | 128 | 71 | last 61 |
| 1935–6 | 124 | Sydney | New South Wales | 94 | 0 | 0 |
| 1936–7 | 130 | Brisbane | England | 58 | 0 | 0 |
| 1936–7 | 131 | Sydney | England | 80 | 0 | 0 |
|  |  |  |  | 324 | 82 | first 57 |
| 1936–7 | 132 | Melbourne | England | 564 | 270 | first 56 |
| 1940–1 | 188 | Melbourne | McCabe's XI | 141 | 12 | 12 |
| 1947–8 | 203 | Brisbane | India | 382(8) | 185 | last 25 |
| 1947–8 | 204 | Sydney | India | 107 | 13 | 13 |
| 1947–8 | 205 | Melbourne | India | 255(4) | 127* | first 23 |

| Year | Match No. | Ground | Opponents | Total | Bradman's full score | Bradman's runs on wet wicket |
|------|-----------|--------|-----------|-------|---------------------|------------------------------|
| 1930 | 32 | Sheffield | Yorkshire | 320 | 78 | 78 |
| 1930 | 36 | Oval | Surrey | 379(5) | 252* | 252* |
| 1930 | 38 | Southampton | Hampshire | 334 | 191 | 191 |
| 1930 | 39 | Lord's | Middlesex | 270 | 35 | 35 |
| 1930 | 41 | Nottingham | England | 144 | 8 | 8 |
| 1930 | 43 | Manchester | Lancashire | 427 | 38 | 38 |
| 1930 | 45 | Bradford | Yorkshire | 302 | 1 | 1 |
| 1930 | 48 | Manchester | England | 345 | 14 | 14 |
| 1930 | 50 | Swansea | Glamorgan | 245 | 58 | 58 |
|      |    |           |           | 71(1) | 19* | 18* |
| 1930 | 51 | Northampton | Northamptonshire | 93 | 22 | 22 |
| 1930 | 52 | Oval | England | 695 | 232 | last 102 |
| 1930 | 53 | Bristol | Gloucester | 157 | 42 | 42 |
|      |    |           |           | 117 | 14 | 14 |
| 1930 | 56 | Scarborough | Leveson-Gower's XI | 238 | 96 | 96 |
| 1934 | 107 | Lord's | England | 118 | 13 | 13 |
| 1938 | 155 | Northampton | Northamptonshire | 406(6) | 2 | 2 |
| 1938 | 157 | Southampton | Hampshire | 320(1) | 145* | 145* |
| 1938 | 158 | Lord's | Middlesex | 132 | 5 | 5 |
|      |    |           |           | 114(2) | 30* | 30* |
| 1938 | 163 | Sheffield | Yorkshire | 222 | 59 | 59 |
|      |    |           |           | 132 | 42 | 42 |
| 1938 | 164 | Birmingham | Warwickshire | 390(8) | 135 | first 116 |
| 1938 | 166 | Leeds | England | 242 | 103 | 103 |
|      |    |           |           | 107(5) | 16 | 16 |
| 1938 | 167 | Taunton | Somerset | 464(6) | 202 | 202 |
| 1938 | 168 | Swansea | Glamorgan | 61(3) | 17 | 17 |
| 1948 | 214 | Manchester | Lancashire | 204 | 11 | 11 |
|      |    |           |           | 259(4) | 43 | 43 |
| 1948 | 218 | Sheffield | Yorkshire | 285(5) | 86 | first 66 |
| 1948 | 219 | Lord's | England | 350 | 38 | 38 |
| 1948 | 221 | Manchester | England | 92(1) | 30* | 30* |
| 1948 | 223 | Leeds | England | 458 | 33 | last 2 |
| 1948 | 225 | Birmingham | Warwickshire | 254 | 31 | 31 |
| 1948 | 227 | Oval | England | 389 | 0 | 0 |

## (c) SUMMARY

Not by any means all the above innings were played on sticky wickets; all, however, were to some extent affected by rain, some, especially in England, so as to be slow and easy, of the 'pudding' variety, others giving the bowlers varying degrees of help. Nor, of course, were these wickets always affected by rain throughout; when, for instance, he made 232 in the fifth Test match at the Oval, in 1930, the wicket was wet on the fourth morning, when Bradman resumed batting with his score 130 not out. Similarly, in his Australian Test innings, he made 223 out of 223 and 92 out of 152 *v* West Indies, 1930–1, and 160 out of 185 *v* India, 1947–8, on good wicket which were affected by rain only at the end; while his 82 and 270 *v* England 1936–7, and 127* *v* India 1947–8, were made on wickets which were rain-affected only at the beginning.

Some of these innings were played on wickets of the genuine 'sticky-dog' variety, such as his 71 *v* MCC in 1932–3, and his 59 and 42 *v* Yorkshire in 1938; many of the others were played on wickets which certainly assisted the bowlers with spin and lift, and his record on them is not to be despised. He also made runs on dry, worn wickets which took spin because they were crumbling.

In comparing the performances of batsmen of different generations, it must be remembered that the practice of covering the ends of the wicket, to protect the bowler's footholds against rain, has made a tremendous difference to a batsman's chances on a sticky wicket; this practice was first permitted in England in 1913, and shortly after that in Australia. Before then, the fast and fast-medium bowlers were unable to stand up on rain-affected pitches, and the slow bowlers were the ones who were apt to do the damage; and a quick-footed batsman such as, for instance, V.T. Trumper, could often, with a bit of luck, make a lot of runs against slow bowlers, however vicious the wicket. Now, however, fast bowlers can bowl at almost their fastest pace despite rain, and this has made batsmanship in such conditions a much more hazardous business, for speed of foot no longer matters; Bradman's two 'ducks' in Test matches against England in 1936–7, for instance, were caused after rain by two fast bowlers, G.O. Allen and W. Voce, neither of whom would have been able to obtain a foothold prior to 1913.

This has particularly affected batting on wet wickets in Australia. In England, a batsman of skill and resource can still, again with a bit of luck, often surmount the difficulties of even the stickiest of wickets, but in Australia, a drying wicket can be almost impossible, with one ball shooting straight along the ground and the next getting straight up; survival and, still more, the scoring of runs, are matters more of chance than of skill, when the fast-medium half-volley is the deadliest wicket-taker, and a tail-ender like W.J. O'Reilly can make top score in a Test match.

These difficulties are not likely to recur, for in virtually all matches in Australia the wickets are now covered from end to end, so that rain cannot affect them. In Sheffield Shield matches, full covering of the wickets was optional from about 1925, and compulsory from 1935–6, which explains why so few of Bradman's

Sheffield Shield innings were played on rain-affected wickets. So far as matches against touring team were concerned, not until after Bradman's retirement was full covering of the pitch introduced, and the infrequency with which he had to bat on a rain-affected wicket in Australia – in effect, the possibility arose only in matches against touring teams or, occasionally, when rain was heavy enough in other matches to penetrate the covers – was another factor militating against his success when he did have to do so.

He certainly played some poor strokes on false turf, had some disappointing failures, and often, even in success, looked uncomfortable; so also did every other batsman in the history of the game, even W.G. Grace being by no means outstanding on wet wickets. Bradman was not, of course, such a master on a sticky wicket as J.B. Hobbs, though even Hobbs, despite all his experience, was not invariably successful in such conditions. Bradman was at least as successful on bad wickets as any other Australian of his time; but Bradman was always expected to make a century, and if he did not do so, whatever the conditions, his failure still captured the headlines when anyone else's failure would have been overlooked.

The suggestion is, therefore, quite untrue that he never, or hardly ever, made runs except when the wicket was fast and true; no one could have an average of 96.44 on four tours of England, the first of which took place in a particularly wet summer, and the last two in normally wet ones, unless he could and often did make runs on wickets affected by rain as well as on those which were dry. Obviously, like anyone else, he preferred batting on good wickets to bad ones, and was more likely to succeed on them, but he was perfectly capable of batting on bowler's wickets and, as will be seen, often did so with success.

# MISCELLANEOUS

## (a) RESULTS OF MATCHES

*All First-class Matches*

|         | P   | W   | L  | D  | T |
|---------|-----|-----|----|----|---|
| 1927–8  | 5   | 1   | 2  | 2  | – |
| 1928–9  | 13  | 4   | 5  | 4  | – |
| 1929–30 | 11  | 5   | 2  | 4  | – |
| 1930    | 27  | 10  | 1  | 15 | 1 |
| 1930–1  | 12  | 7   | 2  | 3  | – |
| 1931–2  | 10  | 7   | 1  | 2  | – |
| 1932–3  | 11  | 3   | 5  | 3  | – |
| 1933–4  | 7   | 2   | 2  | 3  | – |
| 1934    | 22  | 11  | 1  | 10 | – |
| 1935–6  | 8   | 5   | 1  | 2  | – |
| 1936–7  | 12  | 5   | 3  | 4  | – |
| 1937–8  | 12  | 7   | 2  | 3  | – |
| 1938    | 20  | 10  | 1  | 9  | – |
| 1938–9  | 7   | 3   | –  | 4  | – |
| 1939–40 | 9   | 3   | 3  | 3  | – |
| 1940–1  | 2   | 1   | 1  | –  | – |
| 1945–6  | 2   | –   | –  | 2  | – |
| 1946–7  | 9   | 3   | 1  | 5  | – |
| 1947–8  | 9   | 5   | 1  | 3  | – |
| 1948    | 23  | 16  | –  | 7  | – |
| 1948–9  | 3   | 1   | 1  | –  | 1 |
| *Total:* | 234 | 109 | 35 | 88 | 2 |

Only 21 times in his career was a side beaten for which he batted twice on a good wicket in a match limited by time.

Of the 37 matches in which he made a score of 200 or over, his side won 25, drew 11 and lost only one (match no. 21, a Test trial, where the result was of no significance).

Of the 113 matches in which he made a score of 100 or over, his side won 64, drew 41, tied one and lost only seven.

To his side's 109 victories, Bradman contributed a score of at least 50 in one innings or the other in 83 matches and failed to do so in only 26.

Not a single one of the 88 draws, incidentally, was a match which his side might have won had Bradman scored fewer runs or got out earlier; all were either doomed to be drawn in any event, or were matches which his side might well have lost but for him. Personal greed for runs or records irrespective of the state of the game or of his side's interests was certainly not a criticism which could fairly be made against him at any stage of his career.

Bradman's record in the Sheffield Shield was:

|  | P | W | L | D |
|---|---|---|---|---|
| For New South Wales, 1927–34 | 31 | 15 | 5 | 11 |
| For South Australia, 1935–49 | 31 | 14 | 7 | 10 |
| *Total:* | 62 | 29 | 12 | 21 |

New South Wales won the Sheffield Shield three times (1928–9, 1931–2 and 1932–3) in the seven seasons Bradman played for them, and South Australia won the Shield twice in the eight seasons he played for them (1935–6 and 1938–9). In the three post-war seasons, however, he played in only one Shield match each season.

In the four tours he made of England, the 1948 side, under his leadership, was unbeaten; the 1930 and 1934 sides each lost only one match, and the 1938 side (also under his captaincy) lost two matches, in one of which he did not play; in the other he did not bat, though it is unlikely that even two innings by him would have affected the result.

The biggest wins recorded by teams for which he was playing were:
Match no. 152 – Australians *v* Oxford, 1938: innings and 487 runs
Match no. 212 – Australians *v* Essex, 194: innings and 451 runs
Match no. 24 – New South Wales *v* Queensland, 1929–30: 685 runs
Match no. 114 – Australia *v* England, 1934: 562 runs.

The most crushing defeats suffered by teams for which he was playing were:
Match no. 170 – Australia *v* England, 1938: innings and 579 runs
Match no. 10 – Australia *v* England, 1928–9: 675 runs.

*Test Matches*

|  | Opponents | P | W | L | D | Rubber | Ashes |
|---|---|---|---|---|---|---|---|
| 1928–9 | England | 4 | 1 | 3 | 0 | Lost | England |
| 1930 | England | 5 | 2 | 1 | 2 | Won | Australia |
| 1930–1 | W. Indies | 5 | 4 | 1 | 0 | Won | – |
| 1931–2 | S. Africa | 5 | 5 | 0 | 0 | Won | – |

| | Opponents | P | W | L | D | Rubber | Ashes |
|---|---|---|---|---|---|---|---|
| 1932–3 | England | 4 | 1 | 3 | 0 | Lost | England |
| 1934 | England | 5 | 2 | 1 | 2 | Won | Australia |
| 1936–7 | England | 5 | 3 | 2 | 0 | Won | Australia |
| 1938 | England | 4 | 1 | 1 | 2 | Drawn | Australia |
| 1946–7 | England | 5 | 3 | 0 | 2 | Won | Australia |
| 1947–8 | India | 5 | 4 | 0 | 1 | Won | – |
| 1948 | England | 5 | 4 | 0 | 1 | Won | Australia |
| | | | | | | | |
| Total v England: | | 37 | 17 | 11 | 9 | 5 Won | Australia 6 |
| | | | | | | 2 Lost | England 2 |
| | | | | | | 1 Drawn | |
| Total All Tests: | | 52 | 30 | 12 | 10 | 8 Won | – |
| | | | | | | 2 Lost | |
| | | | | | | 1 Drawn | |

To Australia's 30 Test match victories during his career, he contributed a score of at least 100 in one innings or the other in 22 Test matches, and a score of at least 50 in one innings or the other in 25; against England, to 17 Australian victories Bradman contributed a century to 13, and a score of between 50 and 100 to two others. Australia therefore won only four Test matches v England and eight Test matches altogether, in which he failed to make a century; only two Tests v England and five altogether in which he failed to play an innings of at least 50.

Of the 12 matches in which he made a double century, Australia won ten, drew two and lost none; v England he made eight double centuries and Australia won six of these matches, drew two and lost none.

Of the 28 Tests in which he made a century, Australia won 22, drew four and lost two; v England he made centuries in 19 Test matches, of which Australia won 13, drew four and lost two.

### (b) BRADMAN AS CAPTAIN

He first captained a side in a first-class match on the 1934 tour of England when, as vice-captain to W.M. Woodfull, he led the Australians in six games in which the latter was resting. He became captain of South Australia in 1935–6, and of Australia in 1936–7; from 1935–6 onwards he captained every side for which he played, until the last two matches of his career.

The results of matches in which he was captain were:

| | P | W | L | D | T |
|---|---|---|---|---|---|
| All First-class Matches | 120 | 61 | 13 | 45 | 1 |
| All Test Matches | 24 | 15 | 3 | 6 | – |
| Tests v England | 19 | 11 | 3 | 5 | – |

Australia won four Test series under his captaincy (three *v* England and one *v* India) and shared a fifth (*v* England, 1938); Australia retained the Ashes from England throughout his captaincy.

W.M. Woodfull captained Australia 25 times consecutively between 1930 and 1934, the most that any man has led any country in Test matches; only the accident of the Manchester Test match 1938, being abandoned without a ball being bowled, prevented Bradman from also captaining Australia in 25 Tests. The 19 times he captained Australia *v* England is, however, a record, the previous best being 18 by J. Darling; A.C. Maclaren captained England *v* Australia in 22 matches, though not consecutively, as Bradman's were, and Woodfull captained Australia in 15 consecutive Tests *v* England. P.B.H. May has now captained England in 25 consecutive Tests.

He won the toss in 57 of the 120 matches in which he was captain and lost it in 63; in seven (two in Australia and five in England) of the 57 matches in which he won the toss, he put the other side in (and only once regretted it); and in four (one in Australia and three in England) of the 63 matches in which he lost it, the opposing captain gave him first innings.

However, he was a rather unlucky tosser in Tests against England, being successful in only six Test matches out of 19; in nine Tests in England in 1938 and 1948, he won the toss only once. In 1936–7 and 1946–7, in Australia, he won five and lost five tosses; in two of his five successes and one of his five failures in tossing, the toss virtually meant victory, with rain later ruining the pitch. Against India in 1947–8, he won four tosses and lost one.

Australia never lost a Test match in which he won the toss.

(Bradman's successor, A.L. Hassett, won the toss in nine Test matches out of ten *v* England, including all five in England in 1953.)

## The 'Cares of Captaincy'

Bradman's batting showed no sign of being affected by the responsibility of captaincy; in fact, he was slightly more successful in matches when he was captained than otherwise.

*All First-class Matches*

|  |  | Matches | Innings | NO | HS | Runs | Average | Centuries |
|---|---|---|---|---|---|---|---|---|
| In Australia–not captain |  | 71 | 115 | 14 | 452* | 8963 | 88.74 | 34 |
|  | –captain | 71 | 103 | 11 | 369 | 9267 | 100.72 | 42 |
| In England–not captain |  | 43 | 56 | 8 | 334 | 4681 | 97.52 | 17 |
|  | –captain | 49 | 64 | 10 | 278 | 5156 | 95.48 | 24 |
| Total | –not captain | 114 | 171 | 22 | 452* | 13644 | 91.57 | 51 |
|  | –captain | 120 | 167 | 21 | 369 | 14423 | 98.78 | 66 |
| *Total:* |  | 234 | 338 | 43 | 452* | 28067 | 95.14 | 117 |

## Test Matches

|  | Matches | Innings | NO | HS | Runs | Average | Centuries |
|---|---|---|---|---|---|---|---|
| All Tests–not captain | 28 | 42 | 3 | 334 | 3849 | 98.69 | 15 |
| –captain | 24 | 38 | 7 | 270 | 3147 | 101.51 | 14 |
| *Total:* | 52 | 80 | 10 | 334 | 6996 | 99.94 | 29 |
| Tests *v* England–not captain | 18 | 31 | 2 | 334 | 2596 | 89.51 | 9 |
| –captain | 19 | 32 | 5 | 270 | 2432 | 90.07 | 10 |
| *Total:* | 37 | 63 | 7 | 334 | 5028 | 89.78 | 19 |

### (c) BRADMAN AS BOWLER

In his younger days, Bradman was quite often called upon, as a change bowler, to purvey his leg-breaks and 'googlies', and though he was often expensive he sometimes took useful wickets. When he was captain, however, he showed little confidence in his abilities as a bowler and put himself on very rarely.

His season-by-season record was:

|  | 8-ball overs | 6-ball overs | Balls | Maidens | Runs | Wickets | Average |
|---|---|---|---|---|---|---|---|
| 1927–8 | 16 | – | 128 | 0 | 66 | 2 | 33.00 |
| 1928–9 | 19 | – | 152 | 0 | 139 | 3 | 46.33 |
| 1929-30 | 53.7 | – | 431 | 0 | 300 | 4 | 75.00 |
| 1930 | – | 76 | 456 | 12 | 301 | 12 | 25.08 |
| 1930–1 | 37 | 9 | 350 | 4 | 184 | 4 | 46.00 |
| 1931–2 | 6.5 | 1 | 59 | 0 | 54 | 1 | 54.00 |
| 1932–3 | 41.6 | 12 | 406 | 5 | 230 | 6 | 38.33 |
| 1933–4 | 10 | – | 80 | 0 | 69 | 1 | 69.00 |
| 1935–6 | 1 | – | 8 | 1 | 0 | 0 | – |
| 1938 | – | 3 | 18 | 2 | 6 | 0 | – |
| 1938–9 | 0.1 | – | 1 | 0 | 0 | 1 | 0.00 |
| 1947–8 | 1 | – | 8 | 0 | 4 | 0 | – |
| 1948 | – | 1 | 6 | 0 | 2 | 0 | – |
| 1948–9 | 1.7 | – | 15 | 0 | 12 | 2 | 6.00 |
| *Total:* | 188.2 | 102 | 2118 | 24 | 1367 | 36 | 37.97 |

His most successful match as a bowler was for the Australians *v* Cambridge University, 1930 (match no. 39), when he took 6 wickets in the match for 103 runs – 3 wickets in each innings. The only other time he took 3 wickets in an innings was for New South Wales *v* South Australia, 1930–1 (match no. 61), when he took 3 for 54. The longest bowl he had in one innings was 19 eight-ball overs for the Combined Australian XI *v* MCC Team, 1932–3 (match no. 79), when he took 2 for 106.

In Test matches his record was:

| | Opponents | 8-ball overs | 6-ball overs | Balls | Maidens | Runs | Wickets | Average |
|---|---|---|---|---|---|---|---|---|
| 1930 | England | – | 1 | 6 | 0 | 1 | 0 | – |
| 1930–1 | West Indies | – | 9 | 54 | 1 | 15 | 1 | 15.00 |
| 1931–2 | South Africa | – | 1 | 6 | 0 | 2 | 0 | – |
| 1932–3 | England | – | 12 | 72 | 1 | 44 | 1 | 44.00 |
| 1938 | England | – | 3 | 18 | 2 | 6 | 0 | – |
| 1947–8 | India | 1 | – | 8 | 0 | 4 | 0 | – |
| | | | | | | | | |
| Total *v* England: | | – | 16 | 96 | 3 | 51 | 1 | 51.00 |
| *Total All Tests:* | | 1 | 26 | 164 | 4 | 72 | 2 | 36.00 |

His two victims in Test matches were I. Barrow and W.R. Hammond.

It was as a bowler that he sustained his most serious injury on the cricket field, in the Oval Test match, 1938 (match no. 170), when he fractured a bone in his ankle.

### (d) BRADMAN AS FIELDER

At the start of his career, Bradman normally fielded in the deep, where he established a reputation as high as for his batting; he was in the great tradition of Australian outfielders, very fast and sure, and with a long, low and accurate throw. Later on, when his duties as captain required his presence nearer the wicket, he normally fielded as mid-off or extra-cover, and again was very good indeed in these positions, though after the war he was, naturally, a good deal slower, and didn't throw himself about as much as in his younger days.

Perhaps his abilities as a catcher were not quite on the same high plane as his ground fielding and throwing; though possessing a safe pair of hands by normal standards, he did sometimes miss a possible chance. For instance, he dropped some eight possible catches in his 37 Tests against England, including three in 1928–9, his first series; as well as two *v* South Africa in 1931–2. However, in the course of his career as a fieldsman, he caught 122 catches altogether (82 in Australia and 40 in England); in addition, he held one catch when he was fielding as a substitute, and stumped one and caught four in the two matches in which he kept wicket.

In Test matches he caught 32 catches (plus one when substitute); 20 *v* England, four *v* West Indies, two *v* South Africa and six *v* India.

### (e) BRADMAN AS SELECTOR

Bradman was first appointed to the Australian Test Match Selection Committee in the autumn of 1936, and thereafter was one of the three men responsible for the selection of Australian Test teams at home and abroad until he resigned, for family reasons, in the autumn of 1952. He took no part in the selection of the Australian teams which played South Africa in 1952–3, or of the 1953 team which toured England.

He was re-elected to the Selection Committee in the autumn of 1954, and has remained a member of it ever since.